Rethinking the *Filioque* with the Greek Fathers

Rethinking the *Filioque* with the Greek Fathers

GIULIO MASPERO

William B. Eerdmans Publishing Company

Grand Rapids, Michigan

Wm. B. Eerdmans Publishing Co.
4035 Park East Court SE, Grand Rapids, Michigan 49546
www.eerdmans.com

29 28 27 26 25 24 23   1 2 3 4 5 6 7

ISBN 978-0-8028-8305-6

Library of Congress Cataloging-in-Publication Data

A catalog record for this book is available from the Library of Congress.

Contents

Foreword

I am delighted and honored to provide this short introduction to Giulio Maspero's new book, *Rethinking the* Filioque *with the Greek Fathers*, and to commend it with warmth and admiration to all those interested in new developments in patristic theology and in contemporary ecumenical relations—whether they be teachers, students, clergy, or general readers. This book makes several important and original interventions into a new story about "Eastern" and "Western" Christendom in the patristic period up to the fifth century, which has already been developing importantly in recent decades and which this volume further refines and complexifies.

Fr. Maspero, who is a professor at the Pontifical University of Santa Croce in Rome, was originally trained as a physicist, and perhaps something of his sharp analytic mind and pedagogical ambition to probe to the fundamental presumptions of the patristic authors he studies may be attributed to this original formation. For over twenty years he has been well known in the international patristics guild as an astute, original, and probing interpreter of the fourth-century Cappadocian father Gregory of Nyssa, on whom he wrote his dissertation under the late Professor Lucas F. Mateo Secco at the University of Navarre.[1] (Indeed, it was at this period of his theological career that he and I first became fast friends.) Particularly important in Fr. Maspero's reading of Nyssen has been his nuanced account of how "apophaticism" actually *works* in Gregory's doctrinal thinking, and especially in his Trinitarianism (a matter that also features in the core argument of this current book), and his concomitant challenging of the so-called social Trinitarian rendition of Nyssen's thought, which had dominated an earlier generation of scholarship and had led to a misleading thesis about a supposed East-West disjunction in patristic Trini-

1. Giulio Maspero, *Trinity and Man: Gregory of Nyssa's* Ad Ablabium (Leiden: Brill, 2007).

tarianism.[2] Fr. Maspero's more recent work, however, has branched out much more ambitiously into wider themes in contemporary systematic or "dogmatic" theology, while not abandoning his characteristic interest as a patristic scholar in the underlying stories that theologians are inclined to tell about doctrinal development in the history of the church.[3] Indeed, while other theologians in the period of postmodernity have tended to recoil, in line with current fashion, from what they see as the modernistic pretensions of any *Dogmengeschichte* of an earlier generation, Fr. Maspero has remained refreshingly impenitent about seeking *some* such metanarrative of doctrinal development, albeit one suitably chastened by the complexity and breadth of the texts he surveys.[4] For this, and other reasons now to be outlined, however, Maspero's new book is bound to be controversial. That is why it merits your close attention.

We find in this current volume, then, a challenging and original account of the origins of Christian Trinitarian thinking, which—when read with due care and attention to the specific texts which Fr. Maspero covers—contains the following novel contributions that should be underscored.

First, the very title of the book should be heeded, but also not misunderstood, since in a sense it is itself deliberately and provocatively anachronistic. The so-called *Filioque* problem (occasioned by the addition in the West of the phrase "and from the Son" to the Niceno-Constantinopolitan Creed to the clause about the procession of the Holy Spirit "from the Father") did not arise until *after* the patristic period covered in this book;[5] and the impropriety of

2. This line of thinking, which decisively criticizes the earlier-regnant view that the Eastern patristic doctrine of the Trinity is "social" (starting from the three and proceeding to the one), while the Western alternative represents its inverse (starting from the one and proceeding to the three), is especially associated with Lewis Ayres's justly celebrated book *Nicaea and Its Legacy: An Approach to Fourth Century Trinitarian Theology* (Oxford: Oxford University Press, 2004). For a close discussion and assessment of the importance of Ayres's book, see Sarah Coakley, ed., with introduction, *The God of Nicaea: Disputed Questions in Patristic Trinitarianism*, a special issue of *Harvard Theological Review* 100 (2007).

3. See, e.g., Giulio Maspero and Robert Wozniak, eds., *Re-Thinking Trinitarian Theology: Disputed Questions and Contemporary Issues in Trinitarian Theology* (London: T&T Clark, 2012); and Giulio Maspero, *The Mystery of Communion: Encountering the Trinity* (South Bend, IN: St Augustine's Press, 2021).

4. This trait will already be clear from the opening account of Origen's Trinitarianism in chapter 1 in this volume, which schematizes an existing tension in Origen's thinking that, according to Maspero, is then resolved only through the Arian controversy and the crucial contribution of the Cappadocians.

5. Fr. Maspero briefly covers some of this history in the opening to this volume; the "*Filioque* problem" became an open dispute in the ninth century with the Photian schism, but—at least conjecturally—problems were already brewing by the seventh century.

its being added to the creed without the agreement of an ecumenical council must be regarded as a problem distinct from the relevant theological issue of early metaphysical speculation about the immanent "procession" of the Holy Spirit. Well before that fatal credal addition, however—as this book demonstrates with new insight and textual discoveries (but in the wake of many other scholars' previous work in the area)—the idea of a "double procession" of the Spirit, or something like it, was by no means confined to the West; nor should we constrain our investigation of it to the work of Augustine, as older textbooks have often implied. Indeed, the particular contribution of this volume as to the genesis of the "double procession" is Fr. Maspero's argument that we need to focus especially on the late-fourth-century Greek debates with the "Spirit-fighters" (who denied the full divinity of the Spirit) to account for its vindication in quest of a fully-coherent Trinitarian ontology.[6] The vital Cappadocian contribution to this rebuttal of pneumatological late Arianism, then, was—according to Fr. Maspero—the originally *Eastern* locus of the proposal of a view of "relationality" in the Trinity that actually *necessitated* something akin to what later came to be called the *Filioque*; indeed, for those reared on older textbooks, it may still be a surprise to learn that Nyssen himself explicitly described the Spirit as the relational "bond" between Father and Son.[7] But this was a view that subtly, but crucially, distinguished the primal notion of "cause" (a term still reserved for the Father alone) from this new idea of inner-personal relationships of equality in the immanent life of the Trinity, which now logically required an active role for the Son also in the procession of the Spirit. Ultimately, it is *this* patristic "Greek" solution to the (later) "problem of the *Filioque*" that Fr. Maspero wants to commend to the churches for reconsideration, one that need not require the *Filioque* to be excised once more from the Western version of the creed, but rather to be glossed irenically and ecumenically through the lens of Cappadocian thought.

It is most important to stress here, then, that Maspero's is *not* an anachronistic reading of the Cappadocian contribution that forces an Augustinian rendition upon it for reasons of Western *Tendenz*: to presume that would be to continue to kow-tow to the outworn thesis about an East-West disjunction in fourth-fifth Trinitarian thinking, which even now dies hard in some ecumenical circles. Rather, Maspero's painstaking investigation of the Cappadocian Trinitarian heritage, alongside—and in comparison with—the slightly later contribution

6. See chapter 3 in this volume.

7. See chapters 4 and 5 in this volume for Maspero's full and masterful account of Nyssen's Trinitarianism and its development.

of Augustine, stresses both their shared theological instincts and their *philo-sophical* differences on how to construe the notion of divine "substance." What is not necessary, however, is to create any wedge between them on the grounds of their supposedly dichotomous understanding of the Spirit's "procession."

Perhaps even more fascinating still in this book, however (alongside this new proposed *entente* between Greek and Latin patristic views about the Spirit), is the wonderful chapter Fr. Maspero contributes on the Syriac theology of the same period (chapter 6), in which—partly because of the semantic distinctions in Greek on the matter of "procession" that Syriac did not replicate—we again find a remarkable set of witnesses to the idea of "double procession," right from the time of Ephrem, but arising from a richly distinct cultural and theological source.[8]

Because this book contributes to a rising tide in scholarship that already notes the congruence of "pro-Nicene" patristic Trinitarianism, both East and West, it might therefore be easy to miss the very distinctive contributions that Fr. Maspero makes to this ongoing debate, here outlined. That is why I have chosen to underscore these points in this foreword. But Fr. Maspero's own solution to the *contemporary* question of the "*Filioque* problem" is just as bold, and will of course generate further debate: we are bound to ask whether it can really forestall the objection to the underlying canonical inappropriateness of the West's alteration of the creed, and—more importantly—whether the distinction between primal "cause" (the Father) and merely "active" role (the Son) in the procession of the Spirit can finally be maintained *philosophically* as an ecumenical solution without either collapsing the distinction or else leaving a remaining trace of the ontological subordination of the Spirit, which the Cappadocian solution had so urgently sought to erase.[9] Such matters constitute

---

8. It is not only in the Syriac materials of chapter 6 that we encounter important Trinitarian materials that other textbooks have heretofore overlooked. The treatment of the pseudo-Athanasian dialogues in chapter 2 is noteworthy, as is the fascinating treatment of Anastasius of Sinai (as an Eastern exemplar of psychological analogies for the Trinity) in chapter 7.

9. I have accordingly myself recently argued that a more radical solution to the "*Filioque* problem" is therefore required than that proposed by Fr. Maspero, one that—like Maspero's—takes neither side in the supposedly classic East-West disjunction of the ninth century onward, but more daringly follows some of the instincts of select later "mystical theologians," both East and West. What this speculative analysis shares with Fr. Maspero's, however, is a primary inspiration from the Trinitarianism of the later commentary work of Gregory of Nyssa, especially his *Commentary on the Song of Songs*. See Sarah Coakley, "Beyond the Filioque Disputes: Reassessing the Radical Equality of the Spirit through the Ascetic and Mystical Traditions," Duquesne University annual lecture on the Holy Spirit,

the ongoing discussions that Fr. Maspero and I continue to enjoy, as—I do not doubt—will many others.

What is certain, however, is that no careful reader of this enticingly ambitious book will emerge without gaining vividly new perspectives on an age-old theological problem. It deserves to be read in all basic courses on the patristic development of Trinitarian ontology, and, more particularly, in service of the continuing discussions of the future of ecumenical relations between "Western" and "Eastern" denominations on the "*Filioque* problem," as a most creative exercise in *ressourcement* that rightfully returns this matter to its patristic roots.

Sarah Coakley
Oxford, Feast of the Assumption/Dormition,
August 15, 2022

2016; now reprinted in Radu Bordeianu, ed., *It Is the Spirit That Gives Life: New Directions in Pneumatology* (Washington, DC: Catholic University of America Press, 2022), 153–76.

Abbreviations

AW	*Athanasius Werke.* 3 vols. Berlin, 1934
CCSG	Corpus Christianorum: Series Graeca
CCSL	Corpus Christianorum: Series Latina
CPG	*Clavis Patrum Graecorum.* Edited by Maurice Geerard. 5 vols. Turnhout: Brepols, 1974–1987
CSCO	Corpus Scriptorum Christianorum Orientalium
CSEL	Corpus Scriptorum Ecclesiasticorum Latinorum
GCS	Die griechischen christlichen Schriftsteller der ersten [drei] Jahrhunderte
GNO	Gregorii Nysseni Opera
LXX	Septuagint
PG	*Patrologiae Cursus Completus*: Series Graeca. Edited by Jacques-Paul Migne. 162 vols. Paris, 1857–1886
SC	Sources chrétiennes. Paris: Cerf, 1943
SPAW	*Sitzungsberichte der preussischen Akademie der Wissenschaften*

History or Theology?

In 2010 Pope Benedict XVI visited the United Kingdom. Greg Bruke, then a journalist at Fox News, reported that during the Pope's visit a young man could be seen protesting by himself in London carrying a sign made from a pizza box that read: "Drop the *Filioque*." Photos of the protester can still be found on the internet. It may be surprising that someone would feel the need to call public attention to a theological issue that seems to be of interest only to experts in ecumenical dialogue or historians of the Church. Perhaps this protest is an indication of a depth that cannot be relegated to the past, as if it is no longer relevant to us. There are, in fact, fundamental issues from our history that have a significant influence on our present life.

So, do we really have to drop the *Filioque*? Would we lose something? Or would we gain something? This volume was written to answer that question from the standpoint of the Greek fathers of the Church. It stems from the observation that although extraordinary monographs have been written on the historical issue, the theological investigation of such historical data can and should be further developed.[1] In particular, this research has three objectives:

---

1. Some of the most relevant publications of the last decade are A. E. Siecienski, *The Filioque: History of a Doctrinal Controversy* (Oxford: Oxford University Press, 2010); M. Böhnke, A. E. Kattan, and B. Oberdorfer, eds., *Die Filioque-Kontroverse: Historische, ökumenische und dogmatische Perspektiven 1200 Jahre nach der Aachener Synode* (Freiburg im Breisgau: Herder, 2011), Th. G. Weinandy, *The Father's Spirit of Sonship: Reconceiving the Trinity* (Edinburgh: T&T Clark, 1995; repr. Eugene, OR: Wipf & Stock, 2011); M. Coetzee, *The Filioque Impasse: Patristic Roots* (Piscataway, NJ: Gorgias, 2012); M. Gagliardi, ed., *Il Filioque: A mille anni dal suo inserimento nel credo a Roma (1014–2014)* (Vatican City: LEV, 2015). Special attention should be paid to the recent monograph of Ch. Lee, *Gregory of Nyssa, Augustine of Hippo, and the Filioque* (Leiden: Brill, 2021), whose research converges in intention with the present work.

1. To better understand the origins of the tension in the different approaches to the procession of the Holy Spirit and to show how the *Filioque* does not concern an unnecessary appendix of pneumatology, but instead answers an inescapable question posed by the historical development of the doctrine on the divine Third Person.

2. To add an element to the discussion that is mostly neglected in literature; that is, the doctrine developed by the Greek fathers in response to the Pneumatomachians, who accepted the divinity of the Son while denying that of the Holy Spirit.

3. To try to understand the basis of the misunderstanding between the Byzantine world and Augustine's tradition, to see if the new information offered by this research can form the basis of a new ecumenical proposal on the second procession.

When at the end of the eighth century two monks from the Frankish monastery on the Mount of Olives returned to Jerusalem after a trip to Aachen and suggested that the *Filioque* be introduced into the recitation of the Creed in the Mass there, they might not have imagined the scope of the matter, which transcended the question of Charlemagne's patronage over their monastery. The violent reaction of their Greek confreres, who accused them of heresy, led these monks to write to Pope Leo III asking for a selection of quotations from Greek and Latin authorities to support their position. The Pope passed the letter to the emperor, who summoned a council of Frankish bishops who met in Aachen in 809 and decided in favor of including the *Filioque* in the Creed recited in the Mass. But the following year Leo III, after examining the acts of the council and while saying he agreed with the patristic dossier that had been presented to him, strongly defended the exclusion of the formula from the Nicene Creed both to preserve the ancient formula and because the issue was not relevant for the salvation of souls. His approach was apophatic in the sense that the Christian mystery always remains greater than the ability to express it. So the Pope asked that recitation of the *Filioque* be suspended in the Palatine liturgy, considering that little by little it would fall out of use throughout the empire. Moreover, he had the Creed engraved in Greek and Latin without the *Filioque* addition on bronze plates placed beside the door of confession in St. Peter's Basilica and in St. Paul's Basilica.[2]

2. J. Grohe, "Storia del Filioque prima del 1014 e il suo inserimento nel Credo," in Gagliardi, *Il Filioque*, 32–35, and P. Delogu, "Leone III, santo," *Enciclopedia dei papi* (Rome: Treccani, 2000), 700.

The position of Pope Leo III seems very interesting not only for the fact that it is politically balanced but also from a theological and a pastoral perspective. The key point is his acceptance that the patristic doctrine presents a tradition that is favorable to the *Filioque* without contradicting the Eastern position, which is focused on the defense of the paternal monarchy. He dropped and kept the expression simultaneously, distinguishing the level of form from that of content.

This observation is fundamental to the present study in which the term *Filioque*, with the theological discussions it inspires, is not understood in the medieval or contemporary sense, but in the patristic sense as:

1. affirmation of an active role of the Son in the immanent procession of the Spirit;
2. without this role being causal, thereby overshadowing the monarchy of the first divine Person.

This double definition marks a clear difference with respect to the medieval proposals, which in a context already distant from apophatic epistemology conceived the relationship between the Father and the Son as closed, so that the Second Person could be indicated as the cause of the Third Person. Anselm's theology, with its logicalizing defense of the *Filioque*, goes in this direction, which can be dubbed Filioquism. At the same time, the issue analysed here in the context of Greek patristics relates directly to immanence and not only economy,[3] where the role of the Son in the coming of the Spirit is obvious because the gospel indicates beyond a shadow of a doubt that the Spirit is given *per Christum*, as sent by the Father but also by the incarnate Word. The question examined in the present research is whether this *per Christum* is an expression of a *per Filium*, which is the immanent root of the economic origin of the Spirit.

For this reason, the present theological study cannot neglect the question of how the theological reading of God's immanence reflects on the relationship between creation and salvation history, a question which lies at the heart of the very possibility of expressing dogma in human language and in parallel with how icons can represent the mystery of the triune God without ever fully possessing or grasping it.

So, here we will not analyze the literal *Filioque* (i.e., the history of the insertion of the clause into the Symbol of Faith on the Latin side), a matter already

---

3. The reader of the Orthodox perspective should keep in mind that with this distinction we do not refer to Karl Rahner's immanent and economic Trinity, but we mean what, starting from the Cappadocians, the Greek fathers called *theologia* and *oikonomia*.

examined in exemplary fashion by Peter Gemeinhardt[4] and Henry Chadwick.[5] Instead, the object of the present research is the theological *Filioque*, that is, this study analyzes the thought of the Greek fathers concerning the role of the Son in the procession of the Spirit or, in other words, the relationship between the first and second processions in the divine immanence.[6] The epoch studied in this book essentially ends where Gemeinhardt's treatment begins.[7] Therefore, no attempt will be made to explain whether or not and why the Pope inserted the *Filioque* into the Symbol of Faith (that is, the Nicene Creed), nor will any attempt be made to analyze the historical reasons for the ecclesial divisions that originated from it. Instead, we have worked along the lines of a *ressourcement* in search of dogmatic elements that can explain why the Greek fathers were in communion with the Latin fathers while being aware of the mutual differences in their approach to pneumatology. We are, in fact, convinced that the history of dogma offers valuable insights unfortunately absent in the common narrative. Is Augustine really the father of the *Filioque*? Does this follow from the psychological analogy? Was all of this caused by the projection of an anthropology in the Trinity, according to the vulgate present in Eastern manuals?

In the light of these questions, the reader is asked to examine this proposal with an attitude of speculative "virginity" to avoid jumping ahead to the polemical perspectives that characterized the post-patristic era and instead stick to the proposed definition and allow the depth of the pneumatological doctrine of the Eastern fathers to reveal a dogmatic richness that is not reducible to dialectical categories.[8]

This epistemological "virginity" also seems correct from the perspective of history and the critical approach, since the fathers of the Church (despite a certain propensity of early Christian thinkers for confrontation and even

4. P. Gemeinhardt, *Die Filioque-Kontroverse zwischen Ost- und Westkirche im Frühmittelalter* (Berlin: de Gruyter 2002).

5. H. Chadwick, *East and West: The Making of a Rift in the Church; From Apostolic Times until the Council of Florence* (Oxford: Oxford University Press, 2003).

6. This explains why some important authors for Trinitarian theology and pneumatology, such as Irenaeus, Cyril of Jerusalem, and Didymus, are not addressed in this reconstruction.

7. The volume can be considered a theological and documentary deepening of chapters 2–4 of Anthony E. Siecienski's book.

8. From this point of view, the present volume assumes an epistemological option in line with that of Khaled Anatolios in his recent *Deification through the Cross* (Grand Rapids: Eerdmans, 2020). Doxological contrition and the attention to soteriology that characterized the thought of the fathers prevent any dialectical reductionism.

conflict, as the history of the councils shows) have left us a testimony of communion, even in the pneumatological field.[9]

Indeed, epistemology plays a key role. The thesis proposed here is that there is an intimate correspondence between apophaticism, the true foundation of the theological method, and the ontological value of the development of dogma. In fact, the comparison with the various objections to the concrete forms that the formulation of the Christian mystery assumed over the centuries forced the fathers to revise the metaphysical framework inherited from Greek thought in order to reformulate the Aristotelian categories so as to affirm the personal distinction of the Father, the Son, and the Holy Spirit within their perfect substantial identity. This task of reworking and resemantization continued after the fourth century with the deeper examination of christological doctrine,[10] but the methodological approach had already been settled in the development of Trinitarian thought.[11]

For the philosophical and linguistic background of Christian thought is the graduated metaphysical conception of Greek philosophy, which joined the first principle and the world in a single finite and eternal ontological order, internally organized as a descending scale in terms of perfection. In the first attempts of the second- and third-century thinkers, who were also in the wake of the Philonian inheritance, this construction is polarized into an ever clearer distinction between God and the created world, whose relationship is maintained by the *Logos*. The *Logos* is like an intermediary, the thought (and word) of the Father through whom He created the world. Thus, the Son is in an ontologically subordinate position with respect to the Father and has an existence that is at the service of creation. Origen will overcome this *Logos*-theology and open the way to the elaboration on the difference between the Trinity and the world in terms of *physis*, which would emerge in the fourth century as a response to the Arian crisis. From Athanasius onward, only the Father, the Son, and the Spirit are considered eternal because they constitute

9. This option is also relevant from the point of view of postmodernity, as Piet Hein Hupsch notes: "The interplay between doxology and apophasis that we find in Gregory is a salutary example for contemporary theology that can be characterised as postmodern" (P. H. Hupsch, *The Glory of the Spirit in Gregory of Nyssa's* Adversus Macedonianos: *Commentary and Systematic-Theological Synthesis* [Leiden: Brill, 2020], 348).

10. See J. Zachhuber, "Philosophy and Theology in Late Antiquity," in *Eastern Christianity and Late Antique Philosophy*, ed. Ken Parry (Leiden: Brill, 2019), 52–77.

11. See G. Maspero, "The Trinity," in *The Routledge Handbook of Early Christian Philosophy*, ed. M. Edwards (London: Routledge, 2021), 125–38.

the one uncreated nature, while every other being is marked by finiteness in time and space. As we shall see, this *Physis*-theology was the starting point of the Cappadocians, who in their dual response to both the Eunomians and Pneumatomachians transformed it into a *Schesis*-theology, that is, into an ontological conception in which the identification of the three divine Persons is no longer given by the substance which is unique for them but by the relational distinction within this single substance. This marked the shift from the *Logos ut ratio* to the *Logos ut relatio*, that is, from an understanding of the Son as a necessary mediator (who is like an ontological bridge or step between God and the world) to a real relational perspective, where the Second Person is eternally in the divine substance and from there, out of love and in perfect freedom, became flesh, founding the possibility of real relationship between the Trinity and the human being.

But this new metaphysical conception necessarily translated into a new attitude toward knowledge, since the way to approach God could no longer be only the conceptual dimension, climbing the ontological steps going from (necessary) cause to cause, as the nature of the Trinity is totally transcendent with respect to the human being. This means that God radically overcomes the capacities of the latter but should be known through freedom and the personal relationship. This led to a new understanding of the value of history and the corporeal dimension. And this must be kept in mind as we approach this exciting theological epoch, without anachronistically projecting anterior or successive epistemologies onto it.[12]

From this standpoint, the dogmatic explanation proposed in this volume cannot be considered a static image, a kind of surpassing synthesis and *Aufhebung* à la Hegel, which leads to a final solution like an equation or a geometric problem. Instead, one must necessarily resort to a narrative, in which the meaning of each moment is given by their relationships with the other elements of the story, according to a structuring of thought that Gregory of Nyssa indicated with the Greek term *akolouthia*. Therefore, the proposed path should not be followed as if we were observing snapshots in a photo album, from which we choose the one we like best. Here the dynamic development and the set of all the moments count, like an arrow that points in a certain direction.

As Sarah Coakley highlights, we cannot just reduce the fierce disputes of past centuries to bad memories and mistakes in the name of a complementarity

---

12. See Sarah Coakley's criticisms of Maurice Wiles and his thesis of a presumed pneumatological deficit in the first centuries in S. Coakley, *God, Sexuality, and the Self: An Essay 'On the Trinity'* (Cambridge: Cambridge University Press, 2013), 116–21.

between East and West, which is stated in an ideological and irenic way.[13] Like this scholar we should recognize that apophaticism makes it possible to hold together both the spiritual and the metaphysical dimensions among the factors of our analysis, without ever dialectically pitting them against each other: "in and through the Spirit we are drawn to place our binary 'certainties' into the melting pot of the crucible of divine—not human—desire."[14] The dialogue with Sarah Coakley has inspired and encouraged this research, pointing precisely to the Holy Spirit and the related issue of the *Filioque* as a way to rethink the dialectical binary oppositions, which Coakley rightly describes as idolatrous.

So this book is conceived as a contribution to the challenge of taking a fresh look at the relationships between East and West in order to overcome the simplistic vision of the opposition between an essentialist approach and a personalist one.[15]

In the end, this work aims to show the importance of the specific questions that are answered and the particular problems faced by the Greek fathers of the Church in order to reach a correct understanding of dogmatic history. The neverending attempt to formulate the mystery of the triune God in an appropriate way shows how every moment of dogmatic history is an answer to a specific question or a response to a conflict. Thus, in order to reach a full understanding of the theological content of the author's answer, the modern reader must consider this answer within the context in which it arose, looking not only at the author himself but also at those to whom he was responding. Every word is always addressed to someone, and that is also true for dogma.

Thus, we cannot understand the Latin position without considering the contribution of Tertullian, who marked the whole of Western tradition with his *a Patre per Filium*. Every thought is expressed in a certain language, which conditions the thought itself. Thus we can say that the very first point of contact of Latin theology with the mystery of the procession of the Holy Spirit was linked to the role of the Son.[16] This element will also be maintained in the fourth century after the distinction between economy and immanence has been clarified, as witnessed in the thought of Ambrose and Hilary of Poitiers.[17]

13. Coakley, *God, Sexuality, and the Self*, 329.

14. Coakley, *God, Sexuality, and the Self*, 331.

15. Cf. R. Cross, "Two Models of the Trinity?," *Heythrop Journal* 43 (2002): 275–94.

16. Tertullian, *Adversus Praxean*, 4.6 (CCSL 2:1162).

17. On the Latin tradition, see M. Simonetti, "La processione dello Spirito Santo nei Padri Latini," *Maia* 7 (1955): 308–24, and "Il regresso della teologia dello Spirito Santo in Occidente dopo Tertulliano," *Augustinianum* 20 (1980): 655–69, and G. Bendinelli, "Il dibattito sullo Spirito Santo in ambito latino prima di Agostino," in *Pneuma: Il divino in/*

It is significant that when the latter proposes his thought on the relationship between the Son and the procession of the Spirit he always does so in an apophatic context, both when Hilary takes up the *per Filium* of Tertullian[18] and when he formulates an explicit *Filioque*:

> But it is neither appropriate to remain silent about the Holy Spirit, nor is it necessary to talk about Him. In fact, we cannot remain silent because of those who do not know Him, but it is also not necessary to speak of Him who is to be confessed to originate from the Father and the Son.[19]

This Latin father, who knew Greek theology well from direct experience during his exiles, also witnesses the dogmatic connection of John 15:26 and 16:12–15 with the distinction between the two processions, which we will see as fundamental in the response to Pneumatomachians.[20]

Ambrose (another father who is much appreciated in the Eastern tradition) links Sir 24:5, John 1:1, and 14:10 to show that in the procession of the Spirit from the Father and the Son, which the reference to the last verse clearly places in immanence, the Third Person does not separate from the first two:

> Finally, the Wisdom affirms that She proceeds "from the mouth of the Most High," not because She is external to the Father, but rather with the Father, because "the Word was with God," and not only with the Father, but also in the Father. She says, indeed: "I am in the Father and the Father is in me." But when She proceeds from the Father She does not withdraw from a place, nor does She separate herself from Him like a body from a body. Nor when She is in the Father, is She like a body enclosed in another body. And the Spirit, who proceeds from the Father and the Son, does not separate from them.[21]

But if these are some fundamental stages of the Latin path, what were the stages of the Greek one? What linguistic and theological elements defined it?

---

quieto; Lo Spirito santo nelle tradizioni antiche, ed. F. Pieri and F. Ruggiero, Supplementi di Adamantius 6 (Brescia, Italy: Morcelliana, 2018), 195–224; L. F. Ladaria, *El Espíritu Santo en San Hilario de Poitiers* (Madrid: Eapsa, 1977); N. Cipriani, "La processione dello Spirito Santo in sant'Agostino," in Gagliardi, *Il Filioque*, 99–116.

18. Hilary of Poitiers, *De Trinitate*, 12.56.1–8 (SC 462:466).
19. Hilary of Poitiers, *De Trinitate*, 2.29.1–4 (SC 443:322).
20. Hilary of Poitiers, *De Trinitate*, 7.20 (SC 448:408).
21. Ambrose, *De Spiritu Sancto*, 1.11.120.38–44 (CSEL 79:66–67).

What fundamental moments in the elaboration of the relationship between the procession of the Spirit and the Second Person can be found? This is what we will try to show in what follows, proceeding more quickly in the areas already dealt with in the literature and dwelling in more detail on those elements practically absent in previous discussions that seem relevant to the discourse.

The proposed narrative starts from the Trinitarian doctrine of Origen which, as in any other theological field, is an essential reference point. It will show how his reflection can be traced back to two fundamental schemes, one linear and the other triangular (chapter 1). Each of them responds to a different need, but in the fourth century the tension between the two led to a reconstruction of the ontological framework, the aim of which was first to recognize the full divinity of the *Logos* by introducing it into divine immanence, then to repeat this for the Holy Spirit, affirming His active role in the creative act (chapter 2). This last clarification is addressed to the Pneumatomachians, that is, those who accepted the divinity of the Second Person while denying that of the Third. The different responses to their position can be deduced from the analysis of the works of Epiphanius and the *Dialogi adversus Macedonianos* of Pseudo-Athanasius (chapter 3). This will allow us to appreciate the strength of the Cappadocian response, especially that of Gregory of Nyssa and Gregory of Nazianzus, who come to determine the Holy Spirit's own personal *proprium* and, therefore, the difference between the first and the second procession—a difference that remained in the shadows in Athanasius's theology (chapters 4 and 5). After having revealed the dogmatic heart of the pneumatology of the fourth-century Greek fathers and having highlighted how they identify an active, but not causal, role of the Second Person in the procession of the Third Person, we will try both to respond to possible criticism and to explain why the *Filioque* has become a painful point of divergence between Eastern and Western traditions. Three questions will be addressed for the sake of showing how the proposed reading is not simply a Latinizing approach: (1) whether it was only the Latins who felt the need to make explicit the relationship between the first and second procession; (2) whether the Latin *Filioque* is the "offspring" of Augustine's psychological analogy; (3) whether the pneumatological reading in the proposed analysis can be considered a projection onto Greek theology of Augustine's categories of thought. Thus, the geographical and linguistic question will be addressed first by exploring the Syriac tradition so as to show how the need to examine the question about the role of the Son in the procession of the Spirit was not only a Latin requirement (chapter 6). Looking at the dialogue between the Syriac, Greek, and Latin traditions will highlight the theological role of translation as an inescapable element of the process of the handing down of the tradition. Then, we will examine the connection of the *Filioque* with the psychological analogy, a theological element that is also present in the Greek context (chapter 7). Finally, a comparison between the ontological work of Gregory of Nyssa and that of Augustine will aim to highlight the independence of the results obtained from the theological perspective of the bishop of Hippo so as to also explain the Byzantine difficulty in accepting Western formulations (chapter 8).

This path's conclusion leads to a paradox and a proposal. When rereading the claim to count Cyril of Alexandria and Maximus the Confessor in the ranks of the authorities who support the *Filioque* against the backdrop of the suggested path, one comes to the surprising conclusion that their positions appear very different from one another, since the former is closer to Augustine in a more Nicene pneumatological perspective, while the latter remains in the Constantinopolitan line and is linked to Cappadocian theology and their response to Pneumatomachian criticism, which seems to be absent in the discussions related to the so-called Photian schism. Thus, paradoxically, it is precisely this second line of development that appears to be more coherent with the proposed form of *Filioque*, where the divine Second Person plays an active, but not causal, role in the procession of the Spirit. Hence the need to rethink the *Filioque* itself in order to ecumenically verify whether it is possible today to accept this form of *Filioque* as a common faith shared by the Greek and Latin fathers before the ninth century.

The need for this rereading seems to increasingly emerge in both the academic and ecclesial worlds. In fact, two recent conferences have offered extremely interesting material for the topic of the *Filioque* and the research presented in this monograph. In December 2016, the conference "*Contra Latinos et adversus Graecos*: The separation between Rome and Constantinople from the 9th to the 15th century," whose proceedings have just been published,[22] was held in Venice. Then, at the beginning of September 2018 in Paris, at the Collège des Bernardins, the "14th International Colloquium on Gregory of Nyssa" was dedicated to the *Oratio Dominica*—a work which, as will be seen in chapter 5, was the focus of a heated discussion on the issue of the *Filioque*.[23]

22. A. Bucossi and A. Calia, eds., *Contra Latinos et Adversus Graecos: The Separation between Rome and Constantinople from the Ninth to the Fifteenth Century* (Leuven: Peeters, 2020).

23. See the proceedings: M. Cassin, H. Grelier-Deneux, and F. Vinel, eds., *Gregory of*

On both occasions, some moments of the discussion demonstrated the relevance of the purpose that motivates this work, the aim of which is to rethink the question of the role of the Second Person of the Trinity in the procession of the Third. In particular, some exchanges at the Paris conference offered the participants an opportunity to guess what the climate might have been like at the Council of Florence. On both occasions we were struck by the absence of all the work developed by the Greek fathers in response to the Pneumatomachians in the interpretation of the various passages marked by the polemical clash. Thus these two conferences were watershed moments in the completion of this research, which collects ten years of studies, some of which have already been presented and discussed in conferences around Europe, from Granada to Lublin, from Tübingen to Milan, and from Oxford to Cambridge (which is why some subtitles, especially in the first chapter, recall the names of English pubs).

After all, this book was written while imagining what would happen if those two Jerusalem monks of the early ninth century could have a beer with the young man in London who, at the beginning of the third millennium, wrote "Drop the Filioque" on a pizza box before waiting for the Pope to ride past. In fact, the Trinitarian revelation strongly points to the impossibility of getting at the truth if not in communion. That is why it is not possible to conclude this introduction without thanking those who motivated and supported the author throughout the whole process, starting with Sarah Coakley. The dialogue with her has been an inspiration and support from the very beginning of this project. A special thanks also goes to Richard Cross for his challenging remarks, which have pushed this research into new and particularly fertile ground. For the study of the Syriac tradition, Carlos Jódar Estrella deserves special gratitude for his patient and impassioned teachings, along with Peter Bruns and Gregory Kessel for their helpful suggestions. During these years, the conversations with Michael Stavrou and Robert Wozniak, whom I thank especially here, have also been really inspiring. Last but not least, I would also like to thank James Ernest of Eerdmans for his kind and patient help in the publication of this volume and Blake Jurgens for his careful and accurate editing.

The gratitude is all the more sincere and heartfelt because this research has been carried out in the hope of helping us overcome this real scandal which

---

Nyssa: Homilies on the Our Father; An English Translation with Commentary and Supporting Studies (Leiden: Brill, 2021).

leads us Christians to find division in our theology about the Holy Spirit, the Third Person, hypostasis of the very unity of the Blessed Trinity. Both the Greek and Latin fathers' judgment of us would be very pointed and severe.

Of final note, translations of the Greek, Latin, and Syriac text are my own, unless otherwise indicated.

Images and Models: Origen's Legacy

I. INTRODUCTION: *CHRĒSIS* AND *KRISIS*

Theology has a paradoxical nature, as its task is to walk along a tightrope between the desire to communicate the mystery of God and the inability or lack of words to do so. The impossibility of fully expressing this mystery is an essential part of the message of the gospel whose content exceeds human possibilities. This means that any attempt to rethink the *Filioque* should be discussed not only at the level of the relationship between tradition and translation but also more deeply in the framework of the disproportion between the content and a form capable of expressing the mystery of the triune God.

From this perspective, the first fundamental stage of the present account should be Origen. He forged many new concepts and discovered important expressive means of communicating the absolute novelty of the Christian revelation through a true reshaping of the conceptual tools at his disposal. His background is indebted to two principal influences: the Semitic milieu and the Greek philosophical tradition. These areas provided the linguistic tools relevant to his interpretation, although we cannot reduce his thinking to such influences.

At this stage, the key issue is not only the lack of words but, more essentially, the lack of actual concepts. Origen's work is fundamental because he filtered through the different traditions of thought at his disposal. His extraordinary theological method paired *chrēsis* and *krisis*: judging (i.e., *krisis*) which elements could be kept and used (i.e., *chrēsis*) in order to express the mystery of the triune God.[1] The process itself was Trinitarian insofar as the key element for each decision was founded not only in the concepts but also in their

---

1. See Ch. Gnilka, *Chrēsis: Die Methode der Kirchenväter im Umgang mit der antiken Kultur; Der Begriff des "rechten Gebrauchs"* (Basel: Schwabel, 2012).

mutual relations.[2] This chapter will outline this process in Origen's theology with respect to Stoic philosophy, Gnosticism, and the imagery common in the Judeo-Christian world.

We have taken Origen as our starting point because his work also directly reveals the difficulties in the development of authentic Christian thought. From the beginning, the dynamic relationships between the Holy Spirit and the Father and the Son have represented a serious issue together with the distinction between and the correlation of the two divine processions. From a bird's-eye view of the great Alexandrian's Trinitarian images, two main "models" will appear and through them the tension that will later lead to the *Filioque* debate will emerge. Here by "model" we mean a metaphorical and not a logical element, in the sense that every thought, including the theological one, needs representations whose dynamics influence its unfolding. While this is not new, the relevance of these "models" to the question of the Son's role in the procession of the Spirit has not been highlighted before.

So the present chapter aims to present the relational background of Origen's Trinitarian theology, that is, the set of questions to which Origen is responding in developing his theological thought. In this case, the central point is the determination of the absolute distinction between the Trinity and creation in terms of pure spirituality: only the three divine Persons have no material or corporeal dimension. But the elaboration of this point will highlight the tensions underlying the chosen formulation, tensions which become the driving issue in the subsequent theological development.

II. Theological *Intentio*

With his theological and expressive genius, Origen captures and formulates the specific difference between Christian and Jewish prayer.[3] In describing the kinds of prayer, he writes:

> It is good, after having started prayer with a doxology, to end it again with a doxology, praising and glorifying the Father of the Universe through Jesus Christ in the Holy Spirit, to whom be glory forever and ever.[4]

2. The Trinitarian perspective implies the necessity to think at the same time the one and the many, introducing the relational element in the *logos* of being and in epistemology. The following chapters will illustrate this connection.

3. On prayer in Origen's thought, cf. L. Perrone, *La Preghiera Secondo Origine: L'impossibilità Donata* (Brescia: Morcelliana, 2011).

4. εὔλογον δὲ ἀρξάμενον ἀπὸ δοξολογίας εἰς δοξολογίαν καταλήγοντα καταπαύειν τὴν

God is the starting point and the end of every prayer, but for the disciples of Jesus these references are Trinitarian. The perspective of *doxa* is thus, from the outset, the basis of both theological reflection and the identification of the *proprium* of the Christian God. The examples are abundant.[5] Prayer and worship are, in fact, essential for understanding the *Sitz im Leben* of the dogmatic elaboration of the early church and its scope.[6]

Origen pairs the citations of 2 Corinthians 3:18[7] and John 7:39 together. Here, it is written "there was, of course, no Spirit yet, because Jesus had not yet been glorified" (οὔπω γὰρ ἦν πνεῦμα, ὅτι Ἰησοῦς οὐδέπω ἐδοξάσθη). This point becomes particularly important for Origen, who seems to be the first to address the theological puzzle posed by the biblical text, a question that is also particularly relevant for determining the relationship between the Son and the Spirit.[8] In fact, he asks, on several occasions, how some affirmations and prophecies in the course of Christ's life are possible *before* His glorification and thus *before* the subsequent outpouring of the Holy Spirit. Commenting on the Transfiguration in Matthew 17:1–8, the Alexandrian author is aware of the fact that his interpretation might be startling. According to Origen, Peter's words, "it is good that we are here. If you wish, I will make three tents" (Matt 17:4), were pronounced in a state of ecstasy or under the influence of a *spirit* (πνεῦμα), given that Mark and Luke underscore the fact that he did not know what he was saying (cf. Mark 9:6 and Luke 9:33):

> Then you will address the question whether Peter said this either in an ecstatic state or spoke it in a spirit which moved him, a spirit which defi-

---

εὐχήν, ὑμνοῦντα καὶ δοξάζοντα τὸν τῶν ὅλων πατέρα διὰ Ἰησοῦ Χριστοῦ ἐν ἁγίῳ πνεύματι, ᾧ ἡ δόξα εἰς τοὺς αἰῶνας (Origen, *De oratione*, 33.6.1–4 [GCS 3:402]).

5. For example, *Epistula ecclesiae Smyrnensis de martyrio sancti Polycarpi*, 14.3.3–4 (SC 10:228) and *Acta Joannis*, 94.9–14 (M. Bonnet, ed., *Acta Apostolorum Apocrypha* [Leipzig: Mendelssohn, 1903], 2.1:197). In the first case, the Spirit is connected with the Father and the Son with the preposition σύν.

6. In this line, Sarah Coakley's prayer-based approach is also fundamental in avoiding any inappropriate reading of Origen's thought from the systematic perspective. See Sarah Coakley, *God, Sexuality, and the Self: An Essay 'On the Trinity'* (Cambridge: Cambridge University Press, 2013).

7. Cf. J. Dupont, "Le chrétien, miroir de la gloire divine d'après II Cor., III, 18," *Revue biblique* 56 (1949): 392–41; and M. Harl, "From Glory to Glory: L'interprétation de 2 Co 3, 18b par Grégoire de Nysse et la liturgie baptismale," in *Kyriakon: Festschrift Johannes Quasten*, ed. P. Granfield (Münster: Aschendorff, 1970), 2:730–35.

8. The text of *Quaestiones in scripturam sacram* in PG 28:720b–c is clearly Pseudo-Athanasian and later.

nitely cannot be holy. In fact John explained in his Gospel that before the resurrection nobody had received the Holy Spirit, when he said "for there was no Spirit yet because Jesus had not yet been glorified" (John 7:39). If there was no Spirit yet and [Peter] spoke without knowing what he was saying, moved by a spirit, this spirit which was prompting him to say such things would be one of those who were not yet defeated by the wood nor paraded in public together with those of whom it has been written: "and he [Christ] has stripped the sovereignties and the ruling forces, and paraded them in public, behind him in his triumphal procession" (Col 2:15) through the wood. Maybe this was the scandal to which Jesus referred, saying "Get behind me, Satan! You are a scandal in my path" (Matt 16:23).[9]

The Alexandrian asks who this *spirit* could be and concludes it can be none other than a fallen angel; the apostle would have still been under its influence, as confirmed by the sleep that falls upon the apostles and by the rebuke and reproach Jesus directs at Peter.[10]

It is evident that this theme is especially important for Origen; in his commentary on John he returns to it several times. In chapter 28, he mentions John 7:39 as evidence of the fact that Caiaphas, though prophesying, did not have in him the Holy Spirit, citing as an argument *a fortiori* that not even the apostles had received the Spirit yet.[11] In chapter 32 the argument reappears[12] in relation to the one who says "Lord, Lord," but will not enter into the kingdom of heaven (cf. Matt 7:21) and the Pauline teaching that it is only by the Holy Spirit that one can say "Jesus is Lord" (cf. 1 Cor 12:3). In Origen's *logic*, the argument is designed to inspire the reader to follow the *Logos*, as demonstrated by his recourse to these same New Testament verses at the end of the work regarding the apostles and their following of Christ.[13]

---

9. ἐπιστήσεις οὖν εἰ κατ᾽ ἔκστασιν ταῦτα ἐλάλει, πεπληρωμένος του κινοῦντος αὐτὸν πνεύματος πρὸς τὸ εἰπεῖν ταῦτα, ὅπερ ἅγιον μὲν εἶναι οὐ δύναται· ἐδίδαξε γὰρ ἐν τῷ εὐαγγελίῳ ὁ Ἰωάννης πρὸ τῆς ἀναστάσεως τοῦ σωτῆρος μηδένα πνεῦμα ἅγιον ἐσχηκέναι εἰπών· οὔπω γὰρ ἦν πνεῦμα, ὅτι Ἰησοῦς οὐδέπω ἐδοξάσθη. εἰ δὲ οὔπω ἦν πνεῦμα, καὶ ὁ μὴ εἰδὼς τί ἐλάλει ὑπό τινος κινούμενος πνεύματος ἐλάλει, ἕν τι τῶν πνευμάτων ἦν τὸ ταῦτα λέγεσθαι ἐνεργοῦν, ὃ μηδέπω ἐν τῷ ξύλῳ μηδὲ δεδειγμάτιστο μετ᾽ ἐκείνων περὶ ὧν γέγραπται τὸ ἀπεκδυσάμενος τὰς ἀρχὰς καὶ τὰς ἐξουσίας ἐδειγμάτισεν ἐν παρρησίᾳ, θριαμβεύσας ἐν τῷ ξύλῳ. τοῦτο δὲ ἦν τάχα τὸ κληθὲν σκάνδαλον ὑπὸ τοῦ Ἰησοῦ καὶ ὁ εἰρημένος σατανᾶς ἐν τῷ ὕπαγε ὀπίσω μου, σατανᾶ· σκάνδαλόν μου εἶ (Origen, *Commentarium in evangelium Matthaei*, 12.40.11–35 [GCS 40:1.157.18–158.10]).

10. Cf. also Origen, *Commentariorum series in evangelium Matthaei*, 237.1.

11. Origen, *Commentarii in evangelium Joannis*, 28.15.127–128 (SC 385:124–126).

12. Origen, *Commentarii in evangelium Joannis*, 32.11.129 (SC 385:244).

13. Origen, *Commentarii in evangelium Joannis*, 32.32.399 (SC 385:358).

The importance of this exegesis is connected with a structuring principle present in all of Origen's theology: the negation of the materiality of God and thus the anti-Stoic interpretation of *pneuma* in the properly spiritual sense as the distinctive character of the divine nature.[14] To understand this necessity it is important to remember that for the Stoics *pneuma* was essentially material because God coincided with the world. Chrysippus writes: "God is body, even though He is intelligent *pneuma* (πνεῦμα νοερόν) and eternal."[15]

Origen's concern is evident from the presence of this theme in the opening of *De principiis*[16] and also in *Contra Celsum*.[17] In both cases, Origen cites "God is Spirit" from John 4:24. Here *pneuma* is found with reference to adoration, expressed with the verb *proskynein* and not by the semantic family connected with *doxa*, though the theological meaning is the same. The Alexandrian's interest is that of highlighting the absurdity of the attribution of corporeality to God on the basis of the physical images used in Scripture, that is, fire, light, and spirit. At the end of *De principiis* 1.1, Origen asks, with irony, how one could acquire intellectual knowledge and understanding of the truth from material light, concluding that it is necessary to interpret the text in a spiritual, nonliteral sense.[18] In fact, on the basis of an obvious reference to "the Lord is the Spirit" (ὁ δὲ κύριος τὸ πνεῦμά ἐστιν) in 2 Corinthians 3:17, he writes:

> But if "we turn to the Lord" where also the Word of God is and where the Holy Spirit reveals spiritual knowledge, then "the veil is removed" and "with unveiled face" we will "gaze upon the glory of the Lord" in the Sacred Scripture (cf. 2 Cor 3:16, 18).[19]

Only by way of the Spirit, then, is it possible to contemplate the glory in the sacred text with a reading that is not simply material and literal but authentically spiritual.

---

14. Cf. M. Simonetti, "Spirito Santo," in *Dizionario Origene*, ed. A. Monaci Castagno (Rome: Città Nuova, 2000), 451.

15. θεὸς σῶμα, πνεῦμα ὢν νοερόν τε καὶ ἀΐδιον (Chrysippus, *Fragmenta logica et physica*, 310.6–7).

16. Cf. the new critical edition of S. Fernández Eyzaguirre, ed., *Origenes: Sobre los principios*, Fuentes patrísticas 27 (Madrid: Ciudad Nueva, 2015).

17. Origen, *De principiis*, 1.1–4 (GCS 22:16–20), and *Contra Celsum*, 4.70–71 (SC 147:352–60). In the latter, the reference to the Stoics is explicit.

18. Origen, *De principiis*, 1.1 (GCS 22:16.19–17.15).

19. "Si autem 'convertamus nos ad dominum', ubi est et verbum dei, et ubi spiritus sanctus revelat scientiam spiritalem, tunc 'auferetur velamen', et tunc 'revelata facie' in scripturis sanctis 'gloriam domini speculamur'" (Origen, *De principiis*, 1.2 [GCS 22:18.16]).

Origen's reasoning has a properly metaphysical character because it discusses the difference between the participation of doctors in the art of medicine and that in the Holy Spirit, whose "subsistence is intellectual and subsists in the proper sense" (*subsistentia est intellectualis et proprie subsistit et extat*).[20]

Clearly, it is in Origen's commentary on John that we arrive at a key moment in the discussion, precisely when he addresses John 4:24. Yet again, he confronts the metaphysical question of the substance of God, referring to various conceptions among other thinkers: those who held it to be a bodily nature (σωματικῆς φύσεως), albeit subtle and ethereal; those who defined it as incorporeal (ἀσωμάτου); and those, like Plato, who considered it above any substance in its dignity and power (ὑπερέκεινα οὐσίας πρεσβείᾳ καὶ δυνάμει).[21] The affirmation that "God is Spirit" is understood as an indication that the *pneuma* is the "substance" of God.[22] However, this poses a problem because, as in the case of a literal reading of God as fire and light, those who hold His nature to be corporeal—like the Stoics—would be correct. Thus, neither *fire* nor *light* nor *pneuma* can be taken literally but are to be read allegorically, as when the scriptural language uses anthropomorphisms to speak of God. If the terms *light* or *darkness* are taken in their common and corporeal sense or in their intelligible or spiritual sense, so too must *fire* and *pneuma* be understood:[23]

> It seems to me that something similar is true for "God is Spirit." In fact, we receive our life from the *pneuma*, that is, the "intermediate life" commonly called life, when our spirit comes to us, that spirit called "breath of life" (cf. Gen 2:7) in a more physical sense. I hold that it is in this meaning God is said to

20. Origen, *De principiis*, 1.3 (GCS 22:19.7).

21. Origen, *Commentarii in evangelium Joannis*, 13.21.123 (SC 222:94–96). The reference is to Plato, *Respublica*, 509c.

22. Origen, *Commentarii in evangelium Joannis*, 13.21.124 (SC 222:96). The term should not be read in a technical sense, as here the discussion is not on the common *ousia* of the Father and the Son, linked to the definition of the latter as *homoousios* to the First Person. As Manlio Simonetti recommends, it is important to avoid any anachronistic projection of the anti-Arian theology of the fourth century upon the reading of the Alexandrian. See M. Simonetti, "Note sulla teologia trinitaria di Origene," *Vetera Christianorum* 8 (1971): 273–307, esp. 274–75. For the discussion of the *homoousios* in Origen, see Richard P. C. Hanson, "Did Origen Apply the Word 'Homoousios' to the Son?," in *Epektasis: Mélanges Jean Daniélou* (Paris: Beauchesne, 1975), 293–303; Mark J. Edwards, "Did Origen Apply the Word 'Homoousios' to the Son?," *Journal of Theological Studies* 49 (1998): 658–70; and Pier Franco Beatrice, "The Word 'Homoousios' from Hellenism to Christianity," *Church History* 71 (2002): 243–72.

23. Origen, *Commentarii in evangelium Joannis*, 13.21.130–39 (SC 222:100–104).

be *pneuma*, because He brings us true life. In fact, Scripture says that the Spirit gives life, showing that He is giver of life (cf. 2 Cor 3:6) not as "intermediate life," but in reference to the life which is more divine: the letter kills and brings death, but not as separation of the soul from the body, but in reference to the separation of the soul from God and from her Lord and from the Holy Spirit.[24]

Thus, it is this spiritual reading and approach that allows for an ever clearer understanding of the sense in which God is Light, Fire, and Spirit; and this spiritual way is essential for truly worshipping God in the Spirit, and not in the letter that kills, and so in the truth and not in shadows and images.[25]

Origen's statements are also explicitly anti-gnostic, as seen in the reference to Heracleon, who maintained a connaturality between the Father and those who adore in spirit and truth, that is, the pneumatics. Origen maintains it is blasphemous to consider the adorers of God consubstantial with God, whose nature is unbegotten and most blessed (τῇ ἀγεννήτῳ φύσει καὶ παμμακαρίᾳ), because it could thus be affirmed that the divine nature is changeable and subject to sin, as happened with the fornication of the Samaritan woman.[26]

In this context we find a paradigmatic text in Origen's Trinitarian theology which has the great merit of clarifying the purely spiritual nature of the divine processions but still employs a form of expression that must—and will soon afterward—be developed and perfected in light of the distinction between economy and immanence. In particular, in recalling the affirmation of Jesus that "the Father is greater than I" in John 14:28[27] and Jesus's refusal to be called "good" by the rich young man in Mark 10:18, Origen writes:

> We say that the Savior and the Holy Spirit cannot be compared to all the creatures but exceed them by far. Yet they in turn are exceeded by the Father as much and even more with respect as to how He and the Spirit exceed the

---

24. Τοιοῦτόν τί μοι φαίνεται καὶ περὶ τὸ Πνεῦμα ὁ θεός· ἐπεὶ γὰρ εἰς τὴν μέσην καὶ κοινότερον καλουμένην ζωήν, φυσῶντος τοῦ περὶ ἡμᾶς πνεύματος τὴν καλουμένην σω- ματικώτερον πνοὴν ζωῆς, ζωοποιούμεθα ἀπὸ τοῦ πνεύματος, ὑπολαμβάνω ἀπ᾽ ἐκείνου εἰλῆφθαι τὸ πνεῦμα λέγεσθαι τὸν θεὸν πρὸς τὴν ἀληθινὴν ζωὴν ἡμᾶς ἄγοντα· τὸ πνεῦμα γὰρ κατὰ τὴν γραφὴν λέγεται ζωοποιεῖν, φανερὸν ὅτι ζωοποίησιν οὐ τὴν μέσην ἀλλὰ τὴν θειοτέραν· καὶ γὰρ τὸ γράμμα ἀποκτέννει καὶ ἐμποιεῖ θάνατον, οὐ τὸν κατὰ τὸν χωρισμὸν τῆς ψυχῆς ἀπὸ τοῦ σώματος, ἀλλὰ τὸν κατὰ τὸν χωρισμὸν τῆς ψυχῆς ἀπὸ τοῦ θεοῦ, καὶ τοῦ κυρίου αὐτοῦ, καὶ τοῦ ἁγίου πνεύματος (Origen, *Commentarii in evangelium Joannis*, 13.21.140.1–12 [SC 222:106]).

25. Origen, *Commentarii in evangelium Joannis*, 13.24.146 (SC 222:110).

26. Origen, *Commentarii in evangelium Joannis*, 13.25.148–50 (SC 222:110–12).

27. Origen, *Commentarii in evangelium Joannis*, 13.25.151 (SC 222:112–14).

other beings, and not just any ones. Is it necessary to say something on how much the doxology of the greater One [the *Logos*] is superior to Thrones, Dominions, Principalities, Powers and every name spoken not only in this age but in the future one too, and also above the holy angels and the spirits and the souls of the righteous? Nevertheless, even if He is superior to so many and such beings, according to essence, dignity, power, and divinity—that is, the animated *Logos* in person—and wisdom, He cannot at all be compared to the Father. In fact He is image of the Father's goodness and refulgence not of God, but of His glory (cf. Heb 1:3) and of His eternal light, and He is ray not of the Father, but of His power, and pure effusion of His almighty Glory and immaculate mirror of His activity (cf. Wis 7:25). Paul and Peter and those like them see God through this mirror who says "whoever has seen me has seen the one who sent me" (cf. John 12:45).[28]

According to this text, the distance of the Father with respect to the other two divine Persons is greater than that between these divine persons and creatures. The Son, who is superior to all the angelic hosts, is, at the same time, splendour only of the glory of God, not of God Himself.[29] We have here a principle of ontological distinction between the glory and God, something which makes divine knowledge possible directly in the *Logos* without necessarily passing through Christ, that is, through the human nature of the incarnate *Logos*.

This is confirmed by Origen's affirmation that the exchange of glory between the Father and the Son is asymmetrical in that the glory the First Person gives to the Second Person is much greater (πολλῷ γε ὑπερέχουσα) than that which the

28. πάντων μὲν τῶν γενητῶν ὑπερέχειν οὐ συγκρίσει ἀλλ' ὑπερβαλλούσῃ ὑπεροχῇ φαμὲν τὸν σωτῆρα καὶ τὸ πνεῦμα τὸ ἅγιον, ὑπερεχόμενον τοσοῦτον ἢ καὶ πλέον ἀπὸ τοῦ πατρός, ὅσῳ ὑπερέχει αὐτὸς καὶ τὸ ἅγιον πνεῦμα τῶν λοιπῶν, οὐ τῶν τυχόντων ὄντων. Ὅσῃ γὰρ δοξολογία τοῦ ὑπερέχοντος θρόνων, κυριοτήτων, ἀρχῶν, ἐξουσιῶν, καὶ παντὸς ὀνόματος ὀνομαζομένου οὐ μόνον ἐν τῷ αἰῶνι τούτῳ ἀλλὰ καὶ ἐν τῷ μέλλοντι, πρὸς τούτοις καὶ ἁγίων ἀγγέλων καὶ πνευμάτων καὶ ψυχῶν δικαίων, τί δεῖ καὶ λέγειν; Ἀλλ' ὅμως τῶν τοσούτων καὶ τηλικούτων ὑπερέχων οὐσίᾳ καὶ πρεσβείᾳ καὶ δυνάμει καὶ θειότητι – ἔμψυχος γάρ ἐστι λόγος – καὶ σοφία, οὐ συγκρίνεται κατ' οὐδὲν τῷ πατρί. Εἰκὼν γάρ ἐστιν τῆς ἀγαθότητος αὐτοῦ καὶ ἀπαύγασμα οὐ τοῦ θεοῦ ἀλλὰ τῆς δόξης αὐτοῦ καὶ τοῦ ἀϊδίου φωτὸς αὐτοῦ, καὶ ἀτμὶς οὐ τοῦ πατρὸς ἀλλὰ τῆς δυνάμεως αὐτοῦ, καὶ ἀπόρροια εἰλικρινὴς τῆς παντοκρατορικῆς δόξης αὐτοῦ, καὶ ἔσοπτρον ἀκηλίδωτον τῆς ἐνεργείας αὐτοῦ, δι' οὗ ἐσόπτρου Παῦλος καὶ Πέτρος καὶ οἱ παραπλήσιοι αὐτοῖς βλέπουσι τὸν θεὸν λέγοντος· Ὁ ἑωρακὼς ἐμὲ ἑώρακε τὸν πατέρα τὸν πέμψαντά με (Origen, *Commentarii in evangelium Joannis*, 13.25.151.6–153.8 [SC 222:114]).

29. See also C. Blanc, "Jésus est fils de Dieu: L'interprétation d'Origène," *Bulletin de littérature ecclésiastique* 84 (1983): 5–18.

Second gives to the First.[30] In chapter 4 we will see how the response to Pneumatomachians will require the symmetrization of this exchange of glory.[31]

This asymmetry in Origen's picture comes from an underlying tension in the dogmatic reflection at this stage: the affirmation of the unity of nature of the three divine Persons, which Origen expresses by way of pure spirituality, must be brought into harmony with a graduated ontological conception in which the Father, the Son, and the Holy Spirit are on three different metaphysical levels, differentiated by the intensity of their participation in being which is found in absolute fullness only in the First Person.

To avoid any risk of anachronism, however, it is essential to keep firmly in mind the *intentio* of Origen who is engaged in exploring the hermeneutical tension between (a) the *Spirit* understood as God in the substantial—and thus incorporeal—sense; (b) *Spirit* with reference to the Third Person of the Trinity in the personal sense; and, finally (c) *spirit* with reference to the fallen angels. The connection with the glory of God is already evident because it is theologically linked to the affirmation of the divinity but, at the same time, there is still a linguistic imperfection which distinguishes the glory from the person of the Father.[32]

In sum, Origen overcomes the Greek metaphysics picture where God and the world are both finite and eternal, being connected in one graduated chain (see fig. 1a), and presents a theological metaphysics characterized by two levels where the Father, the Son, and the Spirit are absolutely distinct from every other being on account of their perfect spirituality. Between the Trinity and the world there is a real ontological gap[33] (see fig. 1b). However, this bi-level formulation—lacking a key element like the ontological conception of *physis*, as will be developed in the fourth century—creates within the first level a gradation among the divine persons. In fact, the Second and the Third Persons are differentiated from the First in terms of participation and, thus, in substantial terms.[34]

---

30. Origen, *Commentarii in evangelium Joannis*, 32.29.364 (SC 385:344).

31. See pp. 126–34.

32. In the Semitic tradition too, the glory has an ontological character in that the *Kabod* indicates what it most truly is. See, for example, G. M. Porrino, *Le poids et la gloire: Splendeur de Dieu, splendeur de l'homme, de la Genèse aux Psaumes* (Paris: Cerf, 2016).

33. On the importance of the "gap" in later Cappadocian theology, see S. Douglass, *Theology of the Gap: Cappadocian Language Theory and the Trinitarian Controversy* (New York: Lang, 2007).

34. Giovanni Hermanin de Reichenfeld highlights that this "subordination" is only logical and not ontological. See his "The Role of the Holy Spirit in the Gospel of John within Origen's and Augustine's Commentaries" (PhD diss., University of Exeter, 2018), 60.

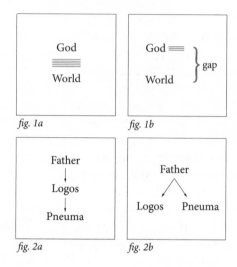

fig. 1a   fig. 1b

fig. 2a   fig. 2b

From this tension, two principal Trinitarian models will arise with an evident value for the question of the *Filioque*. Manlio Simonetti[35] has designated these models the *linear* and the *triangular*. The former describes the inner being of God and presents the Son after the Father, and the Spirit after the Son (see fig. 2a). The Arians will refer to this model as an authority. The *triangular* model is more ancient, recalls divine action, and presents the Son and the Spirit together in mission (see fig. 2b).

The importance of these models for the understanding of the relationship between the Son and the Spirit is obvious. In the linear conception, the Spirit receives being in part from the Second Person in such a way that the procession of the Third Person from the Father and the Son is linked to the imperfection of the Trinitarian formulation. In the triangular conception, however, the two processions appear to be independent yet the distinction between the missions and the processions remains unclear. As it will be seen in the next chapters, the weak points of the linear model will be highlighted by the Arian crisis, whereas the weak points of the triangular model will be highlighted by the Pneumatomachian crisis.

It is essential, therefore, that we deepen the theological study of these views of the background of Origen's *intentio* in order to analyse, in the following chapters, how the tensions and linguistic imperfections we have identified are treated in the development of the history of Trinitarian thought.

35. Simonetti, "Note sulla teologia trinitaria di Origene," 273–307.

III. Dove and Child: The Triangular Model

III.1. Child and Disciples

A very important and almost paradigmatic example of the triangular model is the pneumatological reading of the word *paidion* in Matthew 18:2, something which is clearly motivated by Origen's theological attention to the spiritual dimension. According to this exegesis, the *child* is understood not only with reference to simplicity and the absence of passions, elements that liken children to the more properly spiritual dimension. For after presenting a moral exegesis, Origen makes it clear that he is offering a doctrinally oriented explanation as a sort of exercise (εἴτε ὡς δόγματος εἴτε ὡς γυμνασίου ἕνεκεν):[36]

> You see, then, that it can be said that the child which Jesus called is the Holy Spirit who has humbled himself, called by the Savior and placed at the center of the soul of the disciples of Jesus. And if He wants us to, having abandoned all other things, we turn to the examples proposed by the Holy Spirit in such a way that we become like children—that is the disciples—who have also abandoned those things and have become like the Holy Spirit. Such children has God [the Father] given to the Savior, according to that which Isaiah says: "Behold, I, and the children that the Lord has given me" (Isa 8:18).[37]

This text explicitly refers to a humbling of the Holy Spirit who comes to dwell among men and communicate himself to those who are worthy. The essential point is that the child is not *like* the Holy Spirit but *is* the Holy Spirit. For Origen, the moral dimension is essentially anchored to ontology: only one who has the Holy Spirit can act as Jesus does. This is clarified by what follows in the text:

---

36. Origen, *Commentarium in evangelium Matthaei*, 13.18.3–4 (GCS 40:226.20–21).

37. ὅρα δὲ εἰ δύνασαι τὸ ταπεινῶσαν ἑαυτὸ πνεῦμα ἅγιον, ὑπὸ τοῦ σωτῆρος προσκλη-θὲν καὶ σταθὲν ἐν μέσῳ τῷ ἡγεμονικῷ τῶν μαθητῶν Ἰησοῦ, εἰπεῖν εἶναι ὃ προσεκαλέσατο ὁ Ἰησοῦς παιδίον, εἴτε βούλεται ἡμᾶς πάντα τὰ ἄλλα ἀποστραφέντας στραφῆναι πρὸς τὰ παραδείγματα ὑπὸ τοῦ ἁγίου ὑποβαλλόμενα πνεύματος, ὥστε ἡμᾶς οὕτω γενέσθαι ὡς τὰ παιδία τουτέστι τοὺς ἀποστόλους, τὰ καὶ αὐτὰ στραφέντα καὶ ὁμοιωθέντα τῷ ἁγίῳ πνεύματι· ἅτινα παιδία ἔδωκεν ὁ θεὸς τῷ σωτῆρι κατὰ τὸ ἐν Ἡσαΐᾳ λελεγμένον· ἰδοὺ ἐγὼ καὶ τὰ παιδία ἅ μοι ἔδωκεν ὁ θεός (Origen, *Commentarium in evangelium Matthaei*, 13.18.7–24 [GCS 40:226.24–227.11]).

This Holy Spirit, who, from his perfection, lowered himself to come to men, was called by Jesus and placed as a child among the disciples. It is thus necessary, abandoning desires for worldly things, to humble oneself, not only like a child, but, as is written, like *this* child. And to humble oneself as that child means to humble oneself for God and to imitate the Holy Spirit who lowered himself for men. And that the Savior and the Holy Spirit were sent by the Father for the salvation of men is shown in Isaiah, who says in the name of the Savior: "Now the Lord God has sent me together with his Spirit" (Isa 48:16). But one must pay attention as the expression is double: For either God [the Father] sent, and also the Holy Spirit sent the Savior, or, as it is interpreted, the Father sent both the Savior and the Holy Spirit.[38]

Here the incarnate *Logos* and the Spirit are placed on the same level, creating an implicit identification between the missions of the Second and the Third Person. From the theological point of view, two aspects are worth mentioning:

1. The dimension of *likeness* is not applied at the mere level of image because this child *is* the Holy Spirit and not merely *like* the Spirit. Likeness, instead, is found only on the level of the disciples who must be *like* this child, in that they are called to become ever more spiritual in an *imitatio Spiritus*[39] which, according to Origen, is a condition for the *imitatio Christi*.

2. The reading of Isaiah 48:16, and thus of the possible role of the Third Person in the sending of the Second, is linked to the previous point. This aspect appears to be essential in interpreting the dogmatic value of the images used for the Third Person of the Trinity and for the later theological development of the understanding of the distinction between processions and missions.

---

38. ὅπερ πνεῦμα ἅγιον προσκαλεσάμενος ὁ Ἰησοῦς, ἀπὸ τῆς ἰδίας τελειότητος καταβεβηκὸς πρὸς ἀνθρώπους, ὡς παιδίον ἔστησεν αὐτὸ ἐν μέσῳ τῶν μαθητῶν. δεῖ οὖν στραφέντα ἀπὸ τῶν κοσμικῶν ἐπιθυμιῶν ταπεινῶσαι ἑαυτόν, οὐχ ἁπλῶς ὡς τὸ παιδίον, ἀλλὰ κατὰ τὸ γεγραμμένον ὡς τὸ παιδίον τοῦτο. ἔστι δὲ τὸ ταπεινῶσαι ἑαυτὸν ὡς τὸ παιδίον ἐκεῖνο τὸ ταπεινῶσαι ἑαυτὸν ὑπὲρ θεοῦ καὶ τὸ μιμήσασθαι τὸ ὑπὲρ σωτηρίας ἀνθρώπων ταπεινῶσαν ἑαυτὸ πνεῦμα ἅγιον. ὅτι δὲ ὁ σωτὴρ καὶ τὸ ἅγιον πνεῦμα ἐξαπεστάλη ὑπὸ τοῦ πατρὸς ἐπὶ σωτηρίᾳ τῶν ἀνθρώπων, δεδήλωται ἐν τῷ Ἡσαΐᾳ ἐκ προσώπου τοῦ σωτῆρος λέγοντι· καὶ νῦν κύριος ἀπέστειλέ με καὶ τὸ πνεῦμα αὐτοῦ. ἰστέον μέντοι ὅτι ἀμφίβολός ἐστιν ἡ λέξις· ἢ γὰρ ὁ θεὸς ἀπέστειλεν, ἀπέστειλε δὲ καὶ τὸ πνεῦμα τὸ ἅγιον τὸν σωτῆρα, ἢ (ὡς ἐξειλήφαμεν) ἀμφότερα ἀπέστειλεν ὁ πατήρ, τὸν σωτῆρα καὶ τὸ ἅγιον πνεῦμα (Origen, *Commentarium in evangelium Matthaei*, 12.18.29–56 [GCS 40:227.16–228.24]).

39. Cf. M. Beyer Moser, *Teacher of Holiness: The Holy Spirit in Origen's Commentary on the Epistle to the Romans* (Piscataway, NJ: Gorgias, 2005), 146–69.

The relevance of this image and the underlying Trinitarian model for the discussion on the *Filioque* is evident.

This exegesis of Matthew 18:2 is taken up by Jerome alone and in a clearly dependent manner, in that one finds the same movement from a first moral reading to a more specifically doctrinal one which identifies the child and the Spirit.[40] It is easy to understand why the Greek theology of the fourth century, facing the Arian and Pneumatomachian crises, laid this identification aside. It is worth noting, however, how Origen paved a way for a new and successful path of thought. For, at the end of passage cited above, the text of Matthew is placed parallel to the "He who does not receive the kingdom of God like a child will not enter into it" of Luke 18:17:

> And the expression is double: For, either he who receives the kingdom of God becomes like a child, or he receives the kingdom of God which has become like a child for him.[41]

Origen's identification of the child with the Holy Spirit leads on to the identification of the Third Person with the kingdom of God, which will be found again later in Gregory of Nyssa's response to the Macedonian heresy as an attempt to clarify the role of the Spirit in the relationship between the Father and the Son, as chapter 4 will show.[42] This theological perspective can be also connected with the Syriac tradition through the identification of the Spirit with the kingdom, as occurs in a Lukan variant of the *Our Father*, discussed in chapters 5 and 6.[43]

Chapter 4 will present at the essential difference between the identifications of the Holy Spirit with the kingdom in Origen and in Gregory of Nyssa, showing how the former operates on the economic level, associating the Son and the Spirit with the kingdom in mission, while the latter, in a different polemical context, identifies the Third Person with the kingdom on the immanent level as the Spirit's personal and distinctive characteristic with respect to the Son, who is King in so far as He is the perfect image of the Father who is King.[44]

Origen's economic perspective is also manifest in his reference to the *kenōsis* not only of Christ but also of the Spirit: given that the world itself is a lower

---

40. Jerome, *Commentarii in euangelium Matthaei*, 3.486–92 (CCSL 77:156).

41. καὶ ἔστιν ἀμφίβολος ἡ λέξις, ἢ γὰρ ἵνα ὁ δεχόμενος τὴν τοῦ θεοῦ βασιλείαν γένηται ὡς παιδίον, ἢ ἵνα τὴν τοῦ θεοῦ βασιλείαν παραδέξηται γενομένην αὐτῷ ὡς παιδίον (Origen, *Commentarium in evangelium Matthaei*, 13.19.94–99 [GCS 40:233.18–21]).

42. Gregory of Nyssa, *Adversus Macedonianos*, GNO 3.1:102.26–28. See below on pp. 119–26.

43. See below on pp. 150–60, 198.

44. See below on p. 121.

reality, the presence of the two Trinitarian Persons in time cannot be read as anything other than a *kenōsis*. In the fourth century, the distinction between economy and immanence will bring an understanding of the mission of the Spirit in the world not only as a lowering but as the fullness of the presence of the divinity in history.

In brief, after having considered this first image, three more properly dogmatic aspects underpinning the text can be enumerated:

1. The placement of the Son and the Third Person on the same level, according to the triangular schema.
2. The role of direct imitation of the Spirit, and not of the humanity of Christ, tied to the radical spiritualization of God, and thus of sanctification.
3. The *kenōsis* of the Spirit in mission, parallel to that of the Son.

These three elements are closely connected to one another in the expression of the image in question. Origen presents the Son and the Spirit from a soteriological perspective, stressing the role of their missions, but this seems to imply an imperfect affirmation of the ontological identity of the three divine Persons.[45]

III.2. Doves and Angels

These three dogmatic aspects can be better understood in the context of Origen's Trinitarian doctrine by turning to the Song of Songs, the most spiritual and theological book of the Old Testament according to the Alexandrian tradition.

In chapter 3 of his commentary on the Song of Songs, referring to "How beautiful you are, my friend, how beautiful! Your eyes are doves!" (Song 1:15), Origen argues as follows: the dove is a symbol of the Holy Spirit, and the eyes of the bride are referred to as doves because they are capable of a spiritual gaze, that is, of gazing upon one's interior.[46] However, in a movement analogous to that noted for the image of the child in his *Commentarium in evangelium Matthaei*, immediately following the spiritual exegesis, Origen's attention turns

---

45. For a serious and effective criticism of any interpretation of Origen's theology in the line of a real, and not merely verbal, subordinationism, see I. Ramelli, "Origen's Anti-Subordinationism and Its Heritage in the Nicene and Cappadocian Line," *Vigiliae Christianae* 65 (2011): 21–49.

46. Origen, *In Canticum canticorum*, 3 (GCS 33:173–74).

toward an "even more profound mystery" where he applies "behold you are beautiful" to the Church, offering a completely original interpretation:

> For this reason her eyes are called *doves*, in such a way that the two *doves* that are the two *eyes* are interpreted as the Son of God and the Holy Spirit. And do not be surprised that both are called *doves* since each of them is called *advocate* in the same way. For the evangelist John calls the Holy Spirit *Paraclete*, that is, *advocate* (John 14:16), and in the same way, in his letter he says of Jesus Christ that He is the "advocate with the Father" for our sins (1 John 2:1). But, even more, it is believed that the two olive trees placed at the right and left of the lampstand, according to Zechariah (cf. Zech 4:3), designate the only-begotten One and the Holy Spirit.[47]

In his *Commentarii in evangelium Joannis*,[48] Origen interprets the eyes of the dove in a moral sense with reference to the visual capacity of those who are spiritual. In the fourth century, this exegesis will be taken up again by Gregory of Nyssa in his commentary on the Song of Songs.[49] In the quoted text, however, Origen is stepping into a deeper level of interpretation, reading the scriptural text at the level of dogma, and this is the real foundation for the spiritual interpretation. He is conscious of the surprising nature of his original exegesis. This interpretation is, nevertheless, well-founded in his theology, the main concern of which is the affirmation that "God is Spirit," as we have already seen:[50] The Son and the Spirit are both called *doves* because they belong to the Trinity who is Spirit, that is, *dove*. The entire created world, on the other hand, is typified by materiality, even if that materiality is ethereal, as in the case of the angels. At the same time, however, the Son and the Spirit are distinguished from each other and from the dove itself, without ever being separated from it. This is expressed through the use of the image of the eyes

---

47. "Et ibi dicat esse *oculos* eius *columbas*, ut duorum *oculorum* duae *columbae* intelligantur esse filius Dei et Spiritus sanctus. Et ne mireris, si *columbae* simul dicantur, cum uterque similiter *advocatus* dicatur, sicut Iohannes evangelista declarat *Spiritum* quidem sanctum dicens *paracletum*, quod est advocatus; et de Iesu Christo nihilominus in epistola sua dicit quia ipse sit *advocatus apud patrem* pro peccatis nostris. Sed et apud Zachariam prophetam *duae olivae ad dexteram et ad sinistram candelabri positae* unigenitum nihilominus et Spiritum sanctum designare creduntur" (Origen, *In Canticum canticorum*, 3 [GCS 33:174.13–22]).

48. Origen, *Commentarii in evangelium Joannis*, 10:28.173 (SC 157:488).

49. Gregory of Nyssa, *In Canticum canticorum*, GNO 4:116 and 219.

50. Cf. Simonetti, "Spirito Santo," 451.

of the dove, identified with the Second and Third Persons. Such exegesis is favored by the comparison of John 14:16 and 1 John 2:1 where the title Paraclete is attributed to the Spirit or to Christ.

The origin of the use of the image seems to be rooted in the necessity of placing Christ and the Spirit on the same level, thus clearly working within the triangular Trinitarian model. At the same time, Origen also manifests the need to distinguish the two Persons when, in *De principiis*, the word Paraclete is used with reference to the Third Person in terms of consolation—insofar as He reveals the spiritual sense—while Paraclete is used with reference to the Second Person in terms of the advocate.[51] Looking at Origen's exegesis from the later perspective of the relationship between economy and immanence, it is as though he was seeking the immanent foundation of the missions of the Son and of the Spirit, placed side by side like the eyes of the dove, while at the same time was reading them as belonging to the nature of God Himself, which is Spirit, that is, dove.

The image of the two eyes of the dove is then connected with the clearly Semitic image of the two olive trees of Zechariah 4:3. This dogmatic interpretation, along with that of the child of Matthew 18:1–4 and the eyes of the dove in Song of Songs 1:15, will be abandoned in the fourth century. In his commentary on Zechariah, Didymus reveals his awareness of this exegesis of Origen but interprets it in terms of theological "notions of the Son and of the Spirit" (οἱ περὶ Υἱοῦ καὶ ἁγίου Πνεύματός εἰσιν λόγοι).[52] For this he cites the authority of the church of Alexandria, probably referring to Athanasius.[53] The semantic shift is evident as is Didymus's intention to avoid any possible misunderstanding regarding the divine nature of the Son and the Spirit by moving from the level of being to that of language.

Origen's connecting of the two olive trees with the Son and the Spirit is clearly linked to Judeo-Christian theology and to angelomorphic Christology and pneumatology.[54] This is evident also in his exegesis of the two seraphim:

> For, without a doubt, all those who walk the earth, that is all the earthly and corporeal realities, are participants in the Holy Spirit, receiving Him from God [the Father]. A Hebrew master himself said that those two seraphim,

51. Origen, *De principiis*, 2.7.3 (GCS 22:150).
52. Didymus, *In Zachariam*, 1.286 (SC 83:342).
53. Didymus, *In Zachariam*, 3.343.
54. See Ch. A. Gieschen, *Angelomorphic Christology: Antecedents and Early Evidence* (Leiden: Brill, 1998); B. Bucur, *Angelomorphic Pneumatology: Clement of Alexandria and Other Early Christian Witnesses* (Leiden: Brill, 2009).

that in Isaiah are described with six wings, proclaiming one to the other, saying: "Holy, Holy Holy, the Lord of hosts" (Isa 6:3), are to be understood as the only begotten Son and the Holy Spirit. But we maintain that that which is said in the canticle of Habakkuk must also be understood as referring to Christ and the Holy Spirit: "You will be known among the two animals" (or "living beings") (Hab 3:2, LXX). For every knowledge about the Father is received in the Holy Spirit, by the revelation of the Son, in such a way that both of those beings that are called animals or living beings by the prophet exist for the knowledge of God the Father.[55]

Jean Daniélou traces this reading back to Judeo-Christian circles rather than to Philo.[56] It is interesting to note that Origen not only continues the angelomorphic exegesis present in this background but reinforces it with the reading of the two living beings of Habakkuk 3:2 in terms of the Son and the Spirit.

In fact, in Judeo-Christian circles the image of the Angel of Yahweh was used as a first rudimentary concept of person[57] in order to indicate that God Himself acted in history and had entered into a relationship of intimacy with His people. It was a means of protecting the absolute transcendence of Yahweh while at the same time manifesting His personal dimension. In the first Trinitarian reflection to come from Semitic circles, it is reasonable to suppose that this image would have developed naturally to be applied to the Son and the Spirit in order to indicate their mission in time.

So, in the case of these images, three historical and dogmatic elements can be enumerated:

1. The divine nature is in fact identified with the spiritual dimension.
2. The association of the Son and the Spirit is tied to the Semitic tradition, and in particular to Judeo-Christian circles.

---

55. "Sine dubio enim omnis qui calcat terram, id est terrena et corporalia, particeps est spiritus sancti, a deo eum accipiens. Dicebat autem et Hebraeus magister quod duo alla Seraphin, quae in Esaia senis alis describuntur clamantia adinuicem et dicentia: *Sanctus sanctus sanctus dominus Sabaoth*, de unigenito filio et de spiritu sancto esset intellegendum. Nos uero putamus etiam illud, quod in cantico Ambacum dictum est: *In medio duorum animalium* (uel *duarum uitarum*) *cognosceris*, de Christo et de spiritu sancto sentiri debere. Omnis enim scientia de patre, reuelante filio, in spiritu sancto cognoscitur, ut ambo haec, quae secundum prophetam uel animantia uel uitae dicuntur, causa scientiae dei patris existant" (Origen, *De principiis*, 1.3.4 [GCS 22:52.15–53.13]).

56. J. Daniélou, *Théologie du Judéo-christianisme* (Tournai: Desclée, 1958), 222.

57. Daniélou, *Théologie du Judéo-christianisme*, 205.

3.   For this reason, the images can be related to angelology and early angelo-
     morphic Trinitarian doctrine.

Therefore, in what we have seen thus far, Origen refers to the Holy Spirit using
various images, all biblical and traditional, but read through a pneumatological
lens in the light of the totality of his theology. In addition to the child of Matthew 18:1–4, with which we began, we can also include the eyes of the dove of
Song of Songs 1:15, the olive trees of Zechariah 4:3, the seraphim of Isaiah 6:3,
and the living beings of Habakkuk 3:2. All these images can be presented as
a synthesis of the fundamental themes of the Alexandrian's thought and his
Semitic background.

III.3. Spirit and Mother

Origen is aware that the use of creaturely images to refer to the Third Person,
even images of plants and animals, requires an explanation to avoid misunderstandings. For this reason, he labors to explain the sense of what he is
proposing, changing the meaning and modifying the images in relation to the
tradition from which he draws. In doing so he purifies and criticises them, thus
manifesting the theological value of the images themselves.

One clear case of this reinterpretation is the image of the Holy Spirit as
mother of Christ, an image again derived directly from the Semitic tradition:

> If one accepts the Gospel according to the Hebrews, where the Savior Him-
> self says "My mother, the Holy Spirit, took me by one of my hairs and led
> me to the great mountain, Tabor," he will find himself before the difficulty
> of how the Holy Spirit can be the mother of Christ if He was made by means
> of the Word. But it will not be difficult to explain this thus as well: For if
> "whoever fulfils the will of my Father who is in heaven, is" for Him "brother,
> sister and mother" (Matt 12:50), and if the name of brother of Christ refers
> not only to the race of men, but also to more divine realities than them, it
> will be in no way absurd that, more than any other who receives the title of
> mother of Christ, the Holy Spirit is His Mother in so far as He accomplishes
> the will of the heavenly Father.[58]

58. Ἐὰν δὲ προσίηται τις τὸ καθ' Ἑβραίους εὐαγγέλιον, ἔνθα αὐτὸς ὁ σωτήρ φησιν·
Ἄρτι ἔλαβέ με ἡ μήτηρ μου, τὸ ἅγιον πνεῦμα, ἐν μιᾷ τῶν τριχῶν μου καὶ ἀπήνεγκέ με εἰς
τὸ ὄρος τὸ μέγα Θαβώρ, ἐπαπορήσει, πῶς μήτηρ Χριστοῦ τὸ διὰ τοῦ λόγου γεγενημένον
πνεῦμα ἅγιον εἶναι δύναται. Ταῦτα δὲ καὶ τούτῳ οὐ χαλεπὸν ἑρμηνεῦσαι· εἰ γὰρ ὁ ποιῶν τὸ
θέλημα τοῦ πατρὸς τοῦ ἐν τοῖς οὐρανοῖς ἀδελφὸς καὶ ἀδελφὴ καὶ μήτηρ ἐστὶν αὐτοῦ καὶ

The Alexandrian author is here taking up an image which, in all probability, is linked with the primitive theology of Semitic circles and which is conditioned by the use of the feminine for the word *spirit* in both Hebrew and Syriac.[59] This image was also present in gnostic theology of Egyptian origin.[60] From Origen's perspective, this attribution of maternity to the Spirit would influence the discussion of a possible role of the Third Person in the sending of the Second, something already seen in the commentary on Matthew 18:1–4 with reference to Isaiah 48:16. For this reason, the image is reinterpreted in the light of the concord of will of the three divine hypostases.

This solution, which could appear weak from a fourth-century perspective, can be received in all its force, however, by situating the affirmations in the philosophical background of Middle Platonism. For Origen, God is essentially love, in the sense that the three divine Persons are united in freedom. God moves from the Greek metaphysical dimension of necessity to that of the most pure and true freedom. That this explanation will be interpreted later on the level of moral unity alone cannot overshadow the radical originality introduced here. The doctrinal progress of the fourth century will try to protect the very nucleus of this intuition of Origen by means of the development of the highly sophisticated linguistic tool of *physis*.

Thus, the Alexandrian author reinterprets the Semitic images known to him, moving in the same theological direction that will lead to the disappearance of the feminine images referring to the Spirit, and, in Syriac circles, even to the change of gender of the term *ruhâ* in the fourth century for specifically theological reasons.[61] This is nothing other than an ever more theological understanding of the images themselves and an effort to adapt them

---

φθάνει τὸ ἀδελφὸς Χριστοῦ ὄνομα οὐ μόνον ἐπὶ τὸ τῶν ἀνθρώπων γένος ἀλλὰ καὶ ἐπὶ τὰ τούτου θειότερα, οὐδὲν ἄτοπον ἔσται μᾶλλον πάσης χρηματιζούσης μητρὸς Χριστοῦ διὰ τὸ ποιεῖν τὸ θέλημα τοῦ ἐν τοῖς οὐρανοῖς πατρὸς τὸ πνεῦμα τὸ ἅγιον εἶναι μητέρα (Origen, *Commentarii in evangelium Joannis*, 2.12.87.1– 88.8 [SC 120:262]).

59. Cf. E. Kaniyamparampil, *The Spirit of Life* (Kottayam: OIRSI, 2003), 208–23.

60. The Elkesaites were a heterodox Judeo-Christian group of the second century characterized by gnostic elements. The founder conceived the Holy Spirit as a feminine being. Cf. G. G. Stroumsa, "Le couple de l'Ange et de l'Esprit: Traditions juives et chrétiennes," *Revue biblique* 88 (1981): 43–47, and S. C. Mimouni, *Le judéo-christianisme ancien* (Paris: Cerf, 1998), 287–316.

61. See S. Brock, "The Holy Spirit as Feminine in Early Syriac Literature," in *After Eve: Woman, Theology, and the Christian Tradition*, ed. J. Martin Soskice (London: HarperCollins, 1990), 73–88. Significantly, in Hebrew and Aramaic, this change of gender did not occur because there the theological development and the peculiar dogmatic elaboration were less important. See chapter 6 for more details.

in a continually more perfect manner in order to refer to the mystery, moving beyond the limitations of expressive form and the misunderstandings these can provoke.

An example of a similar exegesis, in a context that is still clearly Semitic, can be found in the commentary on Psalm 122 in the *Selecta in Psalmos*, of dubious attribution to Origen.[62] With reference to the second verse, "Behold, as the eyes of servants are directed to the hands of their masters, and as the eyes of a maidservant to the hands of her mistress; so our eyes are directed to the Lord our God, until He have mercy upon us," it states:

> the spirit and the body are servants of masters, that is of the Father and the Son; while the soul is the handmaid of the mistress, the Holy Spirit. And these three are the Lord our God, because the three are but one. For, the eyes of servants regard the hands of masters, that is, of the Father and the Son, and their powers belong to the mistress, the Holy Spirit.[63]

This text intertwines angelology, anthropology, and Trinitarian reflection in a whole that has a clearly ancient note, as it speaks of the Spirit in feminine terms, identifying Him with the *mistress* of the psalm. The tripartite division of the human being into spirit, body, and soul is placed here in relation to the three divine Persons.

Origen introduces the same tripartite division in his interpretation of the image of the leaven in Luke 13:21. The woman who kneads the dough with leaven is interpreted in an ecclesiological manner while the Spirit is identified with the leaven itself, and the three portions are tied specifically to the human body, spirit, and soul.[64] Once again material symbolism is at the service of the affirmation of the Spirit's presence in the world, particularly in humanity.

---

62. For exegetical writings on the Psalms, see the article "Salmi," by E. Prinzivalli, in Castagno, *Dizionario Origene*, 422–24.

63. Δοῦλοι κυρίων Πατρὸς καὶ Υἱοῦ πνεῦμα καὶ σῶμα· παιδίσκη δὲ κυρίας τοῦ ἁγίου Πνεύματος ἡ ψυχή. Τὰ δὲ τρία Κύριος ὁ Θεὸς ἡμῶν ἐστιν· οἱ γὰρ τρεῖς τὸ ἕν εἰσιν. Ὀφθαλμοὶ γοῦν δούλων εἰς χεῖρας κυρίων ὁρῶντες, ὅτε διὰ χειρῶν νεύοντες κελεύσουσιν. Ἡ χεῖρες κυρίων μὲν Πατρὸς καὶ Υἱοῦ οἱ ἑκατέρου ἄγγελοι· κυρίας δὲ τοῦ ἁγίου Πνεύματος αἱ οἰκεῖαι αὐτοῦ δυνάμεις (Pseudo-Origen, *Selecta in Psalmos*, PG 12:1633c).

64. Ἑτέρως ἔστι λαβεῖν τὴν μὲν γυναῖκα εἰς τὴν ἐκκλησίαν, τὴν δὲ ζύμην εἰς τὸ πνεῦμα τὸ ἅγιον, σάτα δὲ τρία σῶμα, πνεῦμα, ψυχήν. ἁγιάζεται δὲ ταῦτα τῇ ζύμῃ τοῦ ἁγίου πνεύματος, ὥστε γενέσθαι πρὸς τὸ ἅγιον πνεῦμα ἓν φύραμα (Origen, *Fragmenta in Lucam*, 82 [GCS 49:205.1–3]).

This exegesis is taken up by Jerome who refers to the tripartite division of the human being[65] and develops the interpretation in a Trinitarian manner, connecting the three portions of dough to the three divine Persons.[66] In another passage, Jerome connects the woman who kneads with the widow who gives her offering in the temple (cf. Luke 21:1–4; Mark 12:41–44) and with the image of the mustard seed (Matt 13:31–32; Mark 4:30–32; Luke 13:18–19) in order to read the text in a Trinitarian sense and, once again, in relation to Semitic angelology.[67]

However, a quotation from Irenaeus, who refers to the gnostic exegesis of Luke 13:21, can help us better understand Origen's use of the image. According to the heretical reading, the three parts there represent the three classes into which human beings are divided, and the woman represents *Sophia* while the leaven represents the Savior Himself.[68] From this perspective, it can be seen how Origen is engaged in an ecclesiological and anthropological reinterpretation of the Lukan passage in which pneumatological exegesis is at the service of an orthodox reading of the Gospel according to the theological intention already described in the previous section.

Thus, both in the case of the Holy Spirit presented as mother of Christ and in that of the leaven and the three portions of dough, Origen is reinterpreting the images in an anti-gnostic sense for theological reasons.

65. "in cuius farinae satis tribus mittit fermentum euangelica mulier; et ut spiritus quo sentimus et anima qua uiuimus, et corpus quo incedimus, in unum sanctum spiritum redigantur iuxta apostolum: in ipso uiuimus, mouemur et sumus" (Jerome, *Commentariorum in Osee libri III*, 2.8.164–68 [CCSL 76:86]).

66. "mulierem istam et ipsi ecclesiam interpretantur quae fidem hominis farinae satis tribus commiscuerit credulitati patris et filii et spiritus sancti cum que in unum fuerit fermentata non nos ad triplicem deum sed ad unius diuinitatis perducit notitiam" (Jerome, *Commentariorum in Matthaeum libri IV*, 2.912–16 [CCSL 77:109–10]).

67. "uenio ad uidam de euangelio, uidam pauperculam, omni israhelitico populo ditiorem, quae accipiens granum sinapis et mittens fermentum in farinae satis tribus patris et filii confessionem spiritus sancti gratia temperauit et duo minuta misit in gazophylacium quidquid habere poterat in substantia sua uniuersas que diuitias in utroque fidei suae obtulit testamento. haec sunt duo Seraphim ter glorificantia trinitatem et in thesauros ecclesiae condita, unde et forcipe utriusque intrumenti ardens carbo comprehensus purgat labia peccatoris" (Jerome, *Epistulae*, 54.17 [CSEL 54:484]).

68. καὶ τὴν τῆς ζύμης παραβολήν, ἣν ἡ γυνὴ ἐγκεκρυφέναι λέγεται εἰς ἀλεύρου σάτα τρία, τὰ τρία γένη δηλοῦν λέγουσι. γυναῖκα μὲν γὰρ τὴν Σοφίαν λέγεσθαι διδάσκουσιν, ἀλεύρου δὲ σάτα τρία τὰ τρία γένη τῶν ἀνθρώπων, πνευματικὸν ψυχικὸν χοϊκόν (Irenaeus, *Adversus haereses*, 1.1.46–50 [W. W. Harvey, ed., *Adversus Haereses* (Cambridge: Cambridge University Press, 1857)], 71–72).

IV. An Imperfect Success: The Linear Model

IV.1. Order in Order

What we have seen up to this point shows that the use (*chrēsis*) of the various images that refer to the Holy Spirit is charged with immediate theological value which Origen attempts to refine by taking from the tradition known to him and reinterpreting it in the light of the theological errors of his time. It is not by chance that many of these images appear within the context of going deeper into the mystery, what today would be called a properly dogmatic or systematic study.

In this sense, the employment of these images can also be useful in understanding Origen's perspective in the development of his Trinitarian reflection. For him, the fact that the Spirit is listed along with the Father and the Son in the Trinity is an essential aspect of the apostolic tradition, as well as the fact that this same Spirit is He who spoke through the prophets of the Old Testament. This assertion, which is also present in the symbols of faith of the time, aims at affirming the divinity of the Third Person as it links Him with the unique Creator God who saves His people. The triangular model effectively expresses the difference between the three divine Persons and the world together with the kenotic presence of the Son and the Spirit in history. However, another point is not yet clear to the theological reflection of the time, that is, how to characterize the distinction between the *Logos* and the Spirit. For this reason Origen writes:

> [The apostles] have thus transmitted that the Holy Spirit is associated with the Father and the Son in honor and dignity. But it has not been clarified in an explicit manner whether He is engendered or unengendered, and also whether He must be considered Son of God or not. But these things are to be studied according to one's abilities from Sacred Scripture and must be investigated with wise research. The fact is certain that this Holy Spirit inspired each of the saints, prophets and apostles, and that there is not a different spirit in the ancients and in those who were inspired at the coming of Christ. And this is preached in a most clear manner in the Church.[69]

69. "Tum deinde honore ac dignitate patri ac filio sociatum tradiderunt spiritum sanctum. In hoc non iam manifeste discernitur, utrum natus aut innatus, uel filius etiam ipse dei habendus sit, necne; sed inquirenda iam ista pro uiribus sunt de sancta scriptura et sagaci perquisitione inuestiganda. Sane quod iste spiritus sanctus unumquemque sanctorum uel prophetarum uel apostolorum inspirauerit, et non alius spiritus in ueteribus, alius uero in

In this sense, the discussion on the divinity of the Spirit is in direct dialogue with the Hebrew tradition to which the prophets and the narratives regarding the Spirit of Yahweh belong. The same can be said for the special recourse to the angels in order to explain the action of the absolutely transcendent and unique God in history. In this context, one notes Origen's effort to affirm the priority in order of the Second Person in relation to the Third, once again with an exegesis of Isaiah 48:16. The reading of this verse is expanded to underscore the unity of the Spirit in the Old and New Testaments, while at the same time avoids a conception tied to images like that of the mother of Jesus in the Gospel of the Hebrews, something which inverts the position of the Son and the Spirit:

> But since it is the Hebrew who doubts the scriptural narrative of the descent of the Holy Spirit on Jesus in the form of a dove, one could respond to him: You tell me who it is who says in Isaiah "Now the Lord God has sent me together with his Spirit" (Isa 48:16). The text here is ambiguous: was it the Father and the Spirit who sent Jesus, or was it the Father who sent Jesus and the Holy Spirit? The second is true. After the sending of the Savior, the sending of the Holy Spirit took place so that that which the prophet had said be accomplished.[70]

It is in his *Commentarii in evangelium Joannis*[71] that Origen speaks on the issue in a more explicit manner. He affirms there that the Father, the Son, and the Spirit are three persons (τρεῖς ὑποστάσεις)[72] and that only the Father is unengendered (ἀγέννητος),[73] while the Spirit is the greatest of the beings that originated through the mediation of the Word (πάντων διὰ τοῦ λόγου γενομένων)[74] in such a way as to be the first in order among those who have

---

his, qui in adeuntu Christi inspirati sunt, fuerit, manifestissime in ecclesia praedicatur" (Origen, *De principiis*, preface 4 [GCS 22:11.3–10]).

70. Ἐπεὶ δὲ Ἰουδαῖός ἐστιν ὁ περὶ τοῦ ἀναγεγραμμένου ἁγίου πνεύματος κατεληλυθέναι ἐν εἴδει περιστερᾶς πρὸς τὸν Ἰησοῦν ἀπορῶν, λεκτέον ἂν εἴη πρὸς αὐτόν· ὦ οὗτος, τίς ἐστιν ὁ ἐν τῷ Ἡσαΐᾳ λέγων· Καὶ νῦν κύριος ἀπέστειλέ με καὶ τὸ πνεῦμα αὐτοῦ; ἐν ᾧ ἀμφιβόλου ὄντος τοῦ ῥητοῦ, πότερον ὁ πατὴρ καὶ τὸ ἅγιον πνεῦμα ἀπέστειλαν τὸν Ἰησοῦν, ἢ ὁ πατὴρ ἀπέστειλε τόν τε Χριστὸν καὶ τὸ ἅγιον πνεῦμα, τὸ δεύτερόν ἐστιν ἀληθές. Καὶ ἐπεὶ ἀπεστάλη ὁ σωτήρ, εἶτα τὸ πνεῦμα τὸ ἅγιον, ἵνα πληρωθῇ τὸ εἰρημένον ὑπὸ τοῦ προφήτου (Origen, *Contra Celsum*, 1.46.29–38 [SC 132:196–98]).

71. Origen, *Commentarii in evangelium Joannis*, 2.75 (SC 120:254–56).

72. Origen, *Commentarii in evangelium Joannis*, 2.75.1.

73. Origen, *Commentarii in evangelium Joannis*, 2.75.3.

74. Origen, *Commentarii in evangelium Joannis*, 2.75.4–5.

their origin from the Father by means of Christ (καὶ τάξει πρῶτον πάντων τῶν ὑπὸ τοῦ πατρὸς διὰ Χριστοῦ γεγενημένων).[75] For this reason, He is *perhaps* (τάχα) not called Son of God.[76] This *tacha* appears to indicate that Origen is taking a position on an as yet undefined subject, therefore presenting it as his own personal theological reflection. In this way, he can eliminate doubt as to the possible generation and filiation of the Spirit, characterizing the distinction between the Second and Third Persons in a clear way from the theological perspective:

> Insofar as it is only the Only Begotten who is Son by nature from the beginning, in such a manner that it seems that the Holy Spirit needs His mediation in order to subsist, not only to be (τὸ εἶναι), but also to be wise, intelligent, just and all that one must say of Him—by participation in the attributes of Christ that have been already enumerated.[77]

The incompleteness of Origen's Trinitarian thought, that is, his recourse to participation in order to distinguish the divine Persons, is apparent here.[78] He does not have the conceptual and expressive tools at his disposal necessary for avoiding a limited understanding of the communication of being from the Father to the Son and from them to the Spirit. For example, in the text above it is clear that the "being" (τὸ εἶναι) received by the Third Person is not identified with "being wise, rational, just" (τὸ εἶναι σοφόν, λογικόν, δίκαιον), that is, with the divine attributes, as should be the case with Him who is Being itself.

This approach leads to the development of the linear Trinitarian model, which will later be fundamental for the reflection of Athanasius and the Cappadocians in their defense of dogma against the Arians. However, it is important to emphasise that the triangular Trinitarian model connected with the aforementioned images is not independent of the linear one as if it were an

---

75. Origen, *Commentarii in evangelium Joannis*, 2.75.5–7.

76. Origen, *Commentarii in evangelium Joannis*, 2.76.1.

77. μόνου τοῦ μονογενοῦς φύσει υἱοῦ ἀρχῆθεν τυγχάνοντος, οὗ χρήζειν ἔοικε τὸ ἅγιον πνεῦμα διακονοῦντος αὐτοῦ τῇ ὑποστάσει, οὐ μόνον εἰς τὸ εἶναι ἀλλὰ καὶ σοφὸν εἶναι καὶ λογικὸν καὶ δίκαιον καὶ πᾶν ὁτιποτοῦν χρὴ αὐτὸ νοεῖν τυγχάνειν κατὰ μετοχὴν τῶν προειρημένων ἡμῖν Χριστοῦ ἐπινοιῶν (Origen, *Commentarii in evangelium Joannis*, 2.76.2–7 [SC 120:256]).

78. Cf. D. L. Balás, "The Idea of Participation in the Structure of Origen's Thought: Christian Transposition of a Theme of the Platonic Tradition," in *Origeniana* (Bari: Istituto di letteratura cristiana antica, 1975), 1:257–75, esp. 263.

entirely different tradition that later dried up and withered away. The recourse to Isaiah 48:16 in both contexts is a good illustration of this point.[79]

Origen's reflection attempts instead to understand the images and to develop a concept that establishes the dimension that will be called the *economy* in relation to what will be named the *immanence*, thus linking the triangular conceptualization—better suited for speaking of the missions—to the linear one, which tries to express something of the divine immanence. In this sense, Origen's effort will bear fruit in the fourth century, in particular with the in-depth rereading of his heritage. Under pressure from the Arians and the Pneumatomachians, this will lead the Cappadocians and, in particular, the two Gregories to determine the personal *proprium* of the Spirit just as generation characterizes the Son. Origen cannot yet reach this point, mainly because he does not yet have a developed concept of *physis*. For him, the divinity is characterized by pure immateriality and spirituality while all other beings, from angels to men, are characterized by a body to such a point that it can be said that there is no authentic distinction of nature between the angelic and human worlds. It is precisely this line of thought—which can be traced to Philo, for whom angels, demons and men are nothing but souls[80]—that leads Origen to a pneumatological reading of Matthew 18:1–4 and offers him the exegetical space for a Trinitarian rereading of the material and angelic images of the Semitic and Old Testament tradition. A well-known Origenian exegetical principle is behind this:

> For there is no need to think that historical realities are figures of historical realities and that corporeal realities are figures of corporeal realities, but corporeal realities are figures of spiritual realities and historical realities are [figures] of intellectual realities.[81]

This principle is nothing other than a statement of the implications of Origen's cosmological and anthropological views for his exegesis, something which remains in constant play in his theological use of these images.

---

79. These texts can be found at p. 24, n. 38 and p. 35, n. 70.

80. Philo, *De Gigantibus*, 16. For Origen, the terms "angel" and "man" refer to the same reality; cf. Origen, *Commentarii in evangelium Joannis*, 2.23.144.6–7 (SC 120:302) and 2.23.146.6–7 (SC 120:304).

81. Οὐ γὰρ νομιστέον τὰ ἱστορικὰ ἱστορικῶν εἶναι τύπους καὶ τὰ σωματικὰ σωματικῶν, ἀλλὰ τὰ σωματικὰ πνευματικῶν καὶ τὰ ἱστορικὰ νοητῶν (Origen, *Commentarii in evangelium Joannis*, 10.110.4–6 [SC 157:448]).

iv.2. Being and Operation

It should be noted that, despite the apparent subordinationism, Origen manages a clear statement of the consubstantiality and divinity of the Holy Spirit, speaking

> of the Holy Spirit's great authority and dignity as substantial being, so much that the baptism of salvation cannot take place but through the highest authority of the Holy Trinity by the invocation of the Father, of the Son and of the Holy Spirit, so that the Holy Spirit's name is associated with the unbegotten Father and the only-begotten Son.[82]

Only the *Logos* reveals the Father, to whom one cannot come unless through Him, but, at the same time, the Son can only be known in the Spirit.

As is evident, the basis of Origen's pneumatological thought is always Matthew [28:10]. His is a nonsystematic reflection which examines and develops several specific points. As can be understood from the first section of this chapter, his fundamental concern is affirming that the Spirit is incorporeal against the Stoics. In this sense, a basic reference point for his pneumatology is contemporary philosophy. He strives to clarify the content of certain concepts, like that of *pneuma*, which were both employed on a philosophical level and appeared in Scripture.[83]

The reason for his concern and what is at stake in his dialogues with his interlocutors is evident from the following text:

> Some people think that the names are given only according to convention (θέσει) and that they have no natural relation to the reality expressed through them. So these people think that there is no difference between saying "I worship God the highest or Zeus or Jupiter" and "I adore and worship the sun or Apollo, the moon or Artemis, and the spirit of the earth (ἐν τῇ γῇ πνεῦμα) or Demeter" and anything else the Greek wise men say.[84]

---

82. "Ex quibus omnibus didicimus, tantae esse et auctoritatis et dignitatis substantiam spiritus sancti, ut salutare baptismum non aliter nisi exellentissimae omnium trinitatis auctoritate, id est patris et filii et spiritus sancti cognominatione compleatur, et ingenito deo patri et unigenito eius filio nomen quoque sancti spiritus copuletur" (Origen, *De principiis*, 1.3.2 [GCS 22:50.5–9]).

83. Cf. G. Verbeke, *L'évolution de la doctrine du pneuma* (Leuven: Desclée de Brouwer, 1945), 451.

84. Πάλιν τε αὖ ὑπολαμβάνοντές τινες θέσει εἶναι τὰ ὀνόματα καὶ οὐδεμίαν αὐτὰ ἔχειν

To adhere to the biblical text, Origen must clarify absolutely the difference between the materiality of the spirit of the world taught by the Stoics—and closely connected with the pagan polytheistic understanding—and the authentically spiritual nature of the Christian God.

This step was facilitated by the work of Philo for whom the divine transcendence implies that the word and the spirit of Yahweh are sharply differentiated from the material world.[85] However, Origen must push these affirmations even further in order to recognize the authentically personal dimensions of the *Logos* and the Spirit. In doing so, he distances himself from the pneumatological reflections that characterized the thought of the apologist fathers, purifying and fine-tuning their language.

The metaphysical dimension of the theological discussion emerges once again from the commentary on "God is spirit" and the affirmation of the need to adore God in spirit and in truth in John 4:24. Origen criticises those who affirm that the divine substance (οὐσία) is corporeal and instead affirms the necessity of interpreting the passages of Scripture where God is defined as fire, light, and spirit (Deut 4:24, Heb 12:29, and 1 John 1:5) in a spiritual and nonliteral sense.[86] The conclusion of the argument is particularly interesting because it centers on the divine life:

> God is called *light* for his power of enlightening the intellect's eyes, making it possible for one to move from the corporeal light to the invisible and incorporeal one. And He is called *consuming fire*, understood as a corporeal fire in the deep sense, which destroys material realities. Analogous readings, in my opinion, are true also for the sentence "God is *pneuma*." In fact, it is possible to say that we receive the life, which is called "intermediate life" or simply life, by the breath, as the wind (πνεῦμα) around us introduces in us what is called the breath of life (cf. Gen 2:7) in a corporeal meaning. I think that in the same meaning it is said here that God is *pneuma* as He gives us true life. In fact, according to Scripture it is said that the Spirit gives life (cf. 2 Cor 3:6): He obviously gives life not in the sense of what is called "intermediate life," but the more divine life. Also the letter kills and brings

---

φύσιν πρὸς τὰ ὑποκείμενα, ὧν ἐστιν ὀνόματα, νομίζουσι μηδὲν διαφέρειν, εἰ λέγοι τις· σέβω τὸν πρῶτον θεὸν ἢ τὸν Δία ἢ Ζῆνα, καὶ εἰ φάσκοι τις· τιμῶ καὶ ἀποδέχομαι τὸν ἥλιον ἢ τὸν Ἀπόλλωνα καὶ τὴν σελήνην ἢ τὴν Ἄρτεμιν καὶ τὸ ἐν τῇ γῇ πνεῦμα ἢ τὴν Δήμητραν καὶ ὅσα ἄλλα φασὶν οἱ Ἑλλήνων σοφοί (Origen, *Exhortatio ad martyrium*, 46.1–7 [GCS 2:42]).

85. On this point, see G. Maspero, *Dio trino perché vivo: Lo Spirito di Dio e lo spirito dell'uomo nella Patristica greca* (Brescia: Morcelliana, 2018), 15–27.

86. Origen, *Commentarii in evangelium Joannis*, 13.21 (SC 222:44).

death not as separation of the soul from the body, but as separation of the soul from God, her Lord, and from the Spirit.[87]

It is life that is the point of reference for understanding the nature of the Third Person. Similar reasoning, which binds together exegesis and theology, is found in *De principiis*, 1.1–3. The same criterion is expressed in book 4 of *Contra Celsum*, where Origen explicitly places the Stoic conceptions in opposition to the scriptural use of the term spirit, which indicate only truly spiritual and intellectual realities as opposed to those which fall under the dominion of the senses.[88] In his *Homiliae in Ieremiam*, with a particularly original exegesis of the three spirits of Psalm 50:12–14(51:10–12), Origen attributes the term *pneuma* to each of the three divine Persons.[89]

In *Fragmenta in evangelium Joannis*, 37, commenting on the affirmation in John 3:8 that the Spirit blows where it wills, Origen specifies that the Spirit is a true and proper substance (οὐσίαν εἶναι τὸ πνεῦμα) and not only an operation (ἐνέργεια), as held by those who thought the Spirit did not have an existence (ὑπάρξεως) of his own.[90] This affirmation is extremely important because it marks the transition to a properly Christian pneumatological conception and means that Origen's pneumatology must be interpreted from what will later be termed the immanent perspective.

However, the terminological "subordinationism" regarding the Second Person also reflects on the Third, in particular for the hierarchical conception of the divinity which underlies the linear model. Moreover, this view also entails differences in the attribution of power to the three divine Persons. This is seen in the *Commentarii in evangelium Joannis*, 2.10.75.1–76.7 analysed above. The

---

87. Φῶς οὖν ὀνομάζεται ὁ θεὸς ἀπὸ τοῦ σωματικοῦ φωτὸς μεταληφθεὶς εἰς ἀόρατον καὶ ἀσώματον φῶς, διὰ τὴν ἐν τῷ φωτίζειν νοητοὺς ὀφθαλμοὺς δύναμιν οὕτω λεγόμενος· πῦρ τε προσαγορεύεται καταναλίσκον, ἀπὸ τοῦ σωματικοῦ πυρὸς καὶ καταναλωτικοῦ τῆς τοιᾶσδε ὕλης νοούμενος. Τοιοῦτόν τί μοι φαίνεται καὶ περὶ τὸ Πνεῦμα ὁ θεός· ἐπεὶ γὰρ εἰς τὴν μέσην καὶ κοινότερον καλουμένην ζωήν, φυσῶντος τοῦ περὶ ἡμᾶς πνεύματος τὴν καλουμένην σωματικώτερον πνοὴν ζωῆς, ζωοποιούμεθα ἀπὸ τοῦ πνεύματος, ὑπολαμβάνω ἀπ' ἐκείνου εἰλῆφθαι τὸ πνεῦμα λέγεσθαι τὸν θεὸν πρὸς τὴν ἀληθινὴν ζωὴν ἡμᾶς ἄγοντα· τὸ πνεῦμα γὰρ κατὰ τὴν γραφὴν λέγεται ζωοποιεῖν, φανερὸν ὅτι ζωοποίησιν οὐ τὴν μέσην ἀλλὰ τὴν θειοτέραν· καὶ γὰρ τὸ γράμμα ἀποκτέννει καὶ ἐμποιεῖ θάνατον, οὐ τὸν κατὰ τὸν χωρισμὸν τῆς ψυχῆς ἀπὸ τοῦ σώματος, ἀλλὰ τὸν κατὰ τὸν χωρισμὸν τῆς ψυχῆς ἀπὸ τοῦ θεοῦ, καὶ τοῦ κυρίου αὐτοῦ, καὶ τοῦ ἁγίου πνεύματος (Origen, *Commentarii in evangelium Joannis*, 13.23.139.1–140.12 [SC 222:104–6]).

88. Origen, *Contra Celsum*, 6.70–71 (SC 147:352–60).

89. Origen, *Homeliae in Ieremiam*, 8.22–37 (SC 232:354).

90. Origen, *Fragmenta in evangelium Joannis*, 37.8–9 (GCS 10:513).

role of the Third Person is that of communicating the gifts of grace to the holy faithful who are called such precisely because of their participation (μετοχήν) in the Spirit. This grace is produced by God the Father (ἐνεργουμένης μὲν ἀπὸ τοῦ θεοῦ), dispensed by Christ (διακονουμένης δὲ ὑπὸ τοῦ Χριστοῦ), and then comes into existence thanks to the Holy Spirit (ὑφεστώσης δὲ κατὰ τὸ ἅγιον πνεῦμα).[91] Origen applies the same terms *participation* and *dispense* to both Christ in relation to the Spirit and to the Spirit in relation to the holy faithful. In a certain sense, as would be expected, the linguistic limitations that lead to an apparent subordination of the Second Person also reflect on the Third Person in such a way that there is a hierarchical conception of the Trinity in continuity with a hierarchical conception of the world: "The cosmos is thus considered as an ascending hierarchy in which the lower level is made up of the material and the highest is occupied by the immaterial divinity."[92]

There is no possibility of confusion between God and human beings because the operations attributed to the Spirit are divine; but, at the same time, the Spirit and the Son do not enjoy the same fullness of divinity and, consequently, do not enjoy the same power as the Father. The Third Person would have the role of sanctifying and acting only on the level of intelligible beings.

To understand Origen's position, Rufinus's translation of *De principiis*—where Psalm 32:6 appears in an explicitly Trinitarian context—is essential:[93]

> But for the Trinity it is not possible to speak of "more or less," because the one source of the divinity rules everything with the Word and the reason, and sanctifies the worthy realities with the Spirit of His mouth, as it is written in the psalm: "By the Lord's word the heavens were made; by the breath of his mouth all their host" (Ps 32[33]:6).[94]

The expression "more or less" is technical and was used by Aristotle and his commentators to denote the substance and differentiate it from accidents.[95]

---

91. Origen, *Commentarii in evangelium Joannis*, 2.10.77.1–5 (SC 120:256).

92. Verbeke, *L'évolution de la doctrine du pneuma*, 464.

93. On the quality and value of Rufinus's translation, cf. L. Perrone, "Origenes alt und neu: Die Psalmenhomilien in der neuentdeckten Münchner Handschrift," *Zeitschrift für Antikes Christentum* 17.2 (2013): 193–214, and the 2015 edition of the text in GCS 2.19.

94. "Porro autem nihil in trinitate maius minusve dicendum est, cum unus deitatis fons 'verbo' ac ratione sua teneat universa, 'spiritu vero oris sui' quae digna sunt sanctificatione sanctificet, sicut in psalmo scriptum est: 'Verbo domini caeli firmati sunt, et spiritu oris eius omnis virtus eorum'" (Origen, *De principiis*, 1.3.8 [GCS 22:60]).

95. See Aristotle, *Topica*, 115b9–10; *Metaphysica*, 1044a9–11; and *Categoriae*, 3b33–4a9.

This means that Origen really conceived the Trinity as one single ontological entity absolutely different with respect to creation. But at the same time the reference to the "worthy realities" reveals how the Trinitarian action was understood in a nonunitary way in that the action of the Third Person could not be extended to those who are not spiritual in the sense of *pneumatikoi*:

> In fact, I think that the operation of the Father and of the Son undoubtedly takes place both in holy persons and in sinners, in human beings who have reason and in animals which cannot speak, and even in inanimate beings, and in everything that exists. But the operation of the Holy Spirit cannot absolutely affect soulless beings or the ones of animal nature, unable to speak. Nor does that operation take place in those who, being rational, are prone to malice and not at all oriented to the higher realities.[96]

This affirmation could not be clearer and fits perfectly into the whole of Origen's theology.[97] In *De principiis*, 1.3.8 regarding the Trinity this translates into a distinction in the action of each divine person in the creative act: the Father is He who brings created reality from nonbeing into being, the Son makes the rational realities rational, and the Spirit sanctifies the realities that must be made capable of Christ.[98]

See also Porphyry, *Isagoge sive quinque voces*, 9.16–18; 19.21–20.6; *In Aristotelis categorias expositio per interrogationem*, 115.1–4; and Eustratius, *In Aristotelis ethica Nicomachea commentaria*, 47.27–36.

96. "Arbitror igitur operationem quidem esse patris et filii tam in sanctis quam in peccatoribus, in hominibus rationabilibus et in mutis animalibus, sed et in his, quae sine anima sunt, et in omnibus omnino quae sunt; operationem vero spiritus sancti nequaquam prorsus incidere vel in ea, quae sine anima sunt, vel in ea, quae animantia quidem sed muta sunt, sed ne in illis quidem inveniri, qui rationabiles quidem sunt sed 'in malitia positi' nec omnino ad meliora conversi" (Origen, *De principiis*, 1.3.5 [GCS 22:56]).

97. For an in-depth Neoplatonic study of Origen's pneumatology, see J. Dillon, "Origen's Doctrine of the Trinity and Some Later Neoplatonic Theories," in *Neoplatonism and Christian Thought*, ed. D. J. O'Meara (Norfolk, VA: International Society for Neoplatonic Studies, 1982), 19–23.

98. "Cum ergo primo ut sint habeant ex deo patre, secundo ut rationabilia sint habeant ex verbo, tertio ut sancta sint habeant ex spiritu sancto: rursum Christi secundum hoc, quod 'iustitia' dei est, capacia efficiuntur ea, quae iam sanctificata ante fuerint per spiritum sanctum; et qui in hunc gradum proficere meruerint per sanctificationem spiritus sancti, consequuntur nihilominus donum sapientiae secundum virtutem inoperationis spiritus dei" (Origen, *De principiis*, 1.3.8 [GCS 22:61]).

v. Conclusions: Imagining the Unimaginable

The conclusion of the last section explains why some of Origen's pneumato-logical images disappeared in the theology of the fourth century when the distinction between economy and immanence needed to be made more explicit in order to respond to subordinationism. Nevertheless, this did not mean the simple victory of the linear model—more Greek and immanent—over the triangular one—more Semitic and economical—in that for Origen himself these two models are intertwined and interact in the reinterpretation of the images in order to respond to the Stoics and the gnostics. This is all the more evident when one thinks that it was to be a particular reading of the linear model that would provide arguments for the Arians and the interaction of the linear and the triangular that spurs the criticism of the Pneumatomachians.

Instead, the disappearance of the Trinitarian images examined above must be attributed in a decisive manner to the influence on exegesis of the *Physis*-theology, which will be discussed in the next chapter, and the related distinction between economy and immanence. The problem is more than one of Trinitarian theology; it is found in anthropology and the theology of history as well. Origen managed to correct the conception of necessity characteristic of Gnosticism by which human beings are divided into various categories, but he could not refer to a clear distinction of nature in order to separate the purely spiritual world from the material one. He was thus obliged to identify the divinity with the purely spiritual dimension, marking the material world with a negative and transitory significance.

Such a position prompts, on the one hand, a perception of the mission of the Spirit as a lowering in parallel to that of the Son. On the other hand, it leads to a notable allegorical freedom in the use of creaturely images, insofar as the spiritual sense is extra-historical rather than intra-historical. In this way, Origen's interlocutors also partly determined the development of his thought, and this paved the way for the Trinitarian theology of the fourth century where the debate would center on the great Alexandrian author's legacy and its hermeneutics. The dogmatic tensions present in his work would emerge and be the object of the fierce discussions that spanned the entire century.

In Origen's theology, the ontological gap between the Trinity and the world is expressed in terms of spirituality. This implies an imperfect appreciation of the incarnation and the value of the material world. Origen developed an effective response to the Stoic and gnostic objections to Christian revelation, but his thought was still constrained by the metaphysical legacy he received.

The three divine Persons share the perfectly spiritual dimension but are distinguished substantially and not in a purely relational way. The fathers of the fourth century developed new expressive means, including a broader concept of *physis* and a new understanding of the ontological status of relation.

This development facilitated the answers to some crucial questions arising from the tensions present in Origen's theology, in particular those between the triangular and the linear models of the Trinity: Is the Spirit linked to the Father through the Son? Is the linear model only an "imperfect success" that should be superseded on account of its ontological incompleteness? Could the triangular model be applied to the divine immanence, that is, to the processions? In fact, the very existence of a plurality of Trinitarian models points to the difficulty of defining the relationship between the two processions and their connection with the missions. These are the great and fascinating issues faced in later theological discussions, and these very issues would be so important for the different understandings of the role of the Son in the procession of the Holy Spirit.

The Turning Point: From the Third to the Fourth Century

1. Introduction: A Difficult Transition

Origen's contribution to Trinitarian theology was fundamental. At the same time, it was loaded with a tension that would explode in the transition from the third to the fourth century that brought the elaboration of *Physis*-theology in order to overcome the problems raised by *Logos*-theology. From the pneumatological perspective, the critical nature of this phase is especially clear. In the triangular scheme, the immediate origin of the Son and of the Spirit from the Father is evident, but the relationship of the Second and Third Persons with history and the world is too close. This consigns the First Person to an equivocal position in that it leaves the way open to an anti-Trinitarian monism. The linear model made up for this risk by giving a clear demonstration of the unity of the intra-Trinitarian dynamic. Here the Spirit was linked to the Father through the Son who, in His turn, was in direct relationship with the Father. But this was expressed through a distinction of a participatory type that did not end up in a perfect identification of each divine Person with the divine attributes. This tension was exposed, firstly, to Arian criticism that became manifest in 318, and then to that of the Pneumatomachians who were especially active in the second half of the fourth century. It is this period which led from the Council of Nicea in 325 to the clear definition of the divinity of the Third Person in the Council of Constantinople of 381.

The protagonists in this difficult transition were, first, Eusebius and Marcellus, who were followed by Athanasius and Basil. In the present chapter, we shall attempt to highlight those elements of their theologies that seem most important in order to reconstruct the development of pneumatology.[1] Clearly, Arian

1. For an overall view, see R. P. C. Hanson, "The Holy Spirit in Creeds and Confessions

and Pneumatomachian subordinationism are linked in that the first implies the second *a fortiori*. Thus, it is desirable to show the dogmatic connection between the two stages. We shall point out how the denial of the divinity of the Spirit by the Pneumatomachians can be attributed to an imperfect understanding of the first procession. This had its roots in an ontological framework that had not yet been perfectly purified by Christian revelation. This means that the deepest reason for the Pneumatomachian position is really close to the very basis of Arian thought. The mediation of Homoiousians could have performed a fundamental role in this connection.

The chapter opens with the reworking of Origen's heritage by Eusebius and Athanasius.[2] In fact, both found themselves on opposite sides with respect to Arius: the former welcoming the heretic when he was driven out of Alexandria and later causing the exile of the latter. However, beyond these historical considerations, the perspective advanced here is essentially systematic inasmuch as what we want to highlight is the line of development of pneumatological thought with its internal and external connections with respect to both the orthodox development of the doctrine of the divinity of the Holy Spirit and the heterodox position.

II. A TALE OF TWO VERSES: EUSEBIUS AND MARCELLUS

The detailed study of pneumatology between the third and the fourth centuries is closely bound up with the exegesis of the Fourth Gospel. For example, the procession of the Spirit from the Father is commonly based on the reading of John 15:26 so that, as we shall see later, the new term introduced by Gregory of Nazianzus to identify the second procession is based precisely on the *ekporeuetai* in this verse.[3] However, in order to grasp the core of the discussions on the heritage of Origen's thought, it may be useful to address the Trinitarian exegesis of John 16:14 too. In fact, the expression "he will take of mine" (ἐκ

---

of Faith in the Early Church," in *Credo in Spiritum Sanctum: Atti del Congresso Teologico Internazionale di Pneumatologia*, ed. J. Saraiva Martins (Rome: LEV, 1983), 1:291–302, and J. McIntyre, "The Holy Spirit in Greek Patristic Thought," *Scottish Journal of Theology* 7 (1954): 353–75.

2. On the importance of the theological circle connected with Eusebius, see M. DelCogliano, "Eusebius of Caesarea on Asterius of Cappadocia in the Anti-Marcellan Writings: A Case Study of Mutual Defense within the Eusebian Alliance," in *Eusebius of Caesarea: Tradition and Innovations*, ed. A. P. Johnson and J. Schott (Washington, DC: Center for Hellenic Studies Press, 2013), 163–287.

3. Gregory of Nazianzus, *Oratio*, 31.8 (SC 250:291–93).

τοῦ ἐμοῦ λήψεται), which Christ states in reference to the Holy Spirit, points directly toward the relationship between the Second and Third Persons and so requires a rethinking of the distinction and the relation between the first and second processions. It is precisely this question that will be at the center of the controversy with the Pneumatomachians in their different groups, from the Tropici (τροπικοί), with whom Athanasius had to deal, to the Macedonians.

In outline, we can make out two great phases in the dogmatic development: first, the heritage of Origen with the debate between Eusebius and Marcellus; then, even if there is a partial chronological overlap, the theological confrontation begun by Athanasius with the Tropici and carried forward by Basil against the Pneumatomachians.

The first stage starts out from the hermeneutical uncertainty to which, as we have seen, some passages of Origen were exposed. In his commentary on John, Origen describes the Holy Spirit as "generated nature which is found after Him" (τῇ λοιπῇ παρ' αὐτὸν γεννητῇ φύσει) with reference to the Son.[4] Immediately afterward, there appears John 16:14, which is interpreted in the sense of an education carried out by the *Logos* with respect to the Third Person (καὶ αὐτὸ αὐτῷ μαθητεύεται).[5] Thus, the issue is set within the context of the question whether the Spirit knows or does not know everything that the Son knows.[6] The uncertainty is heightened by the association of the Spirit with the angels since Origen specifies that both the Holy Spirit and the heavenly spirits do not speak through their own power but draw on the *Logos*, as shown by the verse cited.[7]

The debate on the pneumatological heritage of Origen at the beginning of the fourth century has been especially intense in German circles with reference to the presumed Binitarianism of Eusebius and the role of Marcellus. The Pneumatomachian heresy is supposed to have been linked with those Eusebian circles[8] where Origen's heritage had been received only in part with regard to the Third Person.[9] The *Logos*-theology that characterized the thought of Eusebius put the role of the Spirit into the shade for Origen's Trinitarian models and presented some ambiguities in this area. To give the briefest of summaries, Kretschmar and Hauschild have each examined the Binitarianism of Eusebius. The former

---

4. Origen, *Commentarii in evangelium Joannis*, 2.18.126.6 (SC 120:290).

5. Origen, *Commentarii in evangelium Joannis*, 2.18.127.2–3 (SC 120:290).

6. Origen, *Commentarii in evangelium Joannis*, 2.18.127.5–7 (SC 120:290).

7. Origen, *Commentarii in evangelium Joannis*, 20.29.263.1–264.1 (SC 290:286).

8. See D. M. Gwynn, *The Eusebians: The Polemic of Athanasius of Alexandria and the Construction of the "Arian Controversy"* (Oxford: Oxford University Press, 2007).

9. See V. H. Drecoll, *Die Entwicklung der Trinitätslehre des Basilius von Cäsarea: Sein Weg vom Homöusianer zum Neonizäner* (Göttingen: Vandenhoeck & Ruprecht, 1996), 140.

attributes the origin of Binitarian thought to Eusebius himself;[10] the latter emphasises its continuity with Origen with a rather severe judgment on the Trinitarian inadequacy of the Alexandrian's position.[11] Subsequently, Strutwolf has criticised these positions, demonstrating the presence of an authentic pneumatology in Eusebius, even if it is insufficient.[12] Finally, Drecoll has shown the role of Marcellus in forcing Eusebius to develop a sketch of his pneumatology.[13]

What is certain is that John 16:14 is found in the fragments of Marcellus recorded by Eusebius in his *Ecclesiastica Theologia* and is at the center of their debate.[14] Eusebius accuses his adversary of Sabellianism because he interprets John 16:13–14 as revelation of the hidden mystery, which consists in the fact that the divine monad (μονάς) expands into a triad (πλατυνομένη μὲν εἰς τριάδα) without there being a real personal distinction (διαιρεῖσθαι).[15] According to Marcellus, the connection with the Johannine text lies in the tension contained in it. He skillfully causes this to emerge when he states that if the Father and the Son were truly two distinct Persons, absurdity would ensue because:

Either the Spirit proceeds (ἐκπορευόμενον) from the Father and, therefore, has no need of the ministry of the Son, in that everything that proceeds from the Father must of necessity be perfect, and absolutely cannot need the help of another; or else if [the Spirit] takes from the Son (cf. John 16:14) and depends on His [of the Son] power, then He [the Spirit] no longer proceeds from the Father.[16]

10. G. Kretschmar, *Studien zur frühchristlichen Trinitätstheologie* (Tübingen: Mohr, 1956), 2–14.

11. W.-D. Hauschild, "Die Pneumatomachen: Eine Untersuchung zur Dogmengeschichte des vierten Jahrhunderts" (PhD diss., Hamburg University, 1967), 131–40 and 151–52.

12. H. Strutwolf, *Die Trinitätstheologie und Christologie des Euseb von Caesarea: Eine dogmengeschichtliche Untersuchung seiner Platonismusrezeption und Wirkungsgeschichte* (Göttingen: Vandenhoeck & Ruprecht, 1999).

13. V. H. Drecoll, "How Binitarian/Trinitarian Was Eusebius?" in *Eusebius of Caesarea: Tradition and Innovations*, ed. A. Johnson and J. Schott (Cambridge: Harvard University Press, 2013), 289–305.

14. See Marcellus, *Fragmenta*, 48, in M. Vinzent, ed., *Markell von Ankyra: Die Fragmente & Der Brief an Jiulius von Rom* (Leiden: Brill, 1997), 42–44.

15. Eusebius, *Ecclesiastica Theologia*, 3.4.2.7–3.1 (GCS 14:158).

16. ἢ τὸ πνεῦμα ἐκ τοῦ πατρὸς ἐκπορευόμενον μὴ δεῖσθαι τῆς παρὰ τοῦ υἱοῦ διακονίας (πᾶν γὰρ τὸ ἐκ πατρὸς ἐκπορευόμενον τέλειον εἶναι ἀνάγκη, μηδαμῶς προσδεόμενον τῆς παρ' ἑτέρου βοηθείας), ἤ, εἰ παρὰ τοῦ υἱοῦ λαμβάνοι καὶ ἐκ τῆς ἐκείνου δυνάμεως διακονίη τὴν χάριν, μηκέτι ἐκ τοῦ πατρὸς ἐκπορεύεσθαι (Eusebius, *Ecclesiastica Theologia*, 3.4.4.3–8 [GCS 14:158]).

Marcellus's reading sets the triangular and linear models in tension, opposing the exegesis of John 15:26 to that of John 16:14 and 20:22. In John 20:22, the sending of the Holy Spirit by Christ is read as clear proof of the fact that the Third Person comes from the Second (ἐκ τοῦ λόγου τὸ πνεῦμα ἐξῆλθεν) and so cannot proceed from the Father (ἐκ τοῦ πατρὸς ἐκπορεύεται).[17] This dogmatic exegesis shows negatively that the distinction and the relation of the two divine processions are essential elements for an authentically Trinitarian conception of God.

Eusebius's response takes its cue precisely from John 16:14. His reading, however, is not dialectic with respect to John 15:26 and 20:22 in that the Son is always with the Father and by Him (ὁ υἱὸς ἀεὶ συνὼν καὶ συμπαρὼν τῷ πατρί). Thus, the Son is the depth of the Father's kingship[18] from whence He is sent into the world.[19] In the same way, the Spirit is always before the throne of God (παρεστὸς ἀεὶ τῷ θρόνῳ τοῦ θεοῦ), together with the myriads of angels, and from there He is sent into the world so that He is said to proceed from the Father (ἐκ τοῦ πατρὸς ἐκπορεύεσθαι).[20] We note that the procession of the divine Persons is interpreted here in the economic sense, following the limitation of Origen's triangular model. That is to be borne in mind when we assess how Eusebius bases the distinction of the Father and the Spirit precisely on his reading of John 16:14:

> The only-begotten Son of God teaches that He [the Son] proceeds (ἐξεληλυθέναι) from the Father through His always being united (συνεῖναι) with Him [the Father], and, in the same way [this goes] for the Holy Spirit who subsists (ὑπάρχον) as distinct with respect to the Son. And the Savior shows this when He says "He will take of mine and declare it to you" (John 16:14). In fact, it is immediately clear that the Son and the Spirit are not one and the same reality in that it is understood that the one who takes from another is distinct from the one who gives.[21]

---

17. Eusebius, *Ecclesiastica Theologia*, 3.4.5.3–5 (GCS 14:158).

18. See chapter 1 (p. 25) and chapter 4 (pp. 119–21). These references highlight the link between the Trinitarian usage of the kingship in Origen, Eusebius, and Gregory of Nyssa with its evolution.

19. Eusebius, *Ecclesiastica Theologia*, 3.4.6.6–10 (GCS 14:159).

20. Eusebius, *Ecclesiastica Theologia*, 3.4.7.3–8.1 (GCS 14:159).

21. ὁ δὲ μονογενὴς υἱὸς τοῦ θεοῦ ἐκ τοῦ πατρὸς ἑαυτὸν διδάσκει διὰ τὸ συνεῖναι αὐτῷ πάντοτε, καὶ τὸ ἅγιον δὲ πνεῦμα ὁμοίως ἕτερον ὑπάρχον παρὰ τὸν υἱόν. ὃ δὴ σαφῶς αὐτὸς ὁ σωτὴρ παρίστησιν λέγων ἐκ τοῦ ἐμοῦ λήψεται καὶ ἀναγγελεῖ ὑμῖν. ἄντικρυς γὰρ παραστατικὸν ἂν εἴη τοῦτο τοῦ μὴ εἶναι ἓν καὶ ταὐτὸν τὸν υἱὸν καὶ τὸ ἅγιον πνεῦμα· τὸ γὰρ παρ' ἑτέρου λαμβάνον τι ἕτερον παρὰ τὸν διδόντα νοεῖται (Eusebius, *Ecclesiastica Theologia*, 3.4.9.2–9 [GCS 14:159]).

The very principle of procession implies that the one who gives and the one who is given (ὁ διδοὺς καὶ τὸ διδόμενον) cannot be the same,[22] just as, in John 15:26, Christ's statement that the Spirit who proceeds from the Father will testify of Him implies a real distinction of the Third Person with respect to the Second.[23] This is the way Eusebius concludes his argument, citing John 16:14 once again as the basis for what he writes:

> In fact, the Savior himself taught explicitly through these words that the Holy Spirit subsists as distinct from Him, and, in honor, glory and merit, is superior to, greater and more worthy than every substance, spiritual and rational—and this is why the Spirit belongs to the holy and thrice-blessed Trinity—without being inferior to Him [the Son]. And He shows this in saying: "He [the Spirit] will not speak of himself, but will say everything that He has heard" (John 16:13). Moreover, the Savior explains from whom He [the Spirit] has heard saying: "He [the Spirit] will take of mine and declare it to you" (John 16:14), that is, from my treasure. For "in Him are hidden all the treasures of wisdom and knowledge" (Col 2:3).[24]

The point is that all three divine Persons can be called *spirit*, but only the Son as such receives from the Father and in His turn leads the Spirit. This shows that John 16:14 is being interpreted as an expression of the personal characteristic of the Second Person rather than as proof of the inferiority of the Third whom Christ calls *Paraclete* precisely to indicate clearly that this is a distinct person who is superior to the angels and belongs to the blessed Trinity.[25]

The personal distinction is stated with great clarity, even if the formulation is still imperfect, in that the fields of action of the three Persons are presented as different,[26] and it is said that the Spirit can be called neither God nor Son since He is not generated by the Father (οὔτε θεὸς οὔτε υἱός, ἐπεὶ μὴ ἐκ τοῦ

---

22. Eusebius, *Ecclesiastica Theologia*, 3.5.3.1 (GCS 14:160).

23. Eusebius, *Ecclesiastica Theologia*, 3.5.8.6–9.1 (GCS 14:161).

24. ἀλλὰ γὰρ σαφῶς διὰ τούτων αὐτὸς ὁ σωτὴρ τὸ πνεῦμα τὸ ἅγιον ἕτερον ὑπάρχειν παρ' ἑαυτὸν ἐδίδαξεν, τιμῇ μὲν καὶ δόξῃ καὶ πρεσβείοις ὑπερέχον καὶ κρεῖττον καὶ ἀνώτε-ρον πάσης τῆς νοερᾶς καὶ λογικῆς τυγχάνον οὐσίας (διὸ καὶ συμπαρείληπται τῇ ἁγίᾳ καὶ τρισμακαρίᾳ τριάδι), ὑποβεβηκός γε μὴν [εἶναι] αὐτοῦ. ὃ δὴ παρίστη εἰπὼν οὐ γὰρ ἀφ' ἑαυτοῦ λαλήσει, ἀλλ' ὅσα ἀκούσει λαλήσει· παρὰ τίνος δὲ ἀκούσει, διασαφεῖ λέγων ἐκ τοῦ ἐμοῦ λήψεται καὶ ἀναγγελεῖ ὑμῖν, ἐκ τοῦ ἐμοῦ δηλαδὴ θησαυροῦ· ἐν αὐτῷ γάρ εἰσιν πάντες οἱ θησαυροὶ τῆς σοφίας καὶ γνώσεως ἀπόκρυφοι (Eusebius, *Ecclesiastica Theologia*, 3.5.17.1–18.5 [GCS 14:162])

25. Eusebius, *Ecclesiastica Theologia*, 3.5.19.1–22.1 (GCS 14:163).

26. Eusebius, *Ecclesiastica Theologia*, 3.6.1.1–3.1 (GCS 14:163–64).

πατρὸς ὁμοίως τῷ υἱῷ).[27] *Theologia* and *oikonomia* are not yet clearly recognized, and the immanent distinction is relegated to the sphere of action as we saw in Origen.[28] However, the transition is extremely important just as the role of John 16:14 in the discussion is evident.

III. ATHANASIUS AND THE FIRST PNEUMATOMACHIANS

In all probability, it was this role that rendered this verse of John a notable element in the confrontation with the Pneumatomachians. The question of the origin of this heresy and its link with Macedonius, bishop of Constantinople, is still open.[29] This historical uncertainty is also reflected from the perspective of the history of dogma, in particular in the assessment of the relationship between the three groups which accepted the divinity of the Son, but not that of the Spirit: (1) the Tropici spoken of by Athanasius, (2) the adversaries of the *homotimia* to whom Basil responds,[30] and (3) the Macedonians whose name appears only at the end of the fourth century. It is not clear why it is only in 380 that people begin to refer to the Macedonians with this name[31] when Macedonius had died in 360 and debates on the Holy Spirit had not been lacking in the previous years.[32] However, still more important from the theological point of view is the clear nature of their connection with the Homoiousians.[33]

At the beginning of his fourth letter to Serapion, Athanasius[34] is witness to the use of John 16:14 by the adversaries. This is their supposed argument:

> If the Holy Spirit is not a creature—they say—then He is a Son and so He and the *Logos* are brothers. Then they add, as you write: if the Spirit takes from the Son (cf. John 16:14) and is given by Him (John 20:22)—in fact, this

27. Eusebius, *Ecclesiastica Theologia*, 3.6.3.3–4 (GCS 14:164).

28. See the final texts cited in the previous chapter, pp. 41–42.

29. See chapter 5 for some remarks on the term *pneumatomachoi* in relation to the blasphemy against the Holy Spirit (p. 146).

30. Cf. M. J. Larson, "A Re-Examination of *De Spiritu Sancto*: Saint Basil's Bold Defence of the Spirit's Deity," *Scottish Bulletin of Evangelical Theology* 19 (2001): 65–84.

31. Jerome, *Chronicon*, GCS 47:235.

32. One of the best overviews of this period is found in M. A. G. Haykin, *The Spirit of God: The Exegesis of 1 and 2 Corinthians in the Pneumatomachian Controversy of the Fourth Century* (Leiden: Brill, 1994).

33. On the complexities of the relationship between the Pneumatomachians, the Macedonians, and the Homoiousians, see P. Meinhold, "Pneumatomachoi," in *Paulys Real Encyclopädie der classischen Altertumswissenschaft* 21.1 (1951): 1066–87.

34. On the pneumatology of Athanasius, see K. Anatolios, *Retrieving Nicaea: The Development and Meaning of Trinitarian Doctrine* (Grand Rapids: Baker Academic, 2011), 133–48.

is what the Scripture says—they immediately conclude, therefore, that the Father is grandfather and the Spirit is his grandson.[35]

Again we see the interaction between the triangular and linear schemes, which is caused by the failure to distinguish the *proprium* of each of the two processions. What leaps to the eyes in the passage just cited is the repeated and simultaneous appearance of John 16:14 and 20:22 following a form of argument which we have already seen in the dispute between Eusebius and Marcellus.

Athanasius's response to this use of John 16:14 can be identified in one of the central points of his pneumatology[36] when, in his third letter to Serapion, he reads the verse in question in the light of the one which immediately follows:

> In fact, the property (ἰδιότητα) of the Son with respect to the Father (πρὸς τὸν Πατέρα) such as we know it is the same that we find with the Spirit with respect to the Son (πρὸς τὸν Υἱόν). And, just as the Son says "All that the Father has is mine" (Jn 16:15), so everything we find to be also in the Spirit through the Son.[37]

Thus, Athanasius favors the linear model since just as everything which is of the Son is of the Father, so too the Spirit, who is the Spirit of the Son, is of the Father.[38] This is both one of the peaks of the Alexandrian's theology and at the same time one of its gravest limitations. In fact, the logical procedure that allows him to state clearly the divinity of the Third Person in the four letters to Serapion consists in extending to the Spirit the arguments developed to affirm the divinity of the Son. However, this symmetrical process obscures the distinction between the two processions, which is the dogmatic crux at which the

---

35. εἰ οὐκ ἔστι κτίσμα τὸ ἅγιον πνεῦμα, οὐκοῦν, φασίν, υἱός ἐστι, καὶ ἀδελφοὶ δύο ὁ λόγος καὶ αὐτό. εἶτα ἐπιλέγουσιν, ὡς γράφεις· εἰ "ἐκ τοῦ υἱοῦ λήψεται τὸ πνεῦμα" καὶ παρ' αὐτοῦ δίδοται (οὕτως γὰρ γέγραπται), εὐθὺς ἐπάγουσιν· οὐκοῦν πάππος ὁ πατὴρ, καὶ ἔκγονόν ἐστιν αὐτοῦ τὸ πνεῦμα (Athanasius, *Epistulae ad Serapionem*, 3.1.3 [AW 1.4:568]).

36. On Athanasius's pneumatology in general, see C. Kannengiesser, "Athanasius of Alexandria and the Holy Spirit between Nicea I and Constantinople I," *Irish Theological Quarterly* 48 (1981): 166–80, and T. F. Torrance, "The Doctrine of the Holy Trinity according to St. Athanasius," *Anglican Theological Review* 71 (1989): 395–405.

37. οἵαν γὰρ ἔγνωμεν ἰδιότητα τοῦ υἱοῦ πρὸς τὸν πατέρα, ταύτην ἔχειν τὸ πνεῦμα πρὸς τὸν υἱὸν εὑρήσομεν. καὶ ὥσπερ ὁ υἱὸς λέγει, "πάντα ὅσα ἔχει ὁ πατὴρ ἐμά ἐστιν," οὕτως ταῦτα πάντα διὰ τοῦ υἱοῦ εὑρήσομεν ὄντα καὶ ἐν τῷ πνεύματι (Athanasius, *Epistulae ad Serapionem*, 2.10.2 [AW 1.4:552]).

38. οὕτως τοῦ πατρός ἐστι τὸ πνεῦμα τὸ ἅγιον, ὅπερ τοῦ υἱοῦ εἴρηται (Athanasius, *Epistulae ad Serapionem*, 2.10.3 [AW 1.4:552]).

Pneumatomachian criticism is aimed.[39] Athanasius succeeds in distinguishing the two processions numerically but is not yet able to explore what it is that characterizes each one and therefore their distinction.

In some ways, this is inevitable because of his approach and the question with which he is dealing. In fact, Athanasius is writing from the starting point of the Arian crisis in which he was involved as a protagonist right from its earliest moments when he was deacon of Alexander, bishop of Alexandria. In this role, he took part in the Council of Nicea and, on account of the authority he gained there, he succeeded Alexander as bishop of Alexandria. Arius's claim that the Son and consequently, *a fortiori*, the Spirit are of a different nature from the Father in that they are creatures implied the need to frame the response precisely in terms of the divine nature and attributes. In fact, the latter were at the center of the debate because the Arians maintained that generation could not be harmonized with the divine immutability, eternity, and simplicity. Athanasius's response constitutes one of the most important stages in the whole of the history of theology. This is because his formulation of the *Physis*-theology allowed for the overcoming of those limitations that were an inherent part of the *Logos*-theology that had marked the thought of the apologists and the later answers by Origen and Eusebius, albeit with their differences.[40]

For glory and eternity interact in the perspective of Athanasius, who identifies the one nature marked by these characteristics with the Father, the Son, and the Holy Spirit. His theological position is dictated by soteriology: if the life communicated in baptism is not the same as the divine life, then Christian salvation is not real in that it does not consist in the communication of eternal life. This is why both the Son and the Spirit must be God, the one divine nature that is identified with the Life without limits. However, this requires that the generation of the second Person must be understood according to a new form never before seen in creation:

> The substance of the Father has never been imperfect as if there had been added to it something which is proper to it. The generation of the Son is

39. In *De communi essentia Patris, Filii et Spiritus Sancti*, 11 (PG 28:45c–d), attributed by some to Athanasius, John 16:14 is employed to affirm the mutual glorification of the divine Persons, but the text is spurious and the pneumatology seems later and close to that of Gregory of Nyssa in *Adversus Macedonianos*, as we shall see in what follows.

40. One thinks also of the theological-political dimension of the concept of the *Logos*: cf. R. Farina, *L'impero e l'imperatore cristiano in Eusebio di Cesarea: La prima teologia politica del cristianesimo* (Zurich: PAS Verlag, 1966), 42–46.

not like human generation, posterior to the existence of the Father. He is indeed generated by God, but being generated by God and being Son of the eternal God, He exists from all eternity.[41]

Athanasius moves forward the theological work of Origen but frees it from the dead weight that the metaphysical apparatus available to him dragged with it. Placing the divine Persons on the same ontological plane of the one eternal nature, Athanasius shows how the same divine attributes, such as immutability, demand that there was never a time in which the First Person was not Father, contrary to the most fundamental Arian thesis. In this way, it is clear theologically that God *is* the Father, and does not just *become* the Father. God has always been Father; He is Father in Himself. However, God has also always been Son and is Son in Himself. Father and Son are, thus, presented as correlatives, starting precisely from the life and the affirmation of Christian salvation.

We are dealing here with the *theologization* of the divine attributes in an effort of thought that aims at showing their intimate connection with the Trinitarian dimension without the same affirmations losing their force when understood on the philosophical level. It is precisely the eternal Sonship which is recognized in God that permits the affirmation of the divine attribute of eternity in all its power. In this way, it becomes clear that the discussion of the properties of the divine nature is inseparable from that of the Persons.

We must not forget that Athanasius is a prudent bishop who is making a real effort to bring his moderate adversaries back into the Church. Thus, he makes little use of the term *homoousios*, which had been at the center of the disputes. The important thing was that the truth expressed by this term be accepted.[42]

With regard to the Holy Spirit, Athanasius limits himself to affirming His divinity, that is, His identity with the one and eternal divine nature, in line with the Symbol of Nicea but without developing the theology of the second procession. However, at the end of the fourth century, the debate was to concentrate on this point. It is then that Basil takes up again the method of Athanasius in order to defend the consubstantial nature of the Holy Spirit. In doing so, he

41. οὐ γὰρ ἀτελὴς οὐσία τοῦ πατρὸς ἦν ποτε, ἵνα καὶ τὸ ἴδιον αὐτῆς ἐπισυμβαίνῃ ταύτῃ· οὐδὲ ὡς ἄνθρωπος ἐξ ἀνθρώπου γεγέννηται ὁ υἱός, ἵνα καὶ ὑστερίζῃ τῆς πατρῴας ὑπάρξεως· ἀλλὰ θεοῦ γέννημά ἐστι, καὶ ὡς θεοῦ τοῦ ἀεὶ ὄντος ἴδιος ὢν υἱὸς ἀιδίως ὑπάρχει (Athanasius, *Oratio I contra Arianos*, 14.5 [AW 1.2:124]).

42. Athanasius, *De synodis*, 41 (AW 2.1:266–67).

took again his starting point from soteriology, as had already happened for the Son. According to the Bishop of Alexandria, if the Spirit is not God, He cannot make us sharers of the divine life.[43]

Athanasius gives a clear formulation of the equality of nature, but he cannot yet offer a clear distinction between the divine Persons for he lacks the conceptual and terminological tools to do this: for Athanasius, *ousia* and *hypostasis* continue to be synonymous, and he does not use *prosōpon* in the sense of person. However, we could say that he had already discerned the way to a solution since he was the one who, at the Council of Alexandria of 362, proposed the distinction between the three hypostases and the one essence, thus strongly favoring the subsequent theological development.[44]

During the first half of the fourth century, the theological dispute focused on the divinity of the Son. The very fact that the Nicene Creed makes a simple mention of the Spirit without any addition indicates that the question of His divinity was not yet being debated at a broad level. However, as we have said, the logic of Arianism led also to the denial of the divinity of the Third Person because, if the Second Person was not divine, then that must be the case, *a fortiori*, for the Spirit. However, the explicit denial of the divinity of the Holy Spirit arose only in the Homoiousian sphere in the years subsequent to Arianism proper.

Here, the contribution of Athanasius was precious once again. The first information about the heresy comes precisely from him in the letters to Serapion, which were written around 360. Athanasius found himself faced with a small group of people in Egypt who denied the divinity of the Holy Spirit. They were former Arians who accepted the true faith about the Son of God but had not accepted the Third Person. Their point was that the Spirit is not generated and so it is difficult to understand how He can be of the same nature as the Father if He is not His Son. One notes immediately, therefore, that the question at stake is how the second procession can transmit identity of nature.[45]

It is interesting to observe that Athanasius calls his opponents Tropici, a play on words that refers both to their volatility and to their exegetical method. In fact, the usual explanation is that the term derives from *tropikos*, which

---

43. Athanasius, *Epistulae ad Serapionem*, 1.24 (AW 1.4:510–12).

44. On the Council of Alexandria, see A. Segneri, ed., *Atanasio: Lettera agli Antiocheni* (Bologna: EDB, 2010), 43–59.

45. For an overview, cf. K. Douglas Hill, *Athanasius and the Holy Spirit: The Development of His Early Pneumatology* (Minneapolis: Fortress, 2016).

means *metaphorical*, since they are supposed to have practised a strongly allegorical type of exegesis. However, it seems more probable that the term refers to the concept of the *logical figure* and of the *syllogism*, since their exegesis is rather literalist. It would be a question, therefore, of the influence of the fundamentalism and rationalism picked up during their Arian phase.[46]

This is perfectly in line with the argument that the Tropici adduced in order to deny the divinity of the Spirit: if He had come from the Son, then the Father would have been the grandfather of the Spirit.[47] For the Tropici, on the other hand, the Third Person was only a heavenly spirit, even if superior to all the angels. Once again, this reveals the influence of the Jewish-Christian world in which angelology played a fundamental role.

As we have seen, Athanasius's response was a simple extension of the arguments employed to defend the divinity of the Son. For him, the Spirit has the same relationship with the Son as the latter has with the Father.[48] The very structure of his third letter to Serapion, which was devoted to the Holy Spirit, retraces the points that were examined for the Son in his first letter to Serapion.

The strong point of his theology is, in fact, the concept of nature. Only the Trinity is uncreated and cannot be a compound of created and uncreated.[49] The distance between the creature and the Creator is infinite, so much so that Origen's hierarchical conception is here radically superseded. The relationship between God and the world is understood in an increasingly theological sense. That is why both the *Logos* and the Spirit cannot be subordinate, not even verbally, since they must be of the same nature and substance as the Father.[50] This is the core of Athanasius's *Physis*-theology.[51] However, this means that the operation or gift that is carried out by the Father, through the Son, in the Holy Spirit is one.[52] The distinction between the divine Persons is based on their reciprocal relations in the immanence. These are not interchangeable because the Son receives the substance directly from the Father,[53] whereas the

46. See L. Iammarrone, ed., *Atanasio: Lettere a Serapione* (Padua: Messaggero, 1983), 16–18.

47. Athanasius, *Epistulae ad Serapionem*, 1.15.1–2 and 3.6.7–7.1 (AW 1.4:489–90 and 574).

48. Athanasius, *Epistulae ad Serapionem*, 1.2.2 and 1.21.1 (AW 1.4:452 and 504).

49. Athanasius, *Epistulae ad Serapionem*, 1.28.2 and 1.29.1 (AW 1.4:520–21).

50. For the Spirit, see Athanasius, *Epistulae ad Serapionem*, 1.2.3 (AW 1.4:452–53).

51. On the relationship between God and the world in Athanasius, see K. Anatolios, *Athanasius: The Coherence of His Thought* (London: Routledge, 1998). The author shows that the bishop of Alexandria's understanding is a relational ontology, explaining also his links with Irenaeus.

52. Athanasius, *Epistulae ad Serapionem*, 1.14.4; 1.20.6; and 3.5.2–3 (AW 1.4:487, 504, and 572).

53. Athanasius, *Epistulae ad Serapionem*, 1.16.4 (AW 1.4:492).

Spirit receives it from the Father through the Son but without any mention of participation.[54]

After having moved the *Logos* from the position of ontological intermediacy between God and the world, inserting Him into divine immanence (see fig. 3), the position of the Spirit still remained to be clarified.

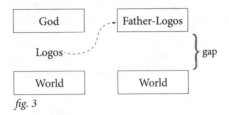

fig. 3

But the Third Person could not yet remain in an intermediate position, as if He were again a metaphysical step between creation and the one nature formed by the Father and the *Logos* together. Thus Athanasius's response to the Pneumatomachians completes the ontological path undertaken in the response to the Arians, presenting a new picture in the relationship between the Trinity and the world through the insertion also of the divine Third Person in the immanence and the formulation of a real and infinite metaphysical gap between the triune Creator and creation (see fig. 4).

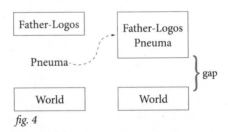

fig. 4

In this way, each Person is immanent to the others: the Father is wholly in the Son who is His Image, and the Son is wholly in the Father; and, in the same way, the Spirit is wholly in the Son and the Son is wholly in the Spirit. Thus, the Spirit is the Image of the Son, just as the Son is the Image of the Father. This argument is the basis of Athanasius's affirmation of the divinity of the Spirit in response to the Tropici:

54. Athanasius, *Epistulae ad Serapionem*, 1.27.2 (AW 1.4:518).

Therefore, since they confess that the Son is not a creature, then neither can His image be a creature. In fact, the image is necessarily the same as that of which it is the image.[55]

It is important to reiterate that Athanasius's argument is fundamentally soteriological and that his starting point is the communication of eternal life. In fact, the neat distinction he establishes between the Trinity and creatures is a way of affirming real human participation in the gift of the divine life. If the Spirit were only an intermediate being, then Christians would not be truly saved in that they would not be divinized, that is, they would not have a share in eternal life, which is something that belongs only to God. Athanasius's axiom is: If He divinizes, there cannot be any doubt that His nature is that of God.[56] The Son is life, as it says in John 14:6, and the Spirit gives life, according to Romans 8:11, and He gives life because through Him it is Christ who lives in us, as Paul affirms in Galatians 2:19–20. Thus, the question is: How can the One who gives life be a creature when creatures are given life by Him? In fact, God alone is life in Himself (αὐτοζωή) and is the author of life (cf. Acts 3:14).[57]

From this point of view, the epilogue of Athanasius's first letter to Serapion is particularly beautiful. There, Athanasius claims to have drawn his doctrine not from sources external to revelation but only from the gospel. To demonstrate this, he interprets the worship in Spirit and Truth in the episode of the Samaritan woman in a Trinitarian sense (cf. John 4:21–24). He says:

> Thus, it is clear that Truth is the Son himself, for he says "I am the Truth" (John 14:6). Moreover, the prophet David calls on him, saying "Send your light and your truth" (Ps 42[43]:3). Thus, the true worshippers worship the Father, but in Spirit and Truth, that is, by confessing the Son and in Him the Spirit. Indeed, the Spirit is inseparable from the Son just as the Son is inseparable from the Father. The Truth Himself bears witness to this, saying: "I will send you the Paraclete, the Spirit of Truth who proceeds from the Father" (John 15:26); "the world cannot receive Him (John 14:17)," that is, those who deny that He is from the Father in the Son. It is necessary, therefore, to confess the faith, in imitation of the true [worshippers] and

55. οὐκοῦν τοῦ υἱοῦ καὶ κατ' ἐκείνους ὁμολογουμένου μὴ εἶναι κτίσματος οὐκ ἂν εἴη οὐδὲ ἡ τούτου εἰκὼν κτίσμα. ὁποία γὰρ ἂν εἴη ἡ εἰκών, τοιοῦτον ἀνάγκη καὶ τὸν, οὗ ἐστιν ἡ εἰκών, εἶναι (Athanasius, *Epistulae ad Serapionem*, 1.24.7 [AW 1.4:512]).
56. Athanasius, *Epistulae ad Serapionem*, 1.24.3 (AW 1.4:510–11).
57. Athanasius, *Epistulae ad Serapionem*, 1.23.2 (AW 1.4:508).

follow the Truth. Let those who then, even after that, do not wish to learn or succeed in understanding at least put an end to uttering blasphemies[58] and not split up the Trinity so that they themselves are not split up from life.[59]

Athanasius thus introduces a basic novelty into Trinitarian doctrine by extending classical metaphysics into a new ontology that now envisages two ontological orders that are radically distinct: the first constituted by the one, eternal and creative divine nature, and the second by the creation. This resemanticization, or reframing of the meaning, has its phenomenological basis in soteriology. On the epistemological level, it translates into apophaticism since it denies the possibility of a necessary reason placed between the world and God which could allow the human intellect to ascend autonomously to the Trinitarian dimension without passing through the Christian revelation. This enormous step forward is formalized in the clear statement of the divinity of the Son and of the Spirit. The two processions are distinct numerically but not pinned down in their reciprocal difference, as the consubstantiality of the Second and the Third Person with the First is expressed in both cases with the concept of "image." In this way, the response to the Pneumatomachian criticism will require a further development, as we shall see in the following.

IV. Basil and Worship

However, the new ontological framework introduced by Athanasius allows Basil to develop two elements which will be essential for the theological grammar of all subsequent patristic thought: firstly, the distinction between economy and immanence, and secondly and inseparably connected with this first element, the affirmation of the unity of action of the three Persons in the divine

58. On the link between the blasphemy against the Holy Spirit and the Pneumatomachians, see chapter 5, pp. 146–47.

59. δέδεικται τοίνυν ἐντεῦθεν, ὡς ἡ ἀλήθεια μὲν αὐτός ὁ υἱός ἐστιν, ὡς αὐτός φησιν· ἐγώ εἰμι ἡ ἀλήθεια. περὶ οὗ καὶ ὁ προφήτης Δαβὶδ ἐπεκαλεῖτο λέγων· ἐξαπόστειλον τὸ φῶς σου καὶ τὴν ἀλήθειάν σου. οἱ ἀληθινοὶ τοίνυν προσκυνηταὶ προσκυνοῦσι μὲν τῷ πατρί, ἀλλ᾽ ἐν πνεύματι καὶ ἀληθείᾳ, ὁμολογοῦντες υἱὸν καὶ ἐν αὐτῷ τὸ πνεῦμα. ἀχώριστον γὰρ τοῦ υἱοῦ τὸ πνεῦμα, ὡς ἀχώριστος ὁ υἱὸς τοῦ πατρός. αὐτὴ ἡ ἀλήθεια μαρτυρεῖ ἡ λέγουσα· πέμψω ὑμῖν τὸν παράκλητον, τὸ πνεῦμα τῆς ἀληθείας, ὃ παρὰ τοῦ πατρὸς ἐκπορεύεται, ὃ ὁ κόσμος οὐ δύναται λαβεῖν, τουτέστιν οἱ ἀρνούμενοι αὐτὸ ἐκ τοῦ πατρὸς ἐν τῷ υἱῷ. χρὴ τοίνυν κατὰ μίμησιν τῶν ἀληθινῶν ὁμολογεῖν [. . .] καὶ προσδραμεῖν τῇ ἀληθείᾳ. ἂν δ᾽ ἄρα καὶ μετὰ ταῦτα μήτε μαθεῖν θέλωσι μήτε νοεῖν δύνωνται, κἂν τῶν δυσφημιῶν παυέσθωσαν καὶ μὴ διαιρείτωσαν τὴν τριάδα, ἵνα μὴ διαιρεθῶσιν ἀπὸ τῆς ζωῆς· (Athanasius, *Epistulae ad Serapionem*, 1.33.4–6 [AW 1.4:533–34]).

acting. The latter element will be examined in the following section, which is devoted to the orthodox response to the Pneumatomachians' denial of the role of the Holy Spirit in the creative act.[60]

Concerning the distinction between economy and immanence, the use of John 16:14 by Basil in his De Spiritu Sancto can serve to set up the question. This treatise was written to demonstrate the orthodoxy of the coordinate doxology, that is, the affirmation that we should worship God giving glory to the Father and to the Son and to the Holy Spirit by coordinating the Persons through the copula "and." Therefore, the discussion about the value of the various prepositions in relation to the divine Persons is essential to the argument. Thus, in connection with "from" (ek), "through" (dia), and "in" (eis) in Romans 11:36, John 16:14 is also cited to show the variety of uses of the preposition indicating provenience when applied to Christ himself.[61] The same thing happens later in the treatise when the unity of the Father, the Son, and the Holy Spirit is based on their mode of origin, expressed precisely by the preposition ek. In fact, the Third Person is united to the First by the Second (δι' ἑνὸς Υἱοῦ τῷ ἑνὶ Πατρὶ συναπτόμενον), thus bringing the most blessed Trinity to its completion (δι' ἑαυτοῦ συμπληροῦν).[62] The natural intimacy of the Spirit with the Father and the Son is such that their absolute unity belongs also to Him, thus creating a radical difference between Him and creatures. Moreover, this is proved also precisely by His origin, and so from what is expressed by the expression "from God" (ἐκ τοῦ Θεοῦ).[63] In fact, one can distinguish two ways of being from God: the first relates to creatures and, therefore, is in the economy, and the second is absolute, that is, on the immanent level, and it characterizes both the generated Son and the Third Person who proceeds from the mouth of God, according to this reading of Psalm 32(33):6, in a sense that is purely spiritual and not in the human sense of the term.[64] These two ways of proceeding from God are matched by two ways of glorifying Him: the first is servile and characteristic of creatures, and the second is free, natural (φυσική), perfect, and intimate (οἰκειακή), precisely the way of the Spirit.[65] In this passage, a series of Johannine texts is produced as proof, with John 16:14 at their center, framed by John 17:4 and 12:28. In this way, it is shown that the Spirit is glorified on account of His common nature with the Father and the Son. This conclusion is reinforced by

60. Cf. B. Pruche, "Autour du traité Sur le Saint-Esprit de saint Basile de Césarée," Revue des sciences religieuses 52 (1964): 204–32.

61. Basil, De Spiritu Sancto, 5.9.15 (SC 17bis:278).

62. Basil, De Spiritu Sancto, 18.45.25–27 (SC 17bis:408).

63. Basil, De Spiritu Sancto, 18.45.33–46.2 (SC 17bis:408).

64. Basil, De Spiritu Sancto, 18.46.2–4 (SC 17bis:408).

65. Basil, De Spiritu Sancto, 18.46.20–26 (SC 17bis:410).

reference to the mutual glorification of the divine Persons and by the text on the blasphemy against the Holy Spirit[66] in Matthew 12:31.[67]

It is apparent, then, that the interpretation of John 16:14 is purely immanent. This forms a neat contrast with the uncertainty of Eusebius where the origin at the base of the personal distinction was situated in the economy. Basil, on the other hand, differentiates absolutely between two ways of being *from* God: that of *theologia*, in which he includes the verse in question, and that of the *oikonomia*, which concerns creatures.

We see, thus, that the theme of glory and its relationship with the divine Third Person are central to Basil's theology.[68] The theological situation is notably different from that in which Origen worked, precisely because of the presence of the Pneumatomachians. In chapters 24–29 of his *De Spiritu Sancto*, Basil argues against those who deny the possibility of coordinating the Third Person in the Trinitarian doxology, requiring instead that the Spirit be subordinated through the preposition *in*.

Starting out from 2 Corinthians 3:8 and relying also on the Psalms and other Pauline passages, Basil affirms that, if the ministry of the Spirit is glorious, and if glory is also promised to Israel and to the just, then how much more necessary it is to attribute glory to the Spirit. The Pneumatomachians' argument is carried *ad absurdum* because their position would imply, from what has been said, that the Third Person would be the only being deprived of glory.[69] This would be absolutely paradoxical since it is precisely through Him that every gift comes to people, and precisely thanks to Him that it is possible to render praise to Christ by recognizing Him as Lord.[70]

This is where the new theological and ontological frame of reference comes in with the power of its distinction of nature between the creature and the Creator. Indeed, in connection with the Spirit, Basil asks:

> But then where shall we put Him? With the creation? But the whole creation is servile while it is the Spirit who makes free. In fact, "where the Spirit of the Lord is, there is freedom" (2 Cor 3:17).[71]

---

66. On this, see E. Cattaneo, "La Bestemmia Contro Lo Spirito Santo (Mt 12,31–32) in S. Atanasio," *Studia Patristica* 21 (1989): 421–25.

67. Basil, *De Spiritu Sancto*, 18.46.27–36 (SC 17bis:410).

68. See M. Brugarolas Brufau, *El espíritu santo: De la divinidad a la procesión; El desarrollo pneumatológico en los escritos dogmáticos de los tres grandes capadocios* (Pamplona: Eunsa, 2012), 77–80.

69. Basil, *De Spiritu Sancto*, 24.55.10–19 (SC 17bis:448–50).

70. Basil, *De Spiritu Sancto*, 24.55.27–31 (SC 17bis:450).

71. Ποῦ τοίνυν φέροντες αὐτὸ τάξομεν, μετὰ τῆς κτίσεως; Ἀλλ᾽ ἡ κτίσις πᾶσα δουλεύει·

The questions and the answer in the text are the basis of Figure 4 above. Once again, the issue is metaphysical and is a powerful indication of the need to exclude every kind of ontological participation in the Trinity. That is why Basil explains that each Person is identified with the divine attributes:

> [The Spirit] is good by nature, just as the Father is good and the Son is good. The creature, on the other hand, shares in goodness by choosing the good. [The Spirit] knows the depth of God, whereas the creature receives the manifestation of the mysteries from the Spirit. He gives life together with God who generates everything with the Son who gives Life.[72]

This implies that one cannot associate the Spirit who gives life with the nature which needs to receive life.[73] The argument aims at showing that the divine Third Person is not only a gift to which to render honor on account of the dignity of the giver, that is, the Father, but that He is due the same glory that is attributed to the other two divine Persons because He is the "gift of life" (δῶρον ζωῆς),[74] that is, He is identified with the one uncreated nature which is Life itself.[75] This is why He should be included in the Trinitarian doxology with the preposition *with* and not only with *in*, as claimed by the Pneumato-machians. The latter wanted to use this to exclude the identity of nature on the linguistic level.[76] Thus, the debate over δοξάζειν becomes an essential stage in the pneumatology of the fourth century.

In connection with the copula *and*, the preposition *with* adds the affirmation of the indivisible communion (τὸ ἀχώριστον τῆς κοινωνίας) which accompa-nies the hypostatic distinction as Basil's adversaries admit happens in the case of the Father and the Son.[77] The point is that all three Persons are not assigned to

---

τὸ δὲ Πνεῦμα ἐλευθεροῖ. Οὐ γὰρ τὸ Πνεῦμα Κυρίου, ἐκεῖ ἐλευθερία (Basil, *De Spiritu Sancto*, 24.55.34–36 [SC 17bis:450]).

72. Φύσει ἐστὶν ἀγαθόν, ὡς ἀγαθὸς ὁ Πατὴρ καὶ ἀγαθὸς ὁ Υἱός. Ἡ κτίσις δὲ ἐν τῇ ἐκλογῇ τοῦ ἀγαθοῦ μέτοχός ἐστι τῆς ἀγαθότητος. Οἶδε τὰ βάθη τοῦ Θεοῦ· ἡ κτίσις δὲ λαμβάνει τὴν φανέρωσιν τῶν ἀπορρήτων διὰ τοῦ Πνεύματος. Ζωοποιεῖ μετὰ τοῦ Θεοῦ τοῦ τὰ πάντα ζωογονοῦντος, μετὰ τοῦ Υἱοῦ τοῦ διδόντος ζωήν (Basil, *De Spiritu Sancto*, 24.56.1–7 [SC 17bis:452]).

73. Basil, *De Spiritu Sancto*, 24.56.14–16 (SC 17bis:452).

74. Basil, *De Spiritu Sancto*, 24.57.1–4 (SC 17bis:452).

75. On the relationship between Basil's pneumatology and life, see P. Luislampe, *Spir-itus vivificans: Grundzüge einer Theologie des Heiligen Geistes nach Basilius von Caesarea* (Münster: Aschendorff, 1981).

76. Basil, *De Spiritu Sancto*, 25.58.1–4 (SC 17bis:456).

77. Basil, *De Spiritu Sancto*, 25.59.41–46 (SC 17bis:460).

temporal periods (χρονικοῖς διαστήμασι),[78] but enjoy the pure and most perfect eternity which is the exclusive characteristic of their one and single nature.[79]

Clearly, the preposition *in* is attributed to the Spirit in Scripture, but it is interesting that this receives a metaphysical reading in Basil's text:

> In fact, it is said that form (εἶδος) is in matter and that power (δύναμις) is in what contains it and that the habitual disposition (ἕξις) in what is organised by it and many similar statements. Given then that the Holy Spirit brings rational beings to perfection, conferring on them their excellence, He is analogous to form. Indeed, *spiritual* is the name of one who lives no longer after the flesh but is led by the Spirit of God and called Son of God and has become conformed to the image of the Son of God.[80]

All this is aimed at showing the attribution of the *in* as a sign of perfection and not as a sign of inferiority. From the metaphysical point of view, the affirmation is not discounted because the *in* indicated precisely the participation and inhering of the accident in the substance, as, for example, the place. That is contrasted with the reference to the form and to the perfection of the power and of the stable disposition but also with reference to the attribute of omnipresence because it is said that the Spirit must be thought of as "the whole in the parts" (ὡς ὅλον ἐν μέρεσι) in the distribution of the charisms, that is, not as the one sharing but as the one shared.[81]

Here, we also find a splendid expression concerning the Trinitarian indwelling in the soul of the just, for to prove that His being is described at times as *place* does not deny the glory of the Spirit but actually proves it, Basil writes:

> Thus, the Spirit is truly *place* of the saints. And the saint is the familiar place for the Spirit since he offers himself to dwell with God and is called His temple.[82]

---

78. Basil, *De Spiritu Sancto*, 25.59.54 (SC 17bis:462).

79. Cf. J. M. Yanguas, "La divinidad del Espíritu Santo en S. Basilio," *Scripta Theologica* 9 (1997): 485–539.

80. Λέγεται μὲν οὖν τὸ εἶδος ἐν τῇ ὕλῃ εἶναι, καὶ ἡ δύναμις ἐν τῷ δεκτικῷ, καὶ ἡ ἕξις ἐν τῷ κατ' αὐτὴν διακειμένῳ, καὶ πολλὰ τοιαῦτα. Οὐκοῦν, καθὸ μὲν τελειωτικὸν τὸ ἅγιον Πνεῦμα τῶν λογικῶν, ἀπαρτίζον αὐτῶν τὴν ἀκρότητα, τὸν τοῦ εἴδους λόγον ἐπέχει. Ὁ γὰρ μηκέτι κατὰ σάρκα ζῶν, ἀλλὰ Πνεύματι Θεοῦ ἀγόμενος, καὶ υἱὸς Θεοῦ χρηματίζων, καὶ σύμμορφος τῆς εἰκόνος τοῦ Υἱοῦ τοῦ Θεοῦ γενόμενος, πνευματικὸς ὀνομάζεται (Basil, *De Spiritu Sancto*, 26.61.5–12 [SC 17bis:466]).

81. Basil, *De Spiritu Sancto*, 26.61.38–39 (SC 17bis:468).

82. Ὥστε τὸ Πνεῦμα, τόπος ἀληθῶς τῶν ἁγίων. Καὶ ὁ ἅγιος, τόπος οἰκεῖος τῷ Πνεύματι

Therefore, the use of *in* applied to the Spirit reveals His greatness, especially when it refers to His relationship with creatures. On the other hand, when He is spoken of in relation to the Father and the Son, it is better to use *with* to indicate their coeternality:

> But when one contemplates the existence which precedes the ages and the ceaseless remaining with the Father and the Son, this requires expressions which indicate the eternal union. In fact "to exist with" is said in a true sense of beings which subsist together in a way that is mutually inseparable. We say that heat is *in* the iron that has been heated in the fire and we say, on the other hand, that the heat itself coexists *with* the fire. And we say that health is in the body but that life coexists with the soul. It follows then that when there is real, connatural and inseparable communion, the more expressive term is *with* since it indicates the idea of indissoluble communion. On the other hand, when there is the possibility that His grace comes and then goes, it is said in a true and proper sense to "exist in," even if His grace often abides in those who have received it on account of their stable and good disposition.[83]

This reference to grace is important because it is possible to adore the Trinity only through the divine gift. The Trinity cannot be known except from the free divine initiative which is given while natural reason on its own cannot reach the immanence. From this perspective, the *in* has great value because the divine Persons contemplate each other in the economy:

> Another meaning which is not to be dismissed is the following: just as the Father is contemplated in the Son, so the Son in the Spirit. Therefore, worship in the Spirit indicates the activity of our mind which takes place in the light, something we can learn from the words spoken to the Samaritan woman.[84]

ἐμπαρέχων ἑαυτὸν πρὸς ἐνοίκησιν τὴν μετὰ Θεοῦ, καὶ ναὸς αὐτοῦ χρηματίζων (Basil, *De Spiritu Sancto*, 26.62.22–24 [SC 17bis:472]).

83. Ἡ δὲ προαιώνιος ὕπαρξις, καὶ ἄπαυστος διαμονὴ μεθ᾽ Υἱοῦ καὶ Πατρὸς θεωρουμένη, τὰς τῆς ἀϊδίου συναφείας προσηγορίας ἐπιζητεῖ. Τὸ γὰρ κυρίως καὶ ἀληθῶς συνυπάρχειν ἐπὶ τῶν ἀχωρίστως ἀλλήλοις συνόντων λέγεται. Τὴν γὰρ θερμότητα τῷ μὲν πυρακτωθέντι σιδήρῳ ἐνυπάρχειν φαμέν· αὐτῷ δὲ τῷ πυρὶ συνυπάρχειν. Καὶ τὴν μὲν ὑγίειαν τῷ σώματι ἐνυπάρχειν, τὴν δὲ ζωὴν τῇ ψυχῇ συνυπάρχειν. Ὥστε ὅπου μὲν οἰκεία καὶ συμφυὴς καὶ ἀχώριστος ἡ κοινωνία, σημαντικωτέρα φωνὴ ἡ σύν, τῆς ἀχωρίστου κοινωνίας τὴν διάνοιαν ὑποβάλλουσα. Ὅπου δὲ προσγίνεσθαι ἡ ἀπ᾽ αὐτοῦ χάρις καὶ πάλιν ἀπογίνεσθαι πέφυκεν, οἰκείως καὶ ἀληθῶς τὸ ἐνυπάρχειν λέγεται, κἂν τοῖς δεξαμένοις πολλάκις διὰ τὸ ἑδραῖον τῆς περὶ τὸ καλὸν διαθέσεως, ἡ ἀπ᾽ αὐτοῦ χάρις διαρκὴς παραμένη (Basil, *De Spiritu Sancto*, 26.63.6–19 [SC 17bis:472–74]).

84. Δεύτερος δὲ νοῦς, οὐδὲ αὐτὸς ἀπόβλητος· ὅτι ὥσπερ ἐν τῷ Υἱῷ ὁρᾶται ὁ Πατήρ,

We see again that John 4 is a privileged point of exegetical reference in the debate over the divinity of the Spirit, as was already the case with Origen.[85] Here, however, we note the power of the new theological tool of the distinction between economy and immanence. This was the fruit of Athanasius's *Physis*-theology and was particularly effective in resolving the tensions of expression that were inherent in the thought of Origen. The power of this tool appears immediately when Basil applies it to the question of the prepositions in the doxology:

> They are not contradictory, but each contributes its own meaning to religion: *in* indicates what concerns us whereas *with* proclaims the communion of the Spirit with God.[86]

This distinction allows for a new way of stating the relationship between Kingdom and Glory which, as we shall see, will be fundamental in Gregory of Nyssa's response to the Pneumatomachians, as it shows that the Third Person is a single thing with the Father and the Son precisely because He reigns and so ought to be included in the doxology:

> I am ashamed to add what follows: you expect to be glorified with Christ, for we suffer with Him to be glorified with Him, but you do not give glory with Christ to the Spirit of holiness, as though even the honours which come to you are not appropriate to Him. And you hope to reign with [Christ], but you outrage the Spirit of Grace, degrading him to the rank of slave and servant. And I say this not in order to show everything that is owed to the Spirit in the doxology but to refute the madness of those who do not admit it and instead reject as if it were impiety the communion of glory of the Spirit with the Son and the Father.[87]

οὕτως ὁ Υἱὸς ἐν τῷ Πνεύματι. Ἡ τοίνυν ἐν τῷ Πνεύματι προσκύνησις, τὴν ὡς ἐν φωτὶ γινο-μένην τῆς διανοίας ἡμῶν ἐνέργειαν ὑποβάλλει, ὡς ἐκ τῶν πρὸς τὴν Σαμαρεῖτιν εἰρημένων ἂν μάθοις (Basil, *De Spiritu Sancto*, 26.64.1–5 [SC 17bis:474–76]).

85. See pp. 17–18.

86. οὐκ ἀπομαχόμεναι πρὸς ἐναντίωσιν, ἀλλ᾽ ἴδιον ἑκατέρα τὸν νοῦν εἰσφερομένη πρὸς τὴν εὐσέβειαν. Ἡ μὲν γὰρ ἐν τὰ πρὸς ἡμᾶς παρίστησι μᾶλλον· ἡ δὲ σὺν τὴν πρὸς Θεὸν κοινωνίαν τοῦ Πνεύματος ἐξαγγέλλει (Basil, *De Spiritu Sancto*, 27.68.3–6 [SC 17bis:488]).

87. Αἰσχύνομαι ἐπαγαγεῖν τὰ λειπόμενα, ὅτι σὺ μὲν συνδοξασθήσεσθαι Χριστῷ προσδο-κᾷς εἴπερ γὰρ συμπάσχομεν ἵνα καὶ συνδοξασθῶμεν, τὸ δὲ Πνεῦμα τῆς ἁγιωσύνης οὐ συν-δοξάζεις Χριστῷ, ὡς οὐδὲ σοὶ τῶν ἴσων τυγχάνειν ἄξιον. Καὶ σὺ μὲν ἐλπίζεις συμβασιλεύειν, τὸ δὲ Πνεῦμα τῆς χάριτος ἐνυβρίζεις, τὴν δούλου αὐτῷ καὶ ὑπηρέτου τάξιν ἀποκληρῶν. Καὶ ταῦτα λέγω, οὐχ ἵνα τοσοῦ τον δείξω ὀφειλόμενον εἶναι εἰς δοξολογίαν τῷ Πνεύματι· ἀλλ᾽ ἵνα τὴν ἀγνωμοσύνην ἐλέγξω τῶν μηδὲ τοσοῦτον διδόντων, ἀλλ᾽ ὡς ἀσέβειαν φευγόντων

Once again, the argument proceeds *ad absurdum* because it shows how the Pneumatomachians place the third Person even below man. The absolute opposition between slavery and royalty, like the distinction of nature between Creator and creature, was formulated earlier when Basil commented on a verse of Psalm 118 (119):

> "All things are subjected to you" (Ps 118:91): and if [the Spirit] is above creation, He shares (ἐστὶ κοινωνόν) the Kingdom.[88]

Here the link between the Third Person and the Kingdom of God resurfaces, after Eusebius and Origen, the latter having identified the Spirit with the Kingdom itself in his exegesis of the child in Matthew 18:2. And this is a point of destination on the route proposed in our analysis of Basil's thought on the Spirit, in particular as it concerns His relationship with the divine attribute of Glory. This connection will become a key element of Gregory of Nyssa's pneumatology that will be presented in chapter 4. The ontological distinction of nature and its exegetical-dogmatic rendering in terms of economy and immanence allow for the superseding of the conception of Origen for whom Glory was distinct from the divine nature, being situated as a Platonic *metaxy* (i.e., an intermediary) among the divine hypostases.[89] Basil was deeply indebted to Origen with whose circle he was linked through Gregory Thaumaturgus, the evangelizer of Cappadocia. At the same time, the battle with the Arians and Pneumatomachians obliged Basil in the direction of a doctrinal development aimed at loosening the tensions of expression inherent in some of Origen's formulations. He is clearly aware of this:

> and we find that Origen, already, in many of his comments on the Psalms, renders glory with the Spirit. In fact, he was someone whose concepts of the Spirit were not wholly sound. Nevertheless, in numerous passages, influenced by the power of tradition, he uttered words about the Spirit that are in harmony with piety. It appears to me that in the sixth of his exegetical comments on John's Gospel he declared clearly that He is to be adored, writing literally: "The washing of water is a symbol of the purification of the soul

---

τὴν τοῦ Πνεύματος πρὸς Υἱὸν καὶ Πατέρα κοινωνίαν τῆς δόξης (Basil, *De Spiritu Sancto*, 28.70.1–11 [SC 17bis:496]).

88. Τὰ γὰρ σύμπαντα, φησί, δοῦλα σά· εἰ δὲ ὑπὲρ τὴν κτίσιν ἐστί, τῆς βασιλείας ἐστὶ κοινωνόν (Basil, *De Spiritu Sancto*, 20.51.49–50 [SC 17bis:428–30]).

89. See the text of the *Commentarii in evangelium Joannis*, cited on pp. 19–20.

which is cleansed from all stain of evil; nonetheless, for the one who offers himself to the divinity of the adorable Trinity, it is the origin and source of graces through the power of the invocations." And again, in his comment on the Epistle to the Romans, he says: "The holy powers are able to contain the Only Begotten and the divinity of the Holy Spirit." I think that thus the power of tradition has led people to contradict even their own teaching.[90]

In the light of this text, Origen's *Homiliae in Psalmos*, which has recently been discovered in the original Greek, seems particularly interesting.[91] We note that, for Basil, Origen is orthodox despite having some concepts that are not wholly in line with subsequent developments in doctrine. He is orthodox because he maintains the praise due to the Third Person of the Trinity which he had received from tradition, so recognizing the divinity of the Spirit along with that of the Son. This is a clear statement of the principle which links the *lex orandi* with the *lex credendi*. From this perspective, theology does not speak on its own authority but seeks to defend the gift received in revelation which is lived out in worship. It is not a question of explaining the divine mystery but of defending it from improper reductions that do not do justice to the surpassing nature of the gift.

90. Ἤδη δὲ καὶ Ὠριγένην ἐν πολλαῖς τῶν εἰς τοὺς ψαλμοὺς διαλέξεων εὕρομεν, σὺν τῷ ἁγίῳ Πνεύματι τὴν δόξαν ἀποδιδόντα, ἄνδρα οὐδὲ πάνυ τι ὑγιεῖς περὶ τοῦ Πνεύματος τὰς ὑπολήψεις ἐν πᾶσιν ἔχοντα· πλὴν ἀλλὰ πολλαχοῦ καὶ αὐτὸς τῆς συνηθείας τὸ ἰσχυρὸν δυσωπούμενος, τὰς εὐσεβεῖς φωνὰς ἀφῆκε περὶ τοῦ Πνεύματος. Ὅς γε κατὰ τὸ ἕκτον οἶμαι τῶν εἰς τὸ κατὰ Ἰωάννην Εὐαγγέλιον ἐξηγητικῶν, καὶ προσκυνητὸν αὐτὸ φανερῶς ἀπεφήνατο, οὑτωσὶ γράφων κατὰ λέξιν· Ὅτι τὸ τοῦ ὕδατος λουτρὸν σύμβολον τυγχάνει καθαρσίου ψυχῆς, πάντα ῥύπον τὸν ἀπὸ κακίας ἀποπλυνομένης· οὐδὲν δὲ ἧττον καὶ καθ' ἑαυτὸ τῷ ἐμπαρέχοντι ἑαυτὸν τῇ θεότητι τῆς προσκυνητῆς Τριάδος, διὰ τῆς δυνάμεως τῶν ἐπικλήσεων, χαρισμάτων ἀρχὴν ἔχει καὶ πηγήν. Καὶ πάλιν ἐν τοῖς εἰς τὴν πρὸς Ῥωμαίους ἐπιστολὴν ἐξηγητικοῖς· Αἱ ἱεραί, φησί, δυνάμεις χωρητικαὶ τοῦ Μονογενοῦς καὶ τῆς τοῦ ἁγίου Πνεύματος θεότητος. Οὕτως, οἶμαι, τὸ τῆς παραδόσεως ἰσχυρὸν ἐνῆγε πολλάκις τοὺς ἄνδρας καὶ τοῖς οἰκείοις αὐτῶν δόγμασιν ἀντιλέγειν (Basil, *De Spiritu Sancto*, 29.73.1–19 [SC 17bis:506–8]). The first text cited is in Origen, *Commentarii in evangelium Joannis*, 4.33.166 (SC 157:254), the second is in Origen, *Commentarii in Epistulam ad Romanos* 3.5(8). The latter text is taken from C. P. Hammond Bammel, ed., *Der Römerbriefkommentar des Origenes: Kritische Ausgabe der Übersetzung Rufins. Buch 1–3* (Freiburg im Breisgau: Herder, 1990), 241 (lines 132–35).

91. See L. Perrone, "Origenes alt und neu: Die Psalmenhomilien in der neuentdeckten Münchner Handschrift," *Zeitschrift für Antikes Christentum* 17.2 (2013): 193–214, and Perrone, "La pneumatologia di Origene alla luce delle nuove 'Omelie sui Salmi,'" in *Pneuma: Il divino in/quieto; Lo Spirito santo nelle tradizioni antiche*, ed. F. Pieri and F. Ruggiero, Supplementi di Adamantius 6 (Brescia: Morcelliana, 2018), 101–17.

v. The Creator Spirit

In addition to the distinction between economy and immanence, the second element developed by Basil and made possible by the theological leap allowed by the new ontological framework introduced by Athanasius is the unity of action. This is directly linked to the response to the Arians. However, for the same reasons, it also takes aim at the criticism of the Pneumatomachians in that they denied that the Holy Spirit was creator.

Athanasius's exegesis of Psalm 32:6 is paradigmatic, even in its chronological development. Whereas in the *Contra gentes* he applies this verse to the Word, as Origen had done already, to deny the power of the idols and affirm the unique action of the Creator,[92] in the somewhat later *Epistulae ad Serapionem*, something new appears. Psalm 32(33):6 is cited three times there. In one case, the reference is to prophecy,[93] but in the other two the reference is precisely to the action of the Third Person in the creative act.

In the first *Epistulae ad Serapionem*, commenting on Wisdom 1:7 where it says that the Spirit of the Lord fills the world, Athanasius affirms the radical difference between the angels and the Third Person of the Trinity, observing that the angels are present where they are sent whereas if the Spirit is everywhere that means that His nature is superior to that of the heavenly creatures (ἄνω τῆς τῶν ἀγγέλων φύσεως). This is due to the fact that the Third Person makes creatures into sharers but does not share (μεθεκτόν ἐστι καὶ οὐ μετέχον), in the sense that the angels owe the perfection which they enjoy to their participation in the Spirit himself while He is always the same.[94] It is noticeable that, having asserted that the Third Person is one while the creatures are many, Athanasius includes the Heavens (οὐρανοί) in the list of heavenly powers, showing that they were being identified with a type of angel.[95]

---

92. διὰ τίνος δὲ δίδωσιν ἢ δι' οὖ καὶ τὰ πάντα γέγονε; δι' οὖ γὰρ γέγονε, δι' αὐτοῦ καὶ ἡ τῶν πάντων ἀκολούθως ἐστὶ πρόνοια. τίς οὖν ἂν εἴη οὗτος ἢ ὁ τοῦ Θεοῦ Λόγος, περὶ οὖ καὶ ἐν ἑτέρῳ λέγει· Τῷ λόγῳ Κυρίου οἱ οὐρανοὶ ἐστερεώθησαν, καὶ τῷ πνεύματι τοῦ στόματος αὐτοῦ πᾶσα ἡ δύναμις αὐτῶν (Athanasius, *Contra gentes*, 46.17–21; text from R. W. Thomson, *Athanasius: Contra gentes and de incarnatione* [Oxford: Clarendon, 1971], 126–28). Cf. also *Epistula ad Marcellinum de interpretatione Psalmorum*, PG 27:16a.

93. Athanasius, *Epistulae ad Serapionem*, 3.3.6 (AW 1.4:570).

94. Athanasius, *Epistulae ad Serapionem*, 1.26.7–8 (AW 1.4:517).

95. καὶ πάλιν· ἕν ἐστι τὸ πνεῦμα τὸ ἅγιον, τὰ δὲ κτίσματα πολλά. ἄγγελοι μὲν γὰρ χίλιαι χιλιάδες καὶ μύριαι μυριάδες, φωστῆρες δὲ πολλοί, καὶ θρόνοι, καὶ κυριότητες καὶ οὐρανοὶ καὶ χερουβὶμ καὶ σεραφὶμ καὶ ἀρχάγγελοι πολλοί· (Athanasius, *Epistulae ad Serapionem*, 1.27.3 [AW 1.4:518–19]). In his edition of the text J. Lebon (SC 15:133n1) reckons the presence of the term οὐρανοὶ is strange and attributes it to a scribal error. However, the context seems to suggest the deliberate choice of Athanasius.

Athanasius's statements are based on a beautiful Trinitarian exegesis of Ephesians 4:6 which speaks of a "single God, Father of all, who is above all (ἐπὶ πάντων), acts through all (διὰ πάντων) and is present in all (ἐν πᾶσι)." Thus, the Father is revealed as Principle (ἀρχή) and as First Person (πατήρ) precisely by the ἐπὶ πάντων, while the διὰ πάντων refers to the Word, and the ἐν πᾶσι to the Spirit in that the Father does everything through the Son in the Spirit (Ὁ γὰρ πατὴρ διὰ τοῦ λόγου ἐν πνεύματι ἁγίῳ τὰ πάντα ποιεῖ).[96]

In this context, Athanasius introduces and comments on 1 Corinthians 12:4–6: the diversity of gifts is brought back to the unicity of the Spirit, just as the multiplicity of ministries to the unicity of the Lord, and the multiplicity of operations to the unicity of God who "is at work in them all (ὁ ἐνεργῶν τὰ πάντα ἐν πᾶσιν)."[97] The source of the gifts is identified with the first two Persons in that grace and the goods bestowed by the Trinity are communicated by the Father and through the Son in the Holy Spirit.[98] This is the point where he cites Psalm 32(33):6:

> In fact, there is nothing which does not come into being and is not accomplished through the Son in the Spirit. That is sung also in the Psalms: "by the word of the Lord were the heavens made, by the breath of his mouth all their hosts" (Ps 32[33]:6).[99]

Then, as examples, he brings forward the indwelling of the Trinity and prophecy,[100] citing also Acts 4:24–25, a text which combines the themes of creation and prophecy,[101] and finally the incarnation, which is once again presented in the light of the mystery of creation:

> Thus too when the Word took up His dwelling in the Holy Virgin Mary, the Spirit entered together with Him, and the Word took form in the Spirit and assumed to Himself the body in order through Himself to unite and

---

96. Athanasius, *Epistulae ad Serapionem*, 1.28.3 (AW 1.4:520).

97. Athanasius, *Epistulae ad Serapionem*, 1.30.4 (AW 1.4:525).

98. ἡ γὰρ διδομένη χάρις καὶ δωρεὰ ἐν τριάδι δίδοται παρὰ τοῦ πατρὸς δι᾽ υἱοῦ ἐν πνεύματι ἁγίῳ (Athanasius, *Epistulae ad Serapionem*, 1.30.6 [AW 1.4:525–26]).

99. οὐδὲν γάρ ἐστιν ὃ μὴ διὰ τοῦ λόγου ἐν τῷ πνεύματι γίνεται καὶ ἐνεργεῖται. τοῦτο καὶ ἐν ψαλμοῖς ᾄδεται· τῷ λόγῳ κυρίου οἱ οὐρανοὶ ἐστερεώθησαν, καὶ τῷ πνεύματι τοῦ στόματος αὐτοῦ πᾶσα ἡ δύναμις αὐτῶν (Athanasius, *Epistulae ad Serapionem*, 1.31.2–3 [AW 1.4:526–27]).

100. Athanasius, *Epistulae ad Serapionem*, 1.31.3–5 (AW 1.4:527).

101. "Lord, you who created the heaven, the earth, the sea and everything in them, who through the Holy Spirit said through the mouth of our father, your servant, David" (Acts 4:24–25).

present the creation (τὴν κτίσιν) to the Father and reconcile in Himself all things, making peace with the things which are in the heavens and on the earth (cf. Col 1:20).[102]

Athanasius's statements are based on the theological principle of the unity of action, which is here affirmed in all its force and extended christologically to power over the corporeal and material dimension. This is confirmed by the third letter to Serapion, the arrangement of which consists, as we have already said, precisely in describing the divine prerogatives of the Son to show then that they belong also to the Holy Spirit. The movement is from the Second Person to the Third one.[103]

Starting from the assertion that the Son is not a creature, Athanasius comments on the reference to the seal of the Spirit in Ephesians 4:30 and claims that He too cannot be a creature. In fact, if creatures are anointed and receive the seal, the Third Person cannot be a creature because the anointment cannot be the same thing as those who are anointed, since the anointment is the breath of the Son (τὸ χρίσμα τοῦτο πνοή ἐστι τοῦ υἱοῦ).[104] That is why, in 2 Corinthians 2:15, it is said that Christians are the fragrance of Christ: the seal represents Christ because it communicates the form of Christ himself.[105] The conclusion of the proof is clear just as is the outline of the argument. This shows, firstly, that it belongs to God to be present everywhere, and then it goes on to claim this for the Son and to point out this is also true of the Spirit. Moreover, the same can be said for the attribute of unity contrasted with the multiplicity of creatures, particularly the angels.[106] Thus, the argument follows the same movement from the Second to the Third Person to arrive at the affirmation that, just as the Son is not a creature, so the Spirit cannot be a creature. At this point, Athanasius's expressions end up being extremely clear. After citing Psalm 103(104):29–30, which links life to the *pneuma* of God, he says:

---

102. οὕτως καὶ ἐπὶ τὴν ἁγίαν παρθένον Μαρίαν ἐπιδημοῦντος τοῦ λόγου συνεισήρχετο τὸ πνεῦμα καὶ λόγος ἐν τῷ πνεύματι ἔπλαττε καὶ ἥρμοζεν ἑαυτῷ τὸ σῶμα, συνάψαι θέλων καὶ προσενεγκεῖν δι' ἑαυτοῦ τὴν κτίσιν τῷ πατρί, καὶ ἀποκαταλλάξαι τὰ πάντα ἐν αὐτῷ, εἰρηνοποιήσας τὰ ἐν τοῖς οὐρανοῖς καὶ τὰ ἐπὶ τῆς γῆς (Athanasius, *Epistulae ad Serapionem*, 1.31.12 [AW 1.4:530–31]).

103. Athanasius, *Epistulae ad Serapionem*, 2.10.1–2 (AW 1.4:551–52).

104. Athanasius, *Epistulae ad Serapionem*, 2.12.2 (AW 1.4:555).

105. ἡ σφραγὶς δὲ τὸν υἱὸν ἐκτυποῖ, ὡς τὸν σφραγιζόμενον ἔχειν τὴν τοῦ Χριστοῦ μορφήν (Athanasius, *Epistulae ad Serapionem*, 2.12.3 [AW 1.4:555]).

106. Athanasius, *Epistulae ad Serapionem*, 2.12.4–5 (AW 1.4:555–56).

And given that it is written thus, it is clear that the Spirit is not a creature (κτίσμα) but that He is present in the act of creating (ἐν τῷ κτίζειν ἐστίν): in fact, the Father creates everything (τὰ πάντα) through the Word in the Spirit (διὰ τοῦ Λόγου ἐν τῷ Πνεύματι) since where the Word is, there too is the Spirit; and what has been created through the Word has the power of being (τὴν τοῦ εἶναι ἰσχύν) from the Spirit (ἐκ τοῦ Πνεύματος) through the Word (παρὰ τοῦ Λόγου). Therefore, it is written in Psalm 32(33): "by the word of the Lord were the heavens made, by the breath of his mouth all their hosts" (Ps 32[33]:6). Certainly, the Spirit remains inseparable from the Son so there is no space for any doubt on the basis of what has been said.[107]

In the rest of the letter, Athanasius cites, by way of example, the cases of prophecy, the infusion of charisms and prayer, and the annunciation of the angel Gabriel to Mary. However, the principle of the unity of action of the Trinity is so clearly expressed that it cannot be doubted that everything that exists comes from the Trinity and that, therefore, the Spirit contributed also to the creation of the material world. Binding the Third Person also to *ta panta* becomes necessary as soon as one intends to ensure that there was no time when the Trinity did not exist.[108]

As has been seen, this clear statement by Athanasius was facilitated by his "proportional" concept of the intra-Trinitarian relations at the basis of which the Spirit is the image of the Son just as the Son is the image of the Father. However, as we have said, it is just such an approach that lays him bare to the criticism of the Tropici that the Father was the grandfather of the Spirit. What was needed to avoid this criticism for Athanasius would have been a clear affirmation of the distinction between the two processions that did not undermine the identity of nature of the three Persons and so fall into the verbal subordinationism of Origen. He had limited the sphere of action of the Second and Third Persons with respect to the First, as a reflection of the participatory

107. Τούτου δὲ οὕτως γεγραμμένου, δῆλόν ἐστιν, ὡς οὐκ ἔστι κτίσμα τὸ πνεῦμα, ἀλλ᾽ ἐν τῷ κτίζειν ἐστίν· ὁ γὰρ πατὴρ διὰ τοῦ λόγου ἐν τῷ πνεύματι κτίζει τὰ πάντα, ἐπεὶ ἔνθα ὁ λόγος, ἐκεῖ καὶ τὸ πνεῦμα· καὶ τὰ διὰ τοῦ λόγου κτιζόμενα ἔχει ἐκ τοῦ πνεύματος παρὰ τοῦ λόγου τὴν τοῦ εἶναι ἰσχύν. οὕτω γὰρ γέγραπται ἐν τῷ τριακοστῷ δευτέρῳ ψαλμῷ· τῷ λόγῳ κυρίου οἱ οὐρανοὶ ἐστερεώθησαν καὶ τῷ πνεύματι τοῦ στόματος αὐτοῦ πᾶσα ἡ δύναμις αὐτῶν. ἀμέλει οὕτως ἐστὶ τὸ πνεῦμα ἀδιαίρετον πρὸς τὸν υἱόν, ὡς μὴ ἀμφιβάλλειν ἐκ τοῦ λεγομένου (Athanasius, *Epistulae ad Serapionem*, 2.14.1–2 [AW 1.4:558]).

108. εἰ τριάς ἐστι καὶ ἐν τριάδι ἐστὶν ἡ πίστις, εἰπάτωσαν, εἰ ἀεὶ τριάς ἐστιν, ἢ ἦν, ὅτε οὐκ ἦν τριάς (Athanasius, *Epistulae ad Serapionem*, 2.16.1 [AW 1.4:562]).

structure within the Trinity. Thus the Spirit could not have any effect on the inanimate beings, on those without intellect, and on sinners.[109]

Starting precisely from Origen's linear scheme and faithful to his pneumatological heritage, Basil avoided exposing himself to the criticism that the Tropici had directed at Athanasius. He did this by limiting the action of the Spirit to all rational beings and no longer only to the saints as in Origen. The equivalence of being called divine and being of the divine nature was linked to the affirmation of the communication of holiness. The Spirit was truly Creator,[110] even if, with respect to the Son, His role was limited solely to the action of sanctifying. It was precisely this that allowed for the distinction between the two, as in the following passage:

> Therefore, while the Word, Creator, Maker of the universe, produced by His own power the coming to being of the angels, the Holy Spirit added their holiness.[111]

The corresponding concept of unity of action is also found in the *De Spiritu Sancto*, showing itself to be a constant feature of Basil's pneumatology:

> Thus, in fact, the Father, who creates by His sole will, has no need of the Son (προσδεηθείη), but nevertheless wills through the Son (διὰ Υίοῦ). Nor has the Son need of collaboration since He acts in the image of the Father, but the Son too wills to make perfect through the Spirit (διὰ τοῦ Πνεύματος): "by the word (λόγος) of the Lord were the heavens made, by the breath of his mouth all their hosts" (Ps 32[33]:6). Therefore, *word* (λόγος) does not indicate a configuration of the air emitted by the organs of speech to signify something; nor does *spirit* indicate a breath of the mouth, emitted by the respiratory organs. But Word (Λόγος) is the [Word] who was in the beginning with God and who was God (cf. John 1:1), and Spirit of the mouth of God (Πνεῦμα δὲ στόματος Θεοῦ) is "the Spirit of Truth who proceeds from the Father" (John 15:26).[112]

---

109. See p. 42.

110. Basil attributes to him a true creative power (δημιουργικῆς δυνάμεως); see Basil, *Homiliae super Psalmos*, PG 29:333a–b.

111. Ἀγγέλων γοῦν τὴν μὲν εἰς τὸ εἶναι πάροδον ὁ δημιουργὸς Λόγος ὁ ποιητὴς τῶν ὅλων παρείχετο· τὸν ἁγιασμὸν δὲ αὐτοῖς τὸ Πνεῦμα τὸ ἅγιον συνεπέφερεν (Basil, *Homiliae super Psalmos*, PG 29:333c).

112. Οὕτω γὰρ ἂν οὔτε Πατὴρ προσδεηθείη Υίοῦ, μόνῳ τῷ θέλειν δημιουργῶν· ἀλλ' ὅμως θέλει διὰ Υίοῦ. Οὔτ' ἂν Υίὸς συνεργίας προσδεηθείη, καθ' ὁμοιότητα τοῦ Πατρὸς

Athanasius had asserted the unity of the nature of the three divine Persons through the procession according to the image, which was extended also to the Spirit. However, this obscured the distinction between the two processions. Basil, on the other hand, seeks to affirm the distinction itself, limiting the action of the Spirit to the sphere of sanctification to which He is called through the pure generosity of the Father and, therefore, of the Son. This whole section of the *De Spiritu Sancto* aims to show that the contribution of the Spirit as Creator is limited to the sanctification of the angels since Basil claims, contrary to the doctrine of Plotinian inspiration, not to be preaching three different hypostatic principles (ἀρχικὰς ὑποστάσεις).[113] Rather, he is affirming the Father as "unique Principle of beings, who creates through the Son and makes perfect in the Holy Spirit."[114]

At this point, it could be extremely interesting to compare Basil's text with a parallel one found in the *Adversus Macedonianos* of Gregory of Nyssa, which will be analyzed in detail in the following chapters. Basil's brother writes:

> Because God who is above all things did not make the universe through the Son because He needed some help, nor did God the only begotten produce everything in the Holy Spirit because He has insufficient power for this purpose. But the Father is the source of power, the Son is power of the Father, and the Holy Spirit is the Spirit of power. And the whole creation, whether perceptible or incorporeal, is the work of the divine power.[115]

ἐνεργῶν· ἀλλὰ καὶ Υἱὸς θέλει διὰ τοῦ Πνεύματος τελειοῦν· Τῷ λόγῳ γὰρ Κυρίου οἱ οὐρανοὶ ἐστερεώθησαν, καὶ τῷ Πνεύματι τοῦ στόματος αὐτοῦ πᾶσα ἡ δύναμις αὐτῶν. Οὔτε οὖν λόγος, ἀέρος τύπωσις σημαντική, διὰ φωνητικῶν ὀργάνων ἐκφερομένη· οὔτε πνεῦμα, στόματος ἀτμός, ἐκ τῶν ἀναπνευστικῶν μερῶν ἐξωθούμενος· ἀλλὰ Λόγος μὲν ὁ πρὸς Θεὸν ὢν ἐν ἀρχῇ, καὶ Θεὸς ὤν. Πνεῦμα δὲ στόματος Θεοῦ, τὸ Πνεῦμα τῆς ἀληθείας, ὃ παρὰ τοῦ Πατρὸς ἐκπορεύεται (Basil, *De Spiritu Sancto*, 16.38.25–36 [SC 17bis:378–80]).

113. Cf. Plotinus, *Enneades*, 5.1. See the phrase in Porphyry, *Vita Plotinii*, 4.41 and 25.36 (text in P. Henry and H. R. Schwyzer, eds., *Plotini Opera, Vol. 1* [Leiden: Brill 1951]), and Proclus, *In Platonis Parmenidem*, 1118, 31; 1135, 21 and 1213, 8 (V. Cousin, ed., *Procli philosophi Platonici opera inedita, pars tertia* [Paris: Durand, 1864; repr. Hildesheim: Olms, 1961]). The expression appears also in Eusebius, *Praeparatio evangelica*, 11.16.4.3 (SC 292:130) and in the Pseudo-Athanasian *Sermo in annuntiationem Deiparae*, PG 28:917c, 920a, and 932a.

114. Ἀρχὴ γὰρ τῶν ὄντων μία, δι' Υἱοῦ δημιουργοῦσα, καὶ τελειοῦσα ἐν Πνεύματι (Basil, *De Spiritu Sancto*, 16.38.21–23 [SC 17bis:378]).

115. ὅτι οὔτε ὁ ἐπὶ πάντων θεὸς συνεργίας τινὸς χρῄζων διὰ τοῦ υἱοῦ τὰ πάντα ἐποίησεν οὔτε ὁ μονογενὴς θεὸς ἐλάττονα τῆς προθέσεως τὴν δύναμιν ἔχων ἐν τῷ ἁγίῳ πνεύματι τὰ πάντα ἐργάζεται. ἀλλὰ πηγὴ μὲν δυνάμεώς ἐστιν ὁ πατήρ, δύναμις δὲ τοῦ πατρὸς ὁ υἱός, δυνάμεως δὲ πνεῦμα τὸ πνεῦμα τὸ ἅγιον· ἡ δὲ κτίσις πᾶσα ὅση τε αἰσθητὴ καὶ ὅση

Gregory's claim seems to follow the lines of his brother. However, it modifies them in a substantial way: its starting point is no longer the unity of action seen from the perspective of the sufficiency of one Person with respect to the others but starts from the full power of each of the Persons. The distinction in action is no longer attributed to what one Person does but to *how* He does it. Thus, the Father creates as source of power; the Son creates in that He is the very power of the Father; and the Holy Spirit creates as the Spirit of power. This shift is significant because it shows clearly the progress made by Gregory compared with Origen and Basil. At the same time, it indicates that this development is possible only because Gregory does not distinguish the processions in a purely numerical way as Athanasius had done.

This solution would be the fruit of intensive theological study that would span the second part of the fourth century. Proof of how difficult this process was is the fact that Gregory's statements mentioned earlier correspond to an internal evolution in his own thought. In fact, the passage ends with a clear assertion of the role of the Holy Spirit in the creation of both spiritual and material beings. However, Gregory had not always followed this doctrine; it is rather the fruit of a development in his thought. In this, his path is intertwined with that of his brother, as is shown by a diachronic analysis.

In fact, at the end of his life, in *Homiliae in hexaemeron* commenting on the action of the *pneuma* on the waters in Genesis 1:2 (καὶ πνεῦμα θεοῦ ἐπεφέρετο ἐπάνω τοῦ ὕδατος), Basil refers to the authority of a Syriac author whose language would have been closer to Hebrew and so more reliable in interpreting the text. This author states that ἐπεφέρετο signifies *warm up* and *make alive* (συνέθαλπε καὶ ἐζωογόνει) so that the Spirit would have communicated to the waters a certain vital force (ζωτικήν τινα δύναμιν) and thus would not be foreign to the creative activity (οὐδὲ τῆς δημιουργικῆς ἐνεργείας τὸ Πνεῦμα τὸ ἅγιον ἀπολείπεται).[116]

The text clearly refers to the material creation and not only to the heavenly powers. It is the only text of Basil that refers the creation of the material world to the Spirit, at least with regard to living beings. It could be argued that Basil's position changed in ways parallel to the gradual transition in his Trinitarian doctrine from Homoiousian positions to ones more properly neo-Nicene. This is also evidenced by the role played by Psalm 32(33):6 in

---

ἀσώματος τῆς θείας δυνάμεώς ἐστιν ἀποτέλεσμα (Gregory of Nyssa, *Adversus Macedonianos*, GNO 3.1:99.29–100.4).

116. Cf. Basil, *Homiliae in hexaemeron*, 2.6 (SC 26bis:166–70).

his thought compared with the thought of Origen, Eusebius, and Athanasius, as Drecoll has clearly shown.[117] Furthermore, extremely interesting is the reference to the Syriac world, which probably had a special role in the formation of Gregory of Nyssa's pneumatological doctrine too. As Parmentier has observed,[118] contact with the world of the Messalians and of Eustathius, together with his journeys and his knowledge of the Syriac sources, which is apparent from various quotations, reveals a certain closeness to this theological tradition. This is also witnessed later by the appreciation of the Bishop of Nyssa's thought in the Syriac sphere, as can be inferred from the numerous Syriac translations of his works.[119] Where pneumatology is concerned, it is noticeable that already in his *De Spiritu Sancto* Basil had quoted a Mesopotamian source for the doxology used by him in order to include the Third Person.[120] Gregory, for his part, is witness in the Greek world to the prebaptismal anointing paralleled only in the Syriac liturgy. Moreover, he cites the *Diatessaron* in the *In Canticum canticorum* and in the *Oratio dominica*, as we shall see later in chapter 5, he reproduces a variant in the Lukan text of the Lord's Prayer that goes back further into the Syrian sphere. To that, as Parmentier observes, we have to add the use of feminine terms to indicate the Holy Spirit, something which could go back to the female gender of the term "spirit" in the Semitic languages.[121]

This reference to the Syriac world and Basil's change at the end of his life could prove interesting for assessing Gregory of Nyssa's position on the creative role of the Holy Spirit from a diachronic point of view. In fact, the clarity of the passage of the *Adversus Macedonianos* which we have quoted had been preceded by a statement by Gregory in the contrary sense. In his *Apologia in hexaemeron*, Gregory interprets Genesis 1:2 with reference to the superior immaterial powers connected with the upper waters, since "the Spirit of God does not hover over earthly and unstable beings" (Τὸ γὰρ πνεῦμα τοῦ Θεοῦ τοῖς χθαμαλοῖς τε καὶ ἀστάτοις οὐκ ἐπιφέρεται).[122] In this passage, it seems

---

117. Drecoll, *Die Entwicklung der Trinitätslehre*, 140 and 169–70.

118. M. Parmentier, "St. Gregory of Nyssa's Doctrine of the Holy Spirit" (PhD diss., University of Oxford, 1972), 310–16.

119. M. Parmentier, "Syriac Translations of Gregory of Nyssa," *Orientalia Lovaniensia Periodica* 20 (1989): 166–73.

120. Basil, *De Spiritu Sancto*, 29.74.45 (SC 17bis:514).

121. Parmentier, "St. Gregory of Nyssa's Doctrine," 313–14. See chapter 6 for more on this topic.

122. Gregory of Nyssa, *Apologia in hexaemeron*, PG 44:81c.

that Gregory is still taking positions closer to Origen. This would indicate a development in his thought since the *Apologia in hexaemeron* is one of his early works and was composed in either 378 or 379 during the first phase of his literary production,[123] which, over the years, was to show an increasing originality and independence with respect to Origen.[124]

The position expressed in the *Adversus Macedonianos* is also found, in fact, in the *Refutatio confessionis Eunomii* and in the *Oratio catechetica magna*,[125] works certainly subsequent to the *Apologia in hexaemeron*.[126] Probably, the challenges in the study of the Trinitarian dimension pressed Gregory into reviewing his initial position. Following in the wake of his brother, he achieved a deepening of doctrine such as to overcome the limits of the formulations of both Origen and Basil, on the one hand, and of Athanasius, on the other. Forced by the Pneumatomachian criticism to make a deep study of the creator role of the Third Person, Gregory's reflection was to penetrate increasingly the distinction and relation between the two processions. However, this journey required intense work and was accompanied by a rich theological development to which the following chapters will be devoted.

VI. Conclusion: The Heart of the Question

Thus, the transition from the third to the fourth century is revealed as a crucial moment for the development of the doctrine of the Trinity and, in particular, for pneumatology. The tensions inherent in Origen's treatment exploded first with the Arian crisis and then with the criticisms of the Pneumatomachians.

The debate between Eusebius and Marcellus highlighted the need to separate the linear model from the concept of participation. However, such an advance required a formidable task, that is, the formulation of a new ontology. Thanks to his theology of the natures, Athanasius managed to overcome the limits of *Logos*-theology, which implied a reading of the position of the

---

123. See P. Maraval, "Chronology of Works," and J. A. Gil-Tamayo, "Hex. Apologia in Hexaemeron," in *The Brill Dictionary of Gregory of Nyssa*, ed. L. F. Mateo-Seco and G. Maspero (Leiden: Brill, 2009), 157 and 387–89.

124. See J. Daniélou, "La chronologie des oeuvres de Grégoire de Nysse," *Studia Patristica* 7 (1966): 159–69, esp. 161.

125. Cf. the reference to the creation both material and immaterial in *Refutatio confessionis Eunomii*, 101.1–13 (GNO 2:354.4–16), and the appellative ποιητικάς of all that has been created referring to the Word and the Spirit in *Oratio catechetica magna*, 4.4–11 (GNO 3.4:14.17–24).

126. See Maraval, "Chronology of Works," 153–69.

Second and Third Persons in terms of a necessary mediation between God and the world. An ontological abyss was opened up between the Creator and the creature, a metaphysical hiatus, which brought together the Father, the Son and the Holy Spirit in a single nature, divine and eternal. The dispute with the Tropici was to be conducted against the background of this same ontological framework: it was precisely the transition to *Physis*-theology that made possible the understanding of the substantial identity of the first two divine Persons since generation always transmits nature. However, precisely this argument became an obstacle to the possibility of understanding the divinity of the Third Person on the basis of the same principle since He does not proceed through generation. Thus, the first response to those who denied the consubstantiality of the Holy Spirit was based on the numerical distinction of the two processions. Yet, this turned out to be insufficient because Athanasius did not have the tools to identify the difference between the generation and procession of the Third Person who was described as the Image of the Image.

However, it was precisely on the new ontology introduced by Athanasius that Basil was able to build and develop the distinction between economy and immanence and make a deeper study of the role of the unity of action. The first treatise devoted to the divine Third Person by the Bishop of Caesarea aimed precisely at defending the divinity of the Holy Spirit against the Pneumatomachians who denied the need to worship the Spirit alongside the Father and the Son. Origen's heritage made itself felt in the development of the linear model by Basil, as we have seen in his interpretation of Psalm 32(33):6 and in his affirmation of the creative role of the Third Person, something denied by the Pneumatomachians. As we shall explain in the next chapters, however, this change permitted the formulation of the correspondence between the intra-Trinitarian *taxis* on the level of being and the *taxis* of the divine Persons in acting. Emphasizing this point, Gregory of Nyssa in his treatise responding to the Pneumatomachians was able to come to an explicit formulation of the role of the Spirit in the creative act. Thus, from pneumatology there arose also a new view of the cosmos. In fact, if the action of the Third Person is not limited to the saints or to rational beings but extends to every created reality, this means that matter too participates in holiness because it was created by the Holy Spirit.[127] The consequences of this dogmatic development turn out to be

---

127. This seems deeply consistent with Olivier Clément's assertion that the world is not profane, but profaned (*profané*). See O. Clément, *The Roots of Christian Mysticism* (New York: New City, 1995), 226.

enormous also in terms of concrete relationships with the world. However, that was the fruit of intense dogmatic study, the principal outcome of which was a series of treatises written with the purpose of refuting the Pneumatomachians. Through the analysis of some of these treatises and the various strategies of response in the next two chapters, we shall see how the difference between the first and second processions was to become even clearer.

The Pneumatomachian Crisis: Generation and Procession

I. Introduction: The Ontological Picture

The Pneumatomachian crisis was an extraordinary moment in the development of Trinitarian dogma as it made Christian thinkers aware of the need to develop a theology capable of distinguishing the two divine processions. This necessity was not determined merely by the confrontation with the different philosophical frameworks of the time or the interaction with the ecclesiastical background, but was intrinsic to the exegetical process necessary for a unitary reading of the most theologically important *loci* of the Gospel of John.

The question about the relationship between the two processions addressed by the *Filioque* is not a Western theological obsession but a decisive issue in the development of Greek pneumatology. Out of the confrontation between Eusebius's Binitarianism and Marcellus's monism a new picture emerged. The main question that arose in the first part of the fourth century was: How is it possible to be God without being generated?

Athanasius and Basil offered a solution within the framework of a *Physis*-theology, showing how the answer to this question was necessarily connected with a development of Origen's linear model. The former's approach was exposed to Pneumatomachian criticism as it clearly distinguished the two processions from the numerical point of view but left the qualitative dimension in the dark. Basil's work was aimed at deepening the understanding of the immanent processions and its essential difference with respect to the economic processions. The role of the Eusebians and their connection with Basil were probably important for this process.

It is apparent that the core of the discussions on the divinity of the Holy Spirit was linked to the work to overcome the merely metaphysical view of philosophy by developing a new ontological picture inspired by the gospel. In some sense the "enemies" of the the Third Person were not able to think theo-logically in a new framework, as Christian revelation could not fit in the old wineskins. The aim of the present chapter is to lay out the dogmatic arguments advanced by the Pneumatomachians and the responses from the orthodox side. We shall not be conducting a detailed historical and philological analysis but we will just underline those elements that play an important role in the background to the discussion of the *Filioque*. But the proposed path will also show how systematic discourse necessarily interacts with ontological reflec-tion, opening the way to new solutions which, in time, will take the form of a new, properly Christian thought.

II. Pneumatomachians: John 15:26 and 16:14 Again

The testimony of Epiphanius is particularly important as regards the core of Pneumatomachian thought and the use of both John 15:26 and 16:14, whose interaction has already been highlighted in the previous chapter. In the *Panar-ion*, John 16:14 appears for a first time with reference to Paul of Samosata. The context is a delineation of the difference between the human *logos* and the divine *Logos*, from which follows the difference between the economy and the imma-nent dimension proper only to God. From here, the reasoning moves to the Holy Spirit, juxtaposing John 14:16 and 16:14 to affirm that each of the three divine Persons is *enypostaton*.[1] Epiphanius is also wont to juxtapose John 15:26 and 16:14,[2] as in his reply to the Anomeans where he interprets Psalm 32(33):6 in the Trinitarian sense,[3] and in his confrontation with the Arians, where again the difference between divine immanence and creation is highlighted.[4]

However, it is in a section dedicated to the Pneumatomachians in an ex-cerpt from the *Ancoratus* that the strength of this connection becomes even more evident:

> But if one believes that Christ is from the Father as God from God (θεὸς ἐκ θεοῦ) and that His Spirit is from Christ or *from both* (παρ' ἀμφοτέρων)— according to the words of Christ [the Spirit] "proceeds from the Father" (John 15:26) and He always "will take from what is mine" (John 16:14)—and

---

1. See Epiphanius, *Panarion*, 57.4.1–10 (GCS 31:348.14–349.21). This passage is also inter-esting because, in the *lectio* cited, λήψεται is replaced by λαμβάνον.

2. See Epiphanius, *Ancoratus*, 7.1 and 8.4 (GCS 25:13.14–22 and 15.3–10).

3. Epiphanius, *Panarion*, 69.34.4 (GCS 37:182.33–183.3).

4. Epiphanius, *Panarion*, 69.56.10 (GCS 37:204.7).

if Christ is from the Holy Spirit— in fact according to the words of the angel "it is through the Holy Spirit that this child has been conceived in her
[Mary]" (Matt 1:20)—then I know the mystery that redeems me in faith,
through simple listening, in the love for the One who came to me. In fact,
God [the Father] is known, Christ is announced, the Holy Spirit is shown
to those who are worthy.[5]

This text is especially rich because the economic mystery is presented in its
Trinitarian roots through the mutual relations between the three divine Persons. The fundamental question is if the "from both" is presented as immanent or just in the sphere of divine action. Subsequently, after having cited
John 16:12–14, Epiphanius explains in a later section:

Therefore, [the Spirit] proceeds (ἐκπορεύεται) from the Father (John 15:26)
and will take (λήψεται) from mine (John 16:14)—says the Lord—then I will
venture to say that, just as "no one knows the Father except the Son and
anyone to whom the Son wishes to reveal him" (Matt 11:27), so also no one
knows the Spirit if not the Son from whom He takes (λαμβάνει) and the
Father from whom He proceeds (ἐκπορεύεται), and no one knows the Son
and the Father if not the Holy Spirit who truly glorifies them, teaches all
things, bears witness (μαρτυροῦν)[6] to the Son, is from (παρά) the Father,
is from (ἐκ) the Son, is the only way to the truth, explains the sacred laws,
instructs in the spiritual law, teaches the prophets, teaches the apostles,
illuminates with the evangelical doctrine, chooses the saints, and is true
light from true light (φῶς τὸ ἀληθινὸν ἐξ ἀληθινοῦ φωτός).[7]

---

5. Εἰ δὲ Χριστὸς ἐκ τοῦ πατρὸς πιστεύεται θεὸς ἐκ θεοῦ καὶ τὸ πνεῦμα αὐτοῦ ἐκ τοῦ
Χριστοῦ ἢ παρ' ἀμφοτέρων (ὥς φησιν ὁ Χριστός, ὁ παρὰ τοῦ πατρὸς ἐκπορεύεται καὶ οὗτος
ἐκ τοῦ ἐμοῦ λήψεται), ὁ δὲ Χριστὸς ἐκ πνεύματος ἁγίου (τὸ γὰρ ἐν αὐτῇ, φησίν, ἐκ πνεύματος ἁγίου, ἀγγέλου φωνή), συνίω τὸ λυτρούμενόν με μυστήριον, πίστει, ἀκοῇ μόνῃ, φιλίᾳ τῇ
πρὸς τὸν ἐλθόντα πρὸς ἐμέ. ἑαυτὸν γὰρ ὁ θεὸς γινώσκει, ἑαυτὸν Χριστὸς κηρύττει, ἑαυτὸ
τὸ πνεῦμα τὸ ἅγιον δηλοῖ τοῖς ἀξίοις (Epiphanius, *Panarion*, 74.4.1 [GCS 37:318.4–10]).

6. The full meaning of the witnessing will become clearer in chapter 5; see pp. 160–67.

7. Εἰ τοίνυν παρὰ τοῦ πατρὸς ἐκπορεύεται καὶ ἐκ τοῦ ἐμοῦ, φησὶν ὁ κύριος, λήψεται,
ὃν τρόπον οὐδεὶς ἔγνω τὸν πατέρα εἰ μὴ ὁ υἱὸς οὐδὲ τὸν υἱὸν εἰ μὴ ὁ πατήρ, οὕτως τολμῶ
λέγειν, ὅτι οὐδὲ τὸ πνεῦμα εἰ μὴ ὁ υἱὸς ἐξ οὗ λαμβάνει, καὶ ὁ πατὴρ παρ' οὗ ἐκπορεύεται, καὶ
οὐδὲ τὸν υἱὸν καὶ τὸν πατέρα εἰ μὴ τὸ πνεῦμα τὸ ἅγιον, τὸ δοξάζον ἀληθῶς, τὸ διδάσκον
τὰ πάντα, τὸ μαρτυροῦν περὶ τοῦ υἱοῦ, ὃ παρὰ τοῦ πατρός, ὃ ἐκ τοῦ υἱοῦ, μόνος ὁδηγὸς
ἀληθείας, νόμων ἐξηγητὴς ἁγίων, πνευματικοῦ νόμου ὑφηγητής, προφητῶν καθηγητής,
ἀποστόλων διδάσκαλος, εὐαγγελικῶν δογμάτων φωστήρ, ἁγίων ἐκλογεύς, φῶς τὸ ἀληθινὸν ἐξ ἀληθινοῦ φωτός (Epiphanius, *Panarion*, 74.10.1–2 [GCS 37:327. 7–16]).

The argumentative strategy of Epiphanius is brilliant because it extends to the Holy Spirit the correlativity that characterizes the relationship between the Father and the Son. This is expressed also in terms of knowledge, the weak point of Marcellus's reading of John 16:14. In Epiphanius's text, there resounds the echo of the Nicene symbol of faith which equates "God from God," confessed in regard to the Second Person, and "true light from true light," applied to the Spirit at the end of the text above. This implies that the "from both" should be read in the immanent sense.

From what has been said, the importance of the interaction between John 15:26 and 16:14 in the response to the Pneumatomachians seems evident[8]: it served as a point of critical comparison for those who did not recognize the divinity of the Third Person and as a catalyst for the solution to the hermeneutical tension present in the development of dogma from Origen to the emergence of a more evolved pneumatology in the fourth century. Epiphanius seems to work on the connection between economy and immanence. In fact, the answer to Pneumatomachian criticism is effective only if the unity of action can be extended to "theology" (i.e., to the divine immanence). This, then, prompts a more detailed analysis of his answer.

III. Epiphanius's Derivative Approach

As said in the introduction, the methodology of the present research attempts to avoid recourse to short, isolated quotations from different authors pulled from their proper context, a procedure common since the Middle Ages. As explained, this seems to be the origin of some of the principal misunderstandings between the Western and Byzantine worlds after the patristic era. With this in mind, the following pages attempt to offer a more thorough analysis of the main works of two of the most important authors who responded to the Pneumatomachians.

As is evident from what was presented above, it is worth analysing Epiphanius of Salamis's works in more detail. He wrote around 375 in Palestine where his monastery was a Nicene stronghold. In chapter 54 of his *Panarion*, he deals with the heretical Pneumatomachians, defining them as monstrous beings who are only half-formed and of a dual nature (τεράστιοι διφυεῖς καὶ ἡμίπλαστοι), like the centaurs, pans, and sirens.[9] According to Epiphanius's

---

8. This is also confirmed by the quotation of John 16:14 in Pseudo-Athanasius, *Dialogus I adversus Macedonianos*, 16.62–63 (E. Cavalcanti, ed., *Dialoghi contro i Macedoniani* [Turin: Società editrice internazionale, 1983], 90), a treatise that will presented later in this chapter.

9. Epiphanius, *Panarion*, 74.1.1 (GCS 37:313.12–13).

description, the crux of the heresy is the equation of the Spirit to a creature while the Son is considered coeternal with the Father.[10]

The body of Epiphanius's counterargument in the *Panarion* consists in the inclusion of a long, more directly pneumatological section from his own *Ancoratus* (65.1–73.9). He begins with the *Logos*, bearing witness to a point held in common with the Semi-Arians. Clearly the argumentative strategy, which is always essentially scriptural, aims at putting the Second and Third Persons of the Trinity on the same level. That is why Epiphanius emphasises how they both (ἀμφότερα) dwell in the righteous,[11] and thus, with reference to John 15:26 and 16:14, he immediately speaks of the procession of the Spirit from both the Father and the Son, as seen in the previous quotations.

Salvation therefore comes from the entire Trinity in such a way that, from the soteriological and economic perspective, one may ascend to the immanent dimension:

> Three Holy Ones who are altogether one holiness, three existences (ὑπαρκτά) that are altogether one single existence, three subjects (ἔμμορφα) who are altogether one single subject, three agents (ἐνεργά) who are altogether one single agent, three subsistences (ἐνυπόστατα) who are altogether one single subsistence, in reciprocal union (ἀλλήλοις συνόντα). And this is called the Holy Trinity, because the three are one divinity inasmuch as they are a single harmony (συμφωνία) of the same substance, of the same divinity, of the same subsistence (ὑποστάσεως), like from like (ὁμοία ἐξ ὁμοίου). In fact, identical is the grace of the Father, of the Son, and of the Holy Spirit that is operative, and it is up to them to teach it.[12]

It is noteworthy that even the Holy Spirit is denoted by *enypostaton*,[13] a term which seems to perform a specific role in this approach. Epiphanius emphasizes the relational unity of the three divine Persons, each of whom is perfectly identified with the unique divine substance and is present in the unique ac-

---

10. Epiphanius, *Panarion*, 74.1.3 (GCS 37:313.19–24).

11. Epiphanius, *Ancoratus*, 66.12.3–5 (GCS 25:81).

12. τρία ἅγια τρία συνάγια, τρία ὑπαρκτὰ τρία συνύπαρκτα, τρία ἔμμορφα τρία σύμμορφα, τρία ἐνεργὰ τρία συνεργά, τρία ἐνυπόστατα τρία συνυπόστατα ἀλλήλοις συνόντα· τριὰς αὕτη ἁγία καλεῖται, τρία ὄντα μία συμφωνία μία θεότης τῆς αὐτῆς οὐσίας τῆς αὐτῆς θεότητος τῆς αὐτῆς ὑποστάσεως, ὁμοία ἐξ ὁμοίου, ἰσότητα χάριτος ἐργαζομένη πατρὸς καὶ υἱοῦ καὶ ἁγίου πνεύματος τὸ δὲ πῶς αὐτοῖς ἀπολείπεται διδάσκειν (Epiphanius, *Ancoratus*, 67.4.3–5.1 [GCS 25:82]).

13. On the history of this key term, see B. Gleede, *The Development of the Term ἐνυπόστατος from Origen to John of Damascus* (Leiden: Brill, 2012).

tion, while the personal distinction is formulated on a prepositional level that expresses reciprocal relations: "because they are three as in tension *from*, *by*, and *toward* (ταῦτα τρία ὄντα ἢ ἐξ αὐτοῦ ἢ παρ' αὐτοῦ ἢ πρὸς αὐτόν)."[14]

The Son and the Spirit are both sent by the Father in such a way that, if the former made Himself a servant (διάκονον), the latter made Himself a servant alongside Him (συνδιακονεῖν), which is why Scripture teaches that both persons speak in the saints, heal, sanctify, and baptize.[15] The text is full of quotations which range from the *Trisagion* in Isaiah 6:3 to the command not to grieve the Spirit in Ephesians 4:30, and the deception of Ananias in Acts 5:3–4, which Epiphanius comments on, using a significant expression:

> So also the Holy Spirit is God as God from God (θεὸς ἐκ θεοῦ), inasmuch as those who had kept a part of the earnings for themselves lied to God Himself.[16]

Through this text, clearly in the wake of Nicea, we arrive, therefore, at the dogmatic core of Epiphanius's theological presentation, which moves from the unity of action of the three divine Persons to their distinction and mutual immanent relation. Psalm 32(33):6, an especially important verse in the Pneumatomachian dispute as already seen,[17] is cited as proof of the *synergy* of the Father, Son, and Holy Spirit by virtue of the dual reference to the creative act and to the distinction with respect to the angels. This citation is immediately linked to John 4:24 as an indication of the necessity of also adoring the Third Person.[18] In fact, it is precisely the creative act that radically differentiates the Father, Son, and Spirit from all creatures:

> But if [the Spirit] makes together these things, a creature does not produce a creature, nor does the divinity become created, nor is He known as God according to a limited and partial sense. In fact, the divinity is without limits, infinite and unknowable (ἀπερίγραφος ἀχώρητος ἀπερινόητος), but embraces all that God has made.[19]

---

14. Epiphanius, *Ancoratus*, 67.6.1–2 (GCS 25:82).

15. Epiphanius, *Ancoratus*, 68.1–2 (GCS 25:82).

16. ἄρα θεὸς ἐκ θεοῦ καὶ θεὸς τὸ πνεῦμα τὸ ἅγιον, ᾧ ἐψεύσαντο οἱ τοῦ τιμήματος τοῦ χωρίου νοσφισάμενοι (Epiphanius, *Ancoratus*, 69.8.17–18 [GCS 25:86]).

17. Cf. G. Maspero, "Dallo Spirito vivificatore allo Spirito Creatore: L'esegesi cappadoce di Sal 32(33),6," in *Creazione e salvezza nella Bibbia*, ed. M. V. Fabbri and M. Tábet (Rome: EDUSC, 2009), 407–26.

18. Epiphanius, *Ancoratus*, 70.1–2 (GCS 25:87).

19. εἰ δὲ συνεργεῖ ταῦτα, κτίσις κτίσιν οὐκ ἐργάζεται οὐδὲ κτιστὴ ἡ θεότης γίνεται οὐδὲ

Therefore, not adoring the Third Person would be equivalent to a violation of the first commandment of Deuteronomy 6:4. The reasoning is simultaneously deeply biblical and authentically ontological. These metaphysical inclusions are particularly surprising in the discourse of Epiphanius, who does not usually work in a philosophically sophisticated way as the Cappadocians do. However, the line of reasoning is similar and clear: "If God and Father is light, the Son will also be light from light" (εἰ δὲ φῶς ὁ θεὸς καὶ πατήρ, φῶς ἄρα ἐκ φωτὸς ὁ υἱός).[20] In the same way, given that God is Wisdom, the Son is "Wisdom from Wisdom" (σοφία ὁ υἱὸς ἐκ σοφίας),[21] and given that God is Life, the Son is "Life from Life" (ζωὴ ἐκ ζωῆς),[22] as John 14:6 confirms.[23] In the same way, applying the fundamental principle of his refutation, Epiphanius adds with regard to the Third Person in His relation to the Father and the Son: "And the Spirit, being *from both*, is Spirit from Spirit" (τὸ δὲ ἅγιον πνεῦμα παρὰ ἀμφοτέρων, πνεῦμα ἐκ πνεύματος).[24] Again, the legacy of the theology of Origen and of Nicea is evident.

It is important to note how in the reasoning proposed by the Bishop of Salamis, the Third Person's relation of origin to *both* of the first two Persons is the basis for his affirmation that *both* the Son and the Spirit are God. For his opponents, the affirmation of the divinity of the Second Person is acceptable, though not with the same strength as the Niceans. Epiphanius's response thus presents the second procession alongside the first in such a way that the fact of the Father and the Son being only one substance implies *per se* that the Spirit proceeds from both because the Spirit proceeds from God as Spirit from Spirit. In this way, the affirmation of the perfection of the first procession is the basis for the full formulation of the second procession.

From here, the necessity of distinguishing the two processions clearly emerges. Thus, Epiphanius responds immediately to a fundamental objection that recurs in his debate with the Pneumatomachians:

ἐν μέτρῳ ἢ περιοχῇ θεὸς γινώσκεται. ἔστι γὰρ ἀπερίγραφος ἀχώρητος ἀπερινόητος, πάντα περιέχων τὰ ποιήματα τοῦ θεοῦ (Epiphanius, *Ancoratus*, 70.2.1–3.1 [GCS 25:87]).

20. Epiphanius, *Ancoratus*, 70.5.2–6.1 (GCS 25:87).

21. Epiphanius, *Ancoratus*, 70.6.3 (GCS 25:88).

22. See G. Maspero, "Life from Life: The Procession of the Son and the Divine Attributes in Ch. VIII of Gregory of Nyssa's *Contra Eunomium III*," in *Gregory of Nyssa's Contra Eunomium III: An English Translation with Commentary and Supporting Studies; Proceedings of the 12th International Colloquium on Gregory of Nyssa (Leuven, 14–17 September 2010)*, ed. J. Leemans and M. Cassin (Leiden: Brill, 2014), 401–28, esp. 423–27.

23. Epiphanius, *Ancoratus*, 70.7.1 (GCS 25: 88).

24. Epiphanius, *Ancoratus*, 70.7.1–2 (GCS 25:88).

One may object: therefore we say that there are two sons, but then how is [the Son] only begotten? "But who indeed are you, a human being, to talk back to God?" (Rom 9:20). In fact, if He calls the Son the one who is from Him, He also calls the Holy Spirit the one who is *from both* (παρ' ἀμφο-τέρων). These two Persons [the Son and the Holy Spirit], who are known by the saints only through faith, are light and they communicate light, and their operation is illumination and production of harmony (συμφωνίαν) with the Father of light. Listen, therefore, with faith, that the Father, who is all Light, is the Father of the true Son, and the Son is Son of the true Father, as Light from Light, not just nominally like what is made or created. And the Holy Spirit is Spirit of Truth, third Light, that is, from the Father and from the Son (παρὰ πατρὸς καὶ υἱοῦ).[25]

Thus, just as the Father neither began to be nor ceases to be Father—unlike the patriarchs and human fathers who, in turn, are someone's son[26]—so also the Holy Spirit neither began to be nor ceases to be the Spirit, as can be said regarding the angels and other spirits, even though Isaiah calls Him "Angel of Great Counsel" (Isa 9:6 [LXX]). In fact, His spiration has neither a beginning nor an end, and it is incomprehensible, unlike what occurs on the level of creatures which are in time but depend on Him who is outside of time itself (οὐκ ἐν χρόνῳ τυγχάνει).[27] Therefore, once again, just as all generally come to be called children of God, but their generation is essentially different from that of the Son in so far as their generation is limited, so also Scripture uses the term *spirit* with diverse meanings, but the Holy Spirit alone is the Spirit of the Father and of the Son.[28]

The entire demonstrative strategy culminates in the theological affirmation that the Holy Spirit is a *subsistent subject*. Epiphanius affirms this with the term *enypostaton* and the expression is typical of his vocabulary.[29] This point is es-

---

25. Ἀλλ' ἐρεῖ τις· οὐκοῦν φαμὲν δύο εἶναι υἱούς, καὶ πῶς μονογενής; μενοῦν γε, σὺ τίς εἶ ὁ ἀντιλογιζόμενος τῷ θεῷ; εἰ γὰρ τὸν μὲν υἱὸν καλεῖ τὸν ἐξ αὐτοῦ, τὸ δὲ ἅγιον πνεῦμα τὸ παρ' ἀμφοτέρων, (ἃ μόνον πίστει νοούμενα ὑπὸ τῶν ἁγίων φωτεινὰ φωτοδότα φωτεινὴν τὴν ἐνέργειαν ἔχει συμφωνίαν τε πρὸς αὐτὸν τὸν πατέρα ποιεῖται φωτός), πίστει ἄκουε, ὦ οὗτος, ὅτι ὁ πατὴρ ἀληθοῦς υἱοῦ ἐστι πατήρ, φῶς ὅλος, καὶ ὁ υἱὸς ἀληθοῦς πατρὸς υἱός, φῶς ἐκ φωτός, οὐχ ὡς τὰ ποιητὰ ἢ κτιστὰ προσηγορίᾳ μόνῃ· καὶ πνεῦμα ἅγιον πνεῦμα ἀληθείας ἐστί, φῶς τρίτον παρὰ πατρὸς καὶ υἱοῦ (Epiphanius, *Ancoratus*, 71.1.1–3.1 [GCS 25:88]).

26. Cf. Epiphanius, *Ancoratus*, 71.4.1–6.1 (GCS 25:89).

27. Epiphanius, *Ancoratus*, 71.7.1–8.2 (GCS 25:89).

28. Epiphanius, *Ancoratus*, 72.6.1–5 (GCS 25:90).

29. Epiphanius, *Ancoratus*, 72.8.3–4 (GCS 25:91).

sential because the divine nature is all spirit and all holy, as revealed in God's own activity, but here we are dealing with the recognition of the divine Third Person as God, beginning from His relations with the other two Persons. In a concise formula in the *Panarion*, taking up again the discussion after the long insertion from the *Ancoratus*, Epiphanius affirms that "As God is one, and just one is the Only-Begotten Son of God, so also the Holy Spirit of God is one: from God and in God" (ἀπὸ δὲ θεοῦ καὶ ἐν θεῷ).[30] The genitive is understood here in the purely immanent sense, stating the divine attributes for each divine Person and then concluding that "the Trinity is eternally Trinity and does not receive any addition" (Ἀεὶ γὰρ ἡ τριὰς τριάς . . . καὶ οὐδέποτε προσθήκην λαμβάνει).[31] From the metaphysical perspective the expression is equivalent to Origen's denial that the more and less could be applied to the Trinity.

In summary, Epiphanius's work seeks to address the heart of the pneumatological question, that is, he affirms not only that God is spirit, but also that the Spirit is God, understood here as a divine person and not as a divine attribute. He is God without being generated. Epiphanius's strategy develops Origen's derivative model in order to show that the Third Person of the Trinity is Spirit from Spirit because, in the divine immanence, He proceeds from both of the first two Persons. The synergy and distinction of the two processions are the main dogmatic elements in this debate. Other possibilities, though, will be added to the response to the Pneumatomachians, as in the case of the Pseudo-Athanasian treatises against the Macedonians.

IV. Pseudo-Athanasius's Relational Approach

IV.1. Earlier Answer

The Pseudo-Athanasian treatises against the Macedonians have a complex history both from a redactional standpoint and from a theological perspective.[32] In her edition of the text and in the analysis that accompanies it, Elena Cavalcanti

---

30. Epiphanius, *Panarion*, 74.11.5 (GCS 37:329.11–13).
31. Epiphanius, *Panarion*, 74.12.1 (GCS 37:329.27–28).
32. The two treatises (CPG 2285) can be found in PG 28:1291 and 1338 respectively. See Ch. Bizer, "Studien zu pseudathanasianischen Dialogen der Orthodoxos und Aëtios" (PhD diss., University of Bonn, 1970); A. Segovia, "Contribucion al estudio de la tradicion manuscrita dei pseudoatanasiano: Dialogo I contra un Macedoniano o pneumatomaco," *Archivio teológico granadino* 1 (1938): 87–107; and A. Günthör, "Die 7 pseudoathanasianischen Dialogen ein Werk Didymus' des Blinden von Alexandrien" (PhD diss., Pontifical Atheneum of St. Anselm, 1940).

emphasizes how the two works can be read in a unitary way from the point of view of the redactor.[33] At the same time, the presence of earlier material in the first dialogue (1–8) is quite evident. According to Friedrich Loofs, this first section presents an anti-Macedonian *dossier* dating back to 381–390.[34] It thus seems appropriate to distinguish the arguments in the two parts of the first treatise. Here we find six main Pneumatomachian objections to the divinity of the Holy Spirit.

1. The first argument of the doctrinal "file" (σχεδάριον)[35] of the heretical part is the clear affirmation that "If the Holy Spirit is God, either He is the Father or He is the Son, otherwise He does not exist."[36] This either-or dichotomy is put in crisis—this word being used here in the etymological Greek sense of judgment—by the orthodox response which distinguishes the ontological dimension of nature from that of person: the Father is not God because He is Father; otherwise the Son could not be God because as Son He is not Father, and vice versa. Therefore, the Holy Spirit is also God, but not because He is Father or Son.[37] The underlying dogmatic and ontological reasoning is as follows:

> God, in fact, indicates a nature (φύσεως) that contemplates and fills the entire universe; Father, rather, is the name of a relation (σχετικόν), as is Son. The name of the relation (τὸ τῆς σχέσεως ὄνομα) does not signify the nature that fills and pervades, nor does the name of the nature that fills and pervades introduce the relation (σχέσιν) of the Father to the Son.[38]

Here, the Macedonian critique of the coordinated doxology makes its appearance, translating the previous exchange in terms of worship (προσκυνητέον).[39] The orthodox response follows with the line of reasoning begun above, distinguishing the plane of nature from that of the person:

33. Cavalcanti, *Dialoghi contro i Macedoniani*.

34. Cf. F. Loofs, "Zwei macedonianische Dialoge," *SPAW* (1914): 526–51.

35. The term appears three times in the first dialogue, in 1.4; 6.30; and 9.4, but it is rather rare. It is found, for example, twice in the *Anacephalaeosis*, which is a work of uncertain attribution to Epiphanius (GCS 37:526.5 and 8), and once in *De eleemosyna* by Pseudo-Chrysostomus (PG 60:710b).

36. Pseudo-Athanasius, *Dialogus I contra Macedonianos*, 1.1 (Cavalcanti, 50).

37. Pseudo-Athanasius, *Dialogus I contra Macedonianos*, 1.2–9 (Cavalcanti, 50).

38. Τὸ γὰρ θεὸς φύσεώς ἐστι θεωρουμένης τι, εἴτουν διαθεούσης τὰ πάντα δηλωτικόν· τὸ δὲ πατήρ, ὄνομα σχετικόν· καὶ τὸ υἱὸς ὁμοίως. Οὔτε δὲ τὸ τῆς σχέσεως ὄνομα τὴν διαθέουσαν ἢ τὴν θεωρουμένην τι φύσιν σημαίνει· οὔτε τὸ τῆς τι θεωρουμένης ἢ διαθεούσης φύσεως ὄνομα τὴν πατρὸς πρὸς υἱὸν σχέσιν εἰσάγει (Pseudo-Athanasius, *Dialogus I contra Macedonianos*, 1.10–14 [Cavalcanti, 52]).

39. Pseudo-Athanasius, *Dialogus I contra Macedonianos*, 1.16 (Cavalcanti, 52).

If this is the reason why you worship the Father, that is, because He is Father, and the Son, that is, because He is Son, then you worship every father and every son.[40]

Rather, one must adore the first two Persons of the Trinity because they have the same nature (δι' αὐτὴν τὴν φύσιν) in such a way that the Third Person too will be adored if He is of the same nature.[41]

On the Macedonian side, the counterargument to the orthodox response is that although John 4:24 says that God is Spirit, it is not to be interpreted to mean that every spirit is God, suggesting in an analogous way that not every father and every son are God.[42] The scriptural standpoint of the orthodox rebuttal is the observation that not even all of what is called God is spirit, so that Moses is called god in Exodus 7:1, and John 10:35 in the New Testament attributes to Christ the statement that the saints are gods. Such citations are many, including Psalms 49:1, 81:1, and 83:8, and Exodus 22:27. The conclusion is that not all of what is called god is also spirit and not all of what is called spirit is god. Also introduced here is the paradoxical example of demons, which are spirits but clearly are not God.[43]

2. In the light of all this, the discussion shifts to the identification of the Spirit with the Lord, taking 2 Corinthians 3:13 as the starting point. The Macedonian objection here is that the Third Person is not God but the Lord.[44] This also introduces the christological theme which, in the final redaction, is developed in the last part of the first treatise and the body of the second because of the need to determine the ontological relationship between the Spirit and Christ. In fact, the Pneumatomachians argue, if the latter is Lord and the Third Person is the Spirit of the Lord, then the Spirit must be Lord. However, their fundamental objection continues to reappear with the denial of the possibility of worshiping Him since it is not written (οὐδὲ γὰρ γέγραπται) that this must be done.[45] The commandment to worship the Lord God in Deuteronomy 6:13 would therefore be limited to the Son toward whom the Spirit would lead, as Matthew 4:10 seems to state.

---

40. εἰ μὲν διὰ τοῦτο προσκυνεῖς τὸν πατέρα, ἐπειδὴ πατήρ ἐστι καὶ τὸν υἱὸν, ἐπειδὴ υἱός ἐστι, προσκυνεῖς καὶ πάντα πατέρα καὶ πάντα υἱόν (Pseudo-Athanasius, *Dialogus I contra Macedonianos*, 2.1–3 [Cavalcanti, 52]).

41. Pseudo-Athanasius, *Dialogus I contra Macedonianos*, 2.5–8 (Cavalcanti, 52).

42. Pseudo-Athanasius, *Dialogus I contra Macedonianos*, 2.10–11 (Cavalcanti, 52).

43. Pseudo-Athanasius, *Dialogus I contra Macedonianos*, 2.27–30 (Cavalcanti, 54).

44. Pseudo-Athanasius, *Dialogus I contra Macedonianos*, 3.1–4 (Cavalcanti, 54).

45. Pseudo-Athanasius, *Dialogus I contra Macedonianos*, 4.2–3 (Cavalcanti, 54).

3. In the background here is present an ontological principle that appears fundamental to the Macedonian view: "Indeed it is necessary that those who approach God do so through another being" (Δεῖ γὰρ ἀληθῶς τὸν προσαγό-μενον θεῷ, δι᾽ ἑτέρου προσάγεσθαι).[46] This is why, in this perspective, even if the Third Person were to be worshiped, one would then have to answer the question of how it would be possible to approach the Spirit Himself. The example of Nathan who worshiped David serves in the orthodox response to show how the prophet did not himself violate the commandment in Deuteronomy 6:13 to worship God alone—which is reproposed by Jesus in Matthew 4:10—because, in worshiping the Anointed of the Lord, the prophet was worshiping the power of the Spirit.[47]

The response continues with the affirmation that the commandment in Deuteronomy 6:13 refers to the divine nature and therefore includes the Father, the Son, and the Holy Spirit:

> If, therefore, it is proved that the Spirit who proceeds (ἐκχυθέν) from the Father Himself through the Son (διὰ τοῦ υἱοῦ) is of the same nature as the Father and the Son, it is also concluded that He must be worshiped and revered.[48]

This point is central to the argument because the Macedonian ontological principle would imply that the worship of a divine person must always be mediated by an intermediate being, that is, by an ontological mediator. Thus, the procession of the Spirit from the Father through the Son in the divine immanence shows that this metaphysical progression is excluded. The impossibility of recognizing Jesus as Lord except by the Holy Spirit, affirmed in 1 Corinthians 12:3, is thus reread in the light of the commandment of John 4:24 to worship God in Spirit and Truth.[49] The text is interpreted in a Trinitarian way, identifying the Truth with the Second Person and the Spirit with the Third. Thus, if worshiping God the Father in Spirit and Truth does not imply the exclusion of the worship of Truth itself (that is, the Son), then, in the same way, worshiping the Father and the Son does not exclude the Spirit. In fact,

---

46. Pseudo-Athanasius, *Dialogus I contra Macedonianos*, 4.12–13 (Cavalcanti, 56).

47. Pseudo-Athanasius, *Dialogus I contra Macedonianos*, 4.15–25 (Cavalcanti, 56).

48. Ἐὰν οὖν δειχθῇ τῆς αὐτῆς εἶναι φύσεως καὶ θεότητος τῷ υἱῷ καὶ τῷ πατρὶ καὶ τὸ πνεῦμα τὸ ἐξ αὐτοῦ τοῦ πατρὸς διὰ τοῦ υἱοῦ ἐκχυθὲν, καὶ προσκυνητὸν καὶ λατρευτὸν ἀποδειχθήσεται (Pseudo-Athanasius, *Dialogus I contra Macedonianos*, 5.11–14 [Cavalcanti, 56–58]).

49. See Origen's recourse to this verse at pp. 17–19 (nn. 17–23) and as Athanasius used it at pp. 58–59 (n. 55).

including the Second Person in worship does not diminish the greatness of the First Person, in that—as John 6:44 states—no one can come to the Son if he or she is not drawn by the Father who is in heaven.[50] Ontologically, this means that the condition for being able to approach God is not external to God Himself, but is the attraction of the highest principle and not of an intermediate being. The possibility of the relation is thus situated not in the divine economy but in the divine immanence, that is, in the eternal relations of the three divine Persons. The conclusion of the argument is very clear in this regard:

> And if we are called to the Son through the Father (διὰ τοῦ πατρὸς πρὸς τὸν υἱόν), but as a result the Father is no less dignified, then we are also called to the Son through the Spirit (διὰ τοῦ πνεύματος πρὸς τὸν υἱόν): and the Latter does not lose anything of His dignity, because you know that we are led to the Spirit through someone and in someone (διὰ τίνος ἢ ἐν τίνι). Read the Scriptures and learn that as we are led by the Father to the Son, also through the Son we are led to the Father; in fact, as was mentioned (προαποδέδοται), they are in reciprocal relations (ἀντιστρέφει). Therefore, just as through the Father we are led to the Son, so by the Father and the Son we are led to the Spirit (διὰ τοῦ πατρὸς καὶ τοῦ υἱοῦ πρὸς τὸ πνεῦμα).[51]

This dogmatic strategy seeks to show the reversibility of the immanent relations according to a method that would be reprised by Gregory of Nyssa, as will be seen in the next chapter.[52]

4. The treatise goes on to discuss baptism, imparted in the name of the Father, and of the Son, and of the Spirit. The issue is framed on the basis of the question of whether either baptism or worship is more important. The superiority of the former over the latter is proved by the fact that catechumens worship the first two divine Persons but they do not reach the fullness of Christian life if they do not receive the Third Person through the sacrament.[53]

---

50. Pseudo-Athanasius, *Dialogus I contra Macedonianos*, 5.17–27 (Cavalcanti, 58).

51. Εἰ δὲ καὶ διὰ τοῦ πατρὸς πρὸς τὸν υἱὸν καλούμεθα, οὐκ ἐλαττοῦσθαι ἄρα τούτου ἕνεκεν τῆς ἀξίας ὁ πατήρ, καὶ διὰ τοῦ πνεματος πρὸς τὸν υἱὸν καλούμεθα· καὶ οὐκ ἐλαττοῦται τῆς ἀξίας τὸ πνεῦμα, ἐπειδὴ δὲ καὶ ἐπιζητεῖς διὰ τίνος ἢ ἐν τίνι προσαγόμεθα τῷ πνεύματι. Ἀνάγνωθι τὰς γραφάς, καὶ μάθε ὅτι ὥσπερ διὰ τοῦ πατρὸς πρὸς τὸν υἱόν, καὶ διὰ τοῦ υἱοῦ πρὸς τὸν πατέρα—ἀντιστρέφει γὰρ καθὼς προαποδέδοται—ὡς οὖν διὰ τοῦ πατρὸς πρὸς τὸν υἱόν, οὕτως διὰ τοῦ πατρὸς καὶ τοῦ υἱοῦ πρὸς τὸ πνεῦμα (Pseudo-Athanasius, *Dialogus I contra Macedonianos*, 5.31–38 [Cavalcanti, 58]).

52. See pp. 119–34.

53. Pseudo-Athanasius, *Dialogus I contra Macedonianos*, 6.2–8 (Cavalcanti, 60).

Linked to baptism is the interpretation of the connumeration (συναριθμεῖται), which, according to the Macedonian reading, is reduced to the nominal level: the Spirit is connumerated as mere spirit and not at the same ontological level as Father, Son, and God.[54]

It is noteworthy that the dispute over the divinity of the Third Person revolves around the identification of the difference between the spiritual nature and the personal characteristic of the Spirit as distinct—in a perfect identity of nature—from the Father and the Son. The orthodox response takes up Psalm 81(82):6 again, rereading it from an angelological perspective in order to show the absurdity of the heretical position, which puts the angels alongside God but excludes the Spirit. All of this is designed to highlight the force of the affirmation of the uniqueness of nature:

> Rather, we do not connumerate on the basis of name, since this is not anything great, but on the basis of the nature itself.[55]

The underlying ontological issue is that nothing can be added to or subtracted from the Father, the Son, and the Spirit because they are perfect in their unique nature.[56]

5. The penultimate Pneumatomachian objection concerns *homotimia*. If one were to admit that the Spirit can be worshiped, then the honor rendered to Him could not be the same as that rendered to the Father and to the Son because this is not written (ἐπειδὴ οὐδὲ γέγραπται).[57] The response reaches a theological peak because it rereads baptism in the name of the three divine Persons as a supreme act of adoration that also involves one's own body, according to what is said in Romans 12:1.[58]

6. Finally, the last and definitive Pneumatomachian objection regards the creaturely nature of the Spirit which is always discussed on the basis of what is or is not written and, therefore, with reference to the exegesis of John 1:3 and 1:10. The orthodox response compares the equivocal nature of this position with the duplicity of the Pharisees when questioned about the baptism of John the Baptist (cf. Matt 21:26). The Macedonian argument consists in affirming

---

54. Pseudo-Athanasius, *Dialogus I contra Macedonianos*, 6.16–18 (Cavalcanti, 60).

55. Ἡμεῖς δὲ οὐ τῷ ὀνόματι συναριθμοῦμεν· οὐδὲν γὰρ τοῦτο μέγα· ἀλλ' αὐτῇ τῇ φύσει, ὡς ὕστερον ἀποδείξομεν (Pseudo-Athanasius, *Dialogus I contra Macedonianos*, 6.27–29 [Cavalcanti, 60]).

56. Pseudo-Athanasius, *Dialogus I contra Macedonianos*, 6.34–36 (Cavalcanti, 62).

57. Pseudo-Athanasius, *Dialogus I contra Macedonianos*, 7.2–3 (Cavalcanti, 62).

58. Pseudo-Athanasius, *Dialogus I contra Macedonianos*, 7.8–18 (Cavalcanti, 62).

the creaturely nature of the Spirit while simultaneously separating Him from all other creatures. The set of different scriptural passages cited to demonstrate the intimate relation between the Father and the Spirit, from Matthew 10:20 to Acts 2:17, converges on the fundamental criticism that the Father could not anoint the Son—who is actually God—with a creature.

From this it follows that the argument of the first and oldest part of the treatise is intended to shortcircuit the relationship between the Father and the Son through the Holy Spirit. The affirmation of the divinity of the Second Person is utilized to show *ad absurdum* that only the uniqueness of nature is a sound basis for the Pneumatomachian reasoning itself in such a way that the divinity of the Holy Spirit can be affirmed starting from the doxological dimension that characterizes the life and liturgy of the Church. In this process, the relational dimension of the divine immanence is perfectly recognized and highlighted together with the role of the Son in the procession of the Third Person. The issue is genuinely metaphysical inasmuch as the Trinitarian revelation excludes the necessity of an ontological mediator in the adoration of the divine person.

The Macedonian objections could be summarized as follows:

1. It is not written that one needs to worship the Spirit.
2. Christological connection: The Spirit is Lord but not God.
3. Ontological core: If He were such, there would be no mediator to approach Him.
4. This is why He is connumerated in name only: The baptismal discourse.
5. Not even *homotimia* can be prescribed.
6. Therefore, the Spirit is created but superior to the creatures.

In the orthodox response, the essential element is the distinction between the personal dimension and the substantial dimension, founded on the attribution of the names of the three divine Persons to the relational sphere. The basis of this is the denial, based on Scripture, of the necessity of an ontological mediator between the faithful and He who is the object of worship. This is deeply coherent because the traces of a graduated metaphysical vision exclude the possibility of direct relational contact between God and the human being, while the relational rereading of the divine immanence introduces a new possibility of expressing the relationship between the creature and the Creator. From this perspective, the mediation of the Son in the procession of the Spirit appears as an intrinsic element of the personal dynamic of the immanent Trinity, and as an element that is intimately connected with the response to the Pneumatomachian heresy.

IV.2. Later Answer

The second part of the first treatise develops arguments with more sophisticated theological tools, and here the influence of the pneumatology of Gregory of Nyssa is evident.[59] In connecting the first and second parts,[60] the redaction of the first treatise reveals the intention of extending the proof of the oneness of nature. The dialogical *fictio* is proposed as an element of continuity with respect to the refutation of the *schedarion* in the first part. Thus, the initiative passes to the orthodox side.

The outline of the proof *ad absurdum* is repeated: (a) Only God is immortal; (b) but the angels are immortal as well; (c) both sides converge on the fact that the angels are immortal owing to participation (μετοχῇ); (d) so, the orthodox lead the Macedonians to recognize that the Son is immortal like the Father and not because of participation; (e) in the end, the argument is repeated about the Holy Spirit—that His immortality is recognized by the Macedonians as being like that of the Father and the Son and not because of participation like the angels; (f) in this way one arrives at the absurd affirmation that God is not the only one to be perfectly immortal, or at least one is compelled to admit as much if it is not accepted that the Father, the Son, and the Spirit are a single nature.[61]

As will be seen, various theological elements recall in particular the *Ad Ablabium* of Gregory of Nyssa, such as the discussion about tritheism which comes immediately after the demonstration of immortality.[62] This treatise by Gregory most likely dates back to the 390s, probably following the composition of the first part of the Pseudo-Athanasian treatise but preceding the second part. The Father, the Son, and the Spirit are identified with the one immortal nature while being three distinct hypostases. The example of Paul, Peter, and Timothy is analogous to this.[63] The Pneumatomachian response seeks to un-

---

59. See the next two chapters.

60. Pseudo-Athanasius, *Dialogus I contra Macedonianos*, 9.1–5 (Cavalcanti, 66).

61. Pseudo-Athanasius, *Dialogus I contra Macedonianos*, 9.6–34 (Cavalcanti, 66–68).

62. For an introduction to the treatise, see G. Maspero, *Trinity and Man: Gregory of Nyssa's Ad Ablabium* (Leiden: Brill, 2007). For the theological discussion on the treatise, see L. Ayres, "Not Three People: The Fundamental Themes of Gregory of Nyssa's Trinitarian Theology as Seen in *To Ablabius: On Not Three Gods*," *Modern Theology* 18 (2002): 445–74, and N. A. Jacobs, "On 'Not Three Gods'—Again: Can a Primary-Secondary Substance Reading of *Ousia* and *Hypostasis* Avoid Tritheism?" *Modern Theology* 18 (2002): 431–58. See also A. Radde-Gallwitz, *Gregory of Nyssa's Doctrinal Works: A Literary Study* (Oxford: Oxford University Press, 2018), 146–60.

63. Pseudo-Athanasius, *Dialogus I contra Macedonianos*, 10.4–7 (Cavalcanti, 68).

dermine this parallelism by highlighting how the men cited have originated from other men while the orthodox argument concludes by affirming that there was nothing prior to the three divine Persons but that their origin is immanent and is linked to the two processions (ἀλλ' ἐκ τοῦ πατρὸς ὁ υἱὸς γεγέννηται, καὶ τὸ πνεῦμα ἐκπορεύεται).[64]

At this point, the reasoning about immortality is repeated with regard to holiness, again proceeding by means of a comparison with the angels in order to conclude with the Holy Spirit's activity as sanctifier.[65] The discussion shifts to activity, that is, *energeia*, which is also the central theme in the *Ad Ablabium*. It is in this direction, focused on activity, that the second part of the first Pseudo-Athanasian treatise seems to move, applying the demonstration regarding immortality to the Holy Spirit's being as a *guide*. Here, the orthodox ontological principle is repeated: where there is identity of action, there must also be identity of nature (ὧν γὰρ ἡ αὐτὴ ἐνέργεια, καὶ ἡ αὐτὴ φύσις).[66]

The equality of the Spirit with regard to the Father and to the Son is put in terms of the identity between gold and gold.[67] Immediately following, the classic Pneumatomachian objection reappears, that is, the statement that if the Spirit were God, then He and the Son would be brothers.[68] The orthodox response rests on the difference between these two processions, generation and *ekporeusis* (ἀλλ' ὁ μὲν υἱὸς γεγέννηται, τὸ δὲ πνεῦμα ἐκπορεύεται).[69] Here, the Spirit as ἐνυπόστατον comes into play. The reasoning springs from the fact that a living being that is characterized by rational activity and is mortal must evidently be a human. In the same way, if the Spirit is hypostatic, sanctifying, and uncreated, then He must necessarily be God (ὡς γὰρ ἐὰν ὁμολογηθῇ πνεῦμα ἐνυπόστατον, ἁγιαστικὸν, ἄκτιστον, θεός ἐστι).[70]

At this point the Pneumatomachian objection is raised through the distinction of being God from being divine.[71] The response, in turn, moves from the unity of action of the three divine Persons, expressed as *synergeia*, to the question about the kingship of the Spirit posed by the orthodox to the Mace-

---

64. Pseudo-Athanasius, *Dialogus I contra Macedonianos*, 10.13–17 (Cavalcanti, 68).

65. Pseudo-Athanasius, *Dialogus I contra Macedonianos*, 11.1–77 (Cavalcanti, 70–74).

66. See Pseudo-Athanasius, *Dialogus I contra Macedonianos*, 12.14–15 (Cavalcanti, 74). The expression is repeated in 12.35–36 (Cavalcanti, 76); 13.24 (Cavalcanti, 80); and 16.8–9 (Cavalcanti, 86).

67. Pseudo-Athanasius, *Dialogus I contra Macedonianos*, 12.57–62 (Cavalcanti, 78).

68. Pseudo-Athanasius, *Dialogus I contra Macedonianos*, 14.21 (Cavalcanti, 82).

69. Pseudo-Athanasius, *Dialogus I contra Macedonianos*, 14.25 (Cavalcanti, 82).

70. Pseudo-Athanasius, *Dialogus I contra Macedonianos*, 15.6–10 (Cavalcanti, 84).

71. Pseudo-Athanasius, *Dialogus I contra Macedonianos*, 15.22 (Cavalcanti, 84).

donians with the latter recognising the kingship of only the first two divine Persons while considering the Spirit as a mere minister (ὑπηρέτης).[72] This point is extremely important, as the next chapter will show, because the link between the Spirit and divine kingship is a key element already in Origen and Basil and will become the fundamental piece of Gregory of Nyssa's response to the Pneumatomachians.[73]

In the following section, the tritheistic objection returns where the essential point of distance is the orthodox equation of *symphōnia* with the identity of nature of the three divine Persons. The Macedonian side, on the other hand, welcomes the First and denies the Second.[74] However, the identity of the attributes that has already been proven should lead to the conclusion that the Third Person cannot be subordinate to the first two.[75] The discussion of the different ways of interpreting the scriptural passages about being beneath another and being greater than another leads to the Macedonian affirmation that the Spirit is not created but made.[76] The scriptural reference is evidently the Johannine Prologue, particularly the affirmation that all things were made through the Son (cf. John 1:3 and 10). Here, we see the literalism that characterizes the Pneumatomachian approach. The orthodox side responds by arguing that, on the basis of this distinction between being made and being created (which the opposition supports), the Macedonians must also then affirm—based on the same verse—that not everything has been created. The Macedonian reveals that the aim of his dogmatic position is to recognize a difference of dignity between different creatures. For the Spirit, this difference with regard to the Father and the Son would be based on His coming into being by means of the Son (ἐκ τοῦ θεοῦ διὰ τοῦ υἱοῦ ἔχει τὸ εἶναι).[77] Once again, a graduated metaphysical conception makes its appearance. This also explains the importance of the role of the Son in the procession of the Spirit, which is emphasised in the first part of the treatise. All of the orthodox reasoning aims to show, on the one hand, the equivalence between being made and being a creature and, on the other hand, the affirmation that only the three divine Persons are not creatures nor are they made, but are distinguished from one another in the divine immanence as the Spirit is *agenēton* but not *anaition* while the Son is

---

72. Pseudo-Athanasius, *Dialogus I contra Macedonianos*, 17.15–20 (Cavalcanti, 90).

73. See pp. 119–26. See also the reference in Eusebius, at p. 49.

74. Pseudo-Athanasius, *Dialogus I contra Macedonianos*, 18.27–29 (Cavalcanti, 94).

75. Pseudo-Athanasius, *Dialogus I contra Macedonianos*, 18.37–40 (Cavalcanti, 94).

76. Pseudo-Athanasius, *Dialogus I contra Macedonianos*, 20.2 (Cavalcanti, 102).

77. Pseudo-Athanasius, *Dialogus I contra Macedonianos*, 20.19 (Cavalcanti, 104).

still *agenētos* but not *apatōr*. Only the First Person can be characterized by all three adjectives.[78]

From the metaphysical perspective, Pneumatomachian criticism extends to the Spirit the operation already performed for the *Logos*, who was recognized as belonging to the divine immanence and not as a mere intermediate ontological degree (see fig. 3 in chapter 2).

In the case of the Holy Spirit the formulation of the distinction of the two processions overcomes the conception of *pneuma* as an intermediate degree, who is now also inserted in the immanence together with the Father and the Son. It is here evident that the linear scheme becomes the reference point and the question of the role of the Second Person in the procession of the Third one becomes inescapable (see fig. 4 in chapter 2).

The treatise concludes with a discussion of the exegesis of the baptism of Jesus in John 1:33 where the Spirit is placed by the Father over the Son. The Macedonian reading suggests that the text refers to God's spiritual dimension while the orthodox response identifies the Spirit in this verse as the Third Person, that is, the Spirit *enypostaton*.[79]

In a very brief summary, the strategy of the response contained in the pneumatology of these treatises apparently aims at discerning the role of the Son in the procession of the Spirit, which the Macedonian reading places on the economic level and the orthodox on the immanent one.[80]

v. Conclusions: The Convergence on Correlativity

Epiphanius's and Pseudo-Athanasius's treatises against the Pneumatomachians present two different lines of development of the orthodox answer before the same objections: the former distinguishes the two immanent processions showing that the Spirit comes from both the Father and the Son, being God precisely because He proceeds from the two divine Persons; the latter's language is more metaphysical as it stresses the role of relation, rereading the derivative model of the procession of the Spirit through the Son in the light of a new ontology typical only of immanence where *schesis* is not accidental.

---

78. Pseudo-Athanasius, *Dialogus I contra Macedonianos*, 20.25–36 (Cavalcanti, 104).

79. Pseudo-Athanasius, *Dialogus I contra Macedonianos*, 20.59 (Cavalcanti, 106).

80. The second treatise seems important for determining the relationship between the Macedonians and the Homoiousians, in addition to the role of Apollinarianism, but its analysis is beyond the scope of the current work: see Pseudo-Athanasius, *Dialogus II contra Macedonianos*, 157–166 (Cavalcanti, 120–22).

Both approaches can be linked to the pneumatology of Gregory of Nyssa and Gregory of Nazianzus, as the next chapters will show. What is fundamental at this stage is that these different strategies converge on correlativity, that is, on the importance of presenting the identity of the first two divine Persons with reference to the Third.

It can be concluded that the anti-Macedonian treatises we have analyzed respond to the same fundamental accusation by the Pneumatomachians, one which is induced by a literalistic exegesis: the Holy Spirit is not to be worshiped because He is not God in that He does not create, as is deduced from the fact that this is not written in any passage in Scripture. The strategies for refuting these claims must avoid a position which allows for a reading of the Second and the Third Persons of the Trinity as though they were two sons. In the same way, the distinction between the procession of the Spirit *ad intra* and the production *ad extra* of the creatures has to be emphasised. For this reason, the ascent to the origin must stop at the Father without extending the Son's generation into another generation as is the case for human beings. At the base of the response, of course, one can see the inspiration of Athanasius who, in the wake of Origen, rereads John 4:24 in an immanent and personal sense, identifying the *pneuma* referred to there with the Holy Spirit and the *alētheia* with the Son.[81]

The more scriptural approach of Epiphanius of Salamis reconnects the affirmation of the divinity of the Third Person with that of the first Two Persons through derivative formulae. This is why he emphasizes that the Spirit proceeds both from the Father and from the Son inasmuch as He is God as Spirit from Spirit. As in Origen, the fundamental exegetical reference is the affirmation that God is *pneuma* in John 4:24, which, however, is now reread in personal terms, concluding that the *pneuma* Himself is God.

The theology that underpins the first *Dialogus contra Macedonianos*, on the other hand, takes a more ontologically refined path, distinguishing the level of nature from that of the persons, through the tool of relation. This implies that for the worship of a divine Person an intermediate metaphysical level is unnecessary—a level which, like substance, separates the worshiper from the deity worshiped. This explains the importance of christological reflection and a deepening of the relationship between economy and immanence through analysis of the divine action. At several points, most of all in the second part, there is noticeable agreement with the pneumatology of Gregory of Nyssa,

---

81. See Athanasius, *Contra gentes*, 46.17–21 (R. W. Thomson, ed., *Athanasius:* Contra Gentes *and* De Incarnatione [Oxford: Clarendon, 1971]). See also pp. 18–19.

especially as it appears in his most mature formulation in *Ad Ablabium*, written at the end of his life. In fact, the heart of the question of the role of the Son in the procession of the Holy Spirit emerges here. If, based on John 1:3 and 10, everything was created by the Word, then it is necessary to determine whether the Third Person is from Him and therefore a creature as the Pneumatomachians tend to affirm, or if the origin of the Spirit through the Son is an immanent one. The process is clearly a discussion on the linear scheme and a development of Origen's heritage. The Cappadocians offered a theological answer to this point that has much to say about the dogmatic core that lies behind the *Filioque* issue, an answer which will be presented in the next chapters.

Gregory of Nyssa: The Spirit's Theologian

I. Introduction: A Summit of Pneumatology

In the previous chapter the main theses of the Pneumatomachians in the second half of the fourth century were analyzed and presented in comparative form together with different possibilities of orthodox response. It has emerged that the common denominator that characterizes the orthodox response is a reformulation of the linear scheme which, without altering the Trinitarian order, highlights the link of the identity of the Third Person with that of the Father and the Son. This required an ontological shift from the level of nature to that of relation. It was precisely this point that the Macedonian perspective could not accept: for their metaphysical view that required a substantial intermediary to get in contact with God. From this point of observation it can be seen that even the affirmation of the Son's divinity on their part was not really fulfilled, confirming the possibility of a Homoiousian origin. As we will see, the Cappadocian strategy will be to connect the Spirit with the completion of the Trinity, inserting Him *between* the First and the Second Person.[1]

In this narrative it is appropriate to dwell on Gregory of Nyssa. The reason is primarily historical, for the special role he played in the Council of Constantinople and, in particular, in the drafting of the pneumatological part of the Symbol.[2]

---

1. The consideration of Pneumatomachian criticism seems to be absent in Thomas G. Weinandy's interesting study. Paradoxically, the very doctrine of Gregory of Nyssa presented in this chapter seems to confirm the thesis of this scholar, who, however, wrote, "The Cappadocians never captured the true metaphysical significance of Nicea's *homoousion* doctrine": Th. G. Weinandy, *The Father's Spirit of Sonship: Reconceiving the Trinity* (Edinburgh: T&T Clark, 1995; repr. Eugene, OR: Wipf & Stock, 2011), 13.

2. See E. D. Moutsoulas, Γρηγόριος Νύσσης. Βίος, Συγγράμματα, Διδασκαλία (Athens:

He pronounced the praise of Meletius and was mentioned, along with Helladius of Caesarea and Otreius of Melitene, as supervisor of the application of the decisions of the Council for the diocese of Pontus by the decree of Theodosius.[3] The reason for the attribution of this role to the Bishop of Nyssa could not be political, as he was not a metropolitan and his diocese was small and unimportant. Gregory's authority must then have been eminently theological.[4] As Michael Haykin wrote, following Werner Jaeger[5] and Jean Daniélou:[6] "Thus, it is not at all improbable that Gregory of Nyssa was the author of the reserved pneumatological statement of the creed issued by the Council of Constantinople."[7]

In the last chapter we saw some references to *Ad Ablabium*, a work to which we will return later. Here it is interesting to analyze *Adversus Macedonianos*, the main work dedicated by Gregory to the Holy Spirit and the response to the Pneumatomachians. It has already been introduced at the end of the second chapter in reference to the creative role of the Holy Spirit. This treatise is a true masterpiece in the pneumatological field, composed in the years of the Council. Therefore this chapter will be dedicated to an analysis of the main themes of this work, presented on the background of the whole of Gregory's theology. This operation will make it possible to appreciate the role of the new ontological conception, which had been developed by Athanasius but whose full theological virtuality was revealed by Gregory of Nyssa and Gregory of Nazianzus, as will also be seen in the next chapter. Their depth and originality, both in terms of philosophical tools and expressive skills, will allow the theology of the second procession to be brought to an authentic completion.

This chapter also serves as an immediate preparation for the next one, in which some original consequences will be drawn regarding the theological line that later would lead to the conflict on the *Filioque* clause.

Eptalophos, 1997), 45, and E. D. Moutsoulas, "Β΄ Οἰκουμενικὴ Σύνοδος καὶ Γρηγόριος ὁ Νύσσης," *Θεολογία* 55 (1984): 384–401. One important source is Nicephorus Callistus, *Historia Ecclesiastica*, 12.13 (PG 146:784b).

3. Gregory kept this eminent role in the years after the Council, as is proved by the invitations to celebrate the funeral rites for the emperor's daughter Pulcheria in 383 and for his wife, Flaccilla, in 385.

4. Cf. J. Daniélou, "Bulletin d'histoire des origines chrétiennes," *Recherches de science religieuse* 55 (1967): 117. W. Jaeger, *Gregor von Nyssas Lehre vom Heiligen Geist* (Leiden: Brill 1966), 59.

5. Jaeger, *Gregor von Nyssas Lehre vom Heiligen Geist*, 51–77.

6. Daniélou, "Bulletin d'histoire des origines chrétiennes," 118.

7. M. A. G. Haykin, *The Spirit of God: The Exegesis of 1 and 2 Corinthians in the Pneumatomachian Controversy of the Fourth Century* (Leiden: Brill, 1994), 201. See, in general, 199–201.

II. The Procession of the Holy Spirit

As we have seen, affirming that the Holy Spirit is Creator with the Father and the Son in the unity of divine action was possible only by developing the relationship between divine economy and divine immanence, accentuating ever more the connection between the being and the action of God: In fact, only a subject of divine nature is capable of divine actions, such as creation.

This however implies that the distinction between divine Persons can no longer be expressed in terms of different spheres of action. The transition to the divine intimacy was thus theologically necessary, to the point of distinguishing the two processions and clarifying their reciprocal relations. This was possible by moving from the consideration of *what* (i.e., essence, nature) to that of *how* (i.e., person, relation), as this chapter and the next one will show. While the divine essence remains absolutely unknowable, the personal dimension is not so, insofar as the Father, the Son and the Holy Spirit intervene in the unique action, each according to His own property. This makes it possible to trace back from the economy to immanence by identifying the personal *proprium* of the Third Person and, therefore, what distinguishes His procession from generation.

This is at the heart of Gregory of Nyssa's treatise *Adversus Macedonianos* that was composed[8] in the period between the spring of 380 and 381 in the context of the theological elaboration of the response to the Pneumatomachians in reference to the Council of Constantinople.[9] Piet Hein Hupsch in a magnificent work, which can be considered a fundamental reference point for any approach to this treatise, states that it is a circular letter sent by Gregory, as *arbiter fidei*, according to the imperial edict *Cunctos populos* of February 28, 380, to ensure the adherence of the various bishops to the Council's decisions.[10]

This is clear from the beginning of the treatise as Gregory, immediately after the introduction, explains their accusations and sketches his arguments.

8. See J. Daniélou, "La chronologie des oeuvres de Grégoire de Nysse." *Studia Patristica* 7 (1966): 159–69, esp. 163, and G. May, "Die Chronologie des Lebens und der Werke des Gregor von Nyssa," in *Ecriture et culture philosophique dans la pensée de Grégoire de Nysse*, ed. M. Harl (Leiden: Brill, 1971), 51–66, esp. 59.

9. For an introduction to the treatise, see V. Drecoll, "Maced: Adversus Macedonianos, De Spiritu Sancto," in *Brill Dictionary of Gregory of Nyssa*, 464–66; Moutsoulas, Γρηγόριος Νύσσης, 189–93; L. F. Mateo-Seco, "El Espíritu Santo en el Adv. Macedonianos de Gregorio de Nisa," *Scripta Theologica* 37 (2005): 475–98, and I. Pochoshajew, *Gregory of Nyssa: De Beatudinibus IV, Ad Ablabium, and Adversus Macedonianos* (Frankfurt am Main: Lang, 2008), 61–72.

10. P. H. Hupsch, *The Glory of the Spirit in Gregory of Nyssa's Adversus Macedonianos: Commentary and Systematic-Theological Synthesis* (Leiden: Brill, 2020), 20–24.

He negates every difference between the divine Persons on the level of nature, while they are distinct because:

> [the Spirit] is confused neither with the Father as the unbegotten nor with the Son as the only begotten, but we envision Him in and of Himself with certain special characteristics.[11]

The text, due to its position at the beginning of the work, is particularly important for the understanding of the treatise, insofar as it presents the content of Gregory's work as the specification of these distinctive properties, declaring the *skopos* of the text. This purpose is also suggested by the parallelism with *Contra Eunomium I*, itself probably written the year before,[12] where Gregory continually specifies the distinctive property of the Third Person in reference to His relationship with creation. Gregory in fact says:

> And the Holy Spirit, who in the uncreated nature is in communion (κοινωνίαν) with the Father and the Son, is nevertheless distinguished in His turn by His proper characteristics. To not be that which is contemplated properly in the Father and the Son is His most proper characteristic and sign: His distinctive property in relation to the procession does not consist in being in an unengendered mode (ἀγεννήτως), nor in an only-begotten mode (μονογενῶς), but despite this in being fully (εἶναι δὲ ὅλως). He is conjoined to the Father by the fact of being uncreated, but is distinguished in His turn by the fact of not being Father as the First Person is. United to the Son by the uncreated nature and by the fact of receiving the cause of existence from the God of the universe, He is distinct from Him in His turn by the peculiarity of not subsisting hypostatically as the only begotten of the Father (μήτε μονογενῶς ἐκ τοῦ πατρὸς ὑποστῆναι) and by the fact of being manifested by the Son himself (δι᾽ αὐτοῦ τοῦ υἱοῦ πεφηνέναι). But further, since creation subsists (ὑποστάσης) by means of the Only Begotten

---

11. οὔτε κατὰ τὸ ἀγέννητον τῷ πατρὶ οὔτε κατὰ τὸ μονογενὲς τῷ υἱῷ συγχεόμενον ἀλλά τισιν ἐξαιρέτοις ἰδιώμασιν ἐφ᾽ ἑαυτοῦ θεωρούμενον (Gregory of Nyssa, *Adversus Macedonianos*, GNO 3.1:90.1–4).

12. According to Pierre Maraval, *Contra Eunomium I* and *Contra Eunomium II* of Gregory of Nyssa were composed in a first form in 379, shortly after the death of Basil at the end of 378 (see SC 363:310.3 and 309n9), and took final form in only seventeen days during 380, after the return to Nyssa from the trip to Armenia (see Gregory of Nyssa, *Epistulae*, 29.2 [SC 363:310.11]). See also A. M. Silvas, *Gregory of Nyssa: The Letters; Introduction, Translation, and Commentary* (Leiden: Brill, 2007), 206–7.

(διὰ τοῦ μονογενοῦς ὑποστάσης), so that one does not think that the Spirit has something in common with it due to the fact that He is manifested (πεφηνέναι) by the Son (διὰ τοῦ υἱοῦ), He is distinguished from creation since He is invariable, immutable and without need of any external good (ἑτέρωθεν).[13]

In this very rich text the formulation of the personal property of the Holy Spirit takes on an apophatic or negative dimension, because He is identified by not being what characterizes the Father and the Son. In fact He is neither unengendered nor only begotten, but in spite of this He is in fullness.

The key point is the interpretation of the Greek expression *einai holōs*, which Gregory also applies to the Son.[14] Here the game of symmetries seems essential, because it shows both what distinguishes and what unites the Spirit in the relation with the First Person, on one hand, and with the Second one, on the other. With respect to the Father, the Third Person is also uncreated, but is distinct because He is not Father.

First Person	Second Person
Uncreated	Uncreated
Father	Not Father

With respect to the Son, instead, there are two elements shared: again the fact of being uncreated, but also having the Father as the only cause. Here it is essential to observe that the Third Person, who is in fullness and not merely by participation, is distinguished from the Son in that He is manifested by the latter.

13. τὸ δὲ πνεῦμα τὸ ἅγιον ἐν τῷ ἀκτίστῳ τῆς φύσεως τὴν κοινωνίαν ἔχον πρὸς υἱὸν καὶ πατέρα τοῖς ἰδίοις πάλιν γνωρίσμασιν ἀπ᾽ αὐτῶν διακρίνεται. γνώρισμα γὰρ αὐτοῦ καὶ ση-μεῖόν ἐστιν ἰδιαίτατον τὸ μηδὲν ἐκείνων εἶναι, ἅπερ ἰδίως τῷ πατρὶ καὶ τῷ υἱῷ ὁ λόγος ἐνε-θεώρησε. τὸ γὰρ μήτε ἀγεννήτως εἶναι μήτε μονογενῶς, εἶναι δὲ ὅλως, τὴν ἐξαίρετον αὐτοῦ ἰδιότητα πρὸς τὰ προειρημένα παρίστησιν. τῷ γὰρ πατρὶ κατὰ τὸ ἄκτιστον συναπτόμενον πάλιν ἀπ᾽ αὐτοῦ τῷ μὴ πατὴρ εἶναι καθάπερ ἐκεῖνος διαχωρίζεται. τῆς δὲ πρὸς τὸν υἱὸν κατὰ τὸ ἄκτιστον συναφείας [καὶ ἐν τῷ τὴν αἰτίαν τῆς ὑπάρξεως ἐκ τοῦ θεοῦ τῶν ὅλων ἔχειν] ἀφίσταται πάλιν τῷ ἰδιάζοντι, ἐν τῷ μήτε μονογενῶς ἐκ τοῦ πατρὸς ὑποστῆναι καὶ ἐν τῷ δι᾽ αὐτοῦ τοῦ υἱοῦ πεφηνέναι. πάλιν δὲ τῆς κτίσεως διὰ τοῦ μονογενοῦς ὑποστάσης, ὡς ἂν μὴ κοινότητά τινα πρὸς ταύτην ἔχειν νομισθῇ τὸ πνεῦμα ἐκ τοῦ διὰ τοῦ υἱοῦ πεφηνέναι, ἐν τῷ ἀτρέπτῳ καὶ ἀναλλοιώτῳ καὶ ἀπροσδεεῖ τῆς ἑτέρωθεν ἀγαθότητος διακρίνεται τὸ πνεῦμα ἀπὸ τῆς κτίσεως (Gregory of Nyssa, *Contra Eunomium I*, 279.5–281.1 [GNO 1:108.7–109.5]).

14. I am grateful to Michel Stavrou for drawing my attention to this point in the discussions during the Colloquium Nyssenum in Paris in 2018, allowing me to correct a previous misinterpretation.

Second Person	Third Person
Uncreated	Uncreated
Father is the only cause	Father is the only cause
Only Begotten	Manifested by the Son

The expression, as will also be seen in the next chapter, clearly concerns the divine immanence. The rest of the quoted passage, in fact, immediately highlights that this characteristic does not coincide with that of the creatures which all, according to the testimony of John's Prologue, receive being through the *Logos*.

The question reveals a great metaphysical depth that implies a sort of ontological enigma. In fact, for Gregory it is clear that what is not *a se* cannot be in full (ὃ γὰρ᾽ ἑαυτοῦ οὐκ ἔστιν, οὐδὲ ἔστιν ὅλως),[15] where the adverb present in *Contra Eunomium I* in reference to the Holy Spirit returns. For this reason in this same work, Eunomius is accused of not being truly Christian and not being able to detach himself from the Jewish background, because he denies that the Son exists in the proper sense (κυρίως) and, therefore, also that He is fully (ὅλως).[16] This means to be *in* the divine substance, without participation as in the case of the accidents.[17] The use of the technical terminology of metaphysics is evident.[18]

At the same time it is also evident how classical metaphysics is radically revised, because the *being in*, which characterized the accident, is reread in a relational sense. This novelty is the very core of the eighth chapter of *Contra Eunomium III*, which shows how being in an absolute and full way does not exclude being in relation because, if it were so, paradoxically not even the Father would be in an absolute way. The line of reasoning is as follows:

1. First of all Gregory accepts the possibility affirmed by Eunomius in the wake of Neoplatonism that only being without relationship (ἄσχετον) is absolute.[19]

2. John, however, not only says that the Son is the *Logos* of the Father and *in* the bosom of the Father, but also that He is God, without adding anything

---

15. Gregory of Nyssa, *In Ecclesiasten*, GNO 5:356.15.

16. Gregory of Nyssa, *Contra Eunomium I*, 179.5–6 (GNO 1:79.25–26).

17. Gregory of Nyssa, *Contra Eunomium I*, 183.1 (GNO 1:80.18). See also 184.1 (GNO 1:80.25), and *Contra Eunomium III*, 8.33.3 (GNO 2:251.4).

18. See Alexander of Aphrodisias, *In Aristotelis metaphysica commentaria*, 285.21–32, and Porphyry, *In Aristotelis categorias expositio per interrogationem*, 1.89.22 and 1.114.18.

19. Gregory of Nyssa, *Contra Eunomium III*, 8.39.6–40.1 (GNO 2:253.12–15).

else. Thus he says that the Second Person is Light and Life in an absolute way (cf. John 1:1–4).

3. Moreover, if it were true that being in the relationship excludes being in an absolute way, not even the Father would be in an absolute way, because John 14:10 says that He is *in* the Son.

The text is very clear and constitutes a point of arrival in Gregory's reply, which leads to the absurdity of Eunomius's arguments. The evangelist John says, in fact:

> that the *Logos* was God, and was Light, and was Life (cf. John 1:1–4), and not only that He was in the beginning and with God and *in* the bosom of the Father, so that by this specification the Lord is deprived of being in the proper sense. By saying that He was God, he [John] cuts the path to those who run toward evil and, more importantly, he proves the evil intention of our adversaries. For if they claim that being *in* something is a sign of not being in the proper sense, they will surely agree that the Father is not in the proper sense either. In fact, they learn from the gospel that just as the Son is *in* the Father, so too the Father is *in* the Son, according to what the Lord says (John 14:10). To say that the Father is *in* the Son and that the Son is *in* the womb of the Father is, in fact, the same.[20]

The name Father also means the concrete way of existing as God of the First Person of the Trinity. It is a name that expresses relationship to the Son. The two divine Persons are correlative: their nature is Being itself (i.e., it is absolute), but at the same time each of them exists in relation to the other. The *pōs einai* is given by the *pros ti*, so that, if it were said absurdly that the Son does not exist, it would necessarily follow the non-existence of the Father too (ἡ τοῦ πατρὸς ἀνυπαρξία).[21]

---

20. θεὸς ἦν ὁ λόγος καὶ ζωὴ ἦν καὶ φῶς ἦν, οὐ μόνον ἐν ἀρχῇ καὶ πρὸς τὸν θεὸν καὶ ἐν κόλποις τοῦ πατρὸς ὤν, ὥστε διὰ τῆς τοιαύτης σχέσεως ἀναιρεῖσθαι τοῦ κυρίου τὸ κυρίως εἶναι· ἀλλὰ τῷ εἰπεῖν ὅτι θεὸς ἦν, τῇ ἀσχέτῳ ταύτῃ καὶ ἀπολύτῳ φωνῇ πᾶσαν περιδρομὴν τῶν εἰς ἀσέβειαν τρεχόντων τοῖς λογισμοῖς ὑποτέμνεται καὶ ἔτι πρὸς τούτοις, ὃ καὶ μᾶλλον, ἐλέγχει τὴν τῶν ἀντικειμένων κακόνοιαν. εἰ γὰρ τὸ ἔν τινι εἶναι σημεῖον ποιοῦνται τοῦ μὴ κυρίως εἶναι, οὐδὲ τὸν πατέρα κυρίως εἶναι πάντως συντίθενται, μεμαθηκότες ἐν τῷ εὐαγγελίῳ ὅτι ὥσπερ ὁ υἱὸς ἐν τῷ πατρί, οὕτω καὶ ὁ πατὴρ ἐν τῷ υἱῷ μένει κατὰ τὴν τοῦ κυρίου φωνήν. ἴσον γάρ ἐστι τῷ ἐν κόλποις εἶναι τοῦ πατρὸς τὸν υἱὸν τὸ ἐν τῷ υἱῷ τὸν πατέρα εἶναι λέγειν (Gregory of Nyssa, *Contra Eunomium III*, 8.40.11–41.6 [GNO 2:253.25–254.11]).

21. Gregory of Nyssa, *Contra Eunomium III*, 6.50.7–51.1 (GNO 2:203.21–23).

It is clear that Gregory of Nyssa moves at ease in the tradition of Aristotle's commentators. In *De infantibus*, speaking of the opposition between knowledge and ignorance of God, linked to that between life and death, he implicitly quotes the Stagirite, writing:

> Let no one force us to make the genealogy of this ignorance, saying where it comes from and from whom but let us understand it from the very meaning of the words that ignorance and knowledge indicate a relation (τὸ πρός τί πως ἔχειν) of the soul. In fact, nothing that is thought and expressed through the relationship (πρός τι) has essence,[22] because one is the discourse of the relationship (πρός τι) and another one is that of the substance.[23]

Here relation is presented as an accident, according to the traditional metaphysical doctrine. But at the same time, as just seen, Gregory affirms something radically different, speaking of the Trinity as for *Logos* who fully is:

> This *Logos* is distinct from the One who is *Logos*: in a certain way it also belongs in the relational sphere (τῶν πρός τι λεγομένων), since it is absolutely necessary to understand the Father of the *Logos* along with the *Logos*: He would not, in fact, be the *Logos*, if He were not the *Logos* of someone.[24]

So the Second Person of the Trinity is, in a perfect sense (ὅλως), being in the divine substance,[25] but belongs to the relative dimension that for classical metaphysics is accidental. The solution to this tension is related to the expression *pros ti pōs echein*, present in Aristotle's definition of relation.[26] This is a categorical formulation that applies only to the diastematic dimension (i.e., to

22. This is a clear reference to Aristotle, *Categoriae*, 8b.

23. Μηδεὶς δὲ γενεαλογεῖν ἡμᾶς ἀναγκαζέτω τὴν ἄγνοιαν, πόθεν αὕτη λέγων καὶ ἀπὸ τίνος, ἀλλ' ἐξ αὐτῆς νοείτω τῆς τοῦ ὀνόματος σημασίας, ὅτι ἡ γνῶσις καὶ ἡ ἄγνοια τὸ πρός τί πως ἔχειν τὴν ψυχὴν ἐνδείκνυται. οὐδὲν δὲ τῶν πρός τι νοουμένων τε καὶ λεγομένων οὐσίαν παρίστησιν· ἄλλος γὰρ ὁ τοῦ πρός τι καὶ ἕτερος ὁ τῆς οὐσίας λόγος (Gregory of Nyssa, *De infantibus praemature abreptis*, GNO 3.2:80.11–16).

24. ὁ δὲ λόγος οὗτος ἕτερός ἐστι παρὰ τὸν οὗ ἐστὶ λόγος· τρόπον γάρ τινα τῶν πρός τι λεγομένων καὶ τοῦτό ἐστιν, ἐπειδὴ χρὴ πάντως τῷ λόγῳ καὶ τὸν πατέρα τοῦ λόγου συνυπακούεσθαι· οὐ γὰρ ἂν εἴη λόγος, μή τινος ὢν λόγος (Gregory of Nyssa, *Oratio cathechetica magna*, 1.73–77 [J. H. Srawley, ed., *The Categorical Oration of Gregory of Nyssa* (Cambridge: Cambridge University Press, 1903), 8–12]).

25. See chapter 8 for more texts and the discussion of this ontological novelty, connected to the transition from the *logos ut ratio* to the *logos ut relatio*, explained in the introduction.

26. See p. 233.

the created world). Gregory is aware that in God there is a different ontology, where the element of substantial identity is flanked by the relational distinction that here has nothing to do with participation and accidents, so as to be defined as *pros ti pōs einai* with a neologism constructed by substituting the verb *to have* with the verb *to be*.

This is extremely important for the interpretation of *Adversus Macedonianos* that, in parallel with the text of the *Contra Eunomium I* just seen, aims to present in an elaborate and detailed way the path to arrive and recognize the distinctive personal property of the Spirit. In the latter work, what distinguishes the Spirit from the Son is that the Spirit is manifested by the Son in the divine immanence. The ontological work carried out by the Bishop of Nyssa to reread the *Logos* from a relational perspective, without lowering Him from His supreme metaphysical level, suggests that the *proprium* of the Third Person, that is His fully being through the manifestation by the Son, should also be interpreted in a relational way. This is confirmed by another parallel, in Gregory Nazianzus, who in *Oratio*, 31.8–9 uses the distinction of manifestation and that of relation as synonyms.[27] The next chapter will discuss these texts and the theological line that links them. We will see that the need of affirming the unity of action leads to a development of the reasons for personal distinction. But, in *Adversus Macedonianos*, there is no immediate elucidation of that which distinguishes the Spirit after the enunciation of *kata to agennēton* and *kata to monogenes*, which correspond to the adverbs *agennētōs* and *monogenōs* in *Contra Eunomium I*. This suggests that the treatise itself as a whole seeks to respond to the Pneumatomachians, specifying precisely this personal characteristic of the Third Person in respect of those of the Father and the Son that in the work against Eunomium is presented in a more concise way.

The link between the definition of the *proprium* of the Third Person and the identification of the difference between the first and second procession can be illustrated through the use of *Ad Ablabium*, as has been already said. This work belongs to the maturity of Gregory's production, as its composition is probably subsequent to 390, close to the writing of both *In canticum* and *De vita Moysis*, in the years that saw a resurgence of discussions with Pneumatomachians.[28]

Here the Bishop of Nyssa presents the personal distinction in Trinitarian immanence, using categories related to the cause (τὸ αἴτιον):

27. See next chapter, p. 170.

28. Cf. G. Maspero, *Trinity and Man: Gregory of Nyssa's Ad Ablabium* (Leiden: Brill, 2007), 30–42.

If then one will falsely accuse the reasoning of presenting a certain mixture (μίξις) of the hypostases and a twisting by the fact of not accepting the difference according to nature, we shall respond to this accusation that, in affirming the absence of the diversity of nature, we do not negate the difference according to that which causes and that which is caused. And we can conceive that the one is distinguished from the other uniquely since we believe that the one is that which causes and the other that which is derived from the cause. And in that which is originated from a cause we conceive yet another difference: one thing it is, in fact, to be immediately from the first (ἐκ τοῦ πρώτου), another to be through (διά) that which is immediately (προσεχῶς) from the first. In this way, the being Only Begotten remains incontestably in the Son and there is no doubt that the Spirit is from the Father, since the mediation of the Son (τῆς τοῦ υἱοῦ μεσιτείας) maintains in Him the being of Only Begotten and does not exclude the Spirit from the natural relation with the Father (τῆς φυσικῆς πρὸς τὸν πατέρα σχέσεως).[29]

Gregory's reasoning moves from the monarchy and is constructed in such a way as never to abandon this basic principle. The Son and the Spirit are, therefore, united and indistinct at this first moment of analysis that corresponds to the double property shared by the Second and the Third Person of being uncreated and having their cause of existence from the Father in the text of *Contra Eunomium I* just analyzed.

Here the discussion of the difference between the two processions comes to the foreground. In fact, the Bishop of Nyssa continues with the second step necessary to arrive at the Trinity of Persons: there is a second distinction between "what is immediately caused by the cause," that is the Son, and what is caused by mediation, that is the Spirit who proceeds through the Son. This is how the one God is triune (see fig. 5). This construction places the Son at the

---

29. Εἰ δέ τις συκοφαντοίη τὸν λόγον ὡς ἐκ τοῦ μὴ δέχεσθαι τὴν κατὰ φύσιν διαφορὰν μίξιν τινὰ τῶν ὑποστάσεων καὶ ἀνακύκλησιν κατασκευάζοντα τοῦτο περὶ τῆς τοιαύτης ἀπολογησόμεθα μέμψεως, ὅτι τὸ ἀπαράλλακτον τῆς φύσεως ὁμολογοῦντες τὴν κατὰ τὸ αἴτιον καὶ αἰτιατὸν διαφορὰν οὐκ ἀρνούμεθα, ἐν ᾧ μόνῳ διακρίνεσθαι τὸ ἕτερον τοῦ ἑτέρου καταλαμβάνομεν, τῷ τὸ μὲν αἴτιον πιστεύειν εἶναι τὸ δὲ ἐκ τοῦ αἰτίου· καὶ τοῦ ἐξ αἰτίας ὄντος πάλιν ἄλλην διαφορὰν ἐννοοῦμεν· τὸ μὲν γὰρ προσεχῶς ἐκ τοῦ πρώτου, τὸ δὲ διὰ τοῦ προσεχῶς ἐκ τοῦ πρώτου, ὥστε καὶ τὸ μονογενὲς ἀναμφίβολον ἐπὶ τοῦ υἱοῦ μένειν, καὶ τὸ ἐκ τοῦ πατρὸς εἶναι τὸ πνεῦμα μὴ ἀμφιβάλλειν, τῆς τοῦ υἱοῦ μεσιτείας καὶ αὐτῷ τὸ μονογενὲς φυλαττούσης καὶ τὸ πνεῦμα τῆς φυσικῆς πρὸς τὸν πατέρα σχέσεως μὴ ἀπειργούσης (Gregory of Nyssa, *Ad Ablabium*, GNO 3.1:55.21–56.10).

center of the immanent dynamic and reproduces in this sphere the economic movement of "from the Father, through the Son, [in relation] to the Spirit" (ἐκ τοῦ πατρὸς διὰ υἱοῦ πρὸς τὸ πνεῦμα).[30] This does imply the presence of a relational element (i.e., a *schesis*) in the eternal substance that is God, an element that corresponds to the connection of the *Logos* with the *pros ti*.

Cause	Caused	
Cause	Caused immediately	Caused mediately
Father unbegotten	Son Only Begotten	Spirit from the Son

fig. 5

It should be noted that the recourse to αἰτία was already present in Origen.[31] In fact, this can also be considered the first father of *dia tou huiou* within his linear scheme.[32] It was Origen who first supported the necessity of a certain *genesis* of the Spirit through the Son to express His hypostatic individuality and to protect, at the same time, the Father as the only unbegotten.[33] However, Gregory's doctrine perfects and purifies Origen's intuition, overcoming the limits of the linear scheme through the ontological analysis of the intradivine relations without losing the connecting force between God and the historical action that characterized the triangular scheme.

The Bishop of Nyssa distinguishes, in fact, with great care the reasoning proposed from that which leads to consubstantiality:

> And by saying "cause" and "from the cause" (αἴτιον καὶ ἐξ αἰτίου), we do not designate with these names a nature—in fact, one could not adopt the same

30. Gregory of Nyssa, *Ad Ablabium*, GNO 3.1:48.23–24.

31. See Origen, *Commentarii in evangelium Joannis*, 2.10.76.1–7 (SC 120:256). Gregory of Nazianzus takes up this category; see Gregory of Nazianzus, *Oratio*, 20.7 (SC 270:72) and 31.14 (SC 250:302).

32. Cf. M. A. Orphanos, "The Procession of the Holy Spirit: According to Certain Greek Fathers," Θεολογία 50 (1979): 763–78, esp. 768.

33. See Origen, *Commentarii in evangelium Joannis*, 2.10.74.1–5 (SC 120:254).

explanation for a cause and for a nature—but we explain the difference according to the mode of being (κατὰ τὸ πῶς εἶναι). For, saying that the one is in a caused mode (αἰτιατῶς), while the other is without cause (ἄνευ αἰτίας), we do not divide the nature according to the understanding of the cause (τῷ κατὰ τὸ αἴτιον λόγῳ), but we only demonstrate that neither is the Son without generation nor is the Father by generation. It is first necessary that we believe something is (εἶναί τι), and only then do we interrogate how that in which we have believed is (πῶς ἐστι). It is different, then, to say "what it is" (τί ἐστι) from saying "how it is" (πῶς ἐστι). So, saying that something is without generation, one sets forth how it is, but, with those words, one does not express what it is as well. And, in fact, if you asked a farmer about a tree whether it was planted or if it grew on its own, and he responded either that the tree was not planted or that it came from a seedling, did he perhaps with the response explain the nature to you? Or instead, saying only how it is, did he not leave obscure and unexplained the discourse on the nature? So, also here, in learning that He is without generation, we have learned to think, as is fitting, that He is, but we have not understood through the word what He is. Therefore, affirming in the Holy Trinity such a distinction, so as to believe that one thing is that which is cause and another that which is from the cause, we will not any longer be able to be accused of confusing the relation of the hypostases in the communion of nature.[34]

Here it is clearly explained that there are two distinct ontological levels: that of nature and that of the person or relation. Nature remains absolutely ineffable, thus referring any possibility of knowledge to the second dimen-

---

34. Αἴτιον δὲ καὶ ἐξ αἰτίου λέγοντες οὐχὶ φύσιν διὰ τούτων τῶν ὀνομάτων σημαίνομεν (οὐδὲ γὰρ τὸν αὐτὸν ἄν τις αἰτίας καὶ φύσεως ἀποδοίη λόγον), ἀλλὰ τὴν κατὰ τὸ πῶς εἶναι διαφορὰν ἐνδεικνύμεθα. εἰπόντες γὰρ τὸ μὲν αἰτιατῶς τὸ δὲ ἄνευ αἰτίας εἶναι οὐχὶ τὴν φύσιν τῷ κατὰ τὸ αἴτιον λόγῳ διεχωρίσαμεν, ἀλλὰ μόνον τὸ μήτε τὸν υἱὸν ἀγεννήτως εἶναι μήτε τὸν πατέρα διὰ γεννήσεως ἐνεδειξάμεθα. πρότερον δὲ ἡμᾶς εἶναί τι πιστεύειν ἐπάναγκες, καὶ τότε πῶς ἐστι τὸ πεπιστευμένον περιεργάσασθαι· ἄλλος οὖν ὁ τοῦ τί ἐστι καὶ ἄλλος ὁ τοῦ πῶς ἐστι λόγος. τὸ οὖν ἀγεννήτως εἶναί τι λέγειν, πῶς μέν ἐστιν ὑποτίθεται, τί δέ ἐστι τῇ φωνῇ ταύτῃ οὐ συνενδείκνυται. καὶ γὰρ εἰ περὶ δένδρου τινὸς ἠρώτησας τὸν γεωργόν, εἴτε φυτευτὸν εἴτε αὐτομάτως ἐστίν, ὁ δὲ ἀπεκρίνατο ἢ ἀφύτευτον εἶναι τὸ δένδρον ἢ ἐκ φυτείας γενόμενον, ἆρα τὴν φύσιν διὰ τῆς ἀποκρίσεως ἐνεδείξατο ὁ μόνον τὸ πῶς ἐστιν εἰπὼν ἢ ἄδηλον καὶ ἀνερμήνευτον τὸν τῆς φύσεως ἀπέλιπε λόγον; οὕτω καὶ ἐνταῦθα ἀγέννητον μαθόντες ὅπως μὲν αὐτὸν εἶναι προσήκει νοεῖν ἐδιδάχθημεν, ὅ, τι δέ ἐστι διὰ τῆς φωνῆς οὐκ ἠκούσαμεν. τὴν οὖν τοιαύτην διαφορὰν ἐπὶ τῆς ἁγίας τριάδος λέγοντες, ὡς τὸ μὲν αἴτιον τὸ δὲ ἐξ αἰτίου εἶναι πιστεύειν, οὐκέτ᾽ ἂν ἐν τῷ κοινῷ τῆς φύσεως τὸν τῶν ὑποστάσεων λόγον συντήκειν αἰτιαθείημεν (Gregory of Nyssa, *Ad Ablabium*, GNO 3.1:56.11–57.7).

sion, which is expressed adverbially since it does not answer the question of *what*, but of *how*. The adverbial identification of the *proprium* of each Person responds precisely to this change of metaphysical level and necessarily implies a clear position on what distinguishes the first from the second procession.

The previous texts of the *Ad Ablabium* are also useful as a frame of reference for the rest of the analysis, since the distinction between the way of proceeding immediately (προσεχῶς) from the Father, which characterizes the Son, and proceeding through the One who proceeds immediately, in which the characteristic of the Spirit consists, sheds some light on the images used by Gregory in the *Adversus Macedonianos* to sketch the intra-Trinitarian dynamic.

The following three elements, which will be analyzed in order, can be considered essential in this treatise. These are (1) the image of *fire* with its communication, (2) *anointing* as the foundation of royal dignity, and (3) *glory* in its dynamic transmission in the divine immanence. From different perspectives, all three of these elements refer to the distinction and correlation of the two processions, expressing the relational dimension within the divine substance.

III. THE TRINITARIAN FIRE

The image of fire is inserted into the context of the comparison of God and light. Martien Parmentier[35] individuates two fundamental images in tradition to express the procession in these terms: the relationship of the sun, the ray, and the splendor, which underscores the divine unity and is more widespread; or that of three torches and three suns, which accentuates personal distinction. These are clearly complementary image types whose remote origin can in both cases be traced to Philo, who speaks, respectively, of the communication of the *Logos* and the effusion of the *Pneuma*.[36]

The propagation of fire was used by Justin[37] and Tatian[38] to explain the relationship between the Father and the Son. Epiphanius is witness of its use in the Arian polemic, reporting on the criticisms of Hierakas by Arius.[39] Gregory extends the image to the Spirit in *Adversus Macedonianos*:

---

35. M. Parmentier, "St. Gregory of Nyssa's Doctrine of the Holy Spirit" (PhD diss., University of Oxford, 1972), 39–42.

36. E.g., Philo, *De opificio mundi*, 51.6–8, and *De gigantibus*, 24–27.

37. Justin, *Dialogus cum Tryphone*, 61 (PG 6:616a).

38. Tatian, *Adversus Graecos*, 5 (PG 6:817a).

39. Epiphanius, *Panarion*, 69.7.6 (GCS 31:158.14–15).

For in the case of entities whose good activity does not diminish or change, how could one reasonably think that numerical order is a sign of some diminution, of an alteration in nature? It is as if someone looking at a flame separated in three lamps—let us assume that the first flame is cause of the third light by lighting the tip from transmission through the middle one (διὰ τοῦ μέσου)—should then conclude that the heat in the first flame is greater, that in the second one is inferior and contains change for the smaller, and that the third is no longer called "fire," even if it burns like fire, looks like fire and does everything else characteristic of fire.[40]

The expressions show that the Pneumatomachians are the real target of the text, as the Spirit is no longer called fire. But at the same time Gregory points also at the connection with the Homoiousians, as a sort of subordination of the Son is implicit in the criticisms. On the contrary his image is built on the affirmation of the monarchy, to which the unity of nature is immediately connected, and on the manifestation of the unity of the divine nature through the explanation of intra-Trinitarian relations of origin. In fact, just before in the text,[41] he had used the reference to the heat of fire in order to underscore the unity of the Divinity, and thus the inseparability of the Spirit from the Father and the Son. Fire, in fact, by its proper nature communicates heat to those who approach it in an equal manner in every part with the same efficacy. The reference to the three torches cannot be in any way understood in a tritheistic sense, since every Person must be God as every flame is fire, without any ontological gradation.

The reference to heat seems specific to Gregory, as well as the application to the Spirit. One might suggest again that it draws on the Syriac tradition, if we take into account that Ephrem's Trinitarian theology is based precisely on the analogy of the sun, its rays, and heat. The assimilation of heat to the Third Person is typical of this author, and Gregory is the closest to this image in the

---

40. ἐφ' ὧν γὰρ ἡ κατὰ τὸ ἀγαθὸν ἐνέργεια οὐδεμίαν ἐλάττωσιν ἢ παραλλαγὴν ἔχει, πῶς ἐστιν εὔλογον τὴν κατὰ τὸν ἀριθμὸν τάξιν ἐλαττώσεώς τινος, τῆς κατὰ φύσιν παραλλαγῆς, οἴεσθαι σημεῖον εἶναι; ὥσπερ ἂν εἴ τις ἐν τρισὶ λαμπάσι διῃρημένην βλέπων τὴν φλόγα αἰτίαν δὲ τοῦ τρίτου φωτὸς ὑποθώμεθα εἶναι τὴν πρώτην φλόγα ἐκ διαδόσεως διὰ τοῦ μέσου τὸ ἄκρον ἐξάψασαν ἔπειτα κατασκευάζοι πλεονάζειν ἐν τῇ πρώτῃ φλογὶ τὴν θερμασίαν, τῇ δὲ ἐφεξῆς ὑποβεβηκέναι καὶ πρὸς τὸ ἔλαττον ἔχειν τὴν παραλλαγήν, τὴν δὲ τρίτην μηδὲ πῦρ ἔτι λέγεσθαι, κἂν παραπλησίως καίῃ καὶ φαίνῃ καὶ πάντα τὰ τοῦ πυρὸς κατεργάζηται (Gregory of Nyssa, *Adversus Macedonianos*, GNO 3.1:92.34–93.10).

41. Gregory of Nyssa, *Adversus Macedonianos*, GNO 3.1:91.13–22.

context of Greek theology.[42] Perhaps the Pneumatomachians were partially tied to the Syriac world, and the Semitic one in general, which was marked by a greater development of angelology, as chapter 6 will show.[43]

From a theological perspective, Gregory affirms the unity of divine nature by referring the distinction of order only to the intra-Trinitarian relations of origin. This is a formulation already present in *Contra Eunomium I*:

> For, firmly anchored in the consideration of the unbegotten light, we still know, according to the continuity in relation, the light [that shines] from that, like a ray that coexists with the sun and whose cause of being (αἰτία τοῦ εἶναι) is from the sun, while its existence (ὕπαρξις) is contemporaneous with the sun, since it does not shine successively in time, but together with the apparition of the sun it is manifested from it (συναναφαινομένη). Thus—since there is absolutely no necessity that, remaining slave to the image, by the weakness of the example, we concede to the calumniators a pretext to contradict the reasoning—we will not think of a ray [that shines] from a sun, but of another sun [that shines] from an unbegotten sun, that together with the conception of the first shines together (συνεκλάμποντα) with it in a generated mode (γεννητῶς) and that is equal to it in all things: in beauty, power, splendor, greatness and luminosity and in whatever is observed in the sun. And still [we will think] in the same way of another of such lights, that is not separated from the light generated without any temporal interval, but that shines by means of it (δι' αὐτοῦ), while it has the cause of the hypostasis (τῆς ὑποστάσεως αἰτίαν) from the original light (ἐκ τοῦ πρωτοτύπου φωτός): a light certainly this one as well that, in likeness to that which we first considered, shines and illuminates and accomplishes all that is proper to light. And in fact there is no difference between one light and another in as much as light, from the moment that this Light does not appear deprived of anything or lacking of the illuminating grace, but is contemplated at the summit of every perfection with the Father and with the Son, It is enumerated in succession along with the Father and the Son and in Itself (δι' ἑαυτοῦ) gives access to the light that is known in the Father and the Son to all those that can participate (μετασχεῖν) in It.[44]

---

42. Cf. E. Beck, *Ephräms Trinitätslehre im Bild von Sonne/Feuer, Licht und Wärme*, CSCO 425 (Leuven: Peeters, 1981), 22–24 and 27.

43. On Eustathius and the Pneumatomachians in general, see Parmentier, "St. Gregory of Nyssa's Doctrine," 166; for the relationship of Judaic angelology, Philo, and Origen, see J. Daniélou, *Théologie du Judéo-Christianisme* (Paris: Desclée, 1991), 221 (the entire chap. 5 "Trinité et angélologie" [203–34] is of interest in general).

44. ἐν περινοίᾳ γὰρ τοῦ ἀγεννήτου φωτὸς καταστάντες ἐκεῖθεν πάλιν τὸ ἐξ αὐτοῦ

This text of *Contra Eunomium I* shows the cross-fertilization of various themes: of light, of the ray, and of the three suns, which, in Gregory's theological intention, are exactly parallel to the three torches of *Adversus Macedonianos*. At the same time the statement that the Third Person shines through (δι' αὐτοῦ) the Second, but has the cause of his hypostasis (τῆς ὑποστάσεως αἰτίαν) in the first, recalls the dynamic traced in the *Ad Ablabium*, with the difference between the Son who proceeds immediately from the Father and the Spirit who proceeds from the Father through the Son himself. It can be seen here that the role of the Second Person in the procession of the Third Person is always affirmed together with the monarchy. The reference to the imagery of light here does not make reference to the economical dimension of revelation, but to the purely spiritual nature of God, as in Origen.

The possibility of referring the divine attributes to the Son is linked to the first procession, cause of His identity of nature to the Father. The same thing is to be found in *Adversus Macedonianos* in reference to the Spirit. In fact, Gregory states, now speaking of the Third Person:

> For He is immortal in every sense; He is unchangeable, unalterable, always beautiful and without need of external (ἑτέρωθεν) favor; He actualizes all things in all creatures as He wishes; He is holy, guiding, righteous, just, true, explores the depths of God (1 Cor 2:10), proceeds from the Father (ἐκ πατρὸς ἐκπορευόμενον) and receives himself from the Son (ἐκ τοῦ υἱοῦ λαμβανόμενον).[45]

φῶς κατὰ τὸ προσεχὲς ἐνοήσαμεν οἷον ἀκτῖνά τινα τῷ ἡλίῳ συνυφισταμένην, ἧς ἡ μὲν αἰτία τοῦ εἶναι ἐκ τοῦ ἡλίου, ἡ δὲ ὕπαρξις ὁμοῦ τῷ ἡλίῳ, οὐ χρόνοις ὕστερον προσγινομένη, ἀλλ' ὁμοῦ τῷ ὀφθῆναι τὸν ἥλιον ἐξ αὐτοῦ συναναφαινομένη· μᾶλλον δὲ (οὐ γὰρ ἀνάγκη πάσῃ τῇ εἰκόνι δουλεύοντας δοῦναι τοῖς συκοφάνταις κατὰ τοῦ λόγου λαβὴν ἐν τῇ τοῦ ὑποδείγματος ἀτονίᾳ) οὐχὶ ἀκτῖνα ἐξ ἡλίου νοήσομεν, ἀλλ' ἐξ ἀγεννήτου ἡλίου ἄλλον ἥλιον ὁμοῦ τῇ τοῦ πρώτου ἐπινοίᾳ γεννητῶς αὐτῷ συνεκλάμποντα καὶ κατὰ πάντα ὡσαύτως ἔχοντα κάλλει δυνάμει λαμπηδόνι μεγέθει φαιδρότητι καὶ πᾶσιν ἅπαξ τοῖς περὶ τὸν ἥλιον θεωρουμένοις. καὶ πάλιν ἕτερον τοιοῦτον φῶς κατὰ τὸν αὐτὸν τρόπον, οὐ χρονικῷ τινι διαστήματι τοῦ γεννητοῦ φωτὸς ἀποτεμνόμενον, ἀλλὰ δι' αὐτοῦ μὲν ἐκλάμπον, τὴν δὲ τῆς ὑποστάσεως αἰτίαν ἔχον ἐκ τοῦ πρωτοτύπου φωτός, φῶς μέντοι καὶ αὐτὸ καθ' ὁμοιότητα τοῦ προεπινοηθέντος λάμπον καὶ φωτίζον καὶ τὰ ἄλλα πάντα τὰ τοῦ φωτὸς ἐργαζόμενον. οὐδὲ γὰρ ἔστι φωτὶ πρὸς ἕτερον φῶς κατ' αὐτὸ τοῦτο παραλλαγή, ὅταν κατ' οὐδὲν τῆς φωτιστικῆς χάριτος ἐνδέον ἢ ὑστερούμενον φαίνηται, ἀλλὰ πάσῃ τελειότητι πρὸς τὸ ἀκρότατον ἐπηρμένον μετὰ πατρὸς καὶ υἱοῦ θεωρεῖται, μετὰ πατέρα καὶ υἱὸν ἀριθμεῖται, καὶ δι' ἑαυτοῦ τὴν προσαγωγὴν πρὸς τὸ ἐπινοούμενον φῶς τὸ ἐν πατρὶ καὶ υἱῷ πᾶσι τοῖς μετασχεῖν δυναμένοις χαρίζεται (Gregory of Nyssa, *Contra Eunomium I*, 532.5–534.7 [GNO 1:180.14–181.11]).

45. ὅτι ἀθάνατόν ἐστι πάντως, ὅτι ἄτρεπτόν τε καὶ ἀναλλοίωτον καὶ ἀεὶ καλὸν καὶ ἀπροσδεὲς τῆς ἑτέρωθεν χάριτος, ὅτι πάντα ἐν πᾶσιν ἐνεργεῖ καθὼς βούλεται, ἅγιον, ἡγε-

Unlike in Origen,[46] divine attributes must be predicated of the Third Person precisely because He proceeds from the Father by means of the Son: the parallelism of *ekporeuomenon* and *lambanomenon* appears to be explicitly desired. The second verb was translated in the context of the image of the three torches and three suns, on the background of the link between John 15:26 and 16:14, as referred to *receive himself,* insofar as Gregory constantly asserts that the Spirit has His origin from the Father, as indicated by the first verb, but through the Son.[47] Another text in *Contra Eunomium I* goes in the same direction:

> But [the Spirit], having the cause of being from the God of the universe, from whom (ὅθεν) also the only begotten light has being, shines through the true light (διὰ δὲ τοῦ ἀληθινοῦ φωτός) and is not separated from the Father or from the Only Begotten, neither in an interval of time, nor in a difference of nature.[48]

The formulation of the role of the Son in the procession of the Spirit reaches later its apex in *Ad Ablabium,* when Gregory affirms the unity of nature of the divine Persons, speaking of the distinction between that which is cause (αἴτιον) and that which is caused (αἰτιατόν), as we have already seen. Gregory has found the manner to distinguish the two processions in recognizing a role for the Son in the origin of the Third Person. This is not a simple repetition of Athanasius's solution, presented in chapter 2, because here the Second Person is recognized as the Only Begotten precisely because His being immediately from the Father is expressed in mediating the natural relation of the Spirit to the Father. The second procession is not a simple copy of generation and it does not simply transmit the nature, as if it were something material. On the contrary, the first and the second processions are linked one to the other and the Son is Himself in His relation not only to the Father, but also to the Spirit.

μονικόν, εὐθές, δίκαιον, ἀληθινόν, τὰ βάθη ἐρευνῶν τοῦ θεοῦ, ἐκ πατρὸς ἐκπορευόμενον, ἐκ τοῦ υἱοῦ λαμβανόμενον (Gregory of Nyssa, *Adversus Macedonianos,* GNO 3.1:97.8–13).

46. See the text at p. 36.

47. The expression reminds us of Epiphanius's *Ancoratus:* ἐκ τοῦ πατρὸς ἐκπορευόμενον καὶ ἐκ τοῦ υἱοῦ λαμβάνον καὶ πιστευόμενον (Epiphanius, *Ancoratus,* 119.10–11 [GCS 25:148.30]). The variant λαμβανόμενον is present in copies of the *Ancoratus* found in Codex Laurentianus VI, 12 and in Codex Jenensis, ms. Bose 1.

48. ἀλλ' ἐκ μὲν τοῦ θεοῦ τῶν ὅλων καὶ αὐτὸ τὴν αἰτίαν ἔχον τοῦ εἶναι, ὅθεν καὶ τὸ μονογενές ἐστι φῶς, διὰ δὲ τοῦ ἀληθινοῦ φωτὸς ἐκλάμψαν, οὔτε διαστήματι οὔτε φύσεως ἑτερότητι τοῦ πατρὸς ἢ τοῦ μονογενοῦς ἀποτεμνόμενον (Gregory of Nyssa, *Contra Eunomium I,* 378.8–11 [GNO 1:138.12–15]).

In this way, the two processions are clearly distinguished from one another without separation.

The present reading is confirmed by another passage in *Adversus Macedonianos*, where a long series of divine attributes is framed by an inclusion in a double affirmation of the procession of the Spirit from the Father and the Son:

> Yet, the Holy Spirit is first of all from those who are holy by nature (ἀπὸ τῶν κατὰ φύσιν ἁγίων), that is, the Father, holy in nature, and the Son, who is the same. Such is the Holy Spirit: giver of life, immortal, unchangeable, eternal, just, wise, righteous, Lord, good, powerful, dispenser of all good things and, before all else, dispenser of life itself. For He is everywhere, is present to each creature, fills the earth and remains in the heavens, flows out in the supercosmic powers, fills all creatures as each deserves and remains fully himself, is with all who deserve Him and is not separate from the Holy Trinity. "He is always searching out the depths of God" (1 Cor 2:10); He is always receiving from the Son (ἀεὶ ἐκ τοῦ υἱοῦ λαμβάνει) and being dispatched and is not separate and glorifies and has glory. For a being that gives glory to another is obviously comprehended in overflowing glory. How does a being that does not partake of glory glorify? If there is no light, how will one manifest the grace (χάριν) of light?[49]

Gregory, at the beginning of the passage, affirms the procession from the Father and the Son, using the verb *to be* and the preposition *apo*, according to a pneumatological line similar to that of Epiphanius, who founded the divinity of the Third Person in the origin of both the first two. But it is precisely this origin from the first two divine Persons that establishes the necessity of predicating the divine attributes of the Third Person. The end of the passage elucidates the relation with the Son, from whom the Spirit

---

49. Τὸ δὲ πνεῦμα τὸ ἅγιον πρῶτον μὲν ἀπὸ τῶν κατὰ φύσιν ἁγίων ἐκεῖνό ἐστιν ὅπερ ὁ πατήρ, κατὰ φύσιν ἅγιος, καὶ ὁ μονογενὴς ὡσαύτως. οὕτω καὶ τὸ πνεῦμα τὸ ἅγιον. καὶ κατὰ τὸ ζωοποιὸν πάλιν καὶ κατὰ τὸ ἄφθαρτόν τε καὶ ἀναλλοίωτον καὶ ἀΐδιον, δίκαιον, σοφόν, εὐθές, ἡγεμονικόν, ἀγαθόν, δυνατόν, ἀγαθῶν πάντων παρεκτικὸν καὶ πρό γε ἁπάντων αὐτῆς τῆς ζωῆς· πανταχοῦ ὂν καὶ ἑκάστῳ παρὸν καὶ τὴν γῆν πληροῦν καὶ ἐν οὐρανοῖς μένον, ἐν ταῖς ὑπερκοσμίοις δυνάμεσιν ἐκχεόμενον, πάντα πληροῦν κατὰ τὴν ἀξίαν ἑκάστου καὶ αὐτὸ πλῆρες μένον, μετὰ πάντων ὂν τῶν ἀξίων, καὶ τῆς ἁγίας τριάδος οὐ χωριζόμενον· ἀεὶ τὰ βάθη τοῦ θεοῦ ἐρευνᾷ, ἀεὶ ἐκ τοῦ υἱοῦ λαμβάνει καὶ ἀποστέλλεται καὶ οὐ χωρίζεται καὶ δοξάζεται καὶ δόξαν ἔχει· ὃ γὰρ ἄλλῳ δόξαν δίδωσιν, δῆλον ὅτι ἐν ὑπερβαλλούσῃ δόξῃ καταλαμβάνεται. πῶς γὰρ δοξάζει τὸ δόξης ἄμοιρον; ἐὰν μή τι φῶς ᾖ, πῶς τὴν τοῦ φωτὸς ἐπιδείξεται χάριν (Gregory of Nyssa, *Adversus Macedonianos*, GNO 3.1:108.18–33).

constantly receives glory, which He can in turn communicate in a superabundant manner, that is, without losing anything because He does not simply participate in it, but instead it is identified with His being. The treatise is in fact constructed upon the identity of glory and the divine nature. Thus the adverb *aei*, present in both the reference to 1 Corinthians 2:10 and next to the *ek tou hyiou lambanei*, suggests an interpretation in the line of the second procession, which is recognized as the immanent foundation of the economic gift. In this manner the parallelism with *ek tou hyiou lambanomenon* seen above becomes clear.

The image of the three torches, contemplated with a background in the other works of Gregory, reveals its depth insofar as it manifests that the Spirit is to be adored with the Father and the Son as Creator, because He proceeds from the Father and receives Himself, that is, His nature, from the Son. In this sense, the Third Person completes the Trinity, bringing it to unity according to a conceptualization which places the *dia tou hyiou* at the center of the Trinity, already present in Basil:

> And one also is the Holy Spirit, He too proclaimed in his individuality (μοναδικῶς), who, united to the unique Father through the unique Son (δι' ἑνὸς Υἱοῦ), carries the Holy Trinity worthy of all praise to completion (συμπληροῦν) in himself.[50]

The theology of *Adversus Macedonianos* can be considered a development of this affirmation, because the Spirit is there presented also as the bond between the Father and the Son, as it will be shown in the following. Thus, the specification of what is proper to the Holy Spirit is primarily developed through the specification of His relation not only with the First Person, but with the Second too. In order to understand Gregory's position, it is important to remember that he directly opposes the teaching of Eunomius, who affirmed the procession of the Spirit from the Father *alone* by means of the Only Begotten.[51] On account of this, Gregory both highlights the active role of the Son in the procession of the Spirit and specifies the relation of the Spirit and the procession

---

50. Ἓν δὲ καὶ τὸ ἅγιον Πνεῦμα, καὶ αὐτὸ μοναδικῶς ἐξαγγελλόμενον, δι' ἑνὸς Υἱοῦ τῷ ἑνὶ Πατρὶ συναπτόμενον, καὶ δι' ἑαυτοῦ συμπληροῦν τὴν πολυύμνητον καὶ μακαρίαν Τριάδα (Basil, *De Spiritu Sancto*, 18.45.24–27 [SC 17bis:408]).

51. Γενόμενος, φησί, ὑπὸ τοῦ μόνου θεοῦ διὰ τοῦ μονογενοῦς (Gregory of Nyssa, *Refutatio confessionis Eunomii*, 190.1–2 [GNO 2:392.23–24]; cf. also 196.2 [GNO 2:395.6]).

of the Son. It is exactly this correlation of the roles of the Son and the Spirit which will be the highest point of Gregory of Nyssa's study of the Trinity.

IV. Anointing and the Kingdom

The analogy of anointing seeks to express the unity of the Trinity in a dynamic, correlational, and personal sense, linking the discussion on processions to that on perichoresis.[52] This term refers to the reciprocal being-in-one-another of the three divine Persons that constitute the One and Triune God.[53] This link is what makes the expression *dia tou hyiou* so essential to Gregory's thought: it serves to distinguish the processions from one another, showing that the Spirit does not proceed as Son, but that He has a proper mode of procession in which is implicated the Son, who is Himself just in uniting the Spirit to the Father. Thus the Trinity is complete and is one only in the Third Person.

This is shown in *Adversus Macedonianos*, in one of the most important passages for Gregory's argument. In fact, after having affirmed that without the confession of the Spirit we cannot call ourselves Christians,[54] as without being rational, living, erect, capable of laughter and with nails on our fingers[55] we cannot be called human beings, he moves on to analyze the name of Christ:[56]

52. In Gregory of Nyssa, as in other fathers of the church of the fourth century, both Eastern and Western, one can find an *ante litteram* form of *perichoresis*; see, in this regard, D. F. Stramara, "Gregory of Nyssa's Terminology for Trinitarian *Perichoresis*," *Vigiliae Christianae* 52 (1998): 257–63, and M. S. Troiano, "Il concetto di *perichoresis* in Gregorio di Nissa," *Studi storico-religiosi* 2 (1978): 81–92.

53. In Gregory of Nyssa, the term is not literally present. The root is introduced by Gregory of Nazianzus in his Christology to express the mutual exchange of the properties of the two natures; later it is used by Maximus the Confessor to formulate divinization, and only with John of Damascus does the expression emerge as a link between Christology, anthropology, and Trinitarian doctrine. See G. Maspero, "La perichoresis e la grammatica teologica dei primi sette Concili ecumenici," *Theologica* (2020): 161–81.

54. Gregory of Nyssa, *Adversus Macedonianos*, GNO 3.1:101.4–102.16.

55. The elements of this definition appear in other writings by the bishop of Nyssa: cf. *Contra Eunomium I*, 421.2, and *Contra Eunomium II*, 381.3–5. They appear to be common terms of the philosophical tradition. See the pseudo-Platonic definition in *Definitiones*, 415a11–12: Ἄνθρωπος ζῷον ἄπτερον, δίπουν, πλατυώνυχον· ὃ μόνον τῶν ὄντων ἐπιστήμης τῆς κατὰ λόγους δεκτικόν ἐστιν (J. Burnet, *Platonis Opera*, Vol. 5 [Oxford: Oxford University Press, 1907]). A text of Alexander of Aphrodisias is also interesting: ἢ διάθεσίν τινα αὐτοῦ σημαίνει, ὡς ἐπὶ τοῦ ἀνθρώπου τὸ πλατυώνυχον καὶ τὸ ὄρθιον, ἢ δύναμιν, ὡς τὸ ἐπιστήμης δεκτικὸν καὶ γελαστικόν, ἢ ἐνέργειαν, ὡς τοῦ θείου σώματος τὸ ἀεικίνητον (Alexander of Aphrodisias, *In Aristotelis topicorum libros octo commentaria*, 45.22–24).

56. The argument is parallel to that of Pseudo-Athanasius; see pp. 91–92.

How will one who does not recognize the chrism along with the Anointed One confess Christ? "God anointed this man," he says, "in the Holy Spirit" (Acts 10:38).[57]

The logical sequence of the text indicates that Gregory intends to present the name and the definition of Christ as relative to the Holy Spirit. To think of Christ necessarily entails thinking of the Holy Spirit, just as thinking of the Father leads one to think of the Son. This step is extremely beautiful and important from a theological perspective. For Gregory turns directly from economy to immanence, showing how the first procession itself is not correctly understood without the Spirit. His argument moves from the anointing with chrism, understood as a symbol of royalty:

> So if the Son is king by nature, and the chrism is a symbol of his kingship, then what does the logic of the reasoning mean to you? That the chrism is not something foreign to the natural king, and we do not classify the Spirit with the Holy Trinity as a stranger and foreigner. Indeed the Son is king. But the Holy Spirit is the living, substantial and subsistent kingship (ζῶσα καὶ οὐσιώδης καὶ ἐνυπόστατος). Since He has been anointed with this kingship, the only begotten Christ is also king of all existing things. So if the Father is king and the Only Begotten is king and the Holy Spirit is kingship, the reason for kingship in the case of the Trinity is absolutely the same.[58]

The connection between the kingship and the divinity of the Spirit is clearly at the heart of the discussion. The topic appears to recur in the treatises directed at the Pneumatomachians, as already pointed out in the previous chapter.[59] In the first Pseudo-Athanasian *Dialogus contra Macedonianos*, the subjects of kingship and glory are dealt with explicitly. In fact, the heretics claim:

---

57. πῶς γὰρ ὁμολογήσει Χριστὸν ὁ μὴ συνεπινοῶν τῷ χρισθέντι τὸ χρίσμα; Τοῦτον ἔχρισε, φησίν, ὁ θεὸς ἐν πνεύματι ἁγίῳ (Gregory of Nyssa, *Adversus Macedonianos*, GNO 3.1:102.14–16).

58. εἰ οὖν τῇ φύσει βασιλεὺς ὁ υἱός, βασιλείας δὲ σύμβολόν ἐστι τὸ χρίσμα, τί σοι διὰ τῆς ἀκολουθίας ὁ λόγος ἐνδείκνυται; ὅτι οὐκ ἀλλότριόν τί ἐστι τοῦ κατὰ φύσιν βασιλέως τὸ χρίσμα οὐδὲ ὡς ξένον τι καὶ ἀλλόφυλον τῇ ἁγίᾳ τριάδι τὸ πνεῦμα συντέτακται. βασιλεὺς μὲν γὰρ ὁ υἱός· βασιλεία δὲ ζῶσα καὶ οὐσιώδης καὶ ἐνυπόστατος τὸ πνεῦμα τὸ ἅγιον, ᾗ χρισθεὶς ὁ μονογενὴς Χριστός ἐστι καὶ βασιλεὺς τῶν ὄντων. εἰ οὖν βασιλεὺς ὁ πατήρ, βασιλεὺς δὲ ὁ μονογενής, βασιλεία δὲ τὸ πνεῦμα τὸ ἅγιον, εἰς πάντως τῆς βασιλείας ἐπὶ τῆς τριάδος ὁ λόγος (Gregory of Nyssa, *Adversus Macedonianos*, GNO 3.1:102.22–31).

59. See pp. 95–96.

And even if I affirm that the Spirit acts together (συνεργόν) with God, I do not render Him glory as (συνδοξάζω) to God.[60]

As is clear, the question is a metaphysical one because here the *synergeia* is not held to be a sufficient reason for claiming the identity of nature. This leads to the following exchange:

> *Macedonian*: We say that the Father is king and that the Son is too, but we say that the Spirit is their minister (ὑπηρέτης). *Orthodox*: You do not even know your own heresy. Actually, even if this is not king, the minister has the same substance as the king. You are affirming, therefore, that the Spirit has the same substance as God.[61]

This debate about kingship, rooted in Origen's and Eusebius's heritage, is probably being played out against the same background as the other texts written by Gregory of Nyssa against the Pneumatomachians, like the third homily of the *De oratione dominica* that will be analyzed in the next chapter. This is confirmed by the presence of the argument over the unity of action which Pseudo-Athanasius expresses with a formula extremely close to that of the Bishop of Nyssa. The latter, in fact, writes in that homily: "the activity is one, and also the power is absolutely the same" (ἡ ἐνέργεια μία, καὶ ἡ δύναμις πάντως ἡ αὐτή ἐστιν),[62] to go on to deduce from this the identity of nature as we will see. In the Pseudo-Athanasian *Dialogi contra Macedonianos*, on the other hand, there appears several times, as if it were a common formula, the expression: "if, in fact, the activity is the same, the nature also is the same" (ὧν γὰρ ἡ αὐτὴ ἐνέργεια, καὶ ἡ αὐτὴ φύσις).[63] This very argument is developed also in the *Ad Ablabium* and the *De deitate Filii et Spiritus Sancti*, theologically linked with the affirmation of the creative power of the Spirit.

In this last text, it is also said that "the Spirit is not called God by Sacred Scripture" (τὸ μὴ προσειρῆσθαι θεὸν τὸ πνεῦμα παρὰ τῆς ἁγίας γραφῆς),[64] which also

---

60. Κἂν εἴπω συνεργὸν τὸ πνεῦμα τῷ θεῷ, ἀλλ᾽ οὐ συνδοξάζω αὐτὸ τῷ θεῷ (Pseudo-Athanasius, *Dialogus I contra Macedonianos*, 17.7–8 (Cavalcanti, 90).

61. ΜΑΚ. Ἡμεῖς λέγομεν ὅτι ὁ πατήρ ἐστι βασιλεὺς καὶ ὁ υἱός, τὸ δὲ πνεῦμα ὑπηρέτης. ΟΡΘ. Οὐδὲ οἶδας σαυτοῦ τὴν αἵρεσιν. Ὁ γὰρ ὑπηρέτης, κἂν μὴ ᾖ βασιλεύς, τῆς αὐτῆς ἐστι τῷ βασιλεῖ οὐσίας. Λέγεις οὖν καὶ αὐτὸς τῆς αὐτῆς οὐσίας εἶναι τῷ θεῷ τὸ πνεῦμα (Gregory of Nyssa, *Adversus Macedonianos*, GNO 3.1:17.19–23 [Cavalcanti, 90]).

62. Gregory of Nyssa, *De oratione dominica*, SC 596:418.2.

63. Cf. Pseudo-Athanasius, *Dialogus I contra Macedonianos*, 12.14–15 (Cavalcanti, 74); 12.35–36 (Cavalcanti, 76); 13.24 (Cavalcanti, 80); and 16.8–9 (Cavalcanti, 86).

64. Gregory of Nyssa, *De deitate Filii et Spiritus Sancti*, GNO 10.2:142.4–5.

recalls the formula *oude gar gegraptai* found in the *Dialogi contra Macedonianos*.[65] The closeness of the polemical context is clear. From the ontological perspective, the discourse on kingship is at the heart of the answer to the Macedonian principle that an intermediate metaphysical degree is necessary to approach God.[66]

This refers also to the relationship of the Pneumatomachians with the Homoiousians. The point was the possibility of an ontological gradation which, in the case of the Son, envisaged an identity of dignity through generation, but for the Spirit implied the divine being but without a share in the divine nature.[67] Gregory of Nyssa, on the contrary, shows that the relationship with the Trinity is possible only for the personal relations of the Son and the Spirit, who are *in* the divine immanence, being one *ousia* with the Father. The identification of the Third Person with the kingship of the Father and the Son, who are one King, is deeply connected with the ontological reshaping of the relational dimension in God.

Basil, in *De Spiritu Sancto*, had already cited Psalm 118(119) to show that the Third Person *participates* in the Kingdom:

> All things are subject to you (Ps 118[119]:91). And if the Spirit is above creation, He is participant (ἐστὶ κοινωνόν) in the Kingdom.[68]

This was not sufficient. Conversely, Gregory does not limit himself to the affirmation of participation, but identifies the Spirit with the Kingdom or the Kingship itself. In this manner the personal property of the Third Person is read in correlational terms in respect to the Father and the Son, who are one King. Gregory's inspiration comes from Scripture. For the invocation "Your Kingdom come" of Matthew 6:10 is considered by him as equivalent to the variant of Luke 11:2, "May your Spirit come upon us and purify us," as he explains in the *De oratione dominica*:

> And perhaps, as the same thought has been more clearly interpreted for us by Luke, he who desires that the Kingdom come should cry, asking the help of the Holy Spirit. In fact, in that Gospel, "Your Kingdom come" becomes "May your Spirit come upon us and purify us."[69]

---

65. Cf. Pseudo-Athanasius, *Dialogus I contra Macedonianos*, 4.2–3 (Cavalcanti, 54) and 7.2–3 (Cavalcanti, 62).

66. Pseudo-Athanasius, *Dialogus I contra Macedonianos*, 4.12–13 (Cavalcanti, 56). See the text at p. 90.

67. Cf. Pseudo-Athanasius, *Dialogus I contra Macedonianos*, 15.22 (Cavalcanti, 84).

68. "Τὰ γὰρ σύμπαντα, φησί, δοῦλα σά"· εἰ δὲ ὑπὲρ τὴν κτίσιν ἐστί, τῆς βασιλείας ἐστὶ κοινωνόν (Basil, *De Spiritu Sancto*, 20.51.49–50 [SC 17bis:30]).

69. "Η τάχα, καθὼς ἡμῖν ὑπὸ τοῦ Λουκᾶ τὸ αὐτὸ νόημα σαφέστερον ἑρμηνεύεται, ὁ τὴν

Gregory is one of the witnesses to this variant[70] that according to Jean Magne[71] belonged to the Q source and had a liturgical context from which the commonly accepted text also gradually developed.[72] It is interesting to observe that the variant has left its traces in the offertory both in the Greek and Syriac liturgies,[73] with which it was specially linked. The variant's belonging to both traditions is confirmed by its presence in the *Acta Thomae*, which was composed at the beginning of the third century in an area that was probably bilingual.[74] According to Tertullian, the variant was known to Marcion, originally from Pontus like Gregory of Nyssa and Evagrius, in whose writing too can be found clear traces of it.[75]

The equivalence of the two verses permits Gregory to identify the Spirit and the Kingdom, specifying the personal property of the Third Person in the unification of the first two. From a systematic perspective, the shift that Gregory makes here is particularly noticeable, since, up to this point he had followed a linear schema, which tied the Spirit to the Father through the Son

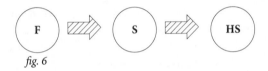

fig. 6

and now inserted the Third Person (see fig. 6) into the relationship between the first two, as a foundation of it

---

βασιλείαν ἐλθεῖν ἀξιῶν τὴν τοῦ ἁγίου πνεύματος συμμαχίαν ἐπιβοᾶται; οὕτω γὰρ ἐν ἐκείνῳ τῷ εὐαγγελίῳ φησὶν, ἀντὶ τοῦ Ἐλθέτω ἡ βασιλεία σου, Ἐλθέτω τὸ πνεῦμά σου τὸ ἅγιον ἐφ' ἡμᾶς καὶ καθαρισάτω ἡμᾶς (Gregory of Nyssa, *De oratione dominica*, GNO 7.2:39.15-19).

70. See M. Alexandre, "La variante de Lc 11, 2 dans la Troisième Homélie sur l'Oraison Dominicale de Grégoire de Nysse et la controverse avec les pneumatomaques," in *Grégoire de Nysse: La Bible dans la construction de son discours*, ed. M. Cassin et al. (Paris: Brepols, 2008), 163–89. See also SC 596:149-55.

71. J. Magne, "La réception de le variante 'Vienne ton Esprit saint sur nous et qu'il nous purifie' (Lc 11,2) et l'origine des épiclèses, du baptême et du 'Notre Père,'" *Ephemerides liturgicae* 102 (1988): 81–106.

72. Cf. Magne, "La réception," 103.

73. Specifically, we are talking about the Greek anaphora of S. Basil, the Maronite anaphora of S. Sixtus and Peter III, and the Nestorian anaphora of Addai and Mari, of Theodore of Mopsuestia and of Nestorius. See chapter 6, p. 198.

74. Cf. *Acta Thomae* 27. See A. F. J. Klijn, *The Acts of Thomas* (Leiden: Brill, 2003), 77 and 83 for the comment.

75. ἐλθέτω ἡ βασιλεία σου, τουτέστι τὸ ἅγιον σου πνεῦμα καὶ ὁ μονογενής σου υἱός. Οὕτω γὰρ καὶ ἐδίδαξε λέγων ἐν πνεύματι καὶ ἀληθείᾳ προσκυνεῖσθαι τὸν πατέρα (Evagrius, *De oratione*, 59 [SC 589:272.3-5]).

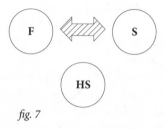

fig. 7

where the double arrow symbol denotes the action of the Spirit (see fig. 7). The Son is King as the Father is, precisely because He receives the chrism that is the Holy Spirit himself. The graphical representation cannot express the fact that the double arrow relationally emerges from a first arrow which starts from the Father and a second arrow that goes back to the First Person from the Second Person, safeguarding the monarchy. In this manner Gregory responds in depth to the Pneumatomachians, whose doctrine was probably a derivation of the Homoiousian doctrine,[76] inserting the Third Person *between* the First and the Second Persons, who were considered divine (see fig. 8). The strategy is common in the response to this confrontation, as seen in the previous chapter.

If one wishes to admit that the Son is the perfect image of the Father, He must then be King as the Father himself, and must possess His unique royal dignity. But this royal dignity is the Spirit himself. The processions cannot be conceived separately from one another, and the intra-Trinitarian order is only one of origin, without any form of subordination whatsoever. The Son cannot be King, that is, Son as eternal and perfect Image of the Father, without the Spirit, so neither can the Father be King without the Son and, therefore, without His Spirit. And the immanent order is perfectly preserved, together with the monarchy.

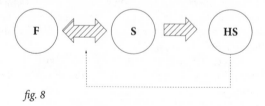

fig. 8

The point is that between the Son and the Spirit there can be no distance, as the surface of the body of one who is anointed is in direct contact with

76. See P. Meinhold, "Pneumatomachoi," *Paulys Real Encyclopädie der classischen Alter-tumswissenschaft* 21.1 (1951), 1066–87.

the chrism.[77] No middle point (μέσον) is admitted that could place itself between (μεταξύ) the one and the other, as the conjunction of the Second and Third Persons is also immediate (ἀδιάστατος). Gregory denies the possibility that one can conceive of an intermediary ontological level between God and the world:

> Reason recognizes nothing intermediary (μέσον), so that some special border (ἐν μεθορίῳ) nature be thought to exist between (μεταξύ) the created and the uncreated, so that it partakes of both and is neither perfectly.[78]

The language is exquisitely metaphysical, and directly denies the foundations of Platonic ontology, which is recalled by the terminology used, in order to affirm that the Spirit is not an intermediary being between God and the world. The Spirit is rather He who, in the Trinity, unites the Father and the Son. Without inverting the Trinitarian order, Gregory affirms that the intermediary between the Father and the Son must be of their very nature. In this manner the two processions are tied to one another in a correlational manner: the Spirit proceeds from the Father through the Son, because His mode of being God is that of uniting the Father and the Son, and because of that He is from the Father, who is His unique cause, and is manifested by the Son. The Spirit makes the Trinity one in His being the communion of the Father and Son: the Second is image of the First (i.e., is King as He is) precisely by the Person of the Holy Spirit.

With the background of the ontological work presented in the introduction to reshape the *Logos*-theology of the apologists as *Physis*-theology, this operation accomplished by Gregory of Nyssa can be read as the final step to overcome the Platonic-Aristotelian and gnostic conception of an ontological ladder that unites God and the world. The first movement of this path was the modification of the philosophical conception of the *Logos* as mediator between heaven and earth. The Johannine Prologue made insertion of the *Logos* into the divinity obligatory, that is, in the *archē*. The dispute with the Arians touched precisely this central point. The following step was to radically exclude the possibility that the Spirit could occupy the position of mediator (*meson, metaxu*) between the Creator and creation. Bringing the *pneuma* into the divine *archē*

---

77. Gregory of Nyssa, *Adversus Macedonianos*, GNO 3.1:103.1–5.

78. μέσον γὰρ τούτων ἐπιγινώσκει ὁ λόγος οὐδέν, ὥστε τινὰ φύσεως ἰδιότητα ἐν μεθορίῳ τοῦ τε κτιστοῦ καὶ τοῦ ἀκτίστου καινοτομηθεῖσαν μεταξὺ τούτων εἶναι νομίζεσθαι, ὡς καὶ ἀμφοτέρων μετέχειν καὶ οὐθέτερον τελείως εἶναι (Gregory of Nyssa, *Adversus Macedonianos*, GNO 3.1:104.8–12).

meant rereading both the mediation of the Son and that of the Holy Spirit in purely immanent terms. Gregory accomplished this task by deepening the understanding of the reciprocal relationship of the two processions.

This all regards the theology of glory as well, insofar as Gregory resolves the question of adoration by presenting glory in its immanent reality. The operation accomplished on the relationship of the King and the Kingdom thus naturally extends to the relationship of God's nature and glory in the framework of Gregory's *Schesis*-theology.

V. THEOLOGY OF GLORY

In order to understand this transition, it is necessary to keep in mind that which has been said on the distinction of processions. Gregory wishes to show the equivalence of glory and the divine nature, distinguishing the procession according to the image that Athanasius had applied to both the Son and the Spirit from the procession of the Third Person. The following texts can be compared, Basil writes, in reference to the Paraclete:

> He, as the sun that reaches the purified eye, will show you in himself the Image of the Invisible. And, in the blessed contemplation of the Image you will see the ineffable beauty of the Archetype.[79]

In *Adversus Macedonianos* a parallel passage is found, where Gregory's attention for the theology of glory can be seen as he uses it to express the relation between the Second and Third Persons. He writes:

> One who reverently accepts the Spirit sees the glory of the Only Begotten in the Spirit, and when he sees the Son he sees the image of the unlimited, and the archetype is impressed in his mind through the image.[80]

It is interesting to note that in the preceding text it is glory and not the image that is now seen in the Spirit. It is as if the refocusing from the Son to the Spirit is expressed in terms of glory.

79. Ὁ δέ, ὥσπερ ἥλιος, κεκαθαρμένον ὄμμα παραλαβών, δείξει σοι ἐν ἑαυτῷ τὴν εἰκόνα τοῦ ἀοράτου. Ἐν δὲ τῷ μακαρίῳ τῆς εἰκόνος θεάματι τὸ ἄρρητον ὄψει τοῦ ἀρχετύπου κάλλος (Basil, *De Spiritu Sancto*, 9.23.9 [SC 17bis:328]).

80. ὁ εὐσεβῶς τὸ πνεῦμα δεξάμενος εἶδεν ἐν τῷ πνεύματι τοῦ μονογενοῦς τὴν δόξαν, τὸν δὲ υἱὸν ἰδὼν τὴν εἰκόνα εἶδε τοῦ ἀορίστου καὶ διὰ τῆς εἰκόνος ἐνετυπώσατο τῇ γνώμῃ ἑαυτοῦ τὸ ἀρχέτυπον (Gregory of Nyssa, *Adversus Macedonianos*, GNO 3.1:107.10–13).

In fact, the Spirit communicates glory because He possesses it in fullness. The gift that flows from His Person is founded on His being God, that is, on His identification with Glory itself. In *Adversus Macedonianos*, Gregory concentrates his attention on the fact that the Spirit certainly gives glory to the Father and the Son, just as the Kingdom constitutes the glory of the King. In this context he uses John 17:5, the study of which is particularly interesting in the diachronic analysis of Gregory's pneumatology. He writes:

> So the Spirit glorifies the Father and the Son. But He is not a liar who says, "I glorify those who glorify me" (1 Sam 2:30). "I glorified you" (John 17:4) says the Lord to the Father. And again, "Glorify me with the glory that I had with you from the beginning before the world existed" (John 17:5). The divine voice responds, "I glorified you and will glorify you again" (John 12:28).[81]

The Spirit glorifies the Father and the Son, but the Son in turn gives glory to the Father and receives from Him that glory that eternally corresponds to Him by nature (see fig. 9). Thus we can see how the Third Person unites the Father and Son as Glory.[82] It can be interesting to read this passage in light of that which has been said on the identification of the Spirit with the Kingdom, and thus with His role in the first procession and His being a foundation of the relation between the Father and the Son.

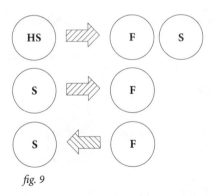

fig. 9

---

81. δοξάζει οὖν τὸν πατέρα καὶ τὸν υἱὸν τὸ πνεῦμα. ἀλλ᾽ ὁ εἰπὼν ἀψευδής ἐστι Τοὺς δοξ-άζοντάς με δοξάζω·Ἐγώ σε ἐδόξασα, φησὶ πρὸς τὸν πατέρα ὁ κύριος· καὶ πάλιν Δόξασόν με τῇ δόξῃ ᾗ εἶχον ἀπ᾽ ἀρχῆς παρὰ σοὶ πρὸ τοῦ τὸν κόσμον εἶναι. ἀποκρίνεται ἡ θεία φωνή· Καὶ ἐδόξασα καὶ πάλιν δοξάσω (Gregory of Nyssa, *Adversus Macedonianos*, GNO 3.1:109.2–7).

82. Khaled Anatolios highlights the importance of this text in K. Anatolios, *Deification through the Cross* (Grand Rapids: Eerdmans, 2020), 185.

In view of this, the perspective of the development of the Bishop of Nyssa's thought can be interesting. In fact, in *Ad Eustathium*, probably composed between 375 and 380,[83] the themes of Kingdom and Glory are placed together precisely when Gregory explains that chrism refers to the dignity of the Third Person. He concludes, "The Holy Spirit shares (κοινωνεῖ) the glory and kingship of the only begotten Son of God."[84] The echo of the already cited τῆς βασιλείας κοινωνόν of Basil in *De Spiritu Sancto* is present here, but later in *Adversus Macedonianos* Gregory identifies the Kingdom with the Spirit, thus going beyond the position of his brother. Alongside the linear conception of the Trinity, centered on the mediation of the Son and His role in the procession of the Holy Spirit, the Bishop of Nyssa adds, through the theology of the Kingdom, a conception of the Holy Trinity that could be called symmetric insofar as it places the Third Person in the center of the relation of image that unites the Son to the Father. As with the Kingdom, Glory too is inserted into this second scheme. This is not yet fully explicit in *Adversus Macedonianos*, but Gregory's later works clearly show this. In fact, while in this treatise the Spirit is identified with *doxa* without the article,[85] since it is consubstantiality that is being affirmed, the article is present in the exegesis of John 17:5 that points directly to the identification of Glory and the Spirit. This is evident in *Antirrheticus adversos Apolinarium*, of uncertain date but certainly composed after 382,[86] where the verse appears[87] with the following comment:

And the Glory that is contemplated before the world and all creation and all the ages, in which the only begotten God is glorified, is nothing other than *the* Glory of the Spirit (τὴν δόξαν τοῦ πνεύματος), according to our thought. In fact, the doctrine of piety teaches that only the Holy Trinity is eternal. "He who exists from before the ages" (Ps 54:20[55:19]) says the

---

83. See Daniélou, "La chronologie," 162, and May, "Die Chronologie," 57–58.

84. τῆς τοῦ μονογενοῦς υἱοῦ τοῦ θεοῦ δόξης καὶ βασιλείας κοινωνεῖ τὸ πνεῦμα τὸ ἅγιο (Gregory of Nyssa, *Ad Eustathium, De sancta Trinitate*, GNO 3.1:16.6–7).

85. In Gregory of Nyssa, *Adversus Macedonianos*, GNO 3.1:108.33–109.2, it is said that there can be no glorifying power that is not glory, honor, and magnificence itself (οὕτως οὐδὲ τὴν δοξαστικὴν δύναμιν ἐπιδείξεται, ὃ ἂν μὴ αὐτὸ ᾖ δόξα καὶ τιμὴ καὶ μεγαλωσύνη καὶ μεγαλοπρέπεια).

86. See Daniélou, "La chronologie," 163. See also P. Maraval, "Cronologia delle opere," in *Dizionario di Gregorio di Nissa*, ed. L. F. Mateo-Seco and G. Maspero (Rome: Città Nuova, 2007), 180–90.

87. See Gregory of Nyssa, *Adversus Macedonianos*, GNO 3.1:222.9–10.

prophecy of the Father; and, in reference to the Son, the Apostle says: "Through Him were made the ages" (Heb 1:2). The glory before the ages, contemplated in the only begotten God, is the Holy Spirit.[88]

Two other texts make this identification even more explicit while also showing the role of connecting the economy and immanence carried out by the Holy Spirit. For He is at once the Person who pours forth the gift of divine life on the human beings and the Person who, in the Trinity, unites the Father and the Son. In *In illud: Tunc et ipse*, written after 385,[89] the succession of commented Johannine texts (John 17:21–23) makes this particularly clear:

> "So that all may be one. As you, Father, are in me and I in you, that they be also one in us." This clearly shows that in uniting us to Himself, He who is in the Father, by means of Himself realizes our union (συνάφειαν) with the Father. But also that which follows in the gospel is in harmony with the explanation: "The glory that you gave me, I have given to them." I maintain in fact that He here calls the Holy Spirit glory (δόξαν γὰρ ἐνταῦθα λέγειν αὐτὸν οἶμαι τὸ πνεῦμα τὸ ἅγιον), whom He gave to the disciples through the act of breathing (cf. John 20:22), since it is not possible that those who were found divided from each other be united, unless guided back to the unity of nature by the unity of the Spirit. For, "if someone has not the Spirit of Christ, he does not belong to him" (Rom 8:9). But the Spirit is *the* Glory (τὸ δὲ πνεῦμα ἡ δόξα ἐστί), as he says in another passage to the Father: "Glorify me near you, with the glory that I had near you before the world was" (John 17:5). For the divine Word, who before the world was created has the glory of the Father, in the last days became flesh (John 1:14); and it was necessary that, due to the union (διὰ τῆς ἀνακράσεως) to the Word, also the flesh became that which the Word is. And the flesh becomes it in receiving that which the Word had before the world was. And this was the Holy Spirit. There is no other eternal being but the Father, the Son and the Holy Spirit.

---

88. ἡ δὲ προκόσμιος καὶ πρὸ πάσης κτίσεως καὶ πρὸ πάντων αἰώνων θεωρουμένη δόξα, ἧ ὁ μονογενὴς θεὸς ἐνδοξάζεται, οὐκ ἂν ἄλλη τις εἴη κατὰ τὸν ἡμέτερον λόγον παρὰ τὴν δόξαν τοῦ πνεύματος· μόνην γὰρ προαιώνιον τὴν ἁγίαν τριάδα ὁ τῆς εὐσεβείας παραδί-δωσι λόγος. Ὁ ὑπάρχων πρὸ τῶν αἰώνων, φησὶ περὶ τοῦ πατρὸς ἡ προφητεία· περὶ δὲ τοῦ μονογενοῦς ὁ ἀπόστολος ὅτι Δι' αὐτοῦ οἱ αἰῶνες ἐγένοντο· καὶ δόξα πρὸ τῶν αἰώνων περὶ τὸν μονογενῆ θεὸν θεωρουμένη τὸ πνεῦμά ἐστι τὸ ἅγιον (Gregory of Nyssa, *Antirrheticus adversos Apolinarium*, GNO 3.1:222.11–19).

89. See Daniélou, "La chronologie," 167.

Therefore He also says: "The glory that You gave Me, I have given to them, so that by means of it they be united to Me and by means of Me to You."[90]

The exegesis of John 17:5 is tied to the salvation realized by Christ in uniting the human being to the Father. But this union is realized in the Holy Spirit, who is the Glory that the Son eternally receives from the Father in generation. The incarnation of the Word is the pouring out of this glory on the world. Trinitarian logic presses Gregory to stress that there is nothing else eternal besides the three divine Persons according to the fundamental ontological principle introduced by Athanasius. This means that the gift received by the human being flows from inside the Trinity. This is applied to unity, to glory itself, and to the love of the Father for the Son, as is said in the continuation of the text, which paraphrases the dialogue of Christ with the Father in John 17:23:

> "So that they be one, as we are one." But how does this happen? Since I am in them. For it is not possible that only I be in them, but it is absolutely necessary that also You be in them, since You and I are one. And thus those who have come to be perfect in Us will be perfect in unity. For we are one. But [the Lord] explains the gift more openly with the words that follow, saying "you have loved them as you have loved me." For if the Father loves the Son and we are all in the Son, as many of us who have become His body by faith in Him, consequently He who loves His own Son loves also the body of the Son, as the Son himself. And we are the body.[91]

90. Ἵνα πάντες ἓν ὦσι καθὼς σύ, πάτερ, ἐν ἐμοὶ κἀγὼ ἐν σοί, ἵνα οὕτω κἀκεῖνοι ἐν ἡμῖν ἓν ὦσιν. σαφῶς γὰρ τοῦτο παρίστησιν ὅτι ἑαυτῷ ἡμᾶς ἑνώσας ὁ ἐν τῷ πατρὶ ὢν δι᾽ ἑαυτοῦ τὴν πρὸς τὸν πατέρα συνάφειαν ἡμῶν ἀπεργάζεται. Ἀλλὰ καὶ τὰ ἐφεξῆς τοῦ εὐαγγελίου συνᾴδει τοῖς εἰρημένοις· Τὴν δόξαν ἣν δέδωκάς μοι δέδωκα αὐτοῖς· δόξαν γὰρ ἐνταῦθα λέγειν αὐτὸν οἶμαι τὸ πνεῦμα τὸ ἅγιον ὃ ἔδωκε τοῖς μαθηταῖς διὰ τοῦ προσφυσήματος. οὐ γὰρ ἔστιν ἄλλως ἑνωθῆναι τοὺς ἀπ᾽ ἀλλήλων διεστηκότας μὴ τῇ ἑνότητι τοῦ πνεύματος συμφυομένους· Εἰ γάρ τις πνεῦμα Χριστοῦ οὐκ ἔχει, οὗτος οὐκ ἔστιν αὐτοῦ. τὸ δὲ πνεῦμα ἡ δόξα ἐστί, καθώς φησιν ἑτέρωθι πρὸς τὸν πατέρα· Δόξασόν με τῇ δόξῃ ᾗ εἶχον ἀπ᾽ ἀρχῆς παρὰ σοὶ πρὸ τοῦ τὸν κόσμον εἶναι. ὁ γὰρ θεὸς Λόγος ὁ πρὸ τοῦ κόσμου ἔχων τὴν τοῦ πατρὸς δόξαν, ἐπειδὴ ἐπ᾽ ἐσχάτων τῶν ἡμερῶν σὰρξ ἐγένετο, ἔδει [δὲ] καὶ τὴν σάρκα διὰ τῆς πρὸς τὸν Λόγον ἀνακράσεως ἐκεῖνο γενέσθαι ὅπερ ὁ Λόγος ἐστίν· γίνεται δὲ ἐκ τοῦ ἐκεῖνο λαβεῖν ὃ πρὸ τοῦ κόσμου εἶχεν ὁ Λόγος· τοῦτο δὲ ἦν τὸ πνεῦμα τὸ ἅγιον· οὐδὲν γὰρ ἄλλο προαιώνιον πλὴν πατρὸς καὶ υἱοῦ καὶ ἁγίου πνεύματος. διὰ τοῦτο καὶ ἐνταῦθά φησιν ὅτι Τὴν δόξαν ἣν δέδωκάς μοι δέδωκα αὐτοῖς, ἵνα δι᾽ αὐτῆς ἐμοὶ ἑνωθῶσιν καὶ δι᾽ ἐμοῦ σοί (Gregory of Nyssa, In illud: Tunc et ipse, GNO 3.2:21.17–22.16).

91. Ἵνα πάντες ἓν ὦσι καθὼς σύ, πάτερ, ἐν ἐμοὶ κἀγὼ ἐν σοί, ἵνα οὕτω κἀκεῖνοι ἐν ἡμῖν ἓν ὦσιν. σαφῶς γὰρ τοῦτο παρίστησιν ὅτι ἑαυτῷ ἡμᾶς ἑνώσας ὁ ἐν τῷ πατρὶ ὢν δι᾽ ἑαυτοῦ

The unity and love that constitute God himself are poured out upon human beings through the gift of the Spirit. One could not think of a closer correlation of economy and immanence. Precisely in the moment in which one recognizes that the Spirit is perfectly of the divine nature, it becomes necessary to find this gift in immanence, which is now completely protected by the affirmation that only the Three Persons are eternal. It is the radicalism of this ontological gap that enables us to recognize the gift as such and allows us to enter into a logic of pure gratuity, something that is fundamental for a proper understanding of worship, as will be seen at the end of this chapter.

For the theology of glory and the understanding of that which follows in *Adversus Macedonianos*, one final text can be of particular interest; it belongs to the most mature phase of the Bishop of Nyssa's works. In his *In Canticum canticorum*, commenting on the same Johannine passages that we have seen, Gregory states:

> It is better to textually cite the divine words of the Gospel: "So that all be one. As You Father, are in Me and I in You, that they be also one in Us" (John 17:21). And the bond of this unity is the Glory (τὸ δὲ συνδετικὸν τῆς ἑνότητος ταύτης ἡ δόξα ἐστίν). But no prudent person could oppose the fact that the Spirit is called 'Glory,' if the words of the Lord are considered. For He says: "The glory that You gave Me I gave to them" (John 17:22). He gave, in fact, that glory to the disciples, saying to them "Receive the Holy Spirit" (John 20:22). He, having embraced human nature, received this glory that He already possessed forever, from before the world was made (cf. John 17:5). And, since this human nature was glorified by the Spirit, the communication of the glory of the Spirit happens to all who belong to the same nature (ἐπὶ πᾶν τὸ συγγενές), starting with the disciples. For this He says: "And the glory that You gave Me, I gave to them, so that they

τὴν πρὸς τὸν πατέρα συνάφειαν ἡμῶν ἀπεργάζεται. Ἀλλὰ καὶ τὰ ἐφεξῆς τοῦ εὐαγγελίου συνάδει τοῖς εἰρημένοις· Τὴν δόξαν ἣν δέδωκάς μοι δέδωκα αὐτοῖς· δόξαν γὰρ ἐνταῦθα λέγειν αὐτὸν οἶμαι τὸ πνεῦμα τὸ ἅγιον ὃ ἔδωκε τοῖς μαθηταῖς διὰ τοῦ προσφυσήματος. οὐ γὰρ ἔστιν ἄλλως ἑνωθῆναι τοὺς ἀπ' ἀλλήλων διεστηκότας μὴ τῇ ἑνότητι τοῦ πνεύματος συμφυομένους· Εἰ γάρ τις πνεῦμα Χριστοῦ οὐκ ἔχει, οὗτος οὐκ ἔστιν αὐτοῦ. τὸ δὲ πνεῦμα ἡ δόξα ἐστί, καθώς φησιν ἑτέρωθι πρὸς τὸν πατέρα· Δόξασόν με τῇ δόξῃ ᾗ εἶχον ἀπ' ἀρχῆς παρὰ σοὶ πρὸ τοῦ τὸν κόσμον εἶναι. ὁ γὰρ θεὸς Λόγος ὁ πρὸ τοῦ κόσμου ἔχων τὴν τοῦ πατρὸς δόξαν, ἐπειδὴ ἐπ' ἐσχάτων τῶν ἡμερῶν σὰρξ ἐγένετο, ἔδει [δὲ] καὶ τὴν σάρκα διὰ τῆς πρὸς τὸν Λόγον ἀνακράσεως ἐκεῖνο γενέσθαι ὅπερ ὁ Λόγος ἐστί· γίνεται δὲ ἐκ τοῦ ἐκεῖνο λαβεῖν ὃ πρὸ τοῦ κόσμου εἶχεν ὁ Λόγος· τοῦτο δὲ ἦν τὸ πνεῦμα τὸ ἅγιον· οὐδὲν γὰρ ἄλλο προαιώνιον πλὴν πατρὸς καὶ υἱοῦ καὶ ἁγίου πνεύματος (Gregory of Nyssa, *In illud: Tunc et ipse*, GNO 3.2:23.3–14).

be one like Us. I in them and You in Me, so that they be perfect in unity"
(John 17:22–23).[92]

Since the disciples are one as the Father and Son are, it is necessary that they receive the Spirit, who is the "bond" (συνδετικόν) of this union.[93] Glory, and thus the Spirit, are recognized as the intra-Trinitarian nexus in which the unity communicated outside the Trinity is founded. The theology of glory here illuminates the theology of the Kingdom, showing how Gregory's conception of immanent relations deepened and developed. The operation is in line with a sort of theologization of divine attributes, because the Bishop of Nyssa shows how the fact of being glory, unity, or life of the triune God is founded both in the being of the divine substance and in the Person of the Holy Spirit, who is the immanent personal foundation of these attributes. God, therefore, is glory, but in God everything is not only substantial but also personal, so one can recognize that the third Person is the hypostatic glory that is eternally exchanged between the Father and the Son. And the same must apply to unity and to every other attribute, especially to that limitless life which the life-giving Spirit communicates to save the human being. The Spirit is personally all that the Trinity is essentially (i.e., He hypostatizes the divine attributes which in God coincide perfectly with one another).

The linear and symmetric schemes interact, giving rise to a dynamic conception based in the correlativity of the Persons and the inseparability of the two processions. In fact, there is no opposition between the two representations because the Spirit proceeds from the Father through the Son and at the same time is the bond of the Father and Son, insofar as the Spirit is the glory that the Father receives back from the Son Himself, Who is His own Image. This is a radical originality in respect to classic ontology because the divine

92. βέλτιον δ' ἂν εἴη αὐτὰς ἐπὶ λέξεως παραθέσθαι τὰς θείας τοῦ εὐαγγελίου φωνάς·
Ἵνα πάντες ἓν ὦσι καθὼς σύ, πάτερ, ἐν ἐμοὶ κἀγὼ ἐν σοί, ἵνα καὶ αὐτοὶ ἐν ἡμῖν ἓν ὦσιν. τὸ δὲ
συνδετικὸν τῆς ἑνότητος ταύτης ἡ δόξα ἐστίν· δόξαν δὲ λέγεσθαι τὸ πνεῦμα τὸ ἅγιον οὐκ
ἄν τις τῶν ἐπεσκεμμένων ἀντείποι πρὸς αὐτὰς βλέπων τὰς τοῦ κυρίου φωνάς· Τὴν δόξαν
γάρ, φησίν, ἣν ἔδωκάς μοι, ἔδωκα αὐτοῖς. ἔδωκε γὰρ ὡς ἀληθῶς τοῖς μαθηταῖς τοιαύτην
δόξαν ὁ εἰπὼν πρὸς αὐτούς· Λάβετε πνεῦμα ἅγιον. ἔλαβε δὲ ταύτην τὴν δόξαν ἣν πάντοτε
εἶχε πρὸ τοῦ τὸν κόσμον εἶναι ὁ τὴν ἀνθρωπίνην φύσιν περιβαλόμενος, ἧς δοξασθείσης διὰ
τοῦ πνεύματος ἐπὶ πᾶν τὸ συγγενὲς ἡ τῆς δόξης τοῦ πνεύματος διάδοσις γίνεται ἀπὸ τῶν
μαθητῶν ἀρξαμένη. διὰ τοῦτό φησι· Τὴν δόξαν, ἣν ἔδωκάς μοι, ἔδωκα αὐτοῖς, ἵνα ὦσιν ἕν,
καθὼς ἡμεῖς ἕν ἐσμεν· ἐγὼ ἐν αὐτοῖς καὶ σὺ ἐν ἐμοί, ἵνα ὦσι τετελειωμένοι εἰς τὸ ἕν (Gregory
of Nyssa, *In Canticum canticorum*, GNO 6:467.2–17).

93. Piet Hein Hupsch analyzes the present passage with great depth in Hupsch, *Glory of the Spirit*, 243–51.

Persons are eternal and thus autonomous, but at the same time each one is Himself only through the other two. The continuation of the text of *Adversus Macedonianos*, cited at the beginning of this section,[94] clearly shows the dynamics of this conceptualization:

> Do you see the cyclical revolution of glory through the same actions? The Son is glorified by (ὑπό) the Spirit. The Father is glorified by (ὑπό) the Son. Again, the Son has glory from (παρά) the Father, and the only begotten becomes the glory of the Spirit. In what will the Father be glorified if not in the true glory of the only-begotten One? In what again will the Son be glorified if not in the grandeur of the Spirit? So, entering this circular movement, reason (ὁ λόγος) glorifies the Son through (διά) the Spirit, and the Father through (διά) the Son.[95]

To realize the theological progress made, one need only think of Origen's affirmation that the glory that the Father would give to the other two divine Persons would not be identical to that which He receives from them.[96] Here we see, instead, the intersection of two movements: that which goes from the Spirit, who is Glory itself, to the Son, and from the Son to the Father; and the opposite one, which goes from the Father to the Son, and thus from Him to the Holy Spirit (see fig. 10 below, reading it on the background of fig. 9).

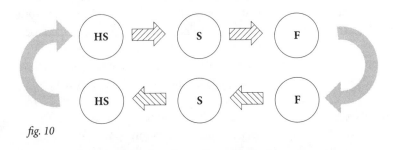

fig. 10

94. Gregory of Nyssa, *Adversus Macedonianos*, GNO 3.1:109.2–7. See p. 127.

95. ὁρᾷς τὴν ἐγκύκλιον τῆς δόξης διὰ τῶν ὁμοίων περιφοράν; δοξάζεται ὁ υἱὸς ὑπὸ τοῦ πνεύματος· δοξάζεται ὑπὸ τοῦ υἱοῦ ὁ πατήρ· πάλιν τὴν δόξαν ἔχει παρὰ τοῦ πατρὸς ὁ υἱὸς καὶ δόξα τοῦ πνεύματος ὁ μονογενὴς γίνεται· τίνι γὰρ ἐνδοξασθήσεται ὁ πατήρ, εἰ μὴ τῇ ἀληθινῇ τοῦ μονογενοῦς δόξῃ; ἐν τίνι δὲ πάλιν ὁ υἱὸς δοξασθήσεται, εἰ μὴ ἐν τῇ μεγαλω-σύνῃ τοῦ πνεύματος; οὕτω πάλιν καὶ ἀνακυκλούμενος ὁ λόγος τὸν υἱὸν μὲν δοξάζει διὰ τοῦ πνεύματος, διὰ δὲ τοῦ υἱοῦ τὸν πατέρα (Gregory of Nyssa, *Adversus Macedonianos*, GNO 3.1:109.7–15).

96. See pp. 20–21.

We may say that the Son is the glory of the Spirit, as the Spirit is the glory of the Son, and the glory of the Father is the very glory of the Son, which is the Spirit Himself. Each Person is Himself in the other, becoming the glory of the other while maintaining His proper personal characteristic: the Father as He who is source of glory and every power, the Son as Son precisely because He receives glory and union from the Father, and the Spirit as the Kingdom and Glory themselves. This is similar to what we have seen in *Adversus Macedonianos*, where the Father was defined as the source of power, the Son as the power of the Father, and the Spirit as the spirit of power.[97]

VI. LATREUTIC THEOLOGY

The text just cited on the "circulation" of glory within the Trinity allows us to move on to the theology of worship, which Gregory has in this way founded from a Trinitarian perspective. Here salvation, liturgy and prayer are convergent epistemological principles. The question is fundamental in the comparison with the Pneumatomachians from the beginning, as demonstrated by Basil's *De Spiritu Sancto*: what is at stake regarding the affirmation of the divinity of the Third Person is not something, but simply everything in Christianity. It is not just a question of the recognition of the almighty nature of a solitary god, itself an extrapolation of human images which, like the idols or powerful ones of the earth, requires submission and recognition of their supremacy. Instead, this is the One and triune God and the conception of worship must correspond to the revealed mystery. For this reason, both the human word and reason are called to insert themselves into this movement, beginning from the gift of the Spirit, in order to reach the Son and arrive to the Father. If one does not recognize and honor the three divine Persons, true worship is not offered. In this way the theological journey started by Origen with his Trinitarian definition of Christian prayer comes to completion. The human mind is called to raise itself from economy to immanence in a linear movement that immerses it in the very mystery of the eternal exchange of intra-Trinitarian glory, recognizing the depth of Being as the eternal dynamic of the relations of intra-Trinitarian origins.

This focus on the relations permits the foundation of a true Trinitarian worship that respects the apophatic limit that absolutely extends to divine nature but, because of the connection between economy and immanence, does not completely cover the personal relations, which can be partially known

97. Gregory of Nyssa, *Adversus Macedonianos*, GNO 3.1:100.1–2.

through their actions (i.e., *energeiai*). As it will be shown in the next chapter, an example of this is the affirmation that blasphemy against the Spirit propagates to the Son, and from Him to the Father, thus penetrating into the divine immanence.[98] Gregory is quite clear on this: revelation permits one not to know but to recognize the three eternal Persons in the divine gift and action. Economy leads to immanence in such a way that human thought can adore the triune God, but immanence itself is always protected by its inexhaustible mystery. Humanity can in no way offer worship that is worthy of God.

In fact, in the first reflection on adoration in Gregory's work,[99] after referring to Isaiah 40:15 where the nations are compared to a drop from a bucket, the Bishop of Nyssa ironically asks what addition to the divine glory could be brought by a drop.[100] The same thing is repeated with reference to Matthew 6:30, which compares the human being to grass: humanity cannot worthily honor the divine nature, as the light of a candle adds nothing to the rays of the sun.[101] At the end of the first partial conclusion on worship, Gregory sums up his position as follows: "the honor that competes in the very sense of divine nature is not realized by our freedom, but exists connaturally with it [i.e. divine nature]."[102] Thus, the Spirit, who is of the divine nature, "is worthy of honor and glory by His own nature" (τῇ ἑαυτοῦ φύσει τίμιον, ἔνδοξον).[103] A second partial conclusion of the treatise develops the same concept, not only from nature but also from the divine Persons and the theology of Glory, which represents the relational dynamic.[104] For this reason, he affirms that worship that neglects the Spirit would be a Judaic, not a Christian, form of worship, as it is not possible to think of the Father and the Son without the Spirit.

The text seeks to answer two questions: (1) what (τί) must one understand by adoration?[105] and, (2) what kind (τίνα τρόπον) of adoration should correspond to God?[106] In the light of what we have already seen, it is clear that "human nature has no gift worthy of God: in fact, our Creator does not need

---

98. See Gregory of Nyssa, *Adversus Macedonianos*, GNO 3.1:106.30–107.2.

99. Gregory of Nyssa, *Adversus Macedonianos*, GNO 3.1:95.27–97.20.

100. Gregory of Nyssa, *Adversus Macedonianos*, GNO 3.1:96.25–28.

101. Gregory of Nyssa, *Adversus Macedonianos*, GNO 3.1:97.1–7.

102. οὐκ ἐκ τῆς προαιρέσεως ἡμῶν πληρουμένη ἡ ἰδίως προσοῦσα τῇ θείᾳ φύσει τιμή, ἀλλὰ προσφυῶς συνυπάρχουσα (Gregory of Nyssa, *Adversus Macedonianos*, GNO 3.1:97.24–26).

103. Gregory of Nyssa, *Adversus Macedonianos*, GNO 3.1:97.28.

104. Gregory of Nyssa, *Adversus Macedonianos*, GNO 3.1:110.21–22.

105. Gregory of Nyssa, *Adversus Macedonianos*, GNO 3.1:110.30–31.

106. Gregory of Nyssa, *Adversus Macedonianos*, GNO 3.1:111.25–26.

our goods."[107] A worship that is worthy of the Creator must begin with the recognition of the gift that has been received and of divine transcendence. For this reason, as in theological language, it is necessary to purify liturgical expressions, which are taken from human customs, and radically alter in meaning when they are turned to the Trinity. The next part of the text for this reason develops an argument similar to that found in *Contra Eunomium II*, where it is said that God can be known only in the moment in which one recognizes Him as unknowable.[108] Analogously, God can only be truly adored when one understands that He is above any possible adoration and thus adopts an attitude of humility. Thus one reaches the response to the first question: "And this is adoration: the request of something desired, occurring in supplication and humility."[109] From the logic of possession one must move to that of gift (i.e., to Trinitarian logic). For this reason the response to the second question begins with the three Persons themselves. One must adore God as Trinity, accepting that only through thanks to His gift can the human being know the Father through the Son in the Spirit. This is so because it is not possible to think of the Father without at the same time thinking of the Son, or to receive the latter into the mind without receiving the Holy Spirit together with Him.[110]

Thus, in the openness to the mystery of the reciprocal correlation of the three divine Persons, authentic Christian worship becomes possible, as explained in the general conclusion of the treatise:

> So the true adorer (cf. John 4:23), after having stripped these corporeal and mundane notions from Him Who rules, is Lord, has authority and actualizes all good things in every creature, will thus honor Him, not as the Spirit deserves, but as much as he [the true adorer] can, like that widow who in donating two simple coins to the sacred treasury (cf. Luke 21:1–4) is portrayed as a model of generosity, not because the material had anything that merited admiration, but because she had no more means. It will thus be concluded that all the practices that humans have conceived of to show honor and glory are inferior to the magnificence of the Spirit since they add nothing to His Glory, as His Glory stays the same both if they honor Him and if they do not. Human nature offers only the gift of its free choice

---

107. θεοῦ μὲν ἄξιον δῶρον ἡ ἀνθρωπίνη φύσις ἔχει οὐδέν· τῶν γὰρ ἀγαθῶν ἡμῶν ὁ ποιητὴς ἡμῶν χρείαν οὐκ ἔχει (Gregory of Nyssa, *Adversus Macedonianos*, GNO 3.1:111.30–32).

108. Gregory of Nyssa, *Contra Eunomium II*, GNO 1:265.23–266.14.

109. τοῦτό ἐστιν ἡ προσκύνησις ἡ μετὰ ἱκεσίας καὶ ταπεινότητος τῶν καταθυμίων τινὸς αἴτησις γινομένη (Gregory of Nyssa, *Adversus Macedonianos*, GNO 3.1:112.22–23).

110. Gregory of Nyssa, *Adversus Macedonianos*, GNO 3.1:113.27–29.

(τὴν προαίρεσιν), for it is only by the will itself that it fulfills the favor it purposed. Besides its will, purposed initiative and motivation, it has nothing in its power.[111]

The text is of a great beauty: humankind is nothing, and the glory of God does not depend on humanity's will. Men and women can however offer their freedom to God. True worship consists precisely in this. We are before a new interpretation of the relationship of the Spirit and those who are worthy of Him. The theme comes from Origen,[112] and is taken up by Basil:[113] the Spirit bears gifts for those who are worthy of sanctification. In *Adversus Macedonianos* this view is repeated, for example when Gregory speaks of the sanctification that flows from the Father and, through the Son, is brought to completion by the Spirit in those who are worthy (τοῖς ἀξιουμένοις),[114] or when Gregory affirms that the Third Person is with "all of those who are worthy" (μετὰ πάντων ὂν τῶν ἀξίων) without ever separating Himself from the Holy Trinity.[115] The conclusion of the treatise however shows, through the example of the widow's mite, that this being worthy consists precisely in recognizing that we are unworthy, an act that is within reach of everyone. Paradoxically, the condition to receive the Spirit is to understand that humanity can do nothing to deserve receiving Him.[116]

---

111. οὐκοῦν ὁ ἀληθινὸς προσκυνητὴς ἀποστὰς τῆς σωματικῆς ταύτης καὶ χαμαιζήλου ταπεινότητος τῶν νοημάτων τὸ ἄρχον καὶ τὸ κυριεῦον καὶ τὸ ἐξουσιάζον καὶ τὸ πάντα τὰ ἀγαθὰ ἐνεργοῦν ἐν πάσῃ τῇ κτίσει οὕτω τιμήσει οὐχ ὡς ἐκείνῳ ἄξιον, ἀλλ᾽ ὅσον αὐτὸς δυνατός ἐστι φέρειν κατὰ τὴν χήραν ἐκείνην, ἢ δύο λεπτοὺς ὀβολοὺς δωροφοροῦσα τοῖς ἱεροῖς θησαυροῖς ἀπεδείχθη τῆς φιλοτιμίας, οὐχ ὅτι ἄξιον τι θαύματος εἶχεν ἡ ὕλη, ἀλλ᾽ ὅτι πλέον οὐκ ἐχώρει ἡ δύναμις. οὕτω τοίνυν λογιεῖται ὄντως ἔχειν, ὅτι πάντα τὰ παρὰ ἀνθρώπων ὅσα εἰς τιμὴν καὶ δόξαν ἐπινενόηται κατώτερά ἐστι τῆς μεγαλοπρεπείας τοῦ πνεύματος οὐδεμίαν προσθήκην τῆς δόξης ποιούμενα. ἡ μὲν γὰρ ὡσαύτως ἔχει καὶ τιμώντων καὶ μή· ἡ δὲ ἀνθρωπίνη φύσις μόνην δωροφορεῖ τὴν προαίρεσιν, αὐτῷ τῷ θελῆσαι μόνον πληροῦσα ἣν προέθετο χάριν· πλέον δ᾽ ἔτι τοῦ θελήματος καὶ τῆς κατὰ πρόθεσιν ὁρμῆς καὶ κινήσεως ἔχει ἐν τῇ δυνάμει οὐδέν (Gregory of Nyssa, *Adversus Macedonianos*, GNO 3.1:114.5–21).

112. For example, while affirming that in the Trinity one cannot speak of "more or less," the Alexandrian states that the Word with His Spirit sanctifies the realities that are worthy of it (*quae digna sunt*) taking from the source of the Father: see Origen, *De principiis*, 1.3.8 (GCS 22:60).

113. E.g., Basil, *Adversus Eunomium III*, 4.27–32 (SC 305:158–60) and the end of *De Spiritu Sancto*, 30.79.27 (SC 17bis:530).

114. Gregory of Nyssa, *Adversus Macedonianos*, GNO 3.1:106.6–8.

115. Gregory of Nyssa, *Adversus Macedonianos*, GNO 3.1:108.27.

116. It seems that the observation of Wolf-Dieter Hauschild, that Gregory of Nyssa would have had a more rigorous position than Basil regarding the spiritual dimension, even in reference to the Messalians and Simeon of Mesopotamia, with elements reminiscent of the

Thus, the first condition for true adoration is the recognition of the absolute transcendence and incomprehensibility of the divine nature:

> But just as the divine and blessed power is inaccessible, the nature itself remains invisible to rational calculation, for it dismisses vain preoccupation with thinking, the power of reason, excitement of the heart, emotional stimulation and all behaviors that are much further beneath it than our bodies are distant from the stars.[117]

Humankind then, perceiving the infinite sublimity of God, will grasp the disproportion and be humble. Thus the perception of the impossibility to worthily adore the Trinity does not lead to renunciation, but to a complete dedication. This is a dynamic analogous to the *logophasis*, presented by Martin Laird in his commentary on *In Canticum canticorum* in order to demonstrate that the meeting of the bride with the spouse is achieved in the apophatic dimension of union, but is transfigured into an overflowing of words of praise.[118] For this reason Gregory, in moving from the perception of the impossibility of praise worthy of the divine nature to the salvation communicated by the three divine Persons, concludes:

> Since he [the true adorer] is so disposed, he will dedicate himself entirely to the service of his superior nature. He will not honor this nature in some ways and refrain from others, but everything in his power that seems to be greater and superior he will dedicate to the God over all, continuously conveying honor, glory, and all the adoration he can to Him who has the authority to save. And this is the Father, Son and Holy Spirit that save.[119]

Syriac environment, can be understood in this sense as well. See W. D. Hauschild, *Gottes Geist und der Mensch: Studien zur frühchristlichen Pneumatologie* (Munich: Chr. Kaiser, 1972), 287–90.

117. αὐτὴ δὲ ἐκείνη καθώς ἐστι ἡ θεία τε καὶ μακαρία δύναμις ἄβατος καὶ ἀθέατος λογισμοῖς μένει καὶ διανοίας πολυπραγμοσύνην καὶ λόγου δύναμιν καὶ καρδίας κίνησιν καὶ ἐνθυμήσεως ὁρμήν, πάντα κάτω ἑαυτῆς ἀφιεῖσα πολὺ μᾶλλον ἢ ὅσον τὰ σώματα ἡμῖν ἀπολιμπάνεται τῆς τῶν ἀστέρων ἁφῆς (Gregory of Nyssa, *Adversus Macedonianos*, GNO 3.1:114.31–115.4).

118. See M. Laird, "Apophasis and Logophasis in Gregory of Nyssa's *Commentarius in Canticum Canticorum*," *Studia Patristica* 37 (2001): 126–32.

119. οὕτω δὲ διακείμενος ὅλον ἑαυτὸν ἀναθήσει τῇ θεραπείᾳ τῆς κρείττονος φύσεως, οὐ τὸ μέν τι ποιῶν τῶν εἰς τιμὴν συντεινόντων, τοῦ δὲ ἀπεχόμενος, ἀλλὰ πᾶν ὅτιπερ ἂν ἐν τῇ καθ᾽ ἑαυτὸν δυνάμει μεῖζον καὶ ὑπερέχον εἶναι φανῇ, τοῦτο ἀναθήσει τῷ ἐπὶ πάντων θεῷ, τιμὴν καὶ δόξαν καὶ προσκύνησιν τὴν ὑπὸ τῆς δυνάμεως χωρουμένην διηνεκῶς ἀναπέμπων τῷ ἔχοντι τοῦ σῴζειν τὴν ἐξουσίαν· σῴζει δὲ ὁ πατὴρ καὶ ὁ υἱὸς καὶ τὸ πνεῦμα τὸ ἅγιον (Gregory of Nyssa, *Adversus Macedonianos*, GNO 3.1:115.14–22).

Nothing less than everything can be enough for God. The scope of theology itself, and thus the scope of the treatise *Adversus Macedonianos*, is that of bringing humanity to perceive this infinite distance that separates them from God, in order to have human beings discover the gift of salvation communicated from the Father, from the Son, and from the Holy Spirit. Recognition of the Spirit as Creator and adoration of Him is then a condition to perceive the infinite transcendence of this God, whose nature remains always absolutely above humankind, but who has willed to enter into relationship with human beings, calling them to partake in the mystery of the eternal glorious dynamism of the intra-Trinitarian relations.

Theology thus reaches its fullness in accomplishing this latreutic function, which places humanity in relation with the one and triune God, leading them to recognize their unworthiness and the infinite depth of the mystery. The purpose of theology, for Gregory, is praise and worship, which occur in the humble renunciation of every pretension of conceptual control before the divine nature in order to discover that the true depth of Being is relation of Persons. True knowledge is achieved not in the possession of concepts that express the nature, but in discovering the unknowability of God in order to open to relationship with the Trinity. This is a personal knowledge that is born as a relation with Him Who is in Himself relations of origin. As an example of Gregory's concept of the role of theology, one could perhaps propose the icon: whoever reveres before the icon recognizes that the divine nature remains infinitely beyond any image, but at the same time it is through the image that one can enter into relation with the mystery itself as personal mystery. It can then be interesting to reread the conclusion of the treatise in light of the affirmation that the cross is *theologos*, insofar as through the form of its four arms it proclaims the absolute power of God.[120]

VII. Conclusion: The Relation of the Processions

The analysis proposed in this chapter for *Adversus Macedonianos* has attempted to manifest its value from a historical and systematic perspective. Hopefully, we have shown its originality with respect to the Trinitarian theology of Origen, Athanasius, and Basil.

The logical development of the treatise, presented on the backdrop of the internal development of Gregory of Nyssa's thought, begins with the recognition that the Spirit is Creator in the fullest sense with the Father and the Son,

---

120. Gregory of Nyssa, *De tridui spatio*, GNO 9:303.2–12.

seen at the end of chapter 2. This surpasses the scheme of Athanasius, who did not perfectly distinguish the two processions, reading both of them in the optic of image.[121] At the same time, Gregory goes beyond Origen and Basil, who both distinguished the processions by limiting the action of the Spirit in respect of the Father and the Son.[122]

This step however required a deepening of the immanent distinction of the two processions and the individuation of the personal property of the Third Person. These elements are, in fact, theologically inseparable because they are mutually connected. Therefore, Gregory uses the image of fire and heat, showing how the Spirit proceeds from the Father through the Son. In this linear scheme Gregory follows Athanasius, but he also overcomes him, breaking the symmetry of the image and highlighting the role of the Son in the procession of the Spirit. In this manner this latter procession is clearly distinguished from generation.

To do this, Gregory introduced a symmetrical scheme in his conception of the Trinity, which reciprocally manifests the role of the Spirit in the procession of the Son: from the image of fire, one moves to that of the Kingdom, symbolized by liturgical anointing. The Second Person is King as the First is, because He receives this Kingship from Him. The Spirit thus becomes the bond between the Father and the Son, revealing himself as foundation of their relation. This step would have been impossible without the new relation-ontology developed by Gregory, since the third Person is placed in a position that, in fact, identifies Him with the hypostatic relation of the first two divine Persons. From the first *Logos*-theology of the apologists, through Athanasius's *Physis*-theology the Bishop of Nyssa develops a *Schesis*-theology, where its relationality presents the previous forms of theologies as inseparable from the result thus achieved.

Finally, the image of glory allows us to summarize the two preceding schemes in a unique representation, showing correlation and reciprocal immanence of the divine Persons. The symmetrical scheme is in fact not opposed to the linear, but instead reveals a further aspect, as the Spirit is bond while proceeding through the Son. The divinity of the Third Person is "protected" before the Macedonian criticism, inserting Him "between" the First and Second Person through the definition of His procession in relative terms with respect to generation. In this way, the symmetrical scheme corrects the linear one and overcomes the tensions caused by it and stressed by the Pneumatomachians,

121. See pp. 56–57.
122. See pp. 42 and 72.

somehow recovering a positive function that was present in the more primitive triangular scheme.

This is visualized by the circulation of glory, which presents the three divine Persons in their mutual being each One Himself through the other two. Gregory's reasoning culminates in the affirmation that this glory, which is absolutely transcendent and independent from the will of man, is constituted by a relational dynamism, from which the Spirit cannot be excluded. Thus, true worship consists in the recognition of the absolute impossibility of the human being to offer worship worthy of the triune God, Who is glorious by nature. This very movement to humility however permits, in an analogous manner to what occurs with cognitive apophaticism, to open oneself to true adoration, understood as supplication and dedication of one's entire self in the praise directed to the three Persons, from whom salvation is communicated to the human being. Thus the response to Pneumatomachians can also be read as a dispute about theological epistemology, which overcomes every rationalist and literalist temptation, stating that there is no true worship without the Holy Spirit.

The argument can be read as an illustration of the role of theology according to Gregory: the essential purpose of theology is worship and fills a latreutic role analogous to that of the icon, insofar as it keeps men and women from foolishly thinking that they comprehend the divine nature. Only in this way can the human being get, through word and thought, to the relation with the Father, the Son, and the Holy Spirit.

The Surprise: A Greek Filioque?

I. Introduction: The Role of the Son

In light of the previous chapter, one can understand why several scholars of different Christian denominations have recognized in the Trinitarian thought of Gregory of Nyssa the presence of a doctrine that points to an active role of the Son in the procession of the Spirit.[1] Claudio Moreschini wrote on the subject: "In our opinion it could be a balanced hypothesis to think that the *Filioque*, even if not explicitly affirmed by the Cappadocians (there is no doubt about this), could appear to later readers—but in any case of Greek environment—as a consequence, more or less justified, of their pneumatology."[2] In fact, any approach that considers the relation between the first two divine Persons complete in itself without regard to the Third, as well as any attribution to the Son of even a minimal causal role in the procession of the Spirit, should be radically excluded as contrary to the Cappadocian theology.

But, if one avoids such defining traits of what in medieval times would become the Filioquist approach, Gregory's theology highlights without hesitation a role of the Second Person in the procession of the Third. And this role is not causal, but purely relational. In a certain sense, one could say that this is

1. See B. Studer, "La foi en l'Esprit Saint dans l'Église Ancienne," in *Mysterium Caritatis: Studien zur Exegese und zur Trinitätslehre in der Alten Kirche* (Rome: Pontificio Ateneo Sant'Anselmo, 1999), 450; J. D. Zizioulas, "The Teaching in the 2nd Ecumenical Council on the Holy Spirit in Historical and Ecumenical Perspective," in *Acts of the International Theological Congress of Pneumatology* (Rome: Libreria Editrice Vaticana, 1983), 1:44; G. Maspero, *Trinity and Man: Gregory of Nyssa's Ad Ablabium* (Leiden: Brill, 2007), 183–84.

2. C. Moreschini, "Osservazioni sulla pneumatologia dei Cappadoci: Preannunci del Filioque?" in *Il Filioque: A mille anni dal suo inserimento nel credo a Roma (1014–2014)*, ed. M. Gagliardi (Vatican City: LEV, 2015), 146.

already implied by the Nicene reading of the *Father* and the *Son* as correlative names, since the name *Father* does not indicate the substance but the relation to the Son Himself,[3] so that in the purest immanence the active role of the Son in the second procession would be implied by the very name of the divine Persons. In fact, according to the Gospel teachings, it is impossible to think of the procession of the Spirit from the Father without reference also to the Son, who founds the very identity of the Father in His mutual relationship with Him. So the role of the Second Person in the procession of the Third is active, but not causal, because it is relational.

This becomes even more relevant if read in the light of the previous chapters. The dogmatic force of Gregory's theology can be fully grasped by rereading what has just been seen from the perspective of the triangular scheme, the object of the Pneumatomachian criticism that approached the Son and the Spirit as if two sons or two brothers, and from the perspective of the linear scheme, criticized on the basis of the identification of the Father with the "grandfather" of the divine Third Person. Here the objections are radically overcome and the two schemes find a synthesis, as the Spirit is presented as the Royal Power and hypostatic Glory that the Father and the Son eternally give each other. The reciprocity of the relation between the Father and the Son, on the one hand, and the Spirit, on the other, which seems to be the focus of Epiphanius's approach, is combined with the more linear conception of the relation between the three divine Persons, in such a way that the giving glory of one Person to the other is always presented in reciprocity. Thus, if the Father gives glory to the Son and the Son to the Father, the Spirit also receives glory from them. This reciprocity of the relation between the first two divine Persons, that is, an ontological translation of their numerical identity of nature from the perspective of correlativity of their personal identities as eternal Father and Son, is extended to the relation between the divine Second and Third Persons through a rereading of the very personal characteristic of the Spirit as correlative to the Father and the Son.

A common strategy in the response to the Pneumatomachian objections is to affirm the divinity of the Third Person by linking it back to the relation between the first two, as also found in Epiphanius and in the Pseudo-Athanasian *Dialogi contra Macedonianos*.

At the same time, the Pneumatomachian positions, read in the light of the identification of the Spirit's personal *proprium* and the difference of His

---

3. ἡ τοῦ πατρὸς κλῆσις οὐκ οὐσίας ἐστὶ παραστατική, ἀλλὰ τὴν πρὸς τὸν υἱὸν σχέσιν ἀποσημαίνει (Gregory of Nyssa, *Refutatio confessionis Eunomii*, 16.4–17.2 [GNO 2:319.1–7]).

procession from the generation of the Son, make visible a line of development that, from Arianism through the Eusebians, culminates with the Pneumatomachians themselves. The correlativity of the divine Persons and, therefore, the connection of the two processions suggest that even the recognition of the divinity of the Second Person was insufficient. From this point of view the affirmation of an active (but not causal) function of the Son in the procession of the Spirit seems consistent, since it aims at strengthening the substantial identity of the Father and the Son.

This discussion recalls what in later, and in some cases dialectical, developments of Trinitarian theology has taken on the name of the *Filioque* question. In the following pages we will try to show how the Greek Trinitarian theology of the second half of the fourth century, with the development of the new ontology of the relation, led to an understanding of the Spirit as a bond between the Father and the Son, without in any way diminishing the monarchy. And this seems to belong to the heart of Cappadocian thought that we will explore in the present chapter as the systematic approach developed thus far will be applied to the analysis of specific texts that have been the object of polemical confrontation in the discussions on the *Filioque*.

II. The Blasphemy against the Holy Spirit

This work requires that, in the first place, our epistemological perspective for approaching these texts should be that which characterized the theological thought of the fourth century, in particular the Cappadocian one. From their very beginning, in fact, theological discussions on the Holy Spirit were linked to liturgy and worship, as in the dispute on doxology in Basil's *De Spiritu Sancto*. To this must also be added the moral perspective, to which the Gospel admonition on blasphemy against the divine Third Person refers. As we saw in the previous chapter, the Lukan variant in Gregory of Nyssa's *De oratione dominica* has shown this deep connection with the dogmatic discourse.[4] If we want to escape the risk of anachronism, we should keep this in mind to avoid any reading shaped by the modern dichotomy between theological theory and Christian praxis, as explained in the introduction.

Without adopting this epistemological perspective, it would be impossible to understand why the Bishop of Nyssa devoted an entire homily to responding to the Pneumatomachians in his commentary on the *Our Father*, where he connects the Third Person to the Kingdom of God. In fact, if this Kingdom is

4. See pp. 122–23.

the triune God's Life in Christians, the equivalence between the Kingdom and the Spirit, invoked in the epiclesis to come and to purify the assembly, suggests a rereading of blasphemy against the Holy Spirit as the action of someone who does not live a truly Christian life despite calling him- or herself a Christian and so placing God as the cause of the evils in his or her own existence. In fact, if it is He who communicates the Trinitarian life to the human being, clothing him or her with the virtues of Christ in such a way as to make him or her able to enter the sanctuary that is the Trinity itself, then the denial of His divinity implies blasphemy in that it excludes in the believer what could be an authentically Christian life.

The pneumatological passage is essential, therefore, so that the prayer can become really Christian (i.e., Trinitarian), as Origen pointed out, in that the reference to the Son in the *Pater Noster* was taken for granted because the Lord's Prayer represented a direct command of the incarnate *Logos* concerning the relationship of Christians with the Father.

It seems very interesting to note that the part devoted to the variant, seen in the previous chapter, begins with "perhaps" (τάχα) as if to indicate a personal suggestion. In Origen too, at times, this expression indicates the passage to a dogmatic treatment of some controversial point.[5] We note here the work's first citation of the Pneumatomachians, called explicitly by their name *Pneumatomachoi* in the conclusion,[6] but indicated here with the elegant and refined expression "those who boldly speak against the Holy Spirit" (οἱ θρασυστομοῦντες κατὰ τοῦ πνεύματος τοῦ ἁγίου).[7] The verb is typical of the tragedians[8] and occurs four times in Gregory of Nyssa, always in a dogmatic context,[9] in particular in relation to those who speak insolently against the divine Third Person in his *De deitate Filii et Spiritus Sancti*,[10] written probably in 383, and always in a liturgical context. This could indicate a constant strategy that Gregory repeats in his struggle with the Pneumatomachians. In fact, also in the last work cited, the dogmatic part addressed against them is preceded by a text

5. Origen, *Commentarii in evangelium Joannis*, 2.10.75.1–76.1 (SC 120:254–56). See p. 36. For the technical value of the term, cf. M. Girardi, *Basilio di Cesarea interprete della Scrittura: Lessico, principi ermeneutici, prassi* (Bari: Edipuglia, 1998), 31–32.

6. Gregory of Nyssa, *De oratione dominica*, SC 596:426.6.

7. Gregory of Nyssa, *De oratione dominica*, SC 596:414.3–4.

8. E.g., Euripides, *Hecuba*, 1286; Sophocles, *Philoctetes*, 380; and Aeschylus, *Supplices*, 203. See also Libanius, *Epistulae*, 81.1.

9. Gregory of Nyssa, *Contra Eunomium I*, 76.3 (GNO 1:48.23), and *Contra Eunomium III*, 1.106.3 (GNO 2:39.17).

10. Gregory of Nyssa, *De deitate Filii et Spiritus Sancti*, GNO 10.2:142.2.

with a midrashic flavor devoted to Abraham,[11] just as Moses is the starting point of the third homily in the commentary on the Lord's Prayer.[12]

It could be interesting to point out that, apart from the title of *Adversus Macedonianos*, the term *Pneumatomachoi* appears six times in Gregory's works. Beyond its occurrence in the already cited conclusion of the *De oratione dominica*, there is one example in the *De Spiritu Sancto sive in Pentecosten*,[13] another in the *De deitate adversus Euagrium*,[14] and three good examples in *In sanctum Stephanum I*,[15] which was delivered probably on December 26, 386 where the context is still of the need, in the face of a Judaising approach, to justify the Trinitarian dimension and divinization by means of a defense of the divinity of the Third Person. This latter work is particularly important because the discussion on the Holy Spirit is connected with the possibility of seeing the Glory of God, precisely that Glory which dwelt in the Holy of Holies and which is now being interpreted in a Trinitarian way, a fundamental topic in *De oratione dominica*. Also, the section in *De deitate adversus Euagrium* where the reference to the Pneumatomachians appears starts out from the figure of the great Moses who erects the tent of the sanctuary (σκηνήν) through the inspiration of the Spirit.[16] The conclusion is that the divine nature is one, and the Holy Spirit is Divine by nature in such a way that what is one in nature (τὸ συνημμένον τῇ φύσει) cannot be divided.[17]

After the appearance of the term *pneumatomachoi* in both the *Epistulae ad Serapionem*, Athanasius's designation of the Tropici of Egyptian origin,[18] and Basil's *De Spiritu Sancto*, both examples coming from the context which led to the Council of Constantinople,[19] it is interesting to see how Epiphanius describes them as "those who blaspheme (βλασφημοῦντες) the Holy Spirit of God."[20]

---

11. On Gregory's authorship of the part devoted to Abraham, found also in the works of Ephraim, see J. Bernardi, *La prédication des Pères Cappadociens: Le prédicateur et son auditoire* (Paris: Presses Universitaires de France, 1968), 327–30, and S. Haidacher, "Rede über Abraham und Isaak bei Ephraem Syrus und Pseudo-Chrysostomus—ein Exzerpt aus Gregor von Nyssa," *Zeitschrift für katholische Theologie* 29 (1905): 764–66.

12. Gregory of Nyssa, *De oratione dominica*, SC 596:386–88.

13. Gregory of Nyssa, *De spiritu sancto sive in Pentecosten*, GNO 10.2:291.4.

14. Gregory of Nyssa, *De deitate adversus Euagrium*, GNO 9:333.11.

15. Gregory of Nyssa, *In sanctum Stephanum I*, GNO 10.1:89.7, 16; 91.2.

16. Gregory of Nyssa, *De deitate adversus Euagrium*, GNO 9:333.1–3.

17. Gregory of Nyssa, *De deitate adversus Euagrium*, GNO 9:334.4.

18. Athanasius, *Epistulae ad Serapionem*, 1.32.2 (AW 1.4:531) and 3.1.3 (AW 1.4:568).

19. Basil, *De Spiritu Sancto*, 11.27.19 and 21.52.7 (SC 17bis:340 and 432). See also *Epistulae*, 140.2 and 263.3.

20. Epiphanius, *Ancoratus*, 13.7.2; see also *Panarion*, 1.161.6.

So blasphemy against the Third Person is a recurrent theme in the battle with the Pneumatomachians and one that has an extremely interesting history.[21] Obviously, the statement about the impossibility of forgiveness for the sin against the Spirit in Matthew 12:31–32 plays a fundamental role; it was used already by Origen to defend the hypostatic identity of the Third Person in relation to the Second.[22] Significantly, however, it is Athanasius who develops the exegetical question of the blasphemy against the Spirit in the ambit of his debates both with the Arians, since to deny the divinity of Christ means blaspheming the Spirit,[23] and with the Pneumatomachians.[24] Here, the blasphemy consists precisely in placing the Third Person in the order of creatures,[25] so that when one blasphemes against the Spirit, one blasphemes against the whole triune God since the blasphemy passes from the Third Person to the Second and from the Second to the Father. One sees clearly the progress achieved compared with Origen, as Athanasius writes:[26]

In fact, since it is not proper to the human nature of itself to cast out devils, except by the power of the Spirit, [Christ], as man, said: "but if I cast out demons in the Spirit" (Matt 12:28); He undoubtedly intended that the blasphemy against the Holy Spirit is greater than that against His humanity and, so He said "He who speaks against the Son of Man will receive forgiveness" (Luke 12:10), like those [that is, the Pharisees] who claimed "is not this the son of the carpenter?" (Matt 13:55). But those who blaspheme against the Holy Spirit and attribute the works of the *Logos* to the devil will not be able to escape punishment.[27]

21. The Cappadocians themselves were accused of blasphemy by the Pneumatomachians; for example cf. Gregory of Nyssa, *Ad Eustathium, De sancta trinitate*, GNO 3.1:5.3–4, and Basil, *De Spiritu Sancto*, 16.38 (SC 17bis:374–84).

22. It is interesting to note how Origen tackles the exegetical problem created by the superiority of the Son to the Spirit compared with the Gospel statement that the sin against the latter will not be forgiven whereas the sin against the former will. Origen explains that the one who sins against the Paraclete is someone who not only shares in the *Logos* like every rational being, but someone who already participates in the life of the Spirit himself. See Origen, *Commentarii in evangelium Joannis*, 2.10.76 (SC 120:258) and 32.11.123–125 (SC 385:240–42).

23. Athanasius, *Oratio III contra Arianos*, 42.1–3 (AW 1.3:353).

24. Athanasius, *Epistulae ad Serapionem*, 1.3.1 and 9.6 (AW 1.4:454 and 474).

25. Athanasius, *Epistula ad Jovianum*, 1.1.6 (AW 2.8:353) and *Epistula ad Afros episcopos*, 11.1 (AW 2.8:338).

26. See the text at p. 20.

27. ὡς γὰρ τῆς ἀνθρώπων φύσεως οὐκ οὔσης ἱκανῆς ἀφ᾽ ἑαυτῆς ἐκβάλλειν τοὺς δαί-

At the same time, the connection of the christological and pneumatological questions is apparent, because only the distinction of natures in the incarnate Word can explain the gravity of the blasphemy against the Third Person compared with that against Christ. As was to become typical, beginning with Athanasius himself, the defense of the Trinitarian dimension is rooted in the soteriological argument: "Let them cease to blaspheme and let them not separate the Trinity so as not to be separated from Life."[28] This is an approach that was to be represented in the connection between the moral and the dogmatic dimensions in Gregory of Nyssa's *De oratione dominica*, even if the perspective was to be still more radical because it is not only a question of a blasphemy that attributes the works of God to the devil, as in Athanasius,[29] but even of one that attributes the works of the devil to God.

Highly important for the interpretation of Gregory is the contribution of Basil, who reads the blasphemy against the Holy Spirit both in a moral sense with reference to the life lived in opposition to charity,[30] and in a dogmatic sense against the Arians[31] and the Pneumatomachians.

The latter are refuted especially in the *De Spiritu Sancto* where Basil introduces the theme of glory, linking John 17:4 with 16:14, 12:18 and, precisely, Matthew 12:31, which represents the denial of *homotomia* in terms of blasphemy against the Third Person.[32] The passage is particularly interesting on the background of the last chapter because it affirms that "the Spirit is glorified by the communion of the Father and the Son" (δοξάζεται τὸ Πνεῦμα διὰ τῆς πρὸς Πατέρα καὶ Υἱὸν κοινωνίας), thus linking the divinity of the Third Person to the relation between the two divine Persons in a hint of what was later to become the most solid and widespread strategy in the struggle against the Pneumatomachians. In this way, the relationship of the Spirit with the communion of the Father and the Son is the foundation of the communion in glory (κοινωνία τῆς δόξης) with them, that is, of the *homotimia* itself.[33]

μονας εἰ μὴ δυνάμει τοῦ πνεύματος, διὰ τοῦτο ὡς ἄνθρωπος ἔλεγεν "εἰ δὲ ἐγὼ ἐν πνεύματι ἐκβάλλω τὰ δαιμόνια" ἀμέλει καὶ τὴν εἰς τὸ πνεῦμα τὸ ἅγιον δυσφημίαν γινομένην μείζονα τῆς ἀνθρωπότητος σημαίνων ἔλεγεν "ὃς ἂν εἴπῃ λόγον εἰς τὸν υἱὸν τοῦ ἀνθρώπου, ἕξει ἄφεσιν," οἷοι ἦσαν οἱ λέγοντες "οὐχ οὗτός ἐστιν ὁ τοῦ τέκτονος υἱός" οἱ δὲ εἰς τὸ πνεῦμα τὸ ἅγιον βλασφημοῦντες καὶ τὰ τοῦ λόγου ἔργα τῷ διαβόλῳ ἐπιγράφοντες ἄφυκτον τιμωρίαν ἕξουσι (Athanasius, *Oratio I contra Arianos*, 50.2–3 (AW 1.2:160).

28. κἂν τῶν δυσφημιῶν παυέσθωσαν, καὶ μὴ διαιρείτωσαν τὴν Τριάδα, ἵνα μὴ διαιρεθῶσιν ἀπὸ τῆς ζωῆς· (Athanasius, *Epistulae ad Serapionem*, 1.33.6 (AW 1.4:534).

29. See also Athanasius, *Epistulae ad Serapionem*, 4.15.5 (AW 1.4:588).

30. Cf. Basil, *Regulae morales*, 35 (PG 31:756).

31. Cf. Basil, *Adversus Eunomium II*, 33 (SC 305:136).

32. Basil, *De Spiritu Sancto*, 18.46 (SC 17bis:196–97).

33. Basil, *De Spiritu Sancto*, 28.70 (SC 17bis:243–44).

With his usual expressive genius and his capacity for synthesis, Gregory of Nazianzus opposed blasphemy to the theological act in the proper sense, extended not only to the Son but also to the Spirit: "it is blasphemy and not theology to deprive [the Spirit] of His divinity" (βλασφημία δὲ, οὐχ ἡ θεολογία, τὸ δὲ ἀλλοτριοῦν τῆς θεότητος).[34] His thought highlights the role of the procession and the need to identify the specific nature of the second in relation to the first:

> Do not fear the procession (πρόοδον): in fact, God has no need either to emit (προβάλλειν), or to emit in an identical way, because He is rich in every aspect. Rather, fear the decay and the threat addressed not to those who profess the theology but to those who blaspheme the Holy Spirit.[35]

Here, the freedom of the immanent processions is affirmed by contrast with the Neoplatonic emanation.[36] Thus, what is common to the Three Persons is identified in their not being created (τὸ μὴ γεγονέναι) and, so, being divine; the Son and the Spirit share the being from the Father (τὸ ἐκ τοῦ Πατρός); and, finally, the distinctive personal characteristics of each Person are *agennēsia* for the First, *gennēsis* for the Second, and *ekpempsis* for the Third.[37] For this second procession, always immanent but distinct from generation, Gregory of Nazianzus was to coin the name of *ekporeusis*.[38]

From here, we can deduce that the blasphemy against the Holy Spirit stimulated theological research in the sense of the deepening of the distinction between the two immanent processions. In fact, the Pneumatomachian critics could not accept the symmetrical model introduced by Athanasius in which the relationship between the Son and the Father was structurally identical to that between the Spirit and the Son, even if the two processions were understood as numerically distinct.[39] In fact, the second could not be a generation, a claim which would have led to the absurdity of two "sons," one of which Scripture called "Only Begotten," or else of the Father as "grandfather" of the third Person.

34. Gregory of Nazianzus, *Oratio*, 34.11 (SC 318:218).

35. Μὴ φοβηθῇς τὴν πρόοδον· οὐ γὰρ ἀνάγκην ἔχει Θεὸς, ἢ μὴ προβάλλειν, ἢ προβάλλειν ὁμοίως, ὁ πάντα πλούσιος· φοβήθητι δὲ τὴν ἀλλοτρίωσιν, καὶ τὴν κειμένην ἀπειλήν, οὐ τοῖς θεολογοῦσιν, ἀλλὰ τοῖς βλασφημοῦσι τὸ Πνεῦμα τὸ ἅγιον (Gregory of Nazianzus, *Oratio*, 25.17 [SC 284:198]).

36. Freedom is the fundamental element that distinguishes the Neoplatonic and the Christian approach to procession, as the reference of Gregory of Nazianzus to Plotinus (*Enneades*, 5.1.6) in *Oratio* 29 shows. See Gregory of Nazianzus, *Oratio*, 29.2.20 (SC 250:180).

37. Gregory of Nazianzus, *Oratio*, 25.16 (SC 284:198).

38. Gregory of Nazianzus, *Oratio*, 31.8 (SC 250:290.17–18).

39. Athanasius, *Epistulae ad Serapionem*, 2.10.2 (AW 1.4:552).

This is the context of Gregory of Nyssa's pneumatology, which is focused on blasphemy in the *Adversus Macedonianos*, where he takes up the claim that the blasphemy itself passes from the Spirit to the Son, and from the latter to the Father, but seeks to escape from the Athanasian scheme that considered the Third Person the image of the Second, just as the Second was image of the First.[40] The definition of the *proprium* of the second procession in relational terms of Glory and Kingship, as the Spirit is the bond (*syndetikon*) of the Father and the Son, accomplished this task. For the solution the connection between divine economy and immanence is fundamental, since the dogmatic definition cannot be disconnected by the moral and liturgical dimensions. And this connection is the core of Gregory of Nyssa's commentary on the Lord's Prayer, where one of the most controversial texts of the patristic dossier on the *Filioque* can be found.

III. The Lord's Prayer

Gregory of Nyssa's *De oratione dominica* is a work composed of five homilies probably written after the Council of Constantinople during the maturity of the author's production.[41] His approach is different with respect to the first commentaries from the North African area, especially those by Tertullian and Cyprian at Carthage and those from the Syriac-speaking world,[42] but their distance from Origen is also pretty clear, as Anthony Meredith has remarked.[43] The key point is that the focus in Gregory's work shifts from baptism—the catechumens used to pray the Lord's Prayer coming out of the water having received the sacrament[44]—to a eucharistic liturgical context in the presence of a community that had already been baptized, as made possible by the end of persecution. According to the Didache, Christians recited three times a day the Lord's Prayer, which had assumed in Christian communities the role of the *Shema*, which was also recited three times each day in Jewish worship.[45]

40. Cf. Gregory of Nyssa, *Adversus Macedonianos*, GNO 3.1:106–7.

41. In the recently published SC 596, the editors propose the years after 385; see pp. 11–29.

42. On the patristic commentaries, see K. Froehlich, "The Lord's Prayer in Patristic Literature," in *A History of Prayer: The First to the Fifteenth Century*, ed. R. Hammerling (Leiden: Brill, 2008), 59–77.

43. See A. Meredith, "Origen and Gregory of Nyssa on the Lord's Prayer," *Heythrop Journal* 43 (2002): 344–56.

44. R. Hammerling, "The Lord's Prayer: A Cornerstone of Early Baptismal Education," in Hammerling, *A History of Prayer*, 167–82.

45. W. Rordorf, *Liturgie, foi et vie des premiers chrétiens: Études patristiques* (Paris: Beauchesne, 1986), 336. The reference is to Didache 8.3.

Precisely in the second half of the fourth century, and in particular in the last quarter, it seems that this prayer had already made its entrance into the eucharistic liturgy in the Greco-Syriac area and would extend itself later to the Latin sphere at the end of the fourth and the beginning of the fifth century.[46]

This information provided by the history of the liturgy supports a proposal to interpret the third homily in Gregory's commentary along the lines of a Trinitarian reading of the *Pater Noster* with an anti-Pneumatomachian objective.[47] But this implied the study of the unity of action—the real core of the Cappadocian thought—so as to show that the link with the liturgical and moral dimension was based on the correspondence between the action and being of the triune God. This was perfectly compatible with apophaticism because such a correspondence is relational.

This enables us to grasp the dogmatic *intentio* of the introduction of the Lukan variant into Gregory of Nyssa's commentary on the Lord's Prayer, as seen in the last chapter, and to follow the line of reasoning proposed by Gregory and others in his time to counter the Pneumatomachians' blasphemy. It is important to stress that the introduction of the variant was not an accident, but obeyed a clear strategy.

Gregory, in fact, employs the Lukan variant in a dogmatic way in two converging directions that follow the theological principle of the connection between nature and *energeia*: (1) firstly, he grasps the opportunity offered by the identification of the Kingdom and the Spirit to show that the divine Third Person cannot be identified with a creature precisely because it is the role of the latter to serve whereas to reign is radically opposed to this activity; (2) Gregory therefore passes to the second part of the variant to show that the Spirit purifies, that is, forgives sins like Christ, an activity proper only to God.

Thus, the nature of the Spirit cannot be linked with what is governed instead of with what governs (τὴν φύσιν τοῦ πνεύματος ἀντὶ τῆς βασιλευούσης τῇ βασιλευομένῃ συγκατατάσσοντες).[48] Given that governing and being subject are opposed, one cannot reckon (συναριθμοῦσιν) the Third Person with the nature which is governed.[49]

46. R. F. Taft, *A History of the Liturgy of St. John Chrysostom: The Precommunion Rites* (Rome: Orientalia Christiana, 2000), 136–37.

47. See G. Maspero, "The Trinitarian Reading of the Lord's Prayer: The Third Homily," in *Gregory of Nyssa: Homilies on the Our Father; An English Translation with Commentary and Supporting Studies*, ed. M. Cassin, H. Grelier-Deneux, and F. Vinel (Leiden: Brill, 2021), 326–54.

48. Gregory of Nyssa, *De oratione dominica*, SC 596:414.8–9.

49. Gregory of Nyssa, *De oratione dominica*, SC 596:415.1–2.

Thus, the Pneumatomachians show that they have not even learned to pray since they do not recognize the One who purifies what is impure through the power and activity (δύναμίς τε καὶ ἐνέργεια) of forgiving sins.[50] The strength of the argument is founded on Hebrews 1:3 where it is said that the Son of God is sitting at His right hand after having purified sins. But the Pneumatomachians recognized the divinity of the Second Person in such a way that their discourse here is severely challenged since the work of forgiveness belongs to both (ἐν ἑκατέρου τὸ ἔργον), that is, both the Son and the Spirit.[51] In fact, there is a metaphysical connection between power, act, and effect[52] in such a way that, if the result of the action is identical, that means that the power and the act are identical in their turn, that is, "the act and the power are one and the same" (ἡ ἐνέργεια μία, καὶ ἡ δύναμις πάντως ἡ αὐτή ἐστιν).[53] However, if the act and the power are identical in the case of the Son and the Spirit, this means that their nature is also the same because one is speaking of actions proper to their nature, as Michel René Barnes has rightly pointed out.[54] For example, a person can carry out the work of a mule, but this is not an action proper to his or her nature, unlike thinking and speaking. In fact, when we recognize such actions in somebody, we are obliged to deduce that we are dealing with a spiritual being, similar to what Moses did before the burning bush (Exod 3:14). Thus reigning and forgiving sins are acts exclusive to the divine nature, which is one.

The argument is identical to that developed in *De deitate Filii et Spiritus Sancti*. Here too, as we have seen, the Pneumatomachians are cited, and here too the treatment of the Third Person is preceded by an explicit reference to the Jewish tradition through the figure of Abraham. The position of those who speak insolently against the Spirit is described as "stupid blasphemy" (τῆς ἀνοήτου βλασφημίας).[55]

As in the *Ad Ablabium*, so too in the *De deitate Filii et Spiritus Sancti* the Aristotelian etymology of *theotēs* from *theaomai* is taken up to ascribe the name of God to the act of seeing,[56] rather than to His nature which, in itself, is

---

50. Gregory of Nyssa, *De oratione dominica*, SC 596:415.6–7.

51. Gregory of Nyssa, *De oratione dominica*, SC 596:416.12–13.

52. "Every effect, in fact, is an act of power": Πᾶσα γὰρ ἐνέργεια δυνάμεώς ἐστιν ἀποτέλεσμα (Gregory of Nyssa, *De oratione dominica*, SC 596:418.3).

53. Gregory of Nyssa, *De oratione dominica*, SC 596:418.2.

54. M. R. Barnes, *The Power of God:* Dunamis *in Gregory of Nyssa's Trinitarian Theology* (Washington, DC: CUA Press, 2001).

55. Gregory of Nyssa, *De deitate Filii et Spiritus Sancti*, GNO 10.2:142.10.

56. Gregory of Nyssa, *De deitate Filii et Spiritus Sancti*, GNO 10.2:142.19–20. See Gregory of Nyssa, *Ad Ablabium*, GNO 3.1:50.1–13.

ineffable and inexpressible (ἄφραστός τε καὶ ἀνεκφώνητος), in that it exceeds (ὑπερβαίνουσα) every human possibility of expression:[57]

> Therefore the name "divinity" does not indicate a nature but the power of seeing. And perhaps they [the Pneumatomachians] do not confess that the Holy Spirit sees? Or do they oppose this too? In fact, if He has seen, He certainly receives the name from this activity.[58]

In this work, the strength of the argument is augmented by the fact that, in the first part, Gregory argues about the divinity of the Son precisely from the starting point of His description as "Power of the Father" (cf. 1 Cor 1:24). If it is impossible to conceive the glory without the splendor, the hypostasis without an image, the sage without wisdom, and the ruler without power, so it is impossible to think of the Father without the Son (οὐκ ἄπαιδα Πατέρα).[59] In this sense, the personal identity of each divine Person is united in a relation to the others:[60] "Each of these [divine Persons] is known as in necessary conjunctions (συζυγίαις), without any being thought of individually alone but both united (συνημμένως) and one with the other."[61]

The comparison with the *De deitate Filii et Spiritus Sancti* can be dogmatically useful. It was delivered in June of 383 at Constantinople in the meeting ordered by Theodosius at which were present both Eunomius (for the Anomei) and Eleusius of Cyzicus (for the Pneumatomachians). According to Michel van Parys, the work is probably linked with the conclusion of Gregory's response to Eunomius, that is, to the *Refutatio*, the pneumatological part of which seems to have been left unfinished in haste.[62]

---

57. Gregory of Nyssa, *De deitate Filii et Spiritus Sancti*, GNO 10.2:15–17.

58. οὐκοῦν οὐχὶ φύσιν, ἀλλὰ τὴν θεατικὴν δύναμιν ἡ τῆς θεότητος προσηγορία παρίστησιν. ἆρ᾽ οὖν οὐχ ὁμολογοῦσι θεᾶσθαι τὸ πνεῦμα τὸ ἅγιον; ἢ καὶ περὶ τούτου ζυγομαχήσουσιν; εἰ μὲν γὰρ τεθέαται, τῇ ἐνεργείᾳ πάντως ἐπονομάζεται (Gregory of Nyssa, *De deitate Filii et Spiritus Sancti*, GNO 10.2:143.5–9).

59. Gregory of Nyssa, *De deitate Filii et Spiritus Sancti*, GNO 10.2:125.2–4.

60. The passage recalls Pseudo-Athanasius where his demonstration that the three divine Persons are not creatures culminates in formulating their distinction in their immanence, affirming that the Spirit is ἀγένητον but not ἀναίτιον, while the Son is, again, ἀγένητος but not ἀπάτωρ, whereas only the First Person is characterized by all three adjectives together. See Pseudo-Athanasius, *Dialogus I contra Macedonianos*, 20.25–36 (Cavalcanti, 104).

61. ὧν ἕκαστον καθάπερ ἐν συζυγίαις τισὶν ἀναγκαίαις οὐδὲν ἀφ᾽ ἑαυτοῦ καταμόνας νοεῖται, ἀλλὰ συνημμένως ἀμφότερα, καὶ μετ᾽ ἀλλήλων καταλαμβάνεται (Gregory of Nyssa, *De deitate Filii et Spiritus Sancti*, GNO 10.2:124.1–5).

62. M. van Parys, "Réfutation, Grégoire de Nysse, Réfutation de la profession de foi d'Eunome" (PhD diss., Université de Paris–Sorbonne, 1968), 170–71.

In the *De oratione dominica*, in fact, there follows the same technique of response to the Pneumatomachians typical also of Epiphanius and Pseudo-Athanasius of the *Dialogi contra Macedonianos*, presented in chapter 3. It starts from the unity of action of the Father and the Son to go on to show that the Second and the Third Persons are characterized by the same activity and concludes with the identity of nature between the Spirit and the Father. This is actually an application of the transitive property (i.e., if A=B and B=C, then A=C) translated in terms of the nature of the divine Persons: (1) if Son's nature = Father's nature, a truth accepted by the Pneumatomachians; and (2) it is shown that Spirit's nature = Son's nature; then (3) the necessary deduction is that Spirit's nature = Father's nature.

The example of fire aims at this because it is characterized by the two activities of giving light and burning and has a single nature, exactly as the activities of reigning and forgiving sins oblige us to conclude that there is no difference of nature between the Spirit and the Son.[63] In fact, the First and the Second Persons are both called "God," so that they cannot have different natures. The Pneumatomachians accepted this conclusion from the point of view of generation, which always transmits the identity of nature. That is why their accusation against the orthodox was that the divinity of the Holy Spirit implied the existence of two Sons,[64] resulting in the contradiction in the title of Only Begotten, as well as the conclusion that the Father was the grandfather of the Spirit.[65] By contrast, Gregory introduces here a series of examples such as the pedestal which cannot be said to have been generated by the carpenter, or the house by the architect.[66] On the other hand, a father and son are united (συνημμένον) according to their nature.[67]

> In an absolutely necessary way (ἀνάγκη πᾶσα),[68] when two realities are in relation (οἰκείως ἔχῃ) to one, I cannot even distinguish (διαφόρως ἔχειν)

63. Gregory of Nyssa, *De oratione dominica*, SC 596:418.6–11. The passage seems close to Didymus, *In Genesim*, 233.25–29.

64. See e.g., Pseudo-Basil, *Homilia de Spiritu Sancto*, PG 31:1433C.

65. E.g., Athanasius, *Epistulae ad Serapionem*, 3.1.3 (AW 1.4:568).

66. These examples are parallel to those in Gregory of Nyssa, *Contra Eunomium III*, 1.95 (GNO 2:36).

67. Gregory of Nyssa, *De oratione dominica*, SC 596:418.13–420.3. In addition to the passage from *De deitate Filii et Spiritus Sancti* just cited, see also *Ad Ablabium*, GNO 3.1:38.10 and *Epistula*, 38.4.65.

68. The expression betrays the influence of Galen on Gregory; the former makes use of the formula more than twenty-five times, while Gregory is the author who makes the most use of it by far among his contemporaries and predecessors.

the one from the other, since, if the Son is united to the Father according to nature, the Spirit, through the identity of acts, is not revealed to be different. Thus it is shown as a consequence that the nature of the Holy Trinity is only one without confusing in each of the hypostases the distinctive properties contemplated in them, or confusing reciprocally the aspects which distinguish them so that the characteristic of the fatherly hypostasis is transferred to the Son and to the Spirit, or that that of the Son, in its turn, is adapted to one of the Persons of whom it is said, or that the property of the Spirit appears (ἐπιφαίνεσθαι) in the Father and the Son.[69]

It is important to note here that the verb *epiphainesthai* does not indicate the economic dimension but the purely immanent one of the intradivine personal distinction, as we shall see in the next section.[70] It concerns the relation of origin which alone distinguishes the Persons within the single nature with which the proper characteristic of each of them is identified perfectly.

What follows is a precise illustration of the distinctive characteristics of each divine Person, starting with the "not being from a cause" (τὸ μὴ ἐξ αἰτίου εἶναι) of the Father.[71] In fact, both the Second and the Third Person proceed from Him according to John 16:28 and 15:26. These two Gospel references point to the distinction between the two processions. This is the real dogmatic question raised by the Pneumatomachians. In fact, the point is to identify a second possibility of proceeding that is absolutely immanent and so does not break the identity of nature but, at the same time, is not a generation.

This is clear in the following text where, on the terminological level, the "not being from a cause" is identified with being *agennētos*:

> The Father's *proprium* is to not exist from a cause, but this is not the *proprium* in the case of the Son and the Spirit, because according to Scripture the Son

---

69. Ἀνάγκη πᾶσα, ὅταν τὰ δύο πρὸς τὸ ἐν οἰκείως ἔχῃ, μηδὲ πρὸς ἄλληλα διαφόρως ἔχειν ὥστε, εἰ τῷ πατρὶ κατὰ τὴν φύσιν ὁ υἱὸς ἥνωται, τῆς δὲ τοῦ υἱοῦ φύσεως διὰ τῆς τῶν ἐνεργειῶν ταυτότητος οὐκ ἀλλότριον ἀπεδείχθη τὸ πνεῦμα τὸ ἅγιον, μία κατὰ τὸ ἀκόλουθον ἀποδέδεικται τῆς ἁγίας τριάδος ἡ φύσις, οὐ συγχεομένης ἐφ᾽ ἑκάστης τῶν ὑποστάσεων τῆς κατ᾽ ἐξαίρετον ἐπιθεωρουμένης αὐταῖς ἰδιότητος οὐδὲ τῶν γνωρισμάτων ἐν ἀλλήλοις ἀλλασσομένων ὥστε τὸ σημεῖον τῆς πατρικῆς ὑποστάσεως ἐπὶ τὸν υἱὸν ἢ τὸ πνεῦμα μετενεχθῆναι, ἢ τοῦ υἱοῦ πάλιν ἐνὶ τῶν προκειμένων ἐφαρμοσθῆναι, ἢ τὴν τοῦ πνεύματος ἰδιότητα τῷ πατρὶ καὶ τῷ υἱῷ ἐπιφαίνεσθαι (Gregory of Nyssa, *De oratione dominica*, SC 596:420.3–14).

70. See pp. 160–71.

71. Gregory of Nyssa, *De oratione dominica*, SC 596:420.15–422.4.

comes from the Father (cf. John 16:28) and "the Spirit is from God" (1 Cor 2:12) and "proceeds from the Father" (John 15:26) (τὸ πνεῦμα ἐκ τοῦ θεοῦ καὶ παρὰ τοῦ πατρὸς ἐκπορεύεται). But as being without a cause (ἄνευ αἰτίας), which is exclusive to the Father, cannot be applied to the Son and to the Spirit, in the same way the inverse, to be from a cause (ἐξ αἰτίας), which is proper to the Son and the Spirit, is not naturally attributed to the Father. And since it is common to the Son and the Spirit to be not without generation (ἀγεννήτως), so that a certain confusion (σύγχυσις) not be maintained regarding the subject (ὑποκείμενον), it is necessary to find another distinction that does not generate confusion in their properties, so that that which is common be kept safe, and that which is proper be not confused. For the Sacred Scripture says that the only begotten Son [comes] from the Father (ἐκ τοῦ πατρός) and this affirmation defines the property. But it is also said that the Holy Spirit is from the Father (ἐκ τοῦ πατρός), as it is also attested that He is from the Son (ἐκ τοῦ πατρὸς λέγεται καὶ ἐκ τοῦ υἱοῦ εἶναι προσμαρτυρεῖται).[72]

This passage is extremely important for the history of the *Filioque* and can be set in parallel both with different pneumatological texts of Gregory as well as with passages of other contemporary authors who are responding to the Pneumatomachian criticisms, as seen in the previous two chapters. In particular, it is apparent that the Bishop of Nyssa is looking for a distinction between the two processions, that is, he has recourse to a relational difference to identify the *proprium* of the Spirit with respect to the Son as both are caused. In *Contra Eunomium I*, the solution was the manifestation by the Second Person, while in *Ad Ablabium* it was the being caused mediately,[73] but in both cases the key element was the relational, and not causal, reading of the role of the Son in the second procession.

72. Ἴδιον τοῦ πατρὸς τὸ μὴ ἐξ αἰτίου εἶναι· τοῦτο οὐκ ἔστιν ἰδεῖν ἐπὶ τοῦ υἱοῦ καὶ τοῦ πνεύματος. Ὅ τε γὰρ υἱὸς ἐκ τοῦ πατρὸς ἐξῆλθεν, καθώς φησιν ἡ γραφή, καὶ τὸ πνεῦμα ἐκ τοῦ θεοῦ καὶ παρὰ τοῦ πατρὸς ἐκπορεύεται. Ἀλλ᾽ ὥσπερ τὸ ἄνευ αἰτίας εἶναι, μόνου τοῦ πατρὸς ὄν, τῷ υἱῷ καὶ τῷ πνεύματι ἐφαρμοσθῆναι οὐ δύναται, οὕτω τὸ ἔμπαλιν τὸ ἐξ αἰτίας εἶναι, ὅπερ ἴδιόν ἐστι τοῦ υἱοῦ καὶ τοῦ πνεύματος, τῷ πατρὶ ἐπιθεωρηθῆναι φύσιν οὐκ ἔχει. Κοινοῦ δὲ ὄντος τοῦ υἱοῦ καὶ τοῦ πνεύματος τοῦ μὴ ἀγεννήτως εἶναι, ὡς ἂν μή τις σύγχυσις περὶ τὸ ὑποκείμενον θεωρηθείη, πάλιν ἔστιν ἄμικτον τὴν ἐν τοῖς ἰδιώμασιν αὐτῶν διαφορὰν ἐξευρεῖν, ὡς ἂν καὶ τὸ κοινὸν φυλαχθείη καὶ τὸ ἴδιον μὴ συγχυθείη. Ὁ γὰρ μονογενὴς υἱὸς ἐκ τοῦ πατρὸς παρὰ τῆς ἁγίας γραφῆς ὀνομάζεται, καὶ μέχρι τούτου ὁ λόγος ἵστησιν αὐτῷ τὸ ἰδίωμα, τὸ δὲ ἅγιον πνεῦμα καὶ ἐκ τοῦ πατρὸς λέγεται καὶ ἐκ τοῦ υἱοῦ εἶναι προσμαρτυρεῖται (Gregory of Nyssa, *De oratione dominica*, SC 596:422.1–424.2).

73. See the texts already analyzed in the previous chapter: *Contra Eunomium I*, 279.5–281.1 (GNO 1:108.7–109.5) at p. 104 and *Ad Ablabium*, GNO 3.1:55.21–56.10, at p. 109.

This is confirmed by the conclusion of the dogmatic argument in *De oratione dominica*, just after the double *ek* in the previous text:

Therefore the Spirit who is from God (ἐκ τοῦ θεοῦ) is also Spirit of Christ. On the other hand, the Son, who is also from God (ἐκ τοῦ θεοῦ), is not and is not said to be "of the Spirit"; and this relational sequence (σχετικὴ ἀκολουθία) is not reversed so as to make it possible to invert the discourse in the same analysis and use the expression "Christ of the Spirit," just as one says "Spirit of Christ."[74]

Gregory's line of reasoning is extremely clear: through their unity of action, the three divine Persons have a nature that is numerically one whereas they are distinguished as persons through their reciprocal relations. In this way, we have to recognize an order in the immanent relation between the Son and the Spirit which cannot be inverted. The reference to the relational dimension is explicit (σχετική), as in *Ad Ablabium*. The new *Schesis*-theology, developed by the Bishop of Nyssa, makes possible the formulation of a purely relational order that exists in the personal characteristics of the Son and the Spirit, so that the latter can be called Spirit of Christ whereas the opposite does not work. This can be read precisely in the light of the end of the previous text in that the Third Person is also from the Son without ceasing absolutely to be from the Father, whereas the Son is not from the Spirit.

At the close, Gregory tackles another possible, or real, objection on the part of the Pneumatomachians to his proof based on the unity of action. In fact, the epicletic invocation introduced by the Lukan variant, on which the proposed proof rests, contains the invocation addressed to the Third Person to "come." This is another activity, but one that appears exclusive to the Spirit. Gregory responds by quoting Psalm 79(80):3 with David's invocation to the Father to come and save. Thus, this activity of the Spirit cannot be an indication of metaphysical inferiority in that it is also characteristic of the Father.

Having taken its cue from Moses and the difference concerning the entry into the Trinitarian sanctuary made possible in Christ, the homily's conclusion returns, thus, to the Jews through the citation of Mark 2:7, according to which

---

74. Οὐκοῦν τὸ μὲν πνεῦμα τὸ ἐκ τοῦ θεοῦ ὂν καὶ Χριστοῦ ἐστι πνεῦμα, ὁ δὲ υἱὸς ἐκ τοῦ θεοῦ ὢν οὐκέτι καὶ τοῦ πνεύματος οὔτε ἐστὶν οὔτε λέγεται, οὔτε ἀντιστρέφει ἡ σχετικὴ αὕτη ἀκολουθία ὡς δύνασθαι κατὰ τὸ ἴσον δι᾽ ἀναλύσεως ἀντιστραφῆναι τὸν λόγον καί, ὥσπερ Χριστοῦ τὸ πνεῦμα λέγομεν, οὕτω καὶ τοῦ πνεύματος Χριστὸν ὀνομάσαι (Gregory of Nyssa, *De oratione dominica*, SC 596:424.3–9).

the Pharisees accused Jesus of blaspheming because only God can forgive sins.[75] The rhetorical path is complete with the identification of the Jews and the Pneumatomachians who fight against their own life (οἱ τῇ ἰδίᾳ προσπολεμοῦντες ζωῇ),[76] in that they are fighting against the Giver of Life, in harmony with what was already seen in the previous section.

Unfortunately, the relational reading of this "being said from the Father and attested from the Son" (ἐκ τοῦ πατρὸς λέγεται καὶ ἐκ τοῦ υἱοῦ εἶναι προσμαρτυρεῖται) in *De oratione dominica* is not present in the literature on the passage, especially considering its value in the dialectic between the East and West. In fact it is a literal parallel of the *Filioque* and its interpretation is a *vexata quaestio* even at the philological level. The presence of a second *ek* inserted into the relationship between the Spirit and the Son, in parallel with that of the Third Person in relation to the Father, is compromised by different variants in the manuscript tradition, even if the philological evidence seems clearly in favor of its presence. This conclusion is strengthened by the appearance of the preposition in the oldest Syriac translations of Gregory's work, which go back to the sixth century,[77] well before any possible polemic concerning the role of the divine Second Person in the procession of the Third. It seems, therefore, that the *ek* belonged to the archetype of the fifth or sixth century, although John Callaghan has put it into square brackets in his edition,[78] deciding that it was added by some copyist on the basis of the arguments of Werner Jaeger,[79] according to whom the presence of this preposition would be inconsistent with Gregory's pneumatology.[80]

However, in light of a contextual reading of the *De oratione dominica* and of both the definition of the personal *proprium* of the Third Person (presented in chapter 4) and the patterns in the responses to the Pneumatomachians in

---

75. Cf. Gregory of Nyssa, *De oratione dominica*, SC 596:426.6–15.

76. The verb appears also in *De oratione dominica*, 332.21. In this case, the whole text of *De oratione dominica*, 332.12–21, with the quote of Psalm 103(104):35, can be found in Pseudo-Eusebius, *Commentaria in Psalmos*, PG 23:1295a–b (CPG 3467). Significant is the parallel use of the verb in Gregory of Nyssa, *Adversus Macedonianos*, GNO 3.1:106.25 and 109.19.

77. Vat. syr. 106 and Brit. syr. 564 (add. 14, 550).

78. Τὸ δὲ ἅγιον πνεῦμα καὶ ἐκ τοῦ πατρὸς λέγεται, καὶ [ἐκ] τοῦ υἱοῦ εἶναι προμαρτυρεῖται (GNO 7.2:43.1–2).

79. W. Jaeger, *Gregor von Nyssas Lehre vom Heiligen Geist* (Leiden: Brill 1966), 122–53.

80. Cf. J. Callaghan, GNO 7.2:x–xiv. This is proof of the importance of methodological exactitude in philology, as various serious scholars were influenced by the choice of the editor; see Moreschini, "Osservazioni sulla pneumatologia dei Cappadoci," 144, and M. Brugarolas Brufau, *El espíritu santo: De la divinidad a la procesión; El desarrollo pneumatológico en los escritos dogmáticos de los tres grandes capadocios* (Pamplona: Eunsa, 2012), 184.

the second half of the fourth century (as seen in chapter 3), it seems possible to claim the exact opposite. In fact the common element of their distinctive approach is the rereading the intra-Trinitarian order in a relational key in order to place the Third Person *between* the Father and the Son, whose divinity was accepted by the adversaries. In this way, the response implied three steps: (1) affirming the monarchy of the Father, the only principle and cause of the other two divine Persons; (2) demonstrating the divinity of the Second Person; and (3) bringing the Third Person into the ontological "space" connecting the First and the Second Persons but in such a way as to preserve the Trinitarian order of the Third Person in relation to the other two.

For this reason, the last critical edition in SC 596, here quoted, is to be greatly appreciated, as it corrects Callaghan's choice, which placed an alleged theological reason before the philological datum with a serious methodological inconsistency. On the contrary, the explanation of the choice in the French edition is extremely convincing.[81] The only criticism that should be made of the French edition in light of the path illustrated here is that its editors read the double *ek* in an Athanasian sense because they consider the relationship between the first two people to be a model (*modèle*) of the relationship between the Second and the Third Persons, so that just as the Father is the cause of the Son so the Son is the cause (*cause*) of the Spirit, even if He is a second cause.[82] From what we have seen, this interpretation cannot be admitted because it misses the core of the response to Pneumatomachians whose criticism was based on the Alexandrian scheme of the symmetry of the two processions. In Gregory's perspective, instead, the double *ek* is perfectly coherent because the *Glory* and the *Kingship* originate from the Father, but are also from the Son. The Pneumatomachian response required the insertion of the Third Person between the first two without diminishing the monarchy. And the double *ek*, read in the whole of Gregory's pneumatology and on the background of response strategies of the time, perfectly fulfills this function. But this is based on relational rereading, also highlighted by the presence of the terminology linked to *schesis*, without any reference to a causality of the Son. This is active in the second procession in a relational and not causal sense.

Even worse and confusing is the reading of Giuliana Caldarelli in her comment on the τὸ πνεῦμα ἐκ τοῦ θεοῦ καὶ παρὰ τοῦ πατρὸς ἐκπορεύεται at the beginning of the text in discussion. She reads the *theou* as a reference to the

81. See SC 598:159–68.
82. See SC 598:166.

Son,[83] a possibility in this case which is really contradictory with respect to the theology of Gregory who is rigorous in his use of *ekporeuetai*. From the other four occurrences of the verb, one could never deduce a generic sense of the Trinitarian procession.[84] All the more since the struggle with the Pneumatomachians demanded precisely the introduction of a clear distinction between the two processions, something which would have been made impossible by the application of the verb in John 15:26 proper to the second procession to the first, when already the origin of the dogmatic tension derived from the presumed application of generation to the second procession.

This necessity of a clear distinction between the two processions is extremely important because it indicates that the anti-Pneumatomachian works are clearly moving in the immanent sphere. Thus, while the statement at the beginning of the text is just part of the list of scriptural quotes relevant for the discussion and does not appear to have any link with a possible role of the Son in the eternal procession of the Spirit, the situation of the last sentence with the double *ek* seems very different.

What we have tried to highlight is that the presence of the second *ek* does not actually contradict Gregory's pneumatology since it is being read from the starting point of the relational conception of the intra-Trinitarian *ordo* which characterizes the response to Eunomius and which is being developed further in an anti-Pneumatomachian key. In fact, the numerical distinction between the two processions was linked dogmatically in a twofold way to the identification of the personal characteristic of the divine Third Person, of His *proprium*.

IV. THE SPIRIT MANIFESTED BY THE SON

This reading is confirmed by the immanent meaning of the terminology of manifestation in Gregory of Nyssa's formula "manifested by the Son" (δι' Υἱοῦ πεφηνός) used in reference to the Holy Spirit. Clearly this is an element received from tradition, as it is proved by the presence of this expression in Gregory Thaumaturgus's Symbol of Faith transmitted by the Bishop of Nyssa in the panegyric dedicated to the first evangelizer of Cappadocia.

83. See G. Caldarelli, *S. Gregorio di Nissa. La preghiera del Signore* (Milan: Edizioni Paoline, 1983), 82n22.

84. See Gregory of Nyssa, *Ad Graecos*, GNO 3.1:24.18 and 25.6; *Refutatio confessionis Eunomii*, 188.5 (GNO 2:392.6); and *In Canticum canticorum*, GNO 6:20.6 (the latter occurs in a context that is not directly Trinitarian). For a detailed discussion, see Maspero, *Trinity and Man*, 160–61.

As already seen in the previous chapter, from a pneumatological point of view the formula is relevant for a deeper understanding of the role of the Second Person in the procession of the Holy Spirit. But the text of the Symbol speaks of the role of the Son in the revelation and in the sending to the world of the Third Person, clearly referring only to the economic dimension.

However, analyzing some passages by Gregory of Nyssa and Gregory of Nazianzus, we can discover that, in the confrontation with the Pneumato-machians, the manifestation of the Spirit by the Son was reinterpreted in an immanent sense, similarly to what happened with the triangular and linear schemes. The key to this rereading is the new ontological value assigned to relation (σχέσις), which follows a path similar to the one that characterized the term *logos*, as seen in the introduction to this book.

In *De vita Gregorii Thaumaturgi*[85] Gregory of Nyssa reports a Symbol of Faith[86] that the Wonderworker would have learned directly during an apparition from the dialogue between the Apostle John and Mary the Mother of Jesus. The debate over the real author of the text does not yet seem to have been resolved.[87] Apart from that, the pneumatology of the Symbol is extremely interesting.[88]

After the first two articles, dedicated respectively to the Father and the Son, the following text appears:

And one is the Holy Spirit who has His subsistence from God, and who has been manifested [to human beings] through the Son (δι' υἱοῦ), the perfect image of the perfect Son, life, cause of life, holy source, holiness that gives sanctification; in Him is manifested (φανεροῦται) God the Father who is above all and is in all, and God the Son who is in all creation.[89]

85. See T. Kochlamazashvili, "Thaum. De vita Gregorii Thaumaturgi," *The Brill Dictionary of Gregory of Nyssa*, ed. L. F. Mateo-Seco and G. Maspero (Leiden: Brill, 2009), 718–20.

86. Gregory of Nyssa, *De vita Gregorii Thaumaturgi*, GNO 10.1:17.24–19.5.

87. See L. Froidevaux, "Le symbole de saint Grégoire le Thaumaturge," *Recherches de science religieuse* 19 (1929): 193–247; L. Abramowski, "The Confession of Gregor Thaumaturgus with Gregor of Nyssa and the Problem of Its Authenticity," *Zeitschrift für Kirchengeschichte* 87 (1976): 145–66; and M. van Esbroeck, "The Credo of Gregory the Wonderworker and Its Influence through Three Centuries," *Studia Patristica* 19 (1989): 255–66.

88. A. Aranda, "El Espíritu Santo en la Exposición de Fe de S. Gregorio Taumaturgo," *Scripta Theologica* 10 (1978): 373–407.

89. Καὶ ἕν Πνεῦμα ἅγιον ἐκ θεοῦ τὴν ὕπαρξιν ἔχον καὶ δι' υἱοῦ πεφηνὸς (δηλαδὴ τοῖς ἀνθρώποις) εἰκὼν τοῦ υἱοῦ τελείου τελεία ζωὴ ζώντων αἰτία ἁγιότης ἁγιασμοῦ χορηγός ἐν ᾧ φανεροῦται θεὸς ὁ πατὴρ ὁ ἐπὶ πάντων καὶ ἐν πᾶσι καὶ θεὸς ὁ υἱὸς ὁ διὰ πάντων (Gregory of Nyssa, *De vita Gregorii Thaumaturgi*, GNO 10.1:18.13–22).

The intimate connection between the attributes of holiness and life is immediately apparent. The expression "to human beings" is absent in Rufinus's Latin translation and in one of the two Syriac codes, the most recent one dating back to the ninth century.[90] The fact that the oldest Syriac tradition included these words seems to suggest that the element was later expunged to encourage an immanent reading of the passage, otherwise referencing the economy.

The antiquity of the theology of the Symbol is also witnessed to by the attribution of the term "image" (εἰκών) to the Spirit, in the line of what Athanasius also did.[91] As seen, in the fourth century the Pneumatomachian crisis forced the procession of the Third Person to be distinguished from the eternal generation, modifying the symmetrical derivative and linear structure, which connected the Spirit to the Son in the same way as the Son was connected to the Father.

Also the second article of the Symbol seems to point to a theology preceding the Nicene Council, as it expresses the derivation of the Second Person from the First through the genitive rather than the preposition *from* (ἐκ). It is said that the Son is "invisible of the invisible" (ἀόρατος ἀοράτου), "incorruptible of the incorruptible" (ἄφθαρτος ἀφθάρτου), "immortal of the immortal" (ἀθάνατος ἀθανάτου) and "eternal of the eternal" (ἀΐδιος ἀϊδίου).[92] Similar formulas are also used by Gregory of Nyssa,[93] who, however, at the same time, declares them equivalent to the derivative Nicene formula φῶς ἐκ φωτὸς and θεὸς ἀληθινὸς ἐκ θεοῦ ἀληθινοῦ.[94]

The theological discussions of the fourth century, in fact, are deeply connected to the hermeneutics of "Light from Light" of Nicea. From the perspective inspired by Arius, the preposition *from* expresses subordination and difference of substance. The root of the question was ontological because metaphysics from Aristotle to Neoplatonism identified the relation with an accident, projecting the categorical and creatural dimension into God, as the theology developed in response to the Arian crisis has shown.[95] The only instrument that made it possible to identify a subject was substance, so that the personal distinction between the Father and the Son required the affirmation of a substantial difference.

---

90. See *Rufini versio latina Eusebii Historiae ecclesiasticae* (GCS 9.2:955s) and Brit. syr. 559 (Ad. 18815).

91. See pp. 57–58.

92. Gregory of Nyssa, *De vita Gregorii Thaumaturgi*, GNO 10.1:18.9–12.

93. See the formula ἄκτιστον ἀκτίστου, ἀγαθοῦ ἀγαθήν, ἀΐδίου ἀΐδιον, in Gregory of Nyssa, *Contra Eunomium III*, 4.26.6–7 (GNO 2:144.7–8).

94. See Gregory of Nyssa, *Contra Eunomium III*, 1.65.12 (GNO 2:27.3) and 1.85.9–10 (GNO 2:33.15–16).

95. See chapter 8 for more details.

Interpreting "Light from Light" as an expression of perfect substantial identity required an extension of the ontology of the time. Basil had already taken this path when he had stressed the difference between God and what is found in the cosmos, reinterpreting the names *Father* and *Son* in such a way as to deny that they implied passion. According to the Bishop of Caesarea, in the Trinity the names Father and Son are not marked by the limits observed at the creatural level but "express only the mutual relation" (τὴν πρὸς ἄλληλα σχέσιν ἐνδείκνυται μόνην).[96] The novelty with respect to Greek metaphysics is situated, therefore, on a relational level.

The instrument of *mutual relation* (ἡ σχέσις πρὸς ἄλληλα) appears several times in the works of Gregory of Nyssa against Eunomius. The latter, in fact, uses precisely this expression to indicate the necessary relationship that would distinguish in the ontological hierarchical scale the second and third substance from the supreme substance.[97] The response of the Bishop of Nyssa ontologically reinterprets the *schesis* in the wake of Basil, reconnecting the mutual relation that unites the Father and the Son to the names of the divine Persons revealed by Scripture and affirming the identity of nature between them.[98] The three divine Persons do not have quantitative and necessary relationships with each other, because they are not like larger and smaller vases put into each other. The Father, the Son, and the Holy Spirit are rather without limit and boundary (πέρατι καὶ ὅρῳ), so that their relational distinction concerns hypostasis and maintains their substantial identity (κοινωνεῖν κατὰ τὴν οὐσίαν καὶ διῃρῆσθαι κατὰ τὸν τῆς ὑποστάσεως).[99] Thus the *mutual relation*, read from the perspective of the names of the first two divine Persons revealed in Scripture, indicates at the same time the unity of nature in the distinction of the two subjects (ἐν δύο τοῖς ὑποκειμένοις τὴν ἑνότητα τῆς φύσεως).[100]

This identification, which is not based on the difference of substance, requires a shift to a new ontological plan, original as the essence because it is eternal but distinct from it, as ground for the personal distinction, that is, the *pōs einai*, already mentioned in chapter 4.[101] The union of the adverb to *einai*

96. Basil, *Adversus Eunomium II*, 22.48 (SC 305:92).

97. Gregory of Nyssa, *Contra Eunomium I*, 154.2 (GNO 1:73.4); 406.1 (GNO 1:145.10–11); 411.8 (GNO 1:146.21–22); 412.3 and 6 (GNO 1:146.25–26 and 28–29).

98. See Gregory of Nyssa, *Contra Eunomium I*, 159 (GNO 1:75.1–7).

99. See Gregory of Nyssa, *Contra Eunomium I*, 410–13 (GNO 1:146–47).

100. See Gregory of Nyssa, *Contra Eunomium I*, 498.1–2 (GNO 1:170.13–14). The theme reappears in the first book of *Contra Eunomium III*, 1.7.6 (GNO 2:6.8–9); 1.9.2 (GNO 2:7.2–3) and 1.112.7 (GNO 2:42.1).

101. See the text of *Contra Eunomium III* on p. 164.

is parallel to the use of prepositions with the same verb in explicit or implicit form,[102] as is the case with the Nicene *ek*. It indicates the plan of the hypostatic distinction, which must be clearly differentiated with respect to the contrast between the created and the uncreated:

> We discover the non-generated through opposition (πρός) with the generated and the incorruptible is known if we put it in front of (πρός) the corruptible and we see the substance with the diversity with respect (πρός) to the insubstantial. . . . Therefore the substance is understood as such in being something (ἐν τῷ εἶναί τι), while the corruptible or incorruptible is understood in being of a certain nature (ἐν τῷ ποδαπὸν εἶναι), the generated and the non-generated in being in a certain way (ἐν τῷ πῶς εἶναι).[103]

The progression of Gregory's analysis is very clear: the substantial identity, which concerns all levels of being, must be flanked by the relational distinction characteristic of the unbegotten Father and the begotten Son, a distinction that is on a different level with respect to the one between created and uncreated, that is, with respect to that between corruptible and incorruptible. So, there are three different metaphysical levels, to which correspond as many distinctions: (1) the immanent one between the unbegotten Father and the begotten Son; (2) the ontological gap that separates the Creator from the creatures (i.e., the Trinity as the only incorruptible nature and the diastematic world marked by corruptibility); and (3) within this, the classical distinction between substance and accident. One could say that the first level is horizontal within divine ontology, the only eternal and uncreated substance that is the Trinity, while the second distinction is vertical. The third, finally, is again horizontal and exclusively characterizes creation (see fig. 11). To each of these levels correspond different questions: to the question on what concerns substance at the creatural level, one must add the question on the difference of nature in the vertical, to conclude with the formulation of the question on the immanent distinction between the divine Persons, which is expressed starting from "how one is" (πῶς εἶναι). This is not a question of quality, which would remain in the accidental sphere, but it is the transition to a real relational level. The

102. See the wonderful text in *Contra Eunomium III*, 8.39.6–41.6 (GNO 2:253.12–254.11).

103. τό τε γὰρ ἀγέννητον τῇ πρὸς τὸ γεννητὸν ἀντιδιαστολῇ ἐξευρίσκομεν καὶ τὸ ἄφθαρτον τῇ πρὸς τὸ φθαρτὸν παραθέσει γνωρίζεται καὶ ἡ οὐσία τῇ πρὸς τὸ ἀνυπόστατον παραλλαγῇ θεωρεῖται. (. . .) οὐκοῦν οὐσία μὲν ἐν τῷ εἶναί τι κατανοεῖται, τὸ δὲ φθαρτὸν ἢ τὸ ἄφθαρτον ἐν τῷ ποδαπὸν εἶναι, τὸ δὲ γεννητὸν ἢ ἀγέννητον ἐν τῷ πῶς εἶναι (Gregory of Nyssa, *Contra Eunomium II*, 386.1–4, 9–11 [GNO 1:338.27–30; 339.3–5]).

definition of the relationship by Aristotle[104] and then by the Stoics in terms of πρός τί πως ἔχειν is reformulated in terms of being, to highlight the ontological stability of the divine Person. The "how one is" thus becomes an expression of the difference of origin that characterizes the divine Persons.

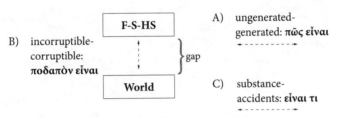

A) ungenerated-generated: πῶς εἶναι

B) incorruptible-corruptible: ποδαπὸν εἶναι

C) substance-accidents: εἶναι τι

fig. 11

This seems to be the necessary context to study the reinterpretation made by the Bishop of Nyssa of the pneumatological formula "manifested by the Son" of the Symbol of Gregory Thaumaturgus. We quote partially the text of *Contra Eunomium I*, already analyzed in chapter 4, where the hypostatic distinction is expressed through the adverbs *agennētos* for the Father and *monogenōs* for the Son.[105] About the Third Person, Gregory writes:

> [The Holy Spirit] united to the Son by the uncreated nature and by the fact of receiving the cause of existence from the God of the universe, He is distinct from Him in His turn by the peculiarity of not subsisting hypostatically as the only begotten of the Father (μήτε μονογενῶς ἐκ τοῦ πατρὸς ὑποστῆναι) and by the fact of being manifested by the Son himself (δι' αὐτοῦ τοῦ υἱοῦ πεφηνέναι). But further, since creation subsists (ὑποστάσης) by means of the Only Begotten (διὰ τοῦ μονογενοῦς ὑποστάσης), so that one does not think that the Spirit has something in common with it due to the fact that He is manifested (πεφηνέναι) by the Son (διὰ τοῦ υἱοῦ), He is distinguished from creation since He is invariable, immutable, and without need of any external good (ἑτέρωθεν).[106]

104. See pp. 232–33.

105. See pp. 103–4.

106. τῆς δὲ πρὸς τὸν υἱὸν κατὰ τὸ ἄκτιστον συναφείας [καὶ ἐν τῷ τὴν αἰτίαν τῆς ὑπάρ-ξεως ἐκ τοῦ θεοῦ τῶν ὅλων ἔχειν] ἀφίσταται πάλιν τῷ ἰδιάζοντι, ἐν τῷ μήτε μονογενῶς ἐκ τοῦ πατρὸς ὑποστῆναι καὶ ἐν τῷ δι' αὐτοῦ τοῦ υἱοῦ πεφηνέναι. πάλιν δὲ τῆς κτίσεως διὰ τοῦ μονογενοῦς ὑποστάσης, ὡς ἂν μὴ κοινότητά τινα πρὸς ταύτην ἔχειν νομισθῇ τὸ πνεῦμα ἐκ τοῦ διὰ τοῦ υἱοῦ πεφηνέναι, ἐν τῷ ἀτρέπτῳ καὶ ἀναλλοιώτῳ καὶ ἀπροσδεεῖ τῆς

The scanning of the different ontological planes clearly separates the immanent "being from the Son," which characterizes the divine Third Person from the "being from God" of creatures. The distinction between the Father, the Son, and the Spirit does not concern the divine nature, since all three are the one uncreated nature, but, as in *Ad Ablabium*, it concerns the *pōs einai*, to which the adverbial expression of the distinctive characteristics of the Father, the Son, and the Spirit refers. The latter is indistinguishable from the other two as far as nature is concerned, but is distinct from them according to the relation indicated by the personal names mentioned in the Scripture, because the Spirit is not the Father and is not the only begotten Son. The Third Person receives the cause of existence from the First, as it is for the Son, but is distinguished from the latter being manifested by Him (δι' αὐτοῦ τοῦ υἱοῦ πεφηνέναι). Thus, the text accurately shows the difference between the latter expression and receiving the being by means (διά) of the *Logos* that characterizes all creatures according to John 1:3. From this we can deduce that the formula "manifested by the Son" has been reread here in an immanent sense.[107]

The manifestation of the Third Person by the Second Person must be linked to the Spirit's hypostatic identity as bond of the Father and the Son in consonance with the following statement by Basil in *De Spiritu Sancto*, which has already been mentioned above:[108]

And one is also the Holy Spirit, also proclaimed in his individuality (μοναδικῶς), who, united with the one Father through the one Son (δι' ἑνὸς Υἱοῦ), brings to completeness (συμπληροῦν) in Himself the Blessed Trinity worthy of all praise.[109]

The Spirit is the One who brings the Trinity to unity, precisely because He receives the being from the Father but in His own personal individuality is manifested by the Son. The Third Person is Himself through the Second one.

ἑτέρωθεν ἀγαθότητος διακρίνεται τὸ πνεῦμα ἀπὸ τῆς κτίσεως (Gregory of Nyssa, *Contra Eunomium I*, 279.4–281.1 [GNO 1:108.16–109.5]).

107. A. de Halleux also agrees with this interpretation, although usually is rather critical of the immanent readings of the role of the Son in the procession of the Spirit in Gregory of Nyssa. See A. de Halleux, "*Manifesté par le Fils*: Aux origines d'une formule pneumatologique," *Revue théologique de Louvain* 20 (1989): 3–31, esp. 25.

108. See p. 118.

109. Ἓν δὲ καὶ τὸ ἅγιον Πνεῦμα, καὶ αὐτὸ μοναδικῶς ἐξαγγελλόμενον, δι' ἑνὸς Υἱοῦ τῷ ἑνὶ Πατρὶ συναπτόμενον, καὶ δι' ἑαυτοῦ συμπληροῦν τὴν πολυύμνητον καὶ μακαρίαν Τριάδα (Basil, *De Spiritu Sancto*, 18.45.24–27 [SC 17bis:408]).

The transition from the economic reading of the manifestation to the immanent reading seems to be linked to the discussion with Pneumatomachians. As we have seen, this forced the development of Basil's pneumatology, going beyond its uncertainties, which Anthony Meredith attributes to a not yet perfectly developed use of the distinction between created and uncreated inherited from the Alexandrian tradition.[110] The Bishop of Caesarea, in fact, had not yet been able to distinguish the two processions by identifying the personal *proprium* of the Holy Spirit, the crucial element to which the adversaries' criticisms pointed.[111] Basil maintains the specularity of the processions, already supported by Athanasius, in the triangular scheme, reproposing the baptismal "syntax" in terms of correspondence of the *disposition* (ἔχει πρός) of the Son with respect to the Father with that of the Spirit with respect to the Son.[112]

As already said, the most effective response to the Pneumatomachians elaborated by Gregory of Nyssa consists, then, in distinguishing without separating the two processions by placing the Third Person *between* the Father and the Son, as the Royal Power and Glory that the two eternally exchange and that constitute the Second Person as the perfect image of the First. But this implies a relational rereading of the manifestation of the Spirit by the Son and therefore a shift to the immanent dimension. While in the Symbol of Gregory the Wonderworker the Spirit was the image of the Son as the latter was the image of the Father, now the being image is not understood simply as an expression of the common identity of nature, according to Athanasius's theology, but as an exclusive reference to the eternal generation.

V. Gregory of Nazianzus's Confirmation

Gregory of Nazianzus's fundamental contribution to pneumatology is well known.[113] Athanasius was the first to point at the numerical distinction of the two immanent processions and Gregory of Nyssa was the first to formulate what distinguishes the procession of the Spirit from the generation of the Son. But it was the Bishop of Nazianzus who coined a proper name for this second procession inspired by John 15:26. Thus, in *Oratio* 39.12, precisely where the

---

110. See A. Meredith, "The Pneumatology of the Cappadocian Fathers and the Creed of Constantinople," *Irish Theological Quarterly* 48 (1981): 196–211.

111. Moreschini, "Osservazioni sulla pneumatologia dei Cappadoci," 118–19.

112. Basil, *De Spiritu Sancto*, 17.43.14–16 (SC 17bis:398).

113. For a diachronic presentation of his pneumatology, see Moreschini, "Osservazioni sulla pneumatologia dei Cappadoci," 129–35.

expression *ekporeusis* is introduced to indicate the procession of the Spirit from the Father, it is said:[114]

> The Spirit is truly the Holy Spirit, in that He proceeds (προϊόν) from the Father, not as a son (υἱκῶς), since He does not [proceed] by generation (γεννητῶς), but by procession (ἐκπορευτῶς), if it is possible to create a new term to be clear.[115]

The Greek text is ingenious in specifying the generic proceeding (προϊόν), which applies to both processions, through the adverb *ekporeutōs* coined for the occasion and referring only to the procession of the Third Person.

Therefore, the confirmation of the reading of the expression "manifested by the Son" in *Oratio* 31 of the Bishop of Nazianzus seems extremely relevant. From the beginning, he declares that his object of investigation is the immanent dimension (i.e., the *theologia*). In the background there is always the intra-Trinitarian interpretation of the Nicene "Light from Light," which must be extended to the Holy Spirit to respond to the Pneumatomachians.[116] Therefore, to the affirmation that if there was a time when there was no Son, then there was not even the Father, typical of the Arian discourse, it must be added that if there was a time when there was no Spirit, then there was not even the Son.[117] The Pneumatomachians' logic is put in check, extending to the Third Person the arguments accepted by them for the Second. This is also reinforced by the soteriological affirmation that if the Spirit is a simple creature then He cannot save the human person by uniting him or her to God and divinizing him or her.[118]

The argument is exquisitely ontological, practically a Porphyrian tree: Gregory wonders whether the Third Person should be placed among the beings that exist *per se* (τῶν καθ᾿ ἑαυτὸ ὑφεστηκότων) or among those which are inherent to another reality (ἐν ἑτέρῳ), that is if He is substance (οὐσίαν) or accident (συμβεβηκός). In the second case He should be a divine operation (ἐνέργεια),

---

114. The date of composition of the theological sermons of Gregory of Nazianzus (*Orationes* 27–31) and *Oratio* 39 is generally placed in the second half of 380 (see SC 250:13–14).

115. Πνεῦμα ἅγιον ἀληθῶς τὸ πνεῦμα, προϊὸν μὲν ἐκ τοῦ Πατρός, οὐχ υἱκῶς δέ, οὐδὲ γὰρ γεννητῶς, ἀλλ᾿ ἐκπορευτῶς, εἰ δεῖ τι καὶ καινοτομῆσαι περὶ τὰ ὀνόματα σαφηνείας ἕνεκεν (Gregory of Nazianzus, *Oratio*, 39.12.14–17 [SC 358:174]).

116. Consider the application of the term "Light" to the three divine Persons in Gregory of Nazianzus, *Oratio*, 31.2 (SC 250:278).

117. See Gregory of Nazianzus, *Oratio*, 31.4 (SC 250:280.28–29).

118. See Gregory of Nazianzus, *Oratio*, 31.4 (SC 250:282.13–14).

that is, one of those realities that concern the substance (τῶν περὶ τὴν οὐσίαν) but are not substance. If the Spirit, on the other hand, is substance, there is no other possibility than to admit that He is either a creature or God Himself, since it is impossible to conceive an intermediate (μέσον) between them or a compound (σύνθετον) of created and uncreated.[119]

After clarifying that the Third Person is divine substance, Gregory puts in crisis the Pneumatomachian reasoning based on the affirmation that then the Spirit must necessarily either be unengendered or generated. In the first case, in fact, there would be two unengendereds, while in the second case there would be two possibilities already seen and both absurd: either He comes directly from the Father, being brother or even twin of the Son, or He comes from the Son, thus becoming a nephew God.[120]

The point is that one must stick to the facts, without fearing names (ἐδεξ-άμην ἂν τὰ πράγματα, οὐ φοβηθεὶς τὰ ὀνόματα) and without applying to the Trinity the human categories and natural kinship relationships (τῆς ἡμετέρας συγγενείας). One must recognize that the Spirit is from God and is consubstantial (ἐκ τοῦ θεοῦ καὶ ὁμοούσιον). For this reason, the category of relation needs to be purified and raised to a higher rank (τινα σχέσιν ὑψηλοτέραν).[121]

After this analysis, Gregory of Nazianzus comes to the conclusion from John 15:26, demonstrating the divinity of the Holy Spirit through His relational position *between* the Father and the Son, the strategy already seen in Gregory of Nyssa:

> Inasmuch as He proceeds (ἐκπορεύεται) from the Father, the Spirit is not a creature; inasmuch as He is not begotten, He is not Son; inasmuch as He is in between (μέσον) the One who is unbegotten and the One who is begotten, He is God.[122]

The ontological reasoning that preceded the statement excludes that *meson* can be read here in an economic sense or as a substantial intermediate degree between creation and the uncreated. Instead, we are before the very solution introduced also by Gregory of Nyssa.[123] The *meson* is here purely relational.

---

119. See Gregory of Nazianzus, *Oratio*, 31.6 (SC 250:286.1–17).

120. See Gregory of Nazianzus, *Oratio*, 31.7 (SC 250:286.26–288.2).

121. See Gregory of Nazianzus, *Oratio*, 31.7 (SC 250:288.6–17).

122. ὃ καθ᾽ ὅσον μὲν ἐκεῖθεν ἐκπορεύεται, οὐ κτίσμα· καθ᾽ ὅσον δὲ οὐ γεννητόν, οὐχ υἱός· καθ᾽ ὅσον δὲ ἀγεννήτου καὶ γεννητοῦ μέσον θεός (Gregory of Nazianzus, *Oratio*, 31.8 [SC 250:290.11–14]).

123. Cf. Gregory of Nyssa, *Adversus Macedonianos*, GNO 3.1:102.22–31; *In illud: Tunc et ipse filius*, GNO 3.2:21.17–22.14; and *In Canticum canticorum*, GNO 6:467.2–17.

This procession of the Spirit cannot be explained in natural terms and the apophatic veil remains. Gregory of Nazianzus writes that it would be madness to try peeking into the mysteries of God (εἰς θεοῦ μυστήρια παρακύπτοντες), when, as it is written in Sirach 1:2, we cannot even count the grains of the sea sand or the drops of rain.[124] But Christian revelation obliges us to affirm the unity of nature and the trinity of Persons with their eternal relations.

Thus we come to a text that seems fundamental for the interpretation of the manifestation of the Spirit by the Son and, therefore, for the question of the *Filioque*:

> What is it, then, that the Spirit lacks, they say, to be Son? If, in fact, He did not miss anything, He would be the Son. We say that He lacks nothing: in fact, God is not incomplete. The difference consists in the manifestation (ἐκφάνσεως), so to speak, and in the mutual relation (τῆς πρὸς ἄλληλα σχέσεως): hence also the difference of their names.[125]

The personal distinction has its foundation in the difference of the revealed names and these names express the mutual relation. The manifestation, then, is placed at the level of relation and specifically of the relations of origin in the pure immanence of the Most Blessed Trinity. The rereading of the formula of Gregory Thaumaturgus operated by Gregory of Nyssa is here confirmed by Gregory of Nazianzus's response to Pneumatomachians.[126]

Therefore, in conclusion, we can say that the formula "manifested by the Son" in the pneumatological article of Gregory the Wonderworker's Symbol of Faith has originally an evident economic value. In the development of the theological response to Pneumatomachians, however, it was reread through the need to place the Spirit *between* the Father and the Son in order to defend His divinity, overcoming the linear representation of the Trinity and any pos-

---

124. Cf. Gregory of Nazianzus, *Oratio*, 31.9 (SC 250:290.25–292.1).

125. Τί οὖν ἐστί, φησιν, ὃ λείπει τῷ πνεύματι, πρὸς τὸ εἶναι υἱόν; εἰ γὰρ μὴ λεῖπόν τι ἦν, υἱὸς ἂν ἦν. οὐ λείπειν φαμέν· οὐδὲ γὰρ ἐλλειπὴς θεός· τὸ δὲ τῆς ἐκφάνσεως, ἵν' οὕτως εἴπω, ἢ τῆς πρὸς ἄλληλα σχέσεως διάφορον, διάφορον αὐτῶν καὶ τὴν κλῆσιν πεποίηκεν (Gregory of Nazianzus, *Oratio*, 31.9.1–5 [SC 250:290–92]).

126. Gregory of Nyssa's *De vita Gregorii Thaumaturgi* is generally dated between 379 and 380 (cf. J. Bernardi, *La prédication des Pères Cappadociens*, 308, and S. Mitchell, "The Life and Lives of Gregorius Thaumaturgus, in Portraits of Spiritual Authority," in *Religious Power in Early Christianity, Byzantium, and the Christian Orient*, ed. J. W. Drijvers and J. W. Watt (Leiden: Brill, 1999), 99–137, esp. 115.

sibility of confusion with the economic dimension inherent to the triangular scheme of Origenian inheritance.

This intermediate being of the Spirit with respect to the Father and the Son was to be understood in a purely relational sense and not as an ontological difference, while maintaining the Trinitarian order and the monarchy of the First Person. This was possible thanks to a reinterpretation of the ontological fundamentals of reality and the opening to a category of relation that was not merely accidental but immanent to the essence itself. From this perspective, the manifestation of the Spirit by the Son should not be understood as a reference to His revelation in history, but as an expression of the eternal *pōs einai* and of the mutual *schesis* of the divine Persons in the purest divine immanence.[127]

VI. A GREEK *FILIOQUE*?

But does this mean that Latin theology can boast a precedent of the *Filioque* in Greek tradition? To respond positively to this question would be at least anachronistic, because it would project medieval understanding onto patristic thinking. However, there is no doubt that, from the perspective of the history of dogma, the dialectic between Western and Eastern traditions regarding the role of the Second Person in the procession of the Third seems improper. The proposed path, in fact, offers a clear indication.

As seen, Origen's pneumatology was centered around the question of the distinction between the spirituality of God, that is, the Trinity with respect to creation, and the being *Spirit* in the personal sense of the divine Third Person. Theologically this is intimately linked to the question of the origin of the Holy Spirit. The two schemes, the more economic triangular one and the more immanent linear one, provided an answer pregnant however with a tension that emerges at the beginning of the fourth century. The expression of the distinction of the Son and the Holy Spirit with respect to the Father in terms of participation, with the resulting difference in the level of divine action, required further elaboration.

Marcellus of Ancyra read the triangular scheme in a dialectical sense to deny the real trinity of the divine persons.[128] Therefore he opposed the proces-

---

127. In this sense, the conclusions of André de Halleux, who writes about δι' υἱοῦ, do not seem to be fully acceptable: "It is always, it seems, an epiphany in him, and when this relationship is understood as eternal, and not only as economic, it could *be* only as a revealing power that is actualized in the history of creation and salvation" (Halleux, "*Manifesté par le Fils*," 31).

128. See pp. 48–49.

sion of the Spirit from the Father to that through the Son. The verses of John 15:26 and 16:14 began here to interact at the heart of Trinitarian theological elaboration. Faced with such criticism, Eusebius of Caesarea defended the doctrine of Origen, reading John 16:14 in the context of the linear scheme, which thus became the main reference point in orthodox Trinitarian teaching. Its limit was a not yet perfect distinction between the economic dimension and the immanent one.

This was overcome by Athanasius through the distinction of two different ontological levels: the first consisting of the one eternal and uncreated nature that identifies with the Most Blessed Trinity, the second represented by created natures marked by temporality and participation.[129] This allowed the Bishop of Alexandria to deepen his approach to divine immanence, now represented according to the linear scheme through the numerical distinction of the two processions but without their authentic qualitative differentiation. The Pneumatomachian criticism was directed precisely to this point: if the second procession is the same as the first then the Father is the grandfather of the Spirit.

Thus, from Epiphanius of Salamis[130] to Gregory of Nyssa, we saw the different attempts to describe the relationship between the two processions.[131] From this point of view the main strategy was to bring back the divinity of the Third Person to the divinity of the first two. The Cappadocians succeeded in formulating a very balanced doctrine by introducing the Spirit *between* the Father and the Son, whose divinity was also accepted by the Pneumatomachians without violating the monarchy: the Spirit is God, God from God because Spirit from Spirit according to the formulation of Epiphanius, as the Royal Power that the First Person, as King, confers on the Second, His image, and so He too is King, and for this reason is returned by the Second Person to the First in perfect imitation of the perfect and eternal act of gift of Self that this one performs. The Bishop of Nyssa repeats the same in terms of Glory

129. See pp. 53–57.

130. See pp. 80–87.

131. As will be seen in the next chapter, it is extremely interesting to note that even in the Syriac sphere, when translating the Symbol of Nicea in Seleucia in 410, there was a need to add the Son in the pneumatological article: cf. P. Bruns, "Bemerkungen zur Rezeption des Nicaenums in der ostsyrischen Kirche," *Annuarium historiae conciliorum* 32 (2000): 1–22. Similarly to the Latin case, a technical verb was missing to indicate the procession of the Third Person from the First, so as to provide additional space for the differentiation of the two processions. See, for the theological meaning, G. Maspero, "Tradition and Translation: The *Filioque* and the Procession of the Holy Spirit in Syriac," *Parole de l'orient* 36 (2011): 87–109.

mutually exchanged between the first two divine Persons, highlighting in his mature works the role of the Son in the procession of the Spirit starting from the category of *aitia*, which clearly stresses the founding role of the Father.

All this is ontologically founded in the reformulation of classical metaphysics made by the Cappadocian Fathers, who redefined the intra-Trinitarian *schesis* in such a way as to break the necessary connection with the accidental dimension it had in the Greek context. Therefore, the achievement of a perspective fully respectful of the excess of the mystery, but at the same time free from the criticism of the formulation of the dogma by the Pneumatomachians, involved the deepening of the personal *proprium* of the Third Person who, not being ascribable to the filiation, escaped more radically from the expressive capacities of the theologians. Thus, the Cappadocians have identified the function of being bond between the Father and the Son, bringing to completeness the Trinity, as the personal characteristic of the Spirit. This implies a relational understanding not only of the first two Persons, whose proper names immediately recall one another, but also of the Third Person,[132] now described in a correlative way with respect to the other two. Thus the Spirit is manifested by the Son. This correlativity makes it possible to recognize a role of the Son in the procession of the Spirit without this meaning a violation of the monarchy, but rather as a deepening of an authentically theological monarchy and not a simple adaptation of the ontological hierarchy typical of Greek metaphysical thought.[133]

Beyond any Filioquist temptation, which in the Middle Ages may have closed the relationship of the first two Persons in itself by making the third one their simple "appendix," the dogmatic development of Greek patristic thought shows the need to overcome all forms of dialectics and conceptualizing reductionism to open up to a new metaphysical vision developed by the fathers, who allowed the mystery to fertilize their thought. In this ontological framework

132. On the Trinitarian understanding of all the divine Persons, that is also of the Father and the Son with respect to the Spirit, see J. Garrigues, "Procession et ekporèse du Saint Esprit: Discernement de la tradition et réception oecuménique," *Istina* 17 (1972): 345–66, and "À la suite de la Clarification romaine sur le 'Filioque,'" *La nouvelle revue théologique* 119 (1997): 321–34.

133. On the comparison between Gregory of Nyssa's thought and the ontology of Eunomius, with a pretty interesting discussion of all relationships with the philosophical and theological tradition of both, see the aforementioned X. Batllo, *Ontologie scalaire et polémique trinitaire: Le subordinatianisme d'Eunome et la distinction κτιστόν/ἄκτιστον dans le Contre Eunome I de Grégoire de Nysse* (Münster: Aschendorff, 2013). Precious is the analysis also in the perspective of a greater understanding of the relationship between the theology of Eunomius and the Pneumatomachians.

relation is a co-principle of being together with substance, so that the very possibility of knowing the truth is rooted in the personal relationship.[134] It seems paradoxical, instead, that the theological discussion on the divine Person who founds unity is a cause of division among Christians. Surely this is a sign of a loss of authentically theological epistemology and a forgetfulness of the ontological gains laboriously elaborated by the fathers.[135]

VII. Conclusion: Theological Epistemology

For this reason, in conclusion of this perhaps bold analysis of the pneumatology of the fourth century, one can put forward the hypothesis that the dialectic that arose around the question of the *Filioque* may be connected to the loss of a properly theological epistemology, that is, one based on apophaticism as gnoseological reflection of the ontological novelty constituted by the *Physis*-theology.

In this chapter we tried to show that the response to the Pneumatomachians was not an abstract dogmatic question, but started biblically from the blasphemy against the Holy Spirit. What has been exposed suggests that this reference was not a mere rhetorical artifice but touched the heart, even epistemology, of the question: the reality of Christian salvation communicated in the liturgy, sacraments, and prayer demanded the affirmation of the divinity of the Third Person.

For this reason, Gregory of Nyssa's commentary on the Lord's Prayer presents a conspicuous pneumatological reflection centered on the relational correspondence between economy and immanence. This is the background that allows us to understand in their real historical-dogmatic content some disputed texts in the history of the *Filioque*. In fact, if we do not take into account *schesis* as a new plane of being identified by the relational Cappadocian re-comprehension of metaphysics, we cannot recognize the immanent meaning of the language of manifestation applied to the Holy Spirit.

When we speak of the Trinity, in fact, we cannot separate the objective dimension from the subjective one because the three divine Persons are the

---

134. See, on this, G. Maspero, *Essere e relazione: L'ontologia trinitaria di Gregorio di Nissa* (Rome: Città Nuova, 2013), 57–61.

135. The perspective is consistent with Sarah Coakley's approach to the *Filioque*, who reads the dogmatic question against the background of theological research of a "Fatherhood beyond patriarchalism." See S. Coakley, *God, Sexuality, and the Self: An Essay 'On the Trinity'* (Cambridge: Cambridge University Press, 2013), 327–34.

origin of the light that, like the sun, makes it possible to see every real object, distinguishing it from idolatrous illusions and our inner projections. Therefore, the conception of *Dogmengeschichte* that inspired the present investigation seeks to be properly theological in the sense that one cannot trace the history of anything without being immersed in it: how, in fact, would it be possible to study the history of philosophy without grasping the desire, passion, and concerns that animate those who dedicate their lives to philosophy? In the same way, here we did not want to propose an aseptic and historicist reconstruction of the different moments that were considered important for the issue, but we tried to offer a narrative that would like to be inspired by the same epistemological perspective of the authors studied.

Thus the essential point of reference is the excess of being over knowledge. As Gregory of Nyssa wrote:

> In fact, the divine Word forbids in the last text (Exod 20:3–7) that humans assimilate the Divinity to any of the created realities, since every concept, elaborated by the cognitive faculty in a sensitive image (περιληπτικὴν φαντασίαν) to know and reach the divine nature, makes an idol (εἴδωλον) of God, and does not give it to know.[136]

Concepts can turn into idols when we overlook apophaticism, that is, when we forget that God is essentially always beyond our cognitive capacity. And since the world and history are the fruit of His creative action and have in Him, indeed precisely in the *Logos* that became flesh, their deepest sense, even the knowledge of reality in its cosmic and historical dimension must always take account of this surplus.

Thus the first epistemological postulate that underlies this research is apophaticism. But from this immediately derives attention to history as a place of encounter with the mystery of the Triune God, which can only be known through personal relationships. The history of salvation, with the plot of encounters and chiaroscuros that characterize it, becomes the fundamental point of reference, so that theological reflection itself on the Mystery is part of

---

136. ἀπαγορεύει γὰρ ἐν πρώτοις ὁ θεῖος λόγος πρὸς μηδὲν τῶν γινωσκομένων ὁμοιοῦσθαι παρὰ τῶν ἀνθρώπων τὸ θεῖον, ὡς παντὸς νοήματος τοῦ κατά τινα περιληπτικὴν φαντασίαν ἐν περινοίᾳ τινὶ καὶ στοχασμῷ τῆς θείας φύσεως γινομένου εἴδωλον θεοῦ πλάσσοντος καὶ οὐ θεὸν καταγγέλλοντος (Gregory of Nyssa, *De vita Moysis*, 2.165.4–9 [M. Simonetti, ed., *Gregorio di Nissa: La vit di Mosè* (Rome: FLV, 2011), 156]).

this history. As Joseph Ratzinger wrote, the *Word*, in German *Wort*, cannot be grasped in its deepest sense without the *Answer*, in German *Antwort*, a term significantly linked to *Word* itself.[137] Therefore, the dogmatic reconstruction sketched here does not aim to be the solution of a conceptual problem, as if it were a mathematical equation, but aspires to trace a series of relationships, which make visible a dogmatic path as a growing immersion of the fathers in that Trinitarian mystery that the encounter with Christ has revealed.

137. Fr. J. Ratzinger, *Theologische Prinzipienlehre: Bausteine zur Fundamentaltheologie* (Donauwörth: Wewel, 2005), 153–54.

The Litmus Test: Syriac Theology and Translations

I. INTRODUCTION: A CONJECTURE

In light of the discussion conducted in the prior chapter, the question remains why the epistemological and ontological approach of the Greek fathers was lost over the centuries, generating the at times fierce dispute over the *Filioque*. Essentially the main reasons can be traced back to the relationship between form and content, which tends to sclerotize over time. This can occur in the process of translation, which is essential for a vital phenomenon that by its own identity must reach all nations (cf. Matt 28:19), or in the process of tradition, where a form of the past is interpreted starting from the meaning it has taken on in a later era. In summary, the two main risks that can move away from a relational epistemology suitable for the object studied (which, in the Trinitarian case, is also subject) are anachronism and anachorism. This latter term is the interpretation of texts of a given geographical area (in Greek *chōra*) starting from the typical forms of a different area. For example, in German *Gift* means "poison" and it would be very dangerous to approach a reality indicated in that linguistic area by this term from its meaning in English. Thus, the study of the Syriac world can be very useful to understand how the Latin question of *Filioque* developed and the comparison with the Greek fathers can serve as confirmation of the interpretative hypothesis presented in the previous chapters.

Every tradition requires a process of translation and that means that the epistemological and hermeneutical issues cannot be avoided: the transmission of a teaching includes making it accessible to people far from those who first received the message, entering into their mentality without wavering from the truth one desires to communicate. This implies a search for the most adequate concepts and terms to serve as the foundation of the relationship between the transmitter and the recipients. This transmission means going beyond the frontiers, both geographically and chronologically, that is, beyond the letter reflecting upon its authentic content, delving deeper into the true meaning of the message. The translation process thus becomes an occasion in which the community transmitting the tradition comes to understand it better in the very act of its transmission.

According to what we have seen in the previous chapters, the *vexata quaestio* of the *Filioque* could be an example of what has just been described. In fact, from a historical perspective, as the conclusions of this volume will suggest, Maximus the Confessor[1] overcomes the perplexity that the *Filioque* aroused in the Orient with the distinction—found already in Cyril of Alexandria— between the *ekporeuesthai* of the Spirit from the Father alone and his *proienai* and *hyparchein* from the Father and Son together.[2] From a philological perspective, the question emerges precisely at the moment of translation: Latin has only the verb *procedere* to express all of the Greek variants, thus losing the specificity of the Greek *ekporeuesthai*, as can be seen in the Latin translations of the Gospel of John (8:42 and 15:26 in particular). This is clearly a limitation; however, it paradoxically permits a greater theological and hermeneutic liberty, offering new degrees of freedom in Trinitarian thought. In fact, this can be used in order to unfold other aspects of the mystery, which always remain beyond any dogmatic formulation.

As explained, apophaticism should be considered the fundamental epistemological law in Trinitarian theology. For this reason our narrative is verified on the Syriac example. The many centuries of dialectical confrontation between the Greek East and the Latin West over the *Filioque* may hinder a clear reading of the sources. Thus we check the reading of the Greek fathers' answer to the Pneumatomachians as presented in the Syriac tradition, which offers a third point of view that sheds new light on the issue, allowing us to rethink the centuries-old polemic. In fact, a dialectic approach necessarily misses the truth because, if true Being is the Trinity, we always need a third perspective to recover a consistent approach to reality.

So the scope of the present chapter is to briefly examine the Syriac case through various examples without any claim of completeness. In this area the situation is analogous to that of the Latin, insofar as the verbs referring to the procession of the Son and the Spirit in the Peshitta (the Syriac New Testament) and in the Vetus Syra (the Syriac Old Testament) are both expressed with

1. Maximus the Confessor, *Opuscula theologica et polemica*, PG 91:136a–c.
2. Cyril of Alexandria, *Thesaurus*, PG 75:585a.

the single verb *npq* (to go out, proceed).[3] For this reason it is interesting to study the manner in which the Syriac theologians resolved the problem. The object of the research presented in this chapter is how the theologians speak of the relation between the Son and the Holy Spirit in this tradition, which is characterized by the absence of two different verbs that distinguish the two intra-Trinitarian processions.

The question is also pertinent due to the geographical proximity to the Greek world as well as the value and originality of the theology developed in this true cultural crossroads. The present study does not thus confront the problem of the *Filioque* debate as it historically emerged in the confrontation between the Latin and Greek worlds attempting to show how the Syriac authors either had or did not have a certain position in relation to it from a purely formal perspective. It instead engages the issue of how the necessity to translate, inserted into the very process of transmission of the tradition, required the resolution of the problem due to the impossibility of the use of two distinct verbs, something which implicated a theological understanding of the transmitted text. In fact, from the doctrinal perspective, in the Syriac world it was also necessary to elucidate three elements:

1. Affirm that the Son is consubstantial to the Father.
2. Affirm that the Spirit is God, stating that He comes from the Father in a unique manner, manifesting His essential difference with respect to creation.
3. Distinguish the procession of the Son from that of the Third Person, which is not generation.

In light of the previous chapters, one should expect that in the Syriac theological writings a role could be assigned to the Son in the procession of the Third Person and that its formulation would oscillate among different forms of expression.

In order to verify this conjecture, the first object of the present analysis is the beginning of the pneumatological and properly Trinitarian thought in the Syriac world, which is situated in the fourth century, particularly with the reflection of Ephrem.[4]

---

3. We find *rwḥ' dšrr' hw dmn lwt 'by npq* for John 15:26 in the Peshitta, while *'n' gyr mn 'lh' npqt w'tyt* is found for John 8:42. In the Vetus Syra manuscript Sinaiticus, the situation is substantially the same, but less servile in respect to the Greek and with the verb in the feminine in John 15:26.

4. For a presentation of earlier Syriac pneumatology, see E. Kaniyamparampil, *The Spirit of Life* (Kottayam: OIRSI, 2003). This is an extremely interesting study, although less relevant from the perspective of Trinitarian immanence. The reflection is initially concentrated on

II. The Beginnings: Profession of Faith

The preoccupation with clarifying the three aforementioned doctrinal points is reflected in Ephrem's theology, even if in a different manner with respect to the Greek world. Instead of working on concepts and their definitions, he prefers to proceed with images,[5] conformed to both his cultural surroundings and the expressive forms at his disposal. It is thanks to this method that he reaches a notable dogmatic depth.[6]

In order to indicate the divinity of the Holy Spirit in his commentary on the *Diatessaron* Ephrem writes in reference to John 21:19:

And because Christ was taken as pledge of life from among men subject to death and from that nature (*mn kyn'*) over which death reigned, [God the Father] elevated Him and seated Him at His right, as hostage taken from those who are inferior. And thus [Christ] sends them [the apostles] a pledge *from* His nature (*mn kyn'*), the Spirit Paraclete, pledge of life.[7]

Both Christ and the Spirit are called *pledge of life*, in the line of the triangular scheme. Consequently, two movements intersect: the ascending one of Christ as man, taken and elevated from the human nature that belongs to Him, and the movement of Christ as God, who sends the Spirit from His divine nature. In this sense the double attribution of the phrase *pledge of life* serves to indicate the unicity of the divine nature, the unique source of life, according to a more linear perspective. For this reason, the second *mn kyn'* is contrasted with the first, and presents the Spirit as consubstantial to the Son precisely because He has His origin from Him, that is, from His divine nature.

---

the more economic aspects, since, as in the Greek and Latin traditions, it is only in the fourth century under Arian pressure that an explicit and complete dogmatic formulation of the Trinitarian dogma becomes necessary. See also R. Murray, *Symbols of Church and Kingdom: A Study in Early Syriac Tradition* (London: T&T Clark, 2006).

5. E. Beck, *Ephräms Trinitätslehre im Bild von Sonne/Feuer, Licht und Wärme*, CSCO 425 (Leuven: Peeters, 1981), 117.

6. On the relationship between Ephrem's pneumatology and the First Council of Constantinople, see C. B. Horn, "Überlegungen zur Rolle der Pneumatologie Ephräm des Syrers im Umfeld des Ersten Konzils von Konstantinopel," in *Syriaca II*, ed. M. Tamcke (Münster: LIT, 2004), 29–52.

7. Ephrem, *Commentarius in diatessaron*, 21.33 (L. Leloir, *Saint Ephrem: Commentaire de l'Évangile concordant texte syriaque (manuscrit Chester Beatty 709)* [Dublin: Hodges Figgis, 1963], 232) (emphasis added).

The Oriental theological conception is particularly concrete and highly spiritual, so much as to place economy and immanence extremely close together, reading the latter in light of the former. This unified conception of procession and mission could play a role in the misunderstandings about monophysitism, which would later be attributed to the Syriac tradition.[8]

Another text of Ephrem could be cited in reference to this, which also serves as an example of the hermeneutical difficulties. In the *Sermo I de reprehensione*, he writes about the unjust condemnation of Christ: "He who had opened the eyes of the blind, people who were blind spat on His face, and He who spirated (*nph*) the Holy Spirit received filthy spit."[9] Edmund Beck[10] excludes the interpretation of Thomas J. Lamy,[11] who reads the text in an intra-Trinitarian manner, taking the verb *nph* (to blow, spirate) as a participle and not as the perfect. It is true that the action is tied with John 20:22, where the breathing on the disciples is expressed with the same verb. The observation of Lamy here that unlike in John 20:22 the verb is not constructed with the preposition *b-* (to, upon) is nevertheless noteworthy. Reading the Gospel text as "He breathed upon them and told them: Receive the Holy Spirit" (*nph bhwn. w'mr lhwn. qblw rwh' dqwdš*) helps us to understand the whole of this passage from Ephrem. Beyond philological and grammatical considerations, the explicit affirmation that Christ is the subject of the action of the infusion of the Holy Spirit seems to be relevant. The Syriac author no longer leaves the origin of the Holy Spirit implicit, as in John 20:22, but refers it immediately to the incarnate Son. It seems that the necessity to affirm, in an anti-Arian context, that the Son has a perfect divine nature is still at play here. This is expressed by connecting the being *from God* of the Spirit to the Son.

A third text is clearer. It is found in the hymn of *De defunctis et Trinitate*, published by Lamy[12] and contained in the manscript Oxon Marsh 711 folios 1–2. The context is explicitly Trinitarian:

8. About monophysitism, see W. H. C. Frend, *The Rise of the Monophysite Movement* (Cambridge: Cambridge University Press, 1972).

9. Ephrem, *Sermo I de reprehensione*, 433–37 (E. Beck, ed., *Des heiligen Ephraem des Syres, Sermones I*, vol. 1, CSCO 305 [Leuven: Secretariat du Corpus Scriptorum Christianorum Orientalium, 1969], 9).

10. E. Beck, ed., *Des heiligen Ephraem des Syrers, Sermones I*, vol. 2, CSCO 306 (Leuven: Secretariat du Corpus Scriptorum Christianorum Orientalium, 1969), 12n6.

11. T. J. Lamy, *Sancti Ephraem Syri hymni et sermones*, 4 vols. (Mechlin: H. Dessain, 1882–1902), 2:353 (see 2:352–56 for the text with complete discussion).

12. Lamy, *Sancti Ephraem Syri hymni et sermones*, 2:240–48.

The Father engenders, the Son is engendered from His bosom, the Holy
Spirit proceeds from the Father and from the Son (*dnpq mnh d'b' wdbr'*).
The Father is the Creator ('*bwd*') who has made the ages from nothing, the
Son is the Creator (*brwy*') who has established everything with his Par-
ent. The Holy Spirit is the Paraclete and the Comforter, in which has been
brought to completion everything that was, that will be and that is. The
Father is the mind, the Son the Word, the Spirit the voice; three names,
one will, one power.[13]

The value of the passage is evident from the point of view of the *Filioque*
clause, here literally present, in connection with the generic nature of the
procession indicated by the verb *npq*. The text, other than the question of its
attribution to Ephrem, also has great value from the perspective of the history
of the development of Trinitarian doctrine, insofar as it is witness to the Syriac
conceptualization of the Trinitarian analogy of mind, word, and voice.[14]

One characteristic of this analogy is the relationship that would unite the
processions of the Second and Third Persons. This is coherent with Ephrem's
principal Trinitarian analogy, that of the sun, sunbeam, and heat,[15] which, as
Edmund Beck states, contains "his entire Trinitarian doctrine."[16] In hymns 40,
73, and 74 the Syriac author specifically develops this analogy, which is truly
original with respect to the Greek world.[17]

A particularly relevant point needs to be added to these considerations: the
pneumatological article in the Symbol of Seleucia of 410 in the act of reception
of the Nicene Creed. In that year, after a period of isolation and persecution,

13. Lamy, *Sancti Ephraem Syri hymni et sermones*, 2:241–43.

14. The next chapter will be devoted to the psychological analogies of the Trinity in
the Greek fathers and to the theological development of this more phonological analogy.

15. Ephrem, *Hymni de fide*, hymn 73, verse 1 (E. Beck, *Des heiligen Ephraem des Syrers
Hymnen de fide*, CSCO 154 [Leuven: Peeters, 1955], p. 223).

16. "Denn es enthält seine ganze Trinitätslehre" (Beck, *Ephräms Trinitätslehre*, 1).

17. "Und nun zum Bilde selber bei Ephräm und bei den Griechen. Hier liegt wohl sicher
die eigne Leistung Ephräms vor allem darin, dass er für den Geist durchgängig und konse-
quent die Wärme als dessen Symbol herausgestellt und durchgeführt hat. Er tritt damit in
Gegensatz zu der Richtung, die von mir als die bei den grossen griechischen Theologen der
Zeit Ephräms herrschende herausgestellt wurde, zwar nur auf Grund einer beschränkten
Zahl ihrer Schriften aber doch wohl hinreichend genug belegt, wo der Geist im Verhältnis
zum Sohn keine eigne, ihn allein charakterisierende Grösse im Bild gefunden hat" (Beck,
Ephräms Trinitätslehre, 117; see also 27 and 91).

the bishops of Syria were able to reunite under the presidency of Marutha of Maipherkat.[18] The text, in the edition of de Halleux,[19] reads:

> And we confess the living and Holy Spirit / the living Paraclete, who is from the Father and the Son (*dmn 'b' wbr'*).[20]

The verse has no variants, as evidenced in the critical edition of Arthur Vöö-bus.[21] The addition of *and the Son* is in perfect accord with Ephrem's commentary on the *Diatessaron*. André de Halleux observes that the absence of the verb *npq* indicates the text must refer to the temporal mission and not to the immanent procession.[22] It nevertheless seems that the polemical context in which this scholar writes may have hindered this scholar from adequately considering the problem of the translation of John 15:26. On the contrary, the immanent reading seems evident from internal arguments, since the Symbol plays on the equivalence of *being from* and consubstantiality. Regarding the Son it states:

> who was generated from Him (*mnh*) [the Father], / that is from the essence (*mn 'ytwt'*) of His Father, / God from (*mn*) God, / Light from (*mn*) Light, / True God from (*mn*) true God, / generated not made, / connatural (*br kyn'*) to his Father.[23]

Throughout the entire Symbol the preposition *mn* is used to indicate consubstantiality through procession, as the insertion of *br kyn'* into the cited text demonstrates. In Syriac, it is as if the very affirmation of connaturality, semantically constructed with the term *br* (son), refers to the procession itself. Self-evident is the meaningfulness of this expression for the theology

---

18. See P. Bruns, "Bemerkungen zur Rezeption des Nicaenums in der ostsyrischen Kirche," *Annuarium historiae conciliorum* 32 (2000): 1–22. For further information on the issue, see the bibliography presented there.

19. A. de Halleux, "Le symbole des évêques perses au synode de Séleucie-Ctésiphon (410)," in *Erkenntnisse und Meinungen*, ed. G. Wiessner (Wiesbaden: O. Harrassowitz, 1977), 161–90.

20. Halleux, "Le symbole des évêques perses," 163.

21. A. Vööbus, "New Sources for the Symbol in Early Syrian Christianity," *Vigiliae Christianae* 26 (1972): 291–96.

22. Halleux, "Le symbole des évêques perses," 172–73.

23. Halleux, "Le symbole des évêques perses," 162–63.

on the *Filioque*. As far as the interpretation of the Symbol is concerned, it seems that this very construction is necessary to understand the content of the pneumatological article in the immanent sense, and not in reference to the mission. At the same time this shows also the difficulty in expressing the second procession.

This is also confirmed by the context of the Trinitarian theology of that period. In addition to that which has been already said of Ephrem, in the *Acts of Sharbil* from the end of the fourth century we find the same phenomenon with expressions that echo the theology of the Symbol:

> Since He who has clothed Himself in flesh is God, is the Son of God, Son of the essence (*br kyn'*) of His Father, is connatural (*br kyn'*) to the One who engendered Him; given that He is the adorable splendor of His divinity and the glorious manifestation of His majesty, He has always existed and for all eternity with His Father as well, His arm and His right, His power and His wisdom and His strength and [with] the Spirit of Life, who is from Him (*dmnh*), the propitiator and sanctifier of all those who adore Him.[24]

In the last lines of this text, it seems that both grammatically and logically the Person from whom the Spirit comes is the Son, due to the proximity and the identification of the adorable One with the source of the procession. Moreover, in the Acts of the martyrdom of Saint Sallita, the verb *npq* appears explicitly stating that the Spirit "proceeds (*npq*) from the Father and the Son."[25]

In synthesis, one can say that the Syriac theology of the fourth century understands the consubstantiality of the Persons in such a way that the procession of the Spirit appears connected to that of the Son. This is habitually expressed with recourse to the preposition *mn*, used in an absolute manner, but also with the verb *npq* thanks to the semantic liberty offered by the fact that this verb cannot become more specific as in the Greek. This theological conceptualization is finally consolidated in the Symbol of Seleucia. The very terminology suggests that divine economy and immanence cannot be thought of as separate, but are perceived in their deep interconnection.

---

24. *Acts of Sharbil*, in W. Cureton, *Ancient Syriac Documents Relative to the Earliest Establishment of Christianity in Edessa and the Neighbouring Countries from the Year after Our Lord's Ascension to the Beginning of the Fourth Century* (London: Williams & Norgate, 1864), 43.

25. P. Bedjan, *Acta martyrum et sanctorum*, 7 vols. (Leipzig: Harrassowitz, 1890–1897), 1:430.

III. The Translations of the Greek Fathers

III.1. Gregory of Nazianzus

The problem created by the lack of a specific verb parallel to the Latin case clearly emerges in the Syriac version of the works of the Cappadocian Fathers,[26] and in particular those of Gregory of Nazianzus,[27] who established the technical terminology in reference to the second procession. Concerning *Oratio* 39.12, discussed earlier in chapter 5, where the expression *ekporeusis* is coined for the first time to indicate the procession of the Spirit from the Father, the Syriac translation of the expression appears almost clumsy since it is incapable of introducing a term that distinguishes the procession of the Son from that of the Spirit. The Greek text has recourse to *proion* to express the procession in general, a term which can be applied to both processions, while the adverb *ekporeutōs*, coined for the occasion, refers only to the second procession.

The Syriac translation, in both the *versio antiqua et media* and the *versio nova*,[28] is incapable of literally rendering the text since the Greek term *ekporeutōs*, newly created in order to indicate the mode of the procession of the Spirit, in Syriac is *npwq'yt* and comes from the same root as the verb that indicates procession in general (*npq*), which corresponds to the Greek *proion*. The linguistic poverty in comparison to the Greek is evident. Everything is resolved through an adverbialization, which in translation appears more or less absurd.

This manifests the necessity of the development of new terminology in the labor of theology. Revelation places man before realities that cannot be known by human effort alone, and it is thus necessary to develop new concepts and words from those that already exist. This however shows how essential interaction with the culture and language in use is. Content and form are inseparable, and each translation requires a theological operation.

---

26. About the influence of the Greek fathers, and the Cappadocians in particular, on Syriac literature, see S. Brock, "L'apport des Pères grecs à la littérature syriaque," 9–26, and D. G. K. Taylor, "Les Pères cappadociens dans la tradition Syriaque," 43–61, both in *Les Pères grecs dans la tradition syriaque*, ed. A. Schmidt and D. Gonnet (Paris: Geuthner, 2007).

27. On Gregory of Nazianzus's presence in the Syriac tradition, see C. Detienne, "Grégoire de Nazianze dans la tradition syriaque," in *Studia Nazianzenica*, ed. B. Coulie, CCSG 41 (Turnhout: Brepols, 2000), 175–83.

28. J.-C. Haelewyck, ed., *Orationes XXVII, XXXVIII et XXXIX*, vol. 3 of *Sancti Gregorii Nazianzeni opera: Versio Syriaca*, CCSG 53 (Turnhout: Brepols, 2005), 12, 15–18, 147–49.

III.2. Basil's *De Spiritu Sancto*

The same phenomenon is evident in the Syriac translation of Basil's *De Spiritu Sancto* edited by David G. K. Taylor.[29] The liberty that typifies the oldest Syriac translations of the Greek fathers,[30] while being philologically a disadvantage, proves to be deeply interesting on the theological level. In fact, an analysis of this text manifests the clearly theological hermeneutic in the intervention of the translator.

The text indicated by *Syr I* in Taylor's edition appears to come from the end of the fourth or the beginning of the fifth century. It is conserved in fifth and sixth century manuscripts.[31] The translator tends to paraphrase the original, integrating numerous points from his own theological perspective. Taylor has shown that the numerous additions are aimed at presenting the Spirit together with the Father and the Son even when Basil does not include Him as well as at making explicit the Third Person's consubstantiality, going beyond the reluctance of the prudent Cappadocian on this point.[32] This is a typical theological operation that perfectly exemplifies the close connection between tradition and translation.

It is interesting to recall that Syriac theology is an important source in Basil's pneumatology.[33] As already mentioned, in *De Spiritu Sancto* he cites the authority of a theologian of Mesopotamian origin in order to maintain *homotimia*.[34] He also, in *Homiliae in hexaemeron*, while interpreting Genesis 1:2, refers to a Syriac author due to his proximity to the biblical language.[35]

The attitude of *Syr I* is that of deepening, in an immanent sense, the considerations that Basil had limited to the economic realm, according to a process parallel to what happened to the Symbol of Gregory Thaumaturgus. For this reason it is of interest here to verify if this tendency also extends to the

---

29. D. G. K. Taylor, ed., *The Syriac Versions of the* De Spiritu Sancto *by Basil of Caesarea*, 2 vols., CSCO 575–576 (Leuven: Peeters, 1999). The Syriac text will henceforth be indicated as *Syr I*. About Syriac translations of Basil's works, see Sebastian Brock, "Traduzioni siriache degli scritti di Basilio," in *Basilio tra oriente ed occidente*, ed. E. Baudry et al. (Bose: Qiqajon, 2001), 165–80.

30. S. Brock, "Towards a History of Syriac Translation Technique," in *III Symposium Syriacum*, ed. R. Lavenant, Orientalia Christiana Analecta 221 (Rome: Pontificium Institutum Orientalium Studiorum, 1983), 1–14.

31. Taylor, *Syriac Versions of the* De Spiritu Sancto, 1:xxv–xxx.

32. Taylor, *Syriac Versions of the* De Spiritu Sancto, 1:xix–xxv.

33. See pp. 74–75.

34. Basil, *De Spiritu Sancto*, 29.74 (SC 17bis:514).

35. Basil, *Homiliae in hexaemeron*, 2.6.21 (SC 26bis:168).

procession of the Holy Spirit, according to a dynamic that is implicated in the very affirmation of consubstantiality. In particular, the passages of the original Greek that have been cited in the discussions on the *Filioque* should be examined. It is precisely in these passages that the problem of the translation of *npq* could most pertinently come into play.

A first indication is found in the citations of Psalm 32(33):6: "By the word of the Lord the heavens were made, and all their host by the breath of his mouth." As already seen, Basil references this verse in a passage that we repeat here to facilitate the comparison:

> This is not a word, that is, modulated air that signifies something, so as to be proffered by the organ of the voice; nor is it a spirit, breath of the mouth, that comes forth from the respiratory tracts. It is, instead, a Word that was with God in the beginning, and that is God (cf. John 1:1) and a Spirit of the mouth of God (cf. Ps 32[33]:6), "The Spirit of truth, who proceeds (ἐκπορεύεται) from the Father" (John 15:26).[36]

John 15:26 appears in the text with the verb *ekporeuetai*. The Syriac translation is more developed, and modifies an essential aspect:

> That (divine) majesty, however, does not have a word which remains in the air, so that by means of a type of the instruments of the (vocal) organ it might convey its message, instructing by its mediation the one who hears on behalf of the one who proclaims. And again, this "Spirit which is *from* the mouth" (Ps 32[33]:6) is not that which is gently exhaled from the parts of the physical organs associated with breathing, but it is that Word of Truth who is with God from the beginning, and is God (cf. John 1:1), for again (it is said): "The Spirit of God, who is the Spirit of Truth who proceeds (*npq'*) from the Father" (John 15:26).[37]

In the first place, *of* the mouth[38] becomes *from* the mouth, explicitly indicating procession according to a tendency to express consubstantiality through the

36. Οὔτε οὖν λόγος, ἀέρος τύπωσις σημαντική, διὰ φωνητικῶν ὀργάνων ἐκφερομένη· οὔτε πνεῦμα, στόματος ἀτμός, ἐκ τῶν ἀναπνευστικῶν μερῶν ἐξωθούμενος· ἀλλὰ Λόγος μὲν ὁ πρὸς Θεὸν ὢν ἐν ἀρχῇ, καὶ Θεὸς ὤν. Πνεῦμα δὲ στόματος Θεοῦ, τὸ Πνεῦμα τῆς ἀληθείας, ὃ παρὰ τοῦ Πατρὸς ἐκπορεύεται (Basil, *De Spiritu Sancto*, 16.31–36 [SC 17bis:378–80]).

37. *Syr I*, 72.25–73.3 (translation in Taylor, *Syriac Versions of the* De Spiritu Sancto, 2:61).

38. In the *Peshitta* the expression used is *of* (*d-*), without any variant; see D. M. Walter, ed., *The Old Testament in Syriac* (Leiden: Brill, 1980), 32.

origin from the divine nature. The surprising element, however, is that John
15:26 appears to be applied to the Word in reference to the spiritual nature
of God. This means that the verb *npq* is understood in a completely generic
manner, and that the two processions are conceived of in a certain unity and
inseparability in their distinction, as will be seen in what follows. Here the text
seeks primarily to distinguish creation and Creator.

Similarly, later in the text, it is specified that each hypostasis is named
individually and correlated to the others: "One is God the Father, one the
only begotten Son, one the Holy Spirit."[39] The Syriac translation includes an
insertion: "One is God the Father, one the only begotten Son *who is from Him*,
one the Holy Spirit."[40] The Syriac author felt the need to insert a reference to
the procession of the Son expressed without the verb, using instead the preposition *from* (*mn*). A little further on, as we know,[41] the Greek text refers to
the relationship between the procession of the Spirit and that of the Son using
the typical Greek preposition διά:

And one also is the Holy Spirit, He too proclaimed in His individuality,
who, united to the unique Father through the unique Son (δι' ἑνὸς Υἱοῦ),
carries the Holy Trinity worthy of all praise to completion in Himself.[42]

The text is obviously particularly pertinent to the question of the *Filioque* in
that it appears to affirm a role of the Son—on the immanent level—in the
relationship of the Spirit with the Father according to a theology similar to
that later presented by Gregory of Nyssa in the *Ad Ablabium*,[43] as chapter 5
has shown. The Syriac version, however, does not translate this passage, but
explains the double procession in another manner: "For just as the Father is,
so also is the Son who is from Him, together with ('*m*) the Holy Spirit."[44] It
seems that the procession of the Third Person is conceived inseparably from
that of the Second, coherently with the necessity of underscoring the consub-

39. Εἷς Θεὸς καὶ Πατὴρ καὶ εἷς μονογενὴς Υἱὸς καὶ ἓν Πνεῦμα ἅγιον (Basil, *De Spiritu Sancto*, 18.44.20–21 [SC 17bis:404]).

40. *Syr* I, 85.21–22 (Taylor, *Syriac Versions of the* De Spiritu Sancto, 2:72).

41. See p. 118.

42. Ἐν δὲ καὶ τὸ ἅγιον Πνεῦμα, καὶ αὐτὸ μοναδικῶς ἐξαγγελλόμενον, δι' ἑνὸς Υἱοῦ τῷ ἑνὶ Πατρὶ συναπτόμενον, καὶ δι' ἑαυτοῦ συμπληροῦν τὴν πολυύμνητον καὶ μακαρίαν Τριάδα (Basil, *De Spiritu Sancto*, 18.45.24–27 [SC 17bis:408]).

43. See G. Maspero, *Trinity and Man: Gregory of Nyssa's Ad Ablabium* (Leiden: Brill, 2007), 153–57.

44. *Syr* I, 86.13–14 (Taylor, *Syriac Versions of the* De Spiritu Sancto, 2:72–73).

stantiality of the Third Person. It is to be noted that the translator employs the preposition *with* (*'m*) and not the prepositional locution *b'd*, which would be the more literal translation of the Greek *through* (διά). In fact, previously, *b'd* had been seen as equivalent to *from* (*mn*) in reference to creation.[45] Here the translator wishes to underscore consubstantiality, and thus the fact that the discourse applies to divine immanence.

The expression is also striking in the work's citation of Psalm 32(33):6, which we have noted above. It appears that the translator applies John 15:26— and thus *npq*—to the Word. Perhaps it is the use of the preposition *with* (*'m*) which explains this peculiarity.

The processions are in fact clearly distinguished, as will be seen in what follows. The Greek text speaks of the communion according to nature (τῆς κατὰ τὴν φύσιν κοινωνίας) founded on being from God (ἐκ τοῦ Θεοῦ), immediately alluding again to Psalm 32(33):6: "Absolutely not as every thing is from God, but in the sense of proceeding (προελθόν) from God; not in a generated manner as the Son, but as Spirit *from* His mouth (cf. Ps 32[33]:6)."[46] The Syriac translator, first of all, speaks of the "one nature of the one glorious Trinity,"[47] then expanding the discourse to the Spirit, saying:

> Thus the Holy Spirit is far removed from the nature of creation since She[48] is the one Spirit who is from God (*mn 'lh'*), and She has never been reckoned with the host of the many spirits. Now She is thus joined to the Father and to the Son, in a way that nothing else apart from Her may be joined to God, because She is from the nature (*mn kyn'*) of God. It was not, however, in the same way as this which is said: "Everything is from God" (1 Cor 11:12) since everything which is made exists on account of His creative power. The Spirit, however, (proceeds) from Him (*mn lwth*) as though She is expressed from His nature, yet not by birth (*ylyd'yt*) like the Son, but like the living breath ('spirit') (*rwḥ' ḥyt'*) which (proceeds) from his mouth (cf. Ps 32[33]:6).[49]

The translation merits a detailed study. In this context it is enough to note that, while for the Son the adverb *ylyd'yt* is employed, the Spirit's being from God

---

45. *Syr* I, 10.20–12.14 (Taylor, *Syriac Versions of the* De Spiritu Sancto, 2:4–6).

46. οὐχ ὡς τὰ πάντα ἐκ τοῦ Θεοῦ, ἀλλ᾽ ὡς ἐκ τοῦ Θεοῦ προελθόν· οὐ γεννητῶς ὡς ὁ Υἱός, ἀλλ᾽ ὡς Πνεῦμα στόματος αὐτοῦ (Basil, *De Spiritu Sancto*, 18.46.2–4 [SC 17bis:408]).

47. *Syr* I, 86.25–26 (Taylor, *Syriac Versions of the* De Spiritu Sancto, 2:73).

48. "Spirit" (*rwḥ'*) is feminine in Syriac, and the grammatical gender has been kept in the translation for the sake of clarity.

49. *Syr* I, 86.27–87.9 (Taylor, *Syriac Versions of the* De Spiritu Sancto, 2:73).

is indicated only with the preposition *from* (*mn*), and not with the adverb or the verb indicating procession. This is reflected in the previously observed modification in the citation of Psalm 32(33):6, where "*of* the mouth" becomes "*from* the mouth." This verse is utilized here in order to distinguish the two processions, while in the previous text it was applied to the Word. The underlying theology is that the Spirit is God because He (in the Syriac She) is from the nature of God, understood in an immanent sense, unlike created realities and angels in particular. Being *from* the divine nature in this manner is possible only for the Third Person of the Trinity, and this in relation to the procession of the Son Himself, in the inseparability of their being from God. It can be remembered that for Ephrem, the Son is *at* the mouth of the Father.[50]

Another fundamental theme is the full recognition of the role of the Spirit as Creator of all things, both spiritual and immaterial, something toward which Basil again shows some uncertainty[51] in the Greek original of *De Spiritu Sancto*. In this work the action of the Third Person is confined to the sanctification and perfecting of intelligible beings. In the Syriac version, the Semitic interest in angelology required great attention in order to distinguish between the Spirit as the divine Person and the angelic spiritual beings. So, from a Trinitarian perspective, the text accentuates the fact that the Spirit is God because He is from the nature of God, in such a way that the Son is implicated in the previously presented affirmation of consubstantiality.

The continuation of the text helps to clarify this last affirmation. The Spirit will manifest the glory of Christ as Spirit of Truth and Wisdom, who shows in His own greatness Christ, Power of God and Wisdom of God:[52]

> and He (the Spirit), who is the Paraclete has in Himself the imprint of the goodness of the Paraclete (Christ) who has sent Him, and manifests in His dignity the greatness of the One from whom He proceeds (προῆλθεν).[53]

Benoît Pruche comments in a note that the originating Paraclete must be the Father, even if the context is completely referred to Christ, and the expression "another Consoler" of John 14:16 would likewise suggest an identification with

---

50. Ephrem, *Sermones de fide*, 1.75 (E. Beck, ed., *Des heiligen Ephraem des Syrers Sermones de fide*, CSCO 212 [Leuven: Secretariat du Corpus Scriptorum Christianorum Orientalium, 1961], 2).

51. See chapter 3.

52. Basil, *De Spiritu Sancto*, 18.46.13–17 (SC 17bis:410).

53. Καὶ ὡς Παράκλητος δὲ ἐν ἑαυτῷ χαρακτηρίζει τοῦ ἀποστείλαντος αὐτὸν Παρακλήτου τὴν ἀγαθότητα· καὶ ἐν τῷ ἑαυτοῦ ἀξιώματι τὴν μεγαλωσύνην ἐμφαίνει τὴν τοῦ ὅθεν προῆλθεν (Basil, *De Spiritu Sancto*, 18.46.17–20 [SC 17bis:410]).

Him. It is noted that the verb used for procession does not necessarily implicate procession from the Father in the sense of *ekporeuetai*. The Syriac text eliminates any doubt:

> and, again, as the Spirit the Paraclete, which She was called, for with this name "Comforter" She has taken upon Herself the likeness of the Son, that through Her benefactions She might comfort the hearts of those to whom She should come, so that by means of the majesty She possessed through Her power She might manifest Her (own) glories, so that She should be known to proceed (and) come forth (*npqt 'tt*) from the Godhead.[54]

The Paraclete is identified with the Son, such that the shift from economy to immanence is clear, with the procession being indicated by the two verbs in the feminine *npqt* and *'tt*. The source of this dynamic is the divinity itself, that is, the "one nature of the one glorious Trinity," as the translator calls it. This origin is clearly in reference to being God, and not only to mission, the being God that also characterizes the Son, and that the Spirit Himself, in His being Comforter, manifests. This is a union of nature founded on an exchange of glory, called "familiar" (οἰκειακή) in the Greek text,[55] which the Syriac text translates "in tenderness and love" (*brḥmt' wbḥwb'*).[56]

A citation of John 14:16 appears immediately afterward, in which Christ says of the Spirit: "He will glorify Me, since He will take of mine and announce it to you." The Greek text comments: "As the Son is glorified by the Father who says: 'I have glorified it [the name] and will glorify it' (John 12:28) so is the Spirit glorified by (διά) His communion with the Father and the Son."[57] The Syriac translator, who typically seeks to follow the text closely, makes significant changes when it refers to the communion of the Father and Son. He writes:

> And, again, just as the Son is glorified by the Father, as He said: "I have glorified and I will glorify" (John 12:28), so also the Holy Spirit is glorified because of (*byd*) the Father by (*mn*) the Son through (*b-*) Her communion with them.[58]

---

54. *Syr I*, 88.2–5 (Taylor, *Syriac Versions of the* De Spiritu Sancto, 2:74).

55. Basil, *De Spiritu Sancto*, 18.46.26 (SC 17bis:410).

56. *Syr I*, 88.13.

57. Καὶ ὡς δοξάζεται Υἱὸς παρὰ τοῦ Πατρός, λέγοντος· Καὶ ἐδόξασα, καὶ πάλιν δοξάσω· οὕτω δοξάζεται τὸ Πνεῦμα διὰ τῆς πρὸς Πατέρα καὶ Υἱὸν κοινωνίας (Basil, *De Spiritu Sancto*, 18.46.30–33 [SC 17bis:410]).

58. *Syr I*, 88.17–19 (Taylor, *Syriac Versions of the* De Spiritu Sancto, 2:74).

The intention appears to be that of making explicit the intra-Trinitarian dynamic, showing how the correspondence of glory and nature—the foundation of the entire argument of the treatise—requires that the communion in nature, and thus in glory, be given from the Father to the Son, and from the Father and Son in their communion to the Spirit. This is in perfect harmony with the conception of the Third Person as bond of the first two Persons seen in Gregory of Nyssa and Gregory of Nazianzus.

In synthesis, the Syriac translator attempts to highlight consubstantiality, and for this reason expresses the divinity of the single divine Person in terms of nature. This however implicates the necessity of further accentuating procession, indicated both by *npq* with a general signification and by recourse to the preposition *mn*. This is an approach that is already present in Syriac theology, which, due to its Semitic background, reads the Trinity in light of the concrete images of Ephrem, manifested by the interaction between the process of translation and properly theological reflection. As will be seen in what follows, from this will emerge again the importance of the "He will take of mine" stated by Christ in John 16:14 in order to distinguish the two processions and specify the role of the Son.

III.3. Gregory of Nyssa and Pseudo-Gregory Thaumaturgus

These remarks can shed some light on the philological *crux* in Gregory of Nyssa's[59] *Oratio Dominica*, seen in the previous chapter. The codex Vaticanus 2066, from the ninth century, inserts the preposition *from* (ἐκ) before the Son as well, but in the *Gregorii Nysseni Opera* critical edition the preposition appears between brackets. The preposition was in fact present in both of the manuscript traditions (Φ and Ψ), but after the ninth century many instances of *ek* were scratched out, clearly for dogmatic reasons. In this context the two Syriac manuscripts that have transmitted the text become especially important for the present discussion, both of them from the sixth century. In fact the manuscripts Vat syr 106 and Brit syr 564 (add. 14, 550) both witness to the presence of a second *from* (*mn*) before the reference to the Son. Here we can show that the Syriac tradition could not read the preposition *mn* of the translation in a polemical sense, because it already knew various examples of this use in its theology.[60] An analogous situation can be found in the *De Sancta*

---

59. On the Syriac translations of Gregory of Nyssa's works, see M. Parmentier, "Syriac Translations of Gregory of Nyssa," *Orientalia Lovaniensia Periodica* 20 (1989): 143–93.

60. In this regard, the observation of Sebastian Brock on the proximity of Ephrem and

Trinitate, where an *ek* referring to the Son is present only in one part of the Greek manuscripts, while it is always transmitted by the Syriac tradition.[61]

A final Greek text will further reveal the richness of the Syriac translations of the Greek originals as well as their theological value. In *Homilia IV in Sancta Theophania*, placed among the dubious works of Gregory Thaumaturgus, the following passage referring to John the Baptist appears:

> And in whose name will I baptize You? In that of the Father? But You have the entire Father in You and You are in the Father entirely. In the name of the Son then? But other than You, there is no other who is Son of God by nature. In the name of the Holy Spirit then? But He is always with You, in so far as consubstantial to You and having the same will, knowledge, power and honour, and adored by all with You.[62]

The Syriac version[63] is virtually identical,[64] except in the case of the Holy Spirit:

> Will I baptize You in the name of the Holy Spirit? But He proceeds from You (*mnk npq*) and is equal to You in eternity and majesty.[65]

As can be seen, the Syriac version adds the procession from the Son, using the verb *npq*, which, given the original Greek text, appears to be the fruit of an interpretation based upon the theological understanding of the translator himself. In fact, the Syriac authors have a similar tendency in the centuries that follow.

Gregory of Nyssa seems extremely interesting. S. Brock, *The Luminous Eye: The Spiritual World Vision of Saint Ephrem* (Kalamazoo, MI: Cistercian, 1992), 145–48.

61. Gregory of Nyssa, *Ad Eustathium, De sancta Trinitate*, GNO 3.1:13.17–18.

62. Εἰς τίνος δὲ ὄνομά σε βαπτίσω; Εἰς τὸ τοῦ Πατρός; Ἀλλ᾽ ὅλον τὸν Πατέρα ἔχεις ἐν ἑαυτῷ, καὶ ὅλος ὑπάρχεις ἐν τῷ Πατρί. Ἀλλ᾽ εἰς τοῦ Υἱοῦ; Ἀλλ᾽ οὐκ ἔστι παρὰ σὲ, ἄλλος φύσει Υἱὸς Θεοῦ. Ἀλλ᾽ εἰς τὸ τοῦ ἁγίου Πνεύματος; Ἀλλὰ σύνεστί σοι διὰ παντός, ὡς ὁμοούσιόν σοι καὶ ὁμόβουλον, καὶ ὁμόγνωμον, καὶ ὁμοδύναμον, καὶ ὁμότιμον, καὶ σὺν σοὶ δέχεται τὴν παρὰ πάντων προσκύνησιν (Pseudo-Gregory Thaumaturgus, *Homilia IV in Sancta Theophania*, PG 10:1184b).

63. It is found in Brit 14515, folio 64 vo, column 2, attributed to Chrysostom. The reference to Arius and Eunomius clearly indicates an epoch posterior to Thaumaturgus. The question is complicated by the fact that the Syriac version appears to be the result of a fusion of the homily attributed to Thaumaturgus and another text: cf. J. B. Pitra, *Analecta sacra Spicilegio Solesmensi parata*, 8 vols. (Paris: Jouby et Roger, 1876–1888), 4:127.

64. See Pitra, *Analecta sacra Spicilegio Solesmensi parata*, 4:130.

65. Pitra, *Analecta sacra Spicilegio Solesmensi parata*, 4:130–31.

IV. THEOLOGY: JOHN 15:26 AND 16:14 RELOADED

The Trinitarian theology of Philoxenus is not widely studied,[66] although it represents a deep and rich synthesis.[67] As for the issue being examined here, his witness is particularly interesting, revealing a leap forward in theological precision. It should be recalled that this author knows and cites the translation of Basil's *De Spiritu Sancto*.[68]

Explaining why the Trinity is one God and thus one nature in three Persons, Philoxenus describes the divine Persons thus:

> The Father who is Father from always and since eternity, not only by will, but also by nature; the Son who is Son in an essential manner together with the Father, Son not by grace, but by natural generation (*bylydwt' dmn kyn'*); and the Spirit who is such neither metaphorically nor temporally, as the other messenger spirits who began to be, but Holy Spirit, [who is] from (*kyn' mn*) the nature of the Father and the Son, and consubstantial with them.[69]

The principle that guides the Trinitarian theology of Philoxenus is the clear distinction between that which is created and the three divine Persons, who are the unique eternal nature and have no beginning. He says of God:

> He is the first and He is the last, and there is no other God or Lord outside of Him. Every Person who is from Him (*mnh*) is God.[70]

From a doctrinal perspective, consubstantiality refers to the relation of origin expressed by the preposition *mn*, such that the Son and the Spirit are God precisely due to their procession from the Father. In the first text cited, it is

66. A. de Halleux, *Philoxène de Mabbog* (Leuven: Imprimerie Orientaliste, 1963), primarily 351–63. A reading of his pneumatology from the spiritual perspective can be found in P. Harb, "La conception pneumatologique chez Philoxène de Mabbug," *Parole de l'orient* 5 (1969): 5–15.

67. See D. A. Michelson, *The Practical Christology of Philoxenos of Mabbug*, Oxford Early Christian Studies (New York: Oxford University Press, 2014).

68. On this see Taylor, *Syriac Versions of the* De Spiritu Sancto, 1:xxxiii–xxxv.

69. Philoxenus, *Epistula ad monachos (Tell'addâ)*, folio 4b column 1.5–21. Manuscript published in I. Guidi, *La lettera di Filosseno ai monaci di Tell'addâ (Taleda)* (Rome: Reale Accademia Nazionale dei Lincei, 1886), 4.

70. Philoxenus, *Tractatus tres de trinitate et incarnatione*, 17.24–26. Text in A. Vaschalde, ed., *Tractatus tres de trinitate et incarnatione*, CSCO 9 (Leuven: Peeters, 1907).

seen how the Spirit proceeding from the Father also implies being *from* the nature of the Son.

This also appears with the recourse to the main Trinitarian analogy in Ephrem's theology that is now inserted into an explicitly dogmatic and systematic theological context in order to clarify the roles of the processions and the Trinitarian perichoresis:

> From the soul and with it are the word and the intellect; from the sun and with it are its ray and heat; from fire and with it are its splendor and heat. Thus, from the Father and with Him are the Son and His Spirit. In fact, if you will learn of the Father, you will find the Son, and if you will keep the Son, you will know the Spirit, from the fact that each of them is from the same nature, and this same nature is recognized as God. One is the nature in three Persons, and again the Persons three in the same nature: the Father is Being itself, the Son is consubstantial and God, and the Spirit, who is from Being itself, is also God; not three gods, but one essence and one divinity.[71]

The psychological analogy and the analogy of light taken from Ephrem are applied to the two processions in a particularly rich and synthetic text. The next chapter will show that the presence of such analogies should not be surprising. The relationship between heat and the ray of sun or the splendor of fire signals again a proceeding together—already seen in the translation of *De Spiritu Sancto*—by which the Spirit is also from the Son without the Father ceasing to be the unique principle.

The close connection in Syriac between procession and consubstantiality is also caused by the necessity of expressing consubstantiality itself with the expression "son of the essence" (*br 'ytwt'*). Reading the above passage in light of this observation will help to better understand the Philoxenian conception of the relationship between the two processions. Assemani affirms that the expression "the Father is Being itself, the Son is consubstantial, and the Spirit is from Being itself,"[72] a parallel to that contained at the end of the passage quoted above, would indicate that Philoxenus does not conceive of the procession of the Spirit in relation to the Son as well[73]. Philoxenus's use of analogies,

---

71. Philoxenus, *Tractatus tres de trinitate et incarnatione*, 25.28–26.9.

72. Philoxenus, *Tractatus tres de trinitate et incarnatione*, 23.31–24.1.

73. Philoxenus would maintain opposing positions *incohaerenter*; see J. S. Assemani, *Bibliotheca Orientalis Clementino-Vaticana*, 4 vols. (Rome: Sacrae Congregationis de Propaganda Fide, 1719–1728), 2:20–21.

however, would prove the contrary. Even Assemani must affirm that the author contradicts himself,[74] in that Philoxenus affirms:

> The Father is distinguished from the Son only by the fact that He engenders and is not engendered, in the same way that the Son is distinguished from the Father because He is engendered but does not engender. Thus the Spirit is distinguished from the Father and the Son in so far as He is always Holy Spirit, and never Father nor Son.[75]

If the only distinction between the Father and the Son regards generation, the procession of the Spirit must also be referred to the Son, not as principle but in His correlation to the Father. This is explained directly afterward, when Philoxenus says:

> For, if someone names the Father, he shows that He [the Father] has a Son. And if he confesses the Son, he manifests that the Son has the Father. Thus, also if he names the Spirit, undoubtedly he indicates that the Spirit is of the Father. For this reason, in Scripture the Spirit of God is called Holy Spirit and Spirit of the Lord.[76]

This text clarifies that saying Father already requires thinking of the Son, in such a manner that to speak of the procession from the Father immediately requires the role of the Son, without whom the Father would not be thus.

The theology of Philoxenus is thus attentive to distinguish the two processions, in order to affirm both the identity of nature and distinction of the divine Persons:

> And since He [the Third Person][77] is called Spirit and recognized [to be] from the nature of God the Father, He who is also called Spirit from the word of our Lord. For the Son is from the Father not in the same manner

---

74. Cf. the discussion in A. A. Vaschalde, *Three Letters of Philoxenus: Bishop of Mabbôgh (485–519); Being the Letter to the Monks, the First Letter to the Monks of Beth-Gaugal, and the Letter to Emperor Zeno* (Rome: Tipografia della R. Accademia dei Lincei, 1902; repr. Whitefish, MT: Kessinger, 2010), 74–76.

75. Philoxenus, *Tractatus tres de trinitate et incarnatione*, 27.4–7.

76. Philoxenus, *Tractatus tres de trinitate et incarnatione*, 27.23–28.

77. In Philoxenus's language, the gender of the Syriac word "Spirit" has already changed for theological reasons.

as the Spirit is from the Son; but both are from the Father: one as Son and the other as Spirit.[78]

The necessity to specify that the Spirit does not come from the Son in the same manner that the Son comes from the Father implies that there is a role of the Son Himself in the communication of the divine nature from the First to the Third Person, without injuring the Father's being the one principle of the Trinity.

Philoxenus expresses procession through the preposition *mn*. In order to distinguish the two processions he chooses to apply "proceed" (*npq*) to the Holy Spirit alone, while indicating the role of the Son in the second procession with "take" (*nsb*) instead, referring to John 16:14:

> We believe that the Father exists because He exists; and that the Son exists because He is engendered; and thus too that the Holy Spirit exists because He proceeds (*npq*) from the Father and takes (*nsb*) from the Son (cf. John 16:14).[79]

The interaction of the two verbs, together with the context of the cited passages, requires that the text be understood in reference to divine immanence. The interaction of John 15:26 and 16:14 comes to the fore again.[80]

This is confirmed by the testimony of Jacob of Sarug. He also combines the verbs *npq* and *nsb*, corresponding to John 15:26 and 16:14, in reference to the Holy Spirit and to the personal characteristic that distinguishes Him from the unbegotten Father and the begotten Son:

> The Father, the Son, and the Spirit are known, seen and preached as the only God who should be worshipped, Who has no other person with Himself who may participate in His adoration. In fact, one alone is the holy Father, one alone the holy Son, one alone the Holy Spirit. The Father is unbegotten,

---

78. Philoxenus, *Tractatus tres de trinitate et incarnatione*, 31.6–11.

79. Philoxenus, *Tractatus tres de trinitate et incarnatione*, 234.21–25.

80. This can be related to the Cappadocian influence on Philoxenus; see D. A. Michelson, "Philoxenos of Mabbug: A Cappadocian Theologian on the Banks of the Euphrates?" in *Motions of Late Antiquity: Essays on Religion, Politics, and Society in Honour of Peter Brown*, ed. J. Kreiner and H. Reimitz, Cultural Encounters in Late Antiquity and the Middle Ages 20 (Turnhout: Brepols, 2016), 151–74.

the Son is begotten, and the Spirit proceeds (*npq*) from the Father and takes (*nsb*) from the Son (cf. John 16:14).[81]

Thus it would seem that between the fifth and sixth centuries the recourse to John 16:14 to specify the relationship between the Holy Spirit and the Son and to distinguish the two processions is not exclusive of Philoxenus' theology but is common at least in Edessa. And this approach is perfectly consistent with the answers to the Pneumatomachians.

v. Liturgy and Spirituality

The importance of the Lukan variant of the Lord's Prayer in Gregory of Nyssa's *De oratione dominica* has already been shown with its connection with Syriac liturgy. The following remarks can suggest the reason of its role in pneumatology. Sebastian Brock, in his study on the epiclesis in the West Syrian anaphoras, identifies six epicleses in which John 16:14 makes an appearance next to "of the proceeding from the Father" expressed with *npq*: Dioscorus of Gazarta (C111or and Renaudot 494–5); Marutha of Tikrit (C151r and 263–4); Peter of Kallinikos (M50r); Matthew the Shepherd (Pampakuda 1986, 171 and 348); Ignatius bar Wahib (C145r and 529); and Xystus (Pampakuda 1986, 208 and 137).

In the final three examples the reference to essence is explicit, as the object of the verb *nsb* is specified in the following way: the Spirit "takes from the Son as regards to the essence" (*wmn br' nsb 'wsy'yt*).[82] We notice, therefore, a noteworthy theological coherence.[83] From here a strict link emerges between John 16:14 and 15:26 in the context of the epiclesis: the Holy Spirit can transform the offerings into Christ precisely because everything the former has belongs to the latter. Further, in the fourth Sunday before Christmas, in the Office called *Of the Annunciation* (*dswbr'*), this formula is found: "The eternal

81. Jacob of Sarug, *Ad Samuelem Abbatem Gabulense*, in Assemani, *Bibliotheca Orientalis Clementino-Vaticana*, 1:302.

82. Assemani, *Bibliotheca Orientalis Clementino-Vaticana*, 1:302.

83. Compare the texts of two of anaphoras cited: "Miserere mei, Deus amator hominum, et mitte super me et super oblationem istam Spiritum Sanctum, Spiritum qui a te procedit et a Filio tuo accipit" (*Anafora di Marutha*, in E. Renaudot, *Liturgiarum orientalium collectio*, 2 vols. [London: John Leslie Bibliopolam, 1847; repr. Westmead: Gregg International, 1970], 2:263); and "Propitius esto mihi Domine, universoque gregi tuo et hereditati suae: placitasque habe et sanctifica oblationes istas per illapsum Spiritus tui Sancti: qui a te procedit ab aeterno et a Filio tuo accipit substantialiter" (Xystus, in Renaudot, *Liturgiarum orientalium collectio*, 2:136).

Father, who has no father. The Son who is from Him (*mnh*), who has no son. And the Holy Spirit who proceeds (*npq*) from them."[84] The text is particularly beautiful from a formal perspective due to its symmetrical structure and is especially rich from a theological perspective due to its extreme synthesis. It can be seen how the verb *npq*, which is applied here to the second procession, can also be referred to the Son in that it is specified that He has no son. In this manner, it is clear that the Father is the Principle without principle and that the Son proceeds by generation, expressed by recourse to *mn*, in such a way that it can safely be said that the Spirit proceeds from both of them due to the general character of the Syriac verb *npq*.

This is also found in the Syriac spiritual tradition. In the seventh century, Dadisho of Qatar again presents the same theology, explicitly applying the verb *npq* to the second procession. In fact, in Discourse 13 of the *Commentarium in Asceticon Abbae Isaiah*, when affirming the identity of the Spirit of penance and the Spirit Paraclete, Dadisho states: "For unique is His Person, consubstantial to the Father and the Son, who proceeds (*npq*) from the Father and the Son, is adored by all and glorified with the Father and the Son."[85] The context is not dogmatic, but spiritual. It is precisely for this reason that the affirmations are all the more striking, since, due to their structure and use, they seem to come from a Symbol. This is confirmed by the fact that, shortly afterward, the same formula is repeated to refer all the charisms to the Spirit through the use of the equality of nature, power, and will of the three divine Persons. In this way Dadisho expresses the greatness of the Spirit Himself, who is "consubstantial with the Father and the Son, and who proceeds (*npq*) from the Father and the Son and has part together with them in the production of creation."[86]

Another example, significantly present in a protological context is by Hazzâyâ, who in the eighth century writes in *Capita scientiae*: "The source that flows from Eden and waters the trees of Paradise is a figure of the Holy Spirit who proceeds (*npq*) from the Father and the Son."[87] In synthesis, the use of the verb *npq* in order to indicate the procession of the Spirit from both the Father and the Son is maintained throughout the Syriac tradition, so much as

84. Assemani, *Bibliotheca Orientalis Clementino-Vaticana*, 3.2:235.

85. Dadisho of Qatar, *Commentarium in Asceticon Abbae Isaiah*, 13. Text in R. Draguet, *Dadišo Qatraya: Commentaire du Livre d'Abba Isaïe*, CSCO 326 (Leuven: Peeters, 1972), 173 (lines 1–2).

86. Dadisho of Qatar, *Commentarium in Asceticon Abbae Isaiah*, 13 (Draguet, *Dadišo Qatraya*, 174 [lines 10–12]).

87. Hazzâyâ, *Capita scientiae*, 35. Text in A. Scher, "Joseph Hazzâyâ, écrivain syrien du VIIIme siècle," *Rivista degli studi orientali* 3 (1910): 45–63, esp. 59.

to be able to be considered the norm. Among the exceptions,[88] the *Liber de Unione* of Babai the Great stands out, which maintains the procession of the Spirit from the Father alone (*lḥwdy'*).[89] The position of this sixth or seventh century author is confirmed by the use of the analogy of the birth of Abel from Adam and the procession of Eve in order to illustrate the two processions.[90]

That the phenomenon of affirming the procession of the Spirit in light of the Son is due to the general nature of the Syriac verb can be confirmed by the Arabic tradition as well, which, in that it is secondary, can only have a verifying role. This can be seen already in the translation of the *Canones* of Hippolytus where the Son appears alongside the Father when the origin of the Spirit is referenced.[91] It is then reflected in later theology, where the situation is more articulated both linguistically and theologically. There nevertheless remains a clear tradition that ties the procession of the Spirit to the Son.[92]

VI. CONCLUSIONS: LANGUAGE AND MYSTERY

In synthesis, the examples presented here from the fourth to eighth centuries appear to permit the conclusion that the Syriac tradition is conscious of the necessity of highlighting the specificity of the Spirit's procession from the Father according to the Greek *ekporeuetai*; at the same time, however, the tradition is at greater liberty to express the role of the Son in this procession, manifesting theological content already present in the Greek Trinitarian doctrine, particularly in Gregory of Nyssa and the confrontation with the Pneumatomachians, as seen. The Syriac phenomenon seems to be explained well through the semantic extension of the verb *npq*, which can be applied to both processions as in the Syriac versions of John 8:42 and 15:26.

88. The exceptions posterior to the ninth century are not considered here, as they are overly marked by polemics. In particular, for the context of the late period, the witness of Barhebraeus does not appear useful for the discussion. Cf. Assemani, *Bibliotheca Orientalis Clementino-Vaticana*, 2:287.

89. Babai the Great, *Liber de unione*. Text in A. Vaschalde, *Babai Magni Liber de unione*, CSCO 79 (Leuven: Peeters, 1915), 30 (line 18).

90. See Vaschalde, *Babai Magni Liber de unione*, 32.

91. D. B. de Haneberg, *Canones S. Hippolyti arabice e codicibus romanis cum versione latina annotationibus et prolegomenis* (Münster: Academiae Regiae Boicae, 1870), 40, 76. See also W. J. Riedel, *Die Kirchenrechtsquellen des Patriarchats Alexandrien* (Leipzig: Wilhelm Johann, 1900), 212.

92. R. Haddad, *La Trinité divine chez les théologiens arabes, 750–1050* (Paris: Beauchesne, 1985), 239–42.

The lack of a specific term to express the procession of the Third Person from the First, who is the only Source and Origin of absolutely everything within and outside God, reflects a linguistic poverty in the Syriac language with respect to the Greek. But, at the same time, analogous to what happened in the Latin world, the translation into a more elementary language obliged the theologians to stress different nuances in the infinite depth of the Trinitarian mystery.

Syriac theology always conceives economy and immanence together without confusing them. This emerges from the very definition of consubstantiality in terms of generation with respect to the divine nature. In this way the Son is God because He proceeds as Son from the nature of the Father. But also the Holy Spirit is God because He ("She" in Syriac) proceeds from the divine nature, not as the Father's Son but in a way that is linguistically expressed as "being son of the divine nature (*br kyn*)." This may explain why Syriac pneumatology has a tendency to speak of the procession of the Holy Spirit from the Father and the Son, stressing that the second procession cannot be thought of without reference to the Second Person. A synthetic formula is that the Spirit proceeds from the Father *with* the Son, where the preposition has an ontological and relational meaning.

This can be considered a sort of litmus test for the narrative presented in the previous chapters. It can also shed some light on the *Filioque* question in general by helping to situate the discussion in a hermeneutic and philological perspective in such a way as to move from the terminological level to that of the meaning that lies behind the terms. In theology, more than in any other field, words are simply arrows pointing to the Trinitarian mystery, a mystery that can never be fully articulated. The Syriac perspective is extremely valuable for a better understanding of pneumatology, so much as to suggest a rethinking of the development of Greek Trinitarian theology and its relationship to the Latin tradition, which, from the ninth century onward, has been somewhat dialectical. This implies a true return to the content and meaning of the greater whole conscious of the limitations of every language before the infinite richness of mystery.

CHAPTER SEVEN

Another Surprise: Greek Psychological Analogies

1. Introduction: A "Logical" Surprise

In this reconsideration of the theological premises of the *Filioque* through the analysis of the pneumatological thought of the Greek fathers, we have seen how anti-Pneumatomachian theology has offered interesting perspectives which broaden the common dialectic approaches. Then, the analysis of the Syriac tradition has shown just how much a different perspective can change our readings, as the discussion about the role of the Son in the procession of Spirit is an issue that cannot be overlooked. Thus arises the doubt that when one adopts an epistemological perspective consistent with apophaticism, other issues that appear to be divisive between East and West may instead turn out to be convergent. This seems to be the case with the psychological analogy, which can be reinterpreted from the relational perspective that is presented here as the core of Cappadocian Trinitarian theology. In chapter 1 we already saw a pseudo-Origenian Greek text where a sort of psychological analogy can be recognized, and in the previous chapter we just witnessed something similar in the study of Philoxenus.[1]

In fact, the human mind needs distinctions and simplifications that allow the complexity of reality to be reduced to some clear and distinct frameworks. Both teaching and the use of maps and charts are based on this process. But always, and above all on a theological level, one must never forget that reality always remains beyond the human capacity for representation. That is why the widespread identification of the Augustinian psychological analogy as a hall-mark of Western Trinitarian theology and the real foundation of the *Filioque* is certainly not baseless, but it cannot be absolutized.[2] In fact, if we observe the

1. See p. 32.
2. Lewis Ayres developed works that help reveal the need to revise some didactic para-

Greek tradition, we can find elements of a psychological analogy of the Trinity that already had a successful formulation in Gregory of Nyssa and Gregory of Nazianzus and would later reach a remarkably rich and elaborate expression in the theology of Anastasius the Sinaite.

The issue is fundamental to the subject of this volume because the procession of the Spirit from the Son in the economy is an undeniable evangelical datum that cannot be denied. The theological point then is how the economy is connected to immanence. Is it only the West that recognizes a correspondence between the two? Does this even go so far as to project an anthropology into God Himself before then deducing the *Filioque* from this, as some Eastern readings of Augustine claim? Or does the relational conception of the gap between the Trinity and the world developed by the Greek fathers suggest another reading confirmed by little known and rarely quoted texts from their works?

What follows is an attempt to answer these questions against the background of what has been presented in the previous chapters. The path taken so far makes it possible to see how the inclusion of the *Pneuma* in divine immanence was based on the development of a new ontology, which interpreted the link between God and the world in a relational way. This was translated into a new vision of the human person and her faculties. From this standpoint, the way was open for a rereading of the human immanence in the light of divine immanence according to the interpretative scheme that the history of theology, especially from the Augustinian heritage,[3] has designated the *psychological analogy*.

This analogy says nothing about God, because it is not a way to "explain" or "prove" the Trinity by introducing necessary reasons. Instead, as has been said, the underlying essential theological dimension is the relation between God and the world. In this context, the creation of humanity in the image and likeness of God (Gen 1:26) and the Pauline identification of the eternal Son with the perfect Image of the Father (Col 1:15) actually compelled a new understanding of the Platonic and Aristotelian categories.

In fact, according to Aristotle, God could not have faculties or virtues, because these are necessarily characterized by potentiality.[4] God and the world

---

digms in the history of Trinitarian dogma; see L. Ayres, *Nicaea and Its Legacy: An Approach to Fourth-Century Trinitarian Theology* (Oxford: Oxford University Press, 2006), and *Augustine and the Trinity* (Cambridge: Cambridge University Press, 2010). On the psychological analogy, see especially 315–18 of the latter volume.

3. The psychological analogy has often been understood as synonymous with Augustinian Trinitarian theology and as its exclusive characteristic. See M. Schmaus, *Die Psychologische Trinitätslehre des Hl. Augustinus* (Münster: Aschendorff, 1927), 79.

4. E.g., Aristotle, *Ethica Nicomachea*, 1178b7–16. See on this, G. Maspero, *Dio trino per-*

belong to a single ontological dimension and for this very reason they must be distinguished, highlighting what separates the human being from God. Instead, from the biblical perspective, the doctrine of creation obliges us to recognize the source of the human faculties and virtues in the Creator. The Prologue of John's Gospel thus offers the scriptural basis for the psychological analogy of the Trinity. The *Logos* is presented from the perspective of divine immanence, bringing all creation back to Him. This implies that God is "logical" and that the divine image imprinted in man must be sought precisely at the level of the *logos*. The eternal *Logos* unites the world to God from *within* the human being to *within* God. Here lie the roots of the capacity to distinguish without separating, avoiding the risks of the subordinationism of the apologist fathers, who bound the *Logos* to the existence of creation according to *Logos*-theology. Origen had succeeded in effectively criticizing this approach, offering a truly theological solution to the question of the relationship between the divine *Logos* and that of the human being. The discussion between Eusebius and Marcellus also touched on this point and is very important for seeing the intimate theological link between pneumatology and the new relational ontology. It is worth briefly analyzing some texts. Marcellus seems to interpret the divine *Logos* as equal to the human one: "The *logos* of man is one and the same as him, and it cannot be distinguished from him except in the performance of an action (ἐνεργείᾳ)."[5] The problem highlighted by Eusebius is precisely that the divine *Logos* is understood by Marcellus in the same sense as the human *logos*. The approach that tries to highlight any correspondence between the human being and the Trinity is radically forbidden here. The vocabulary refers to the terminology of the *logos endiathetos* and *prophorikos*, typical of the apologists. Eusebius denies that this is possible: "To suppose that there is neither an immanent *logos* (ἐνδιάθετον) in God as there is in man, nor an uttered word (προφορικόν) that expresses meanings as there is among us."[6] The second book of *Ecclesiastica Theologia* explains how the very potency that characterizes the human *logos* is the reason for the decisive negation of Marcellus's position. The point is that this *Logos*, similar to the human one, would sometimes be at rest (ἡσυχάζειν) in God, while other times it would proceed from Him (προϊέναι),

---

ché vivo: Lo Spirito di Dio e lo spirito dell'uomo nella Patristica greca (Brescia: Morcelliana, 2018), 193–94.

5. ἓν καὶ ταὐτὸν εἶναι τῷ ἀνθρώπῳ τὸν ἐν αὐτῷ λόγον, οὐδενὶ χωριζόμενον ἑτέρῳ ἢ μόνῃ τῇ τῆς πράξεως ἐνεργείᾳ (Eusebius, *Ecclesiastica Theologia*, 1.17.1.5–6 [GCS 14:77.11–12]).

6. ποτὲ μὲν ἐνδιάθετον ὡς ἐπ᾽ ἀνθρώπῳ λόγον ποτὲ δὲ σημαντικὸν ὡς τὸν ἐν ἡμῖν προφορικὸν καὶ ἐν τῷ θεῷ ὑποτίθεσθαι (Eusebius, *Ecclesiastica Theologia*, 1.17.7.2–3 [GCS 14:178.6–17]).

being both inside and outside (ἐντὸς καὶ ἐκτός).[7] This implies that the *Logos* would be in potency in the Father (δυνάμει ἐν τῷ πατρὶ εἶναι τὸν λόγον).[8] The discussion concerns the exegesis of the first verse of the Johannine Prologue. John would have written "The *Logos* was *with* God" instead of "The *Logos* was *in* God" in order to not lower the *Logos* to the human condition (i.e., at an accidental level):

> In fact, if he had said: "And the *Logos* was in God," as if admitting an accident in the substratum and an entity that is inherent to another, he would have presented God as a compound reality, assuming it as an essence without *Logos* or thinking of the *Logos* as an accident of the essence.[9]

The subtlety of reasoning is based on the discussion of prepositions in Johannine expressions. The use of *in* would have immediately referred to the relation of an accident to the substance. That is why Eusebius explicitly excludes that the divine *Logos* belongs to the relative realities:

> He [the evangelist] says: do not think, in fact, that He [the *Logos*] belongs to the relative realities (τῶν πρός τι), like the *logos* in the soul or like the *logos* that is heard through the voice or like the *logos* that is found in the material seeds or exists in mathematical entities. Indeed, all of these, which are relative realities (τῶν πρός τι), are considered in another substance that exists before them. While the *Logos* that is God does not need anyone else preexisting before Him to be subsisting in it, but He is by Himself, in that He lives and subsists as God.[10]

The final conclusion is that Marcellus makes a mistake by attributing to God a *logos* that is immanent (ἐνδιάθετον), like a sort of reason that is expressed

7. Eusebius, *Ecclesiastica Theologia*, 2.1.1.3–2.1 (GCS 14:99.11–22).

8. Eusebius, *Ecclesiastica Theologia*, 2.11.4.5–6 (GCS 14:113.12–13).

9. εἰ γὰρ εἰρήκει· καὶ ὁ λόγος ἦν ἐν τῷ θεῷ, ὡς ἐν ὑποκειμένῳ συμβεβηκὸς καὶ ὡς ἕτερον ἐν ἑτέρῳ δούς, σύνθετον ὥσπερ εἰσῆγεν τὸν θεόν, οὐσίαν μὲν αὐτὸν ὑποτιθέμενος δίχα λόγου συμβεβηκὸς δὲ τῇ οὐσίᾳ τὸν λόγον (Eusebius, *Ecclesiastica Theologia*, 2.14.4.1–5.1 [GCS 14:115.6–9]).

10. μὴ γὰρ τῶν πρός τι, φησίν, νόμιζε εἶναι καὶ τοῦτον, ὡς τὸν ἐν ψυχῇ λόγον ἢ ὡς τὸν διὰ φωνῆς ἀκουόμενον ἢ ὡς τὸν ἐν σωματικοῖς ὄντα σπέρμασιν ἢ ὡς τὸν ἐν μαθηματικοῖς ὑφεστῶτα θεωρήμασιν· οὗτοι γὰρ πάντες τῶν πρός τι ὄντες ἐν ἑτέρᾳ προϋποκειμένῃ νοοῦνται οὐσίᾳ. ὁ δὲ θεὸς λόγος οὐχ ἑτέρου δεῖται τοῦ προϋποκειμένου, ἵν᾽ ἐν αὐτῷ γενόμενος ὑποστῇ, καθ᾽ ἑαυτὸν δέ ἐστιν ζῶν καὶ ὑφεστὼς ἅτε θεὸς ὤν (Eusebius, *Ecclesiastica Theologia*, 2.14.2.1–3.1 [GCS 14:114.29–35]).

(προφορικόν) in the act of speaking, assuming in this way that the divine *Logos* is identical to the human one.[11]

Over the course of the fourth century this approach would be subverted by the theology of Gregory of Nyssa. As we have already seen, according to him the divine *Logos* belongs to the relative realities thanks to an understanding of ontology that overcomes, in the case of the Trinity, the opposition between relation and substance, with the introduction of the former in the immanence of the latter.[12] In fact, Athanasius's *Physis*-theology paved the way for the work of Gregory of Nyssa and Gregory of Nazianzus, who, thanks to the new ontological framework that was developed, were able to draw real psychological analogies without the risk of binding the Creator and the creature in a necessary way. The spirit of the human being was thus recognized as an image not only of God's pure spirituality but also of that immanence which had been opened up by the Spirit of God, the Third Person of the Trinity. An essential element of this reworking is precisely the new ontological status given to relation. This makes it possible to acknowledge that the psychological analogies are not just a Latin idea, but a possible and coherent consequence of the pneumatological doctrine both in the East and in the West.

This theological doctrine did not remain isolated to Cappadocian thought, but, through the mediation of Maximus the Confessor, had a relevant influence in the Greek tradition, as demonstrated by the work of Anastasius the Sinaite, to whom the second part of this chapter is dedicated. Even Gregory Palamas, as we will see, is a witness to this tradition in the Byzantine era.

II. Cappadocian Analogies

As already stated, while in the Greek philosophical framework there was only one ontology that united the First Principle with the world in such a way as to make it necessary to decisively emphasize what differentiated the two, with the Judeo-Christian revelation the evidence of the infinite ontological distance between the Creator and the creature made it possible to rethink the divine image in humanity by highlighting what unites humanity to God. If for Aristotle, God, as pure Act, can have neither faculty nor virtue because they feature an element of potency, the biblical perception of God and His image in the human being is quite different. Anthropomorphisms are not located at the mere level of language, but they have a profound theological significance linked to the doc-

---

11. Eusebius, *Ecclesiastica Theologia*, 2.15.4.17–19 (GCS 14:119.26–28).
12. See pp. 107–8.

trine of creation in image and likeness, as revealed by the core of the criticism on idolatry. In fact, idols are represented with the organs connected to seeing, hearing, and speaking, but they lack the corresponding faculties. That is why the psalm says that the followers of the idols become like them, that is, lifeless (see Ps 113:12–16[LXX]). The true God is revealed by life and by the correspondence between man's vital and psychological faculties and his Creator, who is their origin. Thus, the psalmist wonders: "Does the one who shaped the ear not hear? The one who formed the eye not see?" (Ps 93[94]:9).

In the New Testament, then, the Prologue of the Fourth Gospel seems fundamental for the path to psychological analogy, describing divine immanence in terms of *Logos*. It can be considered almost an implicit psychological analogy, uniting eternal filiation with the *Logos* itself. That is why in the present narrative a bold statement by Clement of Alexandria can be taken as one of the first and most significant attempts to interpret the human being in the light of the intimate life of the Trinity: "Man becomes an image of God to the extent that he cooperates with Him in the generation of man."[13] The image is related to the faculty of generation that is presented as the seat of resemblance to God through a link between the human being's activity and divine generation in God's immanence. The developments of the analogy will move within the framework of the theology of the *Logos*. However, as already seen, this term was marked by a meaning of subordinate mediation in the Greek philosophical approach, parallel with what also happened with *pneuma*, just as in the Old Testament the language linked to the Word and the Spirit of God pointed to divine speech and action. With the categories of the fourth century we can say that both terms were used on the level of the divine economy and the development of the response to Arianism introduced them into immanence. But this process is long and difficult. In particular, as we have shown, it caused the dropping of some of the images present, for example, in Origen, which could be misunderstood.[14]

In the works of Origen the only text that can be traced back to the logic of psychological analogy has already been presented and is of dubious attribution.[15] The tripartition of the human into spirit, body, and soul in *Selecta in Psalmos* can be read as a real parallel to the Trinity of the divine Persons, but Origen's main concern aimed at distinguishing the divine *Logos* from the human one.[16]

13. καὶ κατὰ τοῦτο εἰκὼν ὁ ἄνθρωπος γίνεται τοῦ θεοῦ, καθὸ εἰς γένεσιν ἀνθρώπου ἄνθρωπος συνεργεῖ (Clement of Alexandria, *Paedagogus*, 2.10.83.2 (SC 108:164).

14. See the image of the Spirit as a child in Matt 18:2: cf. pp. 23–25.

15. See p. 32.

16. See G. Maspero, "Remarks on Origen's Analogies for the Holy Spirit," in *Origeniana Decima*, ed. H. Pietras and S. Kaczmarek (Leuven: Peeters, 2011), 563–78, and Maspero,

Later, through the *Physis*-theology introduced by Athanasius, both the *Logos* and the *Pneuma* were resemantized in terms of the extension of classical ontology, which lies in this new understanding of their relation. Now *schesis* could no longer be considered an accident because the divine Persons are correlative since their names indicate relations. The clear distinction between the Trinity and the world allows, then, for the relationship between the two ontological levels to be interpreted without the risk of confusion. One can look for what unites, because the distinction is ensured by the new metaphysical framework and because relation has been grasped in all its value and reality.

That is why Basil can sketch the principle of psychological analogy, highlighting the peculiarity of the human soul:

> Consider yourself, then, not what you own or what surrounds you, but consider just yourself. In fact, we are one thing, and the things we own and those around us are something different. We are the soul and the mind (ἡ ψυχὴ καὶ ὁ νοῦς), so we were created in the image of the Creator. Instead, the body is what we possess, and through it the senses, while wealth, the arts, and other comforts of life are what surrounds us.[17]

This principle is developed by Gregory of Nyssa, who in his *Oratio catechetica magna* constructs a psychological analogy with a material element, as it corresponds to his sensitivity that tries to recover the body left in shadow in Origen's doctrine. As Jean Daniélou wrote: "According to Gregory, the analogy is that of the relation of the soul with breathing and the word, rather than that of the spirit with the mental verb and the will. This is perfectly in the line of his materialism, which makes him look for the analogies of the divinity between the sensible things rather than the intelligible ones."[18] God, in fact, cannot be *alogos*, so He must have an eternal *Logos* corresponding to His eternal nature, of which the human *logos* is an image, but an image with a changing nature

---

"The Logos in Us and the Logos in the Principle according to Origen," in *Origeniana undecimal: Origen and Origenism in the History of Western Thought*, ed. A-Ch. Jacobsen (Leuven: Peeters, 2016), 843–56.

17. Πρόσεχε οὖν σεαυτῷ, τουτέστι· μήτε τοῖς σοῖς, μήτε τοῖς περὶ σέ, ἀλλὰ σαυτῷ μόνῳ πρόσεχε. Ἄλλο γάρ ἐσμεν ἡμεῖς αὐτοί, καὶ ἄλλο τὰ ἡμέτερα, καὶ ἄλλο τὰ περὶ ἡμᾶς. Ἡμεῖς μὲν οὖν ἐσμεν ἡ ψυχὴ καὶ ὁ νοῦς, καθ᾽ ὃν κατ᾽ εἰκόνα τοῦ κτίσαντος γεγενήμεθα· ἡμέτερον δὲ τὸ σῶμα, καὶ αἱ διὰ τούτου αἰσθήσεις· περὶ ἡμᾶς δὲ χρήματα, τέχναι, καὶ ἡ λοιπὴ τοῦ βίου κατασκευή (Basil, *Homilia in illud: Attende tibi ipsi*, 3 [text in S. Y. Rudberg, ed., *L'homélie de Basile de Césarée sur le mot 'observe-toi toi-même* (Stockholm: Almqvist & Wiksell, 1962), 26–27]).

18. J. Daniélou, *Le IVe siècle: Grégoire de Nysse et son milieu* (Paris: Institut catholique de Paris, 1964), 49.

as is the case for the human being. The same reasoning is applied to *pneuma*, since Life itself cannot lack the vital breath that is inseparable from the eternal *Logos*, of which the breath that always accompanies the word is an image in the human being.[19] What matters most here, from the perspective of the history of dogma, is the underlying theological principle:

> Someone who carefully scrutinizes the depths of the mystery can achieve in his spirit, in an inexpressible way, a proportionate understanding of the doctrine relating to the knowledge of God, without however being able to verbally express this ineffable depth of the mystery; that is, how the same object can be numbered and simultaneously escape numbering, so that it can be considered as distinct in its parts and at the same time be understood as a unity, and once subjected to distinction by the concept of person it is not divided in substance. For the concept of person, the Spirit is a distinct reality from the Word, and He who possesses the Word and the Spirit is also distinct from them. But when we have understood what distinguishes them, we also see how the unity of nature does not admit division: so that the power of the one sovereignty is not divided into different divinities.[20]

As previously mentioned, this conception adheres to a new architectural principle of theological thought, since the clear and absolute distinction between God and the world is ensured by the difference between the two ontological levels: the eternal one, which identifies with the Trinity, and creation. In this way it becomes possible to highlight what unites God and the human being, through the theology of the image, without any more risk of subordinationist tensions still linked to the legacy of Platonism.

This made it possible to apply the concept of virtue both to God and to the human being as a real element of the divine image present in the creature, contrary to what Greek metaphysics did.[21] The psychological analogy indicates,

---

19. Gregory of Nyssa, *Oratio catechetica magna*, 1.79–2.21 (GNO 3.4:11.6–12.24).

20. Ὥστε τὸν ἀκριβῶς τὰ βάθη τοῦ μυστηρίου διασκοπούμενον ἐν μὲν τῇ ψυχῇ κατὰ τὸ ἀπόρρητον μετρίαν τινὰ κατανόησιν τῆς κατὰ τὴν θεογνωσίαν διδασκαλίας λαμβάνειν, μὴ μέντοι δύνασθαι λόγῳ διασαφεῖν τὴν ἀνέκφραστον ταύτην τοῦ μυστηρίου βαθύτητα· πῶς τὸ αὐτὸ καὶ ἀριθμητόν ἐστι καὶ διαφεύγει τὴν ἐξαρίθμησιν, καὶ διῃρημένως ὁρᾶται καὶ ἐν μονάδι καταλαμβάνεται, καὶ διακέκριται τῇ ὑποστάσει καὶ οὐ διώρισται τῷ ὑποκειμένῳ. ἄλλο γάρ τι τῇ ὑποστάσει τὸ πνεῦμα, καὶ ἕτερον ὁ λόγος, καὶ ἄλλο πάλιν ἐκεῖνο, οὗ καὶ ὁ λόγος ἐστὶ καὶ τὸ πνεῦμα· ἀλλ᾽ ἐπειδὰν τὸ διακεκριμένον ἐν τούτοις κατανοήσῃς, πάλιν ἡ τῆς φύσεως ἑνότης τὸν διαμερισμὸν οὐ προσίεται, ὡς μήτε τὸ τῆς μοναρχίας σχίζεσθαι κράτος εἰς θεότητας διαφόρους κατατεμνόμενον (Gregory of Nyssa, *Oratio catechetica magna*, 3.1–14 [GNO 3.4:13.12–26]).

21. See pp. 203–4.

then, that it is possible to find in the human spirit an authentically Trinitarian dimension of the image, starting from two elements: (1) the clear distinction between the divine and created nature; and (2) the connection between immanence and economy, which translates into the possibility of recognizing the characteristic of each divine Person in the unity of their action *ad extra*. This allows us to move on to the even more fundamental level of faculties:

> And if you carefully examine the other elements that characterize the divine beauty, then you will find that even in them the resemblance in the image that is in us is preserved perfectly. The Divinity is Mind (νοῦς) and *Logos*, in fact, "in the beginning was the Logos" (John 1:1). And, according to Paul, the prophets have the spirit (νοῦς) of Christ, who speaks in them (cf. 1 Cor 7:40).[22] But the human being is not far from that. Contemplate both the *logos* and the mind in yourself (διάνοιαν): images of the true Mind (νοῦς) and the true *Logos*. And still God is Love (ἀγάπη) and source of love. In fact, the great John says that "love is from God" and that "God is Love" (1 John 4:7–8). And the Creator of nature has also imprinted this characteristic on us: "By this all will know that you are my disciples: if you have love for one another" (John 13:35). And if that were missing, it would corrupt the whole character of the image. God sees everything, listens to everything, and examines everything. So you too, thanks to sight and hearing, have the perception of reality and the mind (διάνοιαν) that seeks and examines reality.[23]

The text of the Bishop of Nyssa highlights a clear parallelism between the faculties of the human soul and the Trinity. The terms in play are *nous*, *logos*, and *agapē*. This passage led Hans Urs von Balthasar to talk about the possibility

---

22. Here Gregory replaces the *pneuma* that appears in the Pauline text with *nous*.

23. Εἰ δὲ καὶ τὰ ἄλλα συνεξετάζοις, δι' ὧν τὸ θεῖον κάλλος χαρακτηρίζεται· εὑρήσεις καὶ πρὸς ἐκεῖνα δι' ἀκριβείας σωζομένην ἐν τῇ καθ' ἡμᾶς εἰκόνι τὴν ὁμοιότητα. Νοῦς καὶ λόγος ἡ θειότης ἐστίν· ἐν ἀρχῇ τε γὰρ ἦν ὁ Λόγος. Καὶ οἱ προφῆται κατὰ Παῦλον νοῦν Χριστοῦ ἔχουσι, τὸν ἐν αὐτοῖς λαλοῦντα. Οὐ πόρρω τούτων καὶ τὸ ἀνθρώπινον. Ὁρᾷς ἐν σεαυτῷ καὶ τὸν λόγον, καὶ διάνοιαν, μίμημα τοῦ ὄντως νοῦ τε καὶ λόγου. Ἀγάπη πάλιν ὁ Θεός, καὶ ἀγάπης πηγή. Τοῦτο γάρ φησιν Ἰωάννης ὁ μέγας, ὅτι Ἀγάπη ἐκ τοῦ Θεοῦ· καὶ, Ὁ Θεὸς ἀγάπη ἐστί· τοῦτο καὶ ἡμέτερον πεποίηται πρόσωπον ὁ τῆς φύσεως πλάστης. Ἐν τούτῳ γὰρ, φησί, γνώσονται πάντες, ὅτι μαθηταί μου ἐστὲ, ἐὰν ἀγαπᾶτε ἀλλήλους. Οὐκοῦν μὴ παρούσης ταύτης, ἅπας ὁ χαρακτὴρ τῆς εἰκόνος μεταπεποίηται. Πάντα ἐπιβλέπει, καὶ πάντα ἐπακούει τὸ Θεῖον, καὶ πάντα διερευνᾶται. Ἔχεις καὶ σὺ τὴν δι' ὄψεως καὶ ἀκοῆς τῶν ὄντων ἀντίληψιν, καὶ τὴν ζητητικήν τε καὶ διερευνητικὴν τῶν ὄντων διάνοιαν (Gregory of Nyssa, *De opificio hominis*, PG 44:137b–c).

of finding the elements of the Augustinian *imago trinitaris* in Gregory's work.[24] But the Swiss theologian's reasoning also depends on the erroneous attribution of the treatise *Ad imaginem et similitudinem* to the Cappadocian, a work that was actually authored by Anastasius the Sinaite, to whom the last part of this chapter will be dedicated.

The ontological approach allows the theologian to "read" the human in the light of God, grasping the immanence of the former immanence in an analogous way to that of the latter. The virtues and faculties are in the human being as the image of divine life, in which perfect unity is given in the relational distinction of the divine Persons.

This theological development culminates in the work of Gregory of Nazianzus who perfects the principle offering an example of a complete psychological analogy that links the two eternal processions to the faculties of the human soul:

> What we think and believe is that what concerns the mutual relation and order (ταῦτα πρὸς ἄλληλα σχέσεώς τε καὶ τάξεως) is to be reserved to the Trinity alone and to those who are already purified to whom the Trinity reveals it now or later. But we know the one nature of God characterized by being without principle, generation, and the procession, as in us the mind, thought, and spirit (ὡς νῷ τῷ ἐν ἡμῖν, καὶ λόγῳ, καὶ πνεύματι), however much we may conjecture about the intelligible realities starting from the sensible ones and about the great realities starting from the small ones, because no image captures the truth.[25]

The approach moves from divine immanence to the human immanence, characterized by *nous*, *logos*, and *pneuma*.[26] Note how the Bishop of Nazianzus

24. See H. U. von Balthasar, *Présence et pensée: Essai sur la philosophie religieuse de Grégoire de Nysse* (Paris: Beauchesne, 1988), 139. See also M. T.-L. Penido, "Prélude Grec à la Théorie Psychologiche de la Trinité," *Revue thomiste* 45 (1939): 665–74; H. Aldenhoven, "Trinitarische Analogien und Ortskirchenekklesiologie," *Internationale kirchliche Zeitschrift* 92 (2002): 174–75; H. F. Cherniss, *The Platonism of Gregory of Nyssa* (Berkeley: University of California Press, 1930), 37–39.

25. Οὕτω φρονοῦμεν, καὶ οὕτως ἔχομεν, ὥστε ὅπως μὲν ἔχει ταῦτα πρὸς ἄλληλα σχέσεώς τε καὶ τάξεως, αὐτῇ μόνῃ τῇ Τριάδι συγχωρεῖν εἰδέναι, καὶ οἷς ἂν ἡ Τριὰς ἀποκαλύψῃ κεκαθαρμένοις, ἢ νῦν, ἢ ὕστερον· αὐτοὶ δὲ μίαν καὶ τὴν αὐτὴν εἰδέναι φύσιν θεότητος, ἀνάρχῳ, καὶ γεννήσει, καὶ προόδῳ γνωριζομένην, ὡς νῷ τῷ ἐν ἡμῖν, καὶ λόγῳ, καὶ πνεύματι (ὅσον εἰκάσαι τοῖς αἰσθητοῖς τὰ νοητά, καὶ τοῖς μικροῖς τὰ μέγιστα, ἐπειδὴ μηδεμία εἰκὼν φθάνει πρὸς τὴν ἀλήθειαν) (Gregory of Nazianzus, *Oratio*, 23.11.1–9 [SC 270:302]).

26. Gregory of Nazianzus also refers to the tripartition *psychē*, *logos*, *nous*, particularly

explicitly connects the psychological analogy to the mutual relation (πρὸς ἄλληλα σχέσις) of the three divine Persons. It is precisely this formulation that will mark the later theological development, influencing the doctrine followed in the Council of Chalcedon and Maximus. Anastasius the Sinaite's extensive formulation, with the value assigned to the theological principle of relation, seems to be part of this development, as we shall see in the next section.

Maximus knows the psychological analogy of the Trinity and uses it in his work to clarify the difficult exegetical points of the tradition that precedes him. We find the same correspondence as in Gregory of Nazianzus. Indeed, commenting on his expression "the Trinity limited by perfection" (τριάδος ὁρισθείσης διὰ τὸ τέλειον),[27] the Confessor establishes a clear parallelism between the Trinity and the human soul:

> And the expression "the Trinity limited by perfection" means that being is not external to Wisdom and Life. And knowing this, we define Wisdom as the Son, *Logos* of God and Life as the Holy Spirit, because our soul, created in the image of God, is also contemplated in these three: in mind, in *logos*, and in spirit (ἐν νῷ καὶ λόγῳ καὶ πνεύματι).[28]

This correspondence between the immanence of the human and that of God is included in the dogmatic reasoning and anchored to the processions and their reciprocal relations, as can be seen from the following negative answer to the question about the possibility of affirming that the Son is *of* the Spirit:

---

in the context of the anti-Apollinarist controversy, to indicate the completeness of the humanity of Christ. The core of his argument is that spiritual realities are not divided into parts and have no limits on their capacity. In the demonstration, he juxtaposes the triad that characterizes the human soul with the three divine Persons: see Gregory of Nazianzus, *Epistulae theologicae*, 101.38.1–4 (SC 208:52). In the following letter, Gregory uses the same tripartition to counter those who believe that there is a composed unity in the Trinity, like in the human soul. See 102.8.1–9.6 (SC 208:74).

27. See Gregory of Nazianzus, *Oratio*, 23.8 (SC 270:298).

28. Τριάδος δὲ ὁρισθείσης διὰ τὸ τέλειον εἴρηται ὅτι αὐτὸ τὸ ὂν οὐκ ἔξω σοφίας καὶ ζωῆς ἐστιν· ὅπερ νοήσαντες ὡρίσαμεν σοφίαν τὸν υἱὸν καὶ λόγον τοῦ θεοῦ, ζωὴν τὸ πνεῦμα τὸ ἅγιον, ἐπειδὴ καὶ ἡ ψυχὴ ἡμῶν, κατ᾽ εἰκόνα θεοῦ κτισθεῖσα, ἐν τοῖς τρισὶ τούτοις καθορᾶται, ἐν νῷ καὶ λόγῳ καὶ πνεύματι (Maximus the Confessor, *Quaestiones et dubia*, 105.21–26; text in J. H. Declerck, *Maximi Confessoris Quaestiones et dubia*, CCSG 10 [Leuven: Brepols, 1980], 79–80).

Just as the mind is the cause of the *logos* and of the spirit through the *logos*, and just as we cannot say that the *logos* is of the voice, neither can we say that the Son is of the Spirit.[29]

Here it is evident that the psychological analogy is deeply connected with the linear scheme. Trinitarian doctrine, Christology, and anthropology are conceived in a unitary way, starting from the creation in the image and likeness of the triune God who is the archetype of the human being. Maximus stresses that such a resemblance does not just concern one aspect, but that the human being is the image of God in God's entirety.[30] This is particularly true of the saints, who have purified themselves through contemplation so much so that they have, in a mystical way, reached that unity which characterizes the Trinity.[31]

After having summarized some elements of the Greek fathers' theology concerning the psychological analogy, we can recognize some differences in the elements that make up the triad in the human soul, but within a sort of continuity in the doctrinal progression. The authors resort to different choices for the characterization of human immanence based on the psychology and anthropology of their time. If *nous - logos - pneuma* seem to have a certain preponderance, as they are present in Gregory of Nazianzus and Maximus, there are also the variants *nous/dianoia - logos - pneuma/agapē* in Gregory of Nyssa and a reference to *psychē* and *nous* in Basil.

III. A Key Work by Anastasius the Sinaite

From this standpoint, it seems important that the first homily *In creatione hominis*, which today is definitively attributed to Anastasius the Sinaite, has long been considered part of the *corpus* of Gregory of Nyssa's works (see PG 44:257–77). In this sense Anastasius's formulations in terms of *psychē - logos - nous/pneuma* do not literally overlap with the previous cases.[32] But the core of the theological reasoning perfectly follows the development of Greek

29. Ὥσπερ ἐστὶν αἴτιος τοῦ λόγου ὁ νοῦς, οὕτως καὶ τοῦ πνεύματος, διὰ μέσου δὲ τοῦ λόγου· καὶ ὥσπερ οὐ δυνάμεθα εἰπεῖν τὸν λόγον εἶναι τῆς φωνῆς, οὕτως οὐδὲ τὸν υἱὸν λέγειν τοῦ πνεύματος (Maximus the Confessor, *Quaestiones et dubia*, 1.34.4–7 [CCSG 10:151]).

30. See Maximus the Confessor, *Ambigua*, 7 (PG 91:1088a).

31. See Maximus the Confessor, *Ambigua*, 10 (PG 91:1193d–96a).

32. From this standpoint, the following fragment of difficult dating handed down under the name of John of Damascus may be relevant: Τὸ κατ᾽ εἰκόνα καὶ ὁμοίωσιν Θεοῦ εἶναι τὸν ἄνθρωπον, τοῦτο δηλοῖ, τὸ ἐν τρισὶν ἰδιώμασιν εἶναι τὴν τούτου νοερὰν καὶ λογικὴν ψυχήν·

Trinitarian theology, which continuously deepens the Johannine Prologue. In particular, the reference to the correlativity of the names of the parts of the human soul as an analogy of the correlativity of the three divine Persons points directly to the heart of Cappadocian theology.

The treatise was partially reproduced in the Greek Patrology of Migne also under the name of Anastasius the Sinaite[33] (see PG 81:1144–49), who was abbot of the Saint Catherine's Monastery at Mount Sinai in the seventh century. Karl-Heinz Uthemann attributed the work to him in his critical edition.[34] The structure of the work can be outlined as follows:

I. Introductory Part
1. Rhetorical-theological *incipit*: Mirroring oneself in the divine ray (1.1–11).
2. The question: Why did God create humanity in His image and likeness? (1.12–29).
3. The thesis: Humanity, unlike the angels, is the image and likeness of the Trinity in such a way as to refer as a mystery to the incarnation (1.30–57).

II. Formulation of the Answer and Its Limits
1. The Trinitarian image at the beginning of creation: Family analogy (1.58–99).
2. Analogical apophaticism: The soul is incomprehensible because it is the image of the Trinity (2.1–61).

III. Response Development
1. The deepest answer is the psychological analogy: Soul (ψυχή), intelligible word (λόγος), and mind (νοῦς) in the human being constitute the Trinitarian image and indicate the incarnation (3.1–52).
2. Moving on to faculties: Desire, knowledge, and anger (3.53–90).
3. Psychological analogy and history: The development of the human being with the emergence of these faculties corresponds to the history of salvation (4.1–79).

IV. Method and Theological Principles
1. The method: From human immanence to divine immanence (5.1–63).

τουτέστι νοῦς καὶ λόγος καὶ πνεῦμα, οἷον ἐπὶ τῆς θείας οὐσίας, Πατὴρ καὶ Υἱὸς καὶ Πνεῦμα ἅγιον (Pseudo-Damascene, *Qua ratione homo imago dei*, PG 95:232b).

33. For an overview of the author, see K.-H. Uthemann, "Anastasius the Sinaite," in *Patrology: The Eastern Fathers, 451–750*, ed. A. di Berardino (Cambridge: James Clarke, 2006), 313–32.

34. K.-H. Uthemann, ed., *Anastasii Sinaitae Sermones duo in constitutionem hominis secundum imaginem Dei necnon Opuscula adversus Monotheletas*, CCSG 12 (Turnhout: Brepols, 1985).

2. Relation is the theological principle: The names of the faculties in the human being are correlative like those of the divine Persons, and there is an analogous unity of action (5.64–104).

V. Conclusion

1. Limits of the reasoning: Between soul and Trinity no identity is given (6.1–17).
2. Doxological end: The human being is created in image and likeness to reveal the Trinity and give glory to the triune God (6.18–53).

I. The treatise opens with an introductory section that can be divided into three parts, each marked by a reference to image and likeness. The first one (I.1) constitutes a rhetorical-theological *incipit*, which states that in order to know the beauty of one's own face it is necessary to reflect oneself in the divine ray of the spiritual sun in order to come to know that of which our nature is the image and likeness. The next part (I.2) asks the question that the treatise seeks to answer. It is difficult for the soul to understand itself, just as the eye does not know itself, so it is difficult to understand the reason for humanity's creation, which is a kind of world composed of the angelic and material worlds created before him. So the treatise tries to answer the question of why the human being was created in the image and likeness. In order to do this, it is essential to understand that the God who created the human being is the Trinity. Then in the third part, which concludes the introductory section (I.3), the thesis to be demonstrated is presented. Faced with the variety of opinions on the possible answer, the essential element of the proposed argument is that God has called the human being the image and likeness of God and not angels. They have dominion and share the same attributes as Adam. But the human being is the image and likeness for many reasons and on many levels of depth; in fact, he not only refers to the Trinity but also to the incarnation. Thus, the reference to the *image* is understood as a reference to the Trinity, while the *likeness* is linked to the incarnation.

II. After the introduction, a first formulation of the response is made, which also sets the parameters of the validity of the response itself. This section can be divided into two parts. In the first (II.1) the *reason* for the creation of man in the image and likeness is brought back to the beginning, taking up the familiar analogies of the Trinity of Gregory of Nazianzus and Methodius, which is explicitly mentioned.[35] The creation of Adam, Eve, and their son corresponds to the processions and the three relations of origin *in divinis*: without cause like the Father, generation for the Son, and the procession of the Holy Spirit.

35. Cf. Methodius, *Symposium*, 3.8 (SC 95:106–10) and Gregory of Nazianzus, *Oratio*, 39.12 (SC 358:172–76).

It is essential in Anastasius's construction that only the Second Person also has an image in brothers (i.e., all the members of human nature) because of the incarnation. Thus, creation in image and likeness would be a symbol of the Trinity in the unity of the three divine Persons. It is important to highlight that the creation of the human being is here connected from the beginning to the incarnation of the Word. This answer, however, is subject to limits that actually coincide with the answer itself (II.2), since the soul is incomprehensible precisely because it is the image of the incomprehensible Trinity.

III. The third section elaborates on the arguments in a threefold movement that places the psychological analogy as the foundation of the family analogy. In the first part (III.1) Anastasius explains how in the human being there are soul (ψυχή), intelligible word (λόγος), and mind (νοῦς), the last of which Paul in 1 Thessalonians 5:23 and 1 Corinthians 7:34 calls spirit (πνεῦμα). This tripartition once again corresponds to the intra-trinary way of proceeding: the Father, not proceeding from anyone without cause, proceeds by generation for the Son and proceeds by procession for the Spirit. Then the text repeats the idea that the image of the *logos* in the human being refers to the incarnation, because the generation of the human *logos* is twofold: in the heart on an immanent level and when the word is known on the outside but without separation from the heart. This is similar to the two generations of the Word: the eternal one in God and the one in history. The mystery of the Trinity is thought together with that of the incarnation in the light of the two Chalcedonian generations. Thus, when Paul speaks of the human being as the image of God, it is because the human soul bears the image of the three hypostatic properties. Here Colossians 1:15 is significantly applied to humanity and not only to Christ. Therefore, in the second part (III.2) the psychological analogy develops from the perspective of the faculties, as even pagans, in fact, affirm a tripartition in human psychology comprised of desire, knowledge, and anger. From the Christian perspective they correspond to the three faculties of uniting with God's love, of accepting knowledge from Him, and of opposing evil spirits. This places the psychological analogy in a cosmological context, since the three faculties of the human being are the image of the faculty of the Trinity to dominate the three parts of the cosmos: heaven, earth, and the underworld. The Trinity creates, provides, and chastises, just as a man or woman desires by being driven to action, provides by reasoning, and chastises by anger. And this is also observed in childhood development, in which the desire for the mother's breast arises first, and words and the ability to be angry only come afterward. Thus, the image of unity in the Trinity extends to the faculties and parts of the human soul. Finally, in the third section (III.3), the psychological analogy, after being placed in a cosmological context, is reread through a historical lens. The diachronic perspective of the development of the human's faculties offers the possibility of presenting the history of the human soul as a symbol of the whole history of salvation. The emergence of the faculties in the child, specifically that of speech, would be a prophecy of the incarnation. It is a subsequent manifestation of what is already in the soul from the beginning. In this way the human immanence is placed in analogical correspondence with the divine immanence. Word and soul are contemporary just as the Father, the Son, and the Holy Spirit are coeternal. The three divine Persons are inseparable as the soul cannot be mute or beastly, without *logos*, or dead and without the spirit. In fact, if God were not triune, He would not be living.

IV. After having articulated the answer in the three aforementioned stages, the fourth section is dedicated to the method and theological principles underlying the reasoning. The first part (IV.1) clarifies that in order to philosophize about the Trinity one must start from one's own inner life, from human immanence and not from exteriority. The reason for humanity's creation is, in fact, precisely the revelation of the Trinity. The human being is the answer to a series of questions that summarize the history of Trinitarian doctrine, precisely as symbol of the Trinity itself. Everything that is said in the Trinitarian dogma about God is found in the human being: trinity of hypostases, uniqueness of nature, simultaneity of origin and contemporaneity, invisibility, and indescribability, the three hypostatic properties and divine activities and attributes. According to Anastasius, Arius and Macedonius would not have spoken heresies if they had looked at the human being, for they would not have subjected the One being that is above nature to natural reasons. Thus, he clearly states the need to reason on the basis of an extension of classical metaphysics, which does not seek the first principle only in nature (*physis*), but recognizes the transcendent origin of humanity itself in the Trinitarian dimension of its Creator. In the ontology implied in Christian doctrine, relation is elevated to a theological principle along with the substance and is no longer a mere accident. The distinction of the divine Persons, in fact, cannot be based on a substantial difference, but must be purely relational. Thus, in the second part of the section (IV.2), Athanasius explains that the soul possesses the being image figuratively and not naturally, even in the names of the faculties which are correlative, just as it happens with the names of the divine Persons. From an ontological point of view, Anastasius the Sinaite explains that the correlativity in the Trinity is based on God's unlimited being. In the human being, by analogy, where there is a rational soul there is also *logos*, just as "mind" also refers to a soul and a word. Likewise, as with correlativity, so we have unity of action both in the human soul and in God. The analogy is based on the relational correspondence between the two ontologies: the eternal one that is the Trinity and the one of created human nature.

V. Possible criticisms of the proposed reasoning and the point of arrival are laid out in the final part. In the first section (V.1) the author responds to the possibility that the discourse is rejected because it does not take into consideration the body or is accused of affirming an identity between the Trinity and the soul. On the other hand, it is necessary to bear in mind that this line of reasoning is not about equality but about a figurative image. Then, it is possible to get to the actual conclusion of the treatise (V.2). The same word of wisdom and theological research refer to the Trinity and the incarnation together. There is an analogous immanence and an analogous "incarnation" and "revelation" in the human being through his or her cognitive process and word, which correspond to how God made everything and redeemed the human being with His Word. Therefore, humanity's greatness is superior to that of the angels and its most authentic structure is doxological, because the purpose of the human being is to communicate and reveal the glory of the Trinity.

IV. Anastasius's Trinitarian Analogies

The richness of the images and the profound doctrinal elaboration of the theme of psychological analogy is immediately apparent. The simultaneous focus on the mystery of the Trinity, the incarnation, and the cosmos, which characterizes the patristic reflection of the time, is also evident.[36]

Trinitarian analogies follow one another in a crescendo that starts at the moment of creation and extends throughout history. The family analogy that had characterized the theology of the fourth century is reinterpreted in the light of the psychological analogy. So, the first answer Anastasius proposes is traditional:

> But let us instead return to the very beginning of the discourse, from which, as from a very deep source, we try first of all to discover why God created the existences of our progenitors and forefathers, Adam, Eve, and the son born of them, with characteristics not in the likeness of the other rational beings, namely the angels, or to the equality of living beings. But He created Adam without cause and without generation, his son the second

---

36. See B. Studer, *Trinity and Incarnation: The Faith of the Early Church* (Collegeville, MN: Liturgical Press, 1994), 232–38.

man, by generation, while to Eve He mysteriously gave existence neither by generation nor without cause, but by assumption or procession out of the substance of the uncaused Adam. And these three consubstantial existences of the ancestors of all mankind are types of the holy and consubstantial Trinity according to a certain image, as Methodius also says. In fact, to Adam (without cause and without generation) corresponds a type and an image of the almighty God and Father who is uncaused and cause of all; Adam's begotten Son foreshadows an image of the begotten Son and Word of God; while Eve, created by procession, means the proceeding Person of the Holy Spirit, so that God did not even breathe a breath of life into her because she is a symbol of the breath and life of the Holy Spirit and because she is destined to receive, through the Holy Spirit, God, who really is breath and life of all.[37]

Life is at the center of the theological rereading that presents the intra-Trinitarian processions as the communication of divine life, similarly to what happens in Gregory of Nazianzus and Methodius. Rather than a familial analogy in the sense of members that make up the family, it must be read as an analogy of the family relations that characterized the first family with all its uniqueness. In fact, no other family after Adam, Eve, and Seth originated from the relations of origin constituted directly by the creative act.

Anastasius the Sinaite is aware of this and uses the uniqueness to extend the analogy to incarnation. In fact, he clarifies that:

37. Μᾶλλον δὲ ἐπ' αὐτὴν τὴν ἀρχὴν τοῦ λόγου ἀναδράμωμεν, ἐκεῖθεν ὥσπερ ἔκ τινος βαθυτάτης πηγῆς πρῶτον ζητοῦντες, τὸ τί δήποτε μὴ καθ' ὁμοιότητα τῶν λοιπῶν λογικῶν ἤγουν τῶν ἀγγέλων, ἢ πάλιν κατ' ἰσότητα τῶν ἐμψύχων ζῴων ὁμοιοτρόπους τὰς προπατορικὰς καὶ κορυφαίας ἡμῶν ὁ θεὸς ὑποστάσεις, τοῦ Ἀδὰμ λέγω καὶ τῆς Εὔας καὶ τοῦ προελθόντος ἐξ αὐτῶν υἱοῦ, πεποίηκεν, ἀλλὰ τὸν μὲν Ἀδὰμ ἀναιτίως καὶ ἀγεννήτως ὑπέστησε, τὸν δὲ δεύτερον αὐτοῦ ἄνθρωπον τὸν υἱὸν γεννητόν, τὴν δὲ Εὔαν οὔτε γεννητῶς οὔτε πάλιν ἀναιτίως, ἀλλὰ ληπτῶς ἤτοι ἐκπορευτῶς ἐκ τῆς οὐσίας τοῦ ἀναιτίου Ἀδὰμ ἐξελθοῦσαν ἀρρήτως οὐσίωσε, καὶ μήπως ἄρα αἱ τρεῖς αὗται τῶν πρωγόνων κεφαλαὶ πάσης τῆς ἀνθρωπότητος ὁμοούσιοι ὑποστάσεις κατ' εἰκόνα τινά, ὡς Μεθοδίῳ δοκεῖ, τυπικῶς γεγόναν τῆς ἁγίας καὶ ὁμοουσίου τριάδος, τοῦ μὲν ἀναιτίου καὶ ἀγεννήτου Ἀδὰμ τύπον καὶ εἰκόνα ἔχοντος τοῦ ἀναιτίου καὶ πάντων αἰτίου παντοκράτορος θεοῦ καὶ πατρός, τοῦ δὲ γεννητοῦ υἱοῦ αὐτοῦ εἰκόνα προδιαγράφοντος τοῦ γεννητοῦ υἱοῦ καὶ λόγου τοῦ θεοῦ, τῆς δὲ ἐκπορευτῆς Εὔας σημαινούσης τὴν τοῦ ἁγίου πνεύματος ἐκπορευτὴν ὑπόστασιν· διὸ οὐδὲ ἐνεφύσησεν αὐτῇ ὁ θεὸς πνοὴν ζωῆς διὰ τὸ τύπον αὐτὴν εἶναι τῆς τοῦ ἁγίου πνεύματος πνοῆς καὶ ζωῆς, καὶ διὰ τὸ μέλλειν αὐτὴν δι' ἁγίου πνεύματος δέξασθαι θεόν, τὸν ὄντως ὄντα πάντων πνοὴν καὶ ζωήν (Anastasius the Sinaite, *Ad imaginem dei et ad similitudinem*, 1.58–82 [CCSG 12:9–11]).

Therefore, it is also possible to understand and admire the fact that the ungenerated Adam did not have a similar ungenerated and uncaused one among men, as well as Eve who was born by procession, being they the true symbols of the ungenerated Father and the Holy Spirit. Whereas the begotten son had all men as equal brothers and sisters, who were begotten sons, being in the image and symbolic likeness of Christ the begotten Son, who became the firstborn man without seed among many brothers and sisters.[38]

This development of the traditional doctrine is brought back, according to the logic of the treatise, to the psychological analogy, since this indicates the image of the Trinity in the soul of every man, not just in the original couple and their descendants. Therefore, according to Anastasius the Sinaite, the deepest answer to why God created man in His image and likeness is the following:

But let us come therefore to the most authentic sense of the expression "in image and likeness," so that according to the promises we may demonstrate the Unity of the Divinity in the Trinity. And what is this? Evidently it is still our soul and its intelligible word and mind (ψυχὴ καὶ ὁ ταύτης νοερὸς λόγος καὶ ὁ νοῦς) that the Apostle calls spirit (πνεῦμα), when he exhorts us to be saints in body and soul. In fact, the soul (ψυχή) is neither generated nor caused as the image of the ungenerated and uncaused God and Father, while its intelligible word is not without generation, but is generated mysteriously, invisibly, inexplicably, and impassively by the soul. The mind is neither uncaused nor generated, but proceeding, it spreads everywhere and observes everything and invisibly investigates in the image and likeness of the most holy and proceeding Spirit, of whom it has been said "the Spirit scrutinizes everything, even the depths of God" (1 Cor 2:10). The soul is not proceeding as long as it is in the body, because if it were proceeding, we would die instantly. Our word is not without generation, because we would be without reason and like animals.[39]

---

38. Ὅθεν καὶ ἔστιν ἰδέσθαι καὶ θαυμάσαι ὅτι ὁ μὲν ἀγέννητος Ἀδὰμ ἄλλον ἀγέννητον ἢ ἀναίτιον ἐν ἀνθρώποις οὐκ ἔσχεν ὅμοιον, ὥσπερ οὐδὲ ἡ ἐκπορευτὴ Εὔα, ὡς τύποι ἀληθεῖς ὑπάρχοντες τοῦ ἀγεννήτου πατρὸς καὶ τοῦ ἁγίου πνεύματος· ὁ δὲ γεννητὸς υἱὸς πάντας ἀνθρώπους, γεννητοὺς υἱοὺς ὄντας, ἀδελφοὺς ὁμοίους ἔσχεν, ὡς κατ᾽ εἰκόνα καὶ ὁμοίωσιν τυπικὴν ὑπάρχων Χριστοῦ τοῦ γεννητοῦ υἱοῦ, ὃς ἐγένετο ἄνθρωπος πρωτότοκος ἄνευ σπορᾶς ἐν πολλοῖς ἀδελφοῖς (Anastasius the Sinaite, Ad imaginem dei et ad similitudinem, 1.83–91 [CCSG 12:11]).

39. Ἀλλ᾽ ἄγε δὴ ἐπ᾽ αὐτὸ τὸ κυριώτατον τοῦ κατ᾽ εἰκόνα καὶ καθ᾽ ὁμοίωσιν ἔλθωμεν, ὅπως κατὰ τὰς ὑποσχέσεις δείξωμεν τὸ μοναδικὸν τῆς ἐν τριάδι θεότητος. Ποῖον δέ ἐστι

The terms that indicate the components of the image are *psychē*, *logos*, and *nous*, which is declared equivalent to *pneuma*. As in the case of the family analogy, the focus is on the processions and relations of origin of the divine Persons. In this case, however, the image of the Trinity is placed in every human, in every soul, in such a way that "the most authentic sense" appears to be precisely the psychological analogy. And once again, immediately, this is extended to the incarnation:

And what is most wonderful among these wonders is the fact that we have a simple soul, as well as a single, non-composite mind, but a double word, which has a double genesis, which remains one and undivided. For the word is born in the heart with an incomprehensible and incorporeal birth and remains unknown within; however, it is born with a second corporeal genesis through the lips and then becomes known to all. Yet it does not separate itself from the soul that generated it, so that through the two generations of our word we may learn the two generations of the Word of God according to image and likeness. It was in fact generated invisibly, inexplicably, and incomprehensibly before time by the Father and was unknown as in a soul to the Father, until as from a heart it was generated according to the flesh by the holy Virgin without corruption and without suffering, and it appeared to the world, not separated from the paternal and mysterious substance of God the Father. So that in the unity of the immortal and spiritual substance of our soul, three hypostatic properties are shown as in an image: the soul's quality of "not being generated," the "generation" of the word, and the "procession" of the spirit, that is, of the mind.[40]

τοῦτο; Εὔδηλον ὅτι ἡ ἡμετέρα πάλιν ψυχὴ καὶ ὁ ταύτης νοερὸς λόγος καὶ ὁ νοῦς, ὅντινα ὁ Ἀπόστολος πνεῦμα προσηγόρευσεν, ὅτε διακελεύεται ἁγίους ἡμᾶς εἶναι τῇ ψυχῇ καὶ τῷ σώματι καὶ τῷ πνεύματι. Ἀγέννητος μὲν γὰρ πάλιν ἐστὶν ἡ ψυχὴ καὶ ἀναίτιος εἰς τύπον τοῦ ἀγεννήτου καὶ τοῦ ἀναιτίου θεοῦ καὶ πατρός, οὐκ ἀγέννητος δὲ ὁ νοερὸς αὐτῆς λόγος, ἀλλ' ἐξ αὐτῆς γεννώμενος ἀρρήτως καὶ ἀοράτως καὶ ἀνερμηνεύτως καὶ ἀπαθῶς. Ὁ δὲ νοῦς οὐδὲ ἀναίτιός ἐστιν, οὐδὲ γεννητός, ἀλλ' ἐκπορευτός, παντὶ διατρέχων καὶ τὰ πάντα διασκοπῶν καὶ ἀοράτως ψηλαφῶν κατ' εἰκόνα καὶ ὁμοίωσιν τοῦ παναγίου καὶ ἐκπορευτοῦ πνεύματος, περὶ οὗ εἴρηται ὅτι *Τὸ πνεῦμα πάντα ἐρευνᾷ, καὶ τὰ βάθη τοῦ θεοῦ.* Οὐκ ἔστιν ἐκπορευτὴ ἡ ψυχή, ἕως οὗ ἐστιν ἐν τῷ σώματι, ἐπεὶ εἰ ἐκπορευτὴ ἦν, ἄρα ἂν καθ' ὥραν ἀπεθνήσκαμεν. Οὐκ ἔστιν ἀγέννητος ὁ λόγος ἡμῶν, ἐπεὶ ἄλογοί τινες καὶ κτηνώδεις ὑπήρχομεν (Anastasius the Sinaite, *Ad imaginem dei et ad similitudinem*, 3.1–19 [CCSG 12:17–18]).

40. Τὸ δὲ παραδοξότερον τῶν παραδόξων τούτων ἐκεῖνό ἐστιν, ὅτι ψυχὴν μὲν ἁπλὴν τινα ἔχομεν, ὁμοίως καὶ νοῦν μοναδικὸν, καὶ ἀσύνθετον, λόγον δὲ διπλοῦν, διπλὴν ἔχοντα τὸν αὐτὸν τὴν γέννησιν, καὶ ἕνα καὶ ἀμέριστον φυλαττόμενον. Γεννᾶται γὰρ ὁ λόγος ἐν τῇ καρδίᾳ γέννησίν τινα ἀκατάληπτον καὶ ἀσώματον, καὶ μένει ἔνδον ἀγνώριστος· καὶ

Anastasius's theology combines the history of salvation and the human soul in a surprising way, comparing human speech to the incarnation. The very root of the human capacity for speech can be recognized, from this perspective, in the love of the Father who sends His Son to be incarnated in the Virgin Mary through the Holy Spirit. Eremitical thought and monastic theology show all their strength here.

Anastasius the Sinaite refers to a couple of the adjectives connected to the four adverbs of the Chalcedonian christological formula to indicate the tripartition of the divine image in the human being. Indeed, he writes: "our soul has a certain unique tripartition without division and confusion (ἀδιαίρετον καὶ ἀσύγχυτον) in the image of the holy and consubstantial Trinity."[41]

The reference to Chalcedon and the deepened understanding of the christological dimension of the cosmos itself and of human history can also explain the arrival point and the summit of exploration done by Anastasius. In fact, the reformulation of the Trinitarian analogy in terms of faculties allows him to diachronically interpret the emergence of the very faculties of the soul as a symbol of the progressive Trinitarian revelation in the history of salvation:

> Therefore, the nature of children, as soon as they are born out of darkness into the light and have progressed, shows that they have a soul in the image of God the Father, an intellectual soul in potency and having essentially the word and intelligence in themselves; then, as the body develops and grows, it, secondly, manifests the word and does so not all at once and suddenly, but first stammering and as foretelling and announcing the birth of the Word in the flesh and the most perfect revelation, after which the presence of the intellect is revealed, when the child becomes an accomplished man. "But—it will be said—what does all this matter to the present question of being man in the image and likeness?" Very much, friend; from this we

---

γεννᾶται δευτέραν γέννησιν σωματικὴν διὰ χειλέων, καὶ τότε τοῖς πᾶσι γνωρίζεται· τῆς δὲ γεννησάσης αὐτὸν ψυχῆς οὐ χωρίζεται, ἵνα διὰ τῶν δύο τοῦ λόγου ἡμῶν γεννήσεων σαφῶς τὰς δύο τοῦ θεοῦ λόγου γεννήσεις κατ᾿ εἰκόνα τινὰ καὶ ὁμοίωσιν μάθωμεν. Γεγέννηται γὰρ ἀοράτως καὶ ἀνερμηνεύτως καὶ ἀκαταλήπτως πρὸ τῶν αἰώνων ἐκ πατρός, καὶ ἦν ἄγνωστος ὡς ἔν τινι ψυχῇ πρὸς τὸν πατέρα, ἕως ὥσπερ ἐκ καρδίας τινὸς τῆς ἁγίας παρθένου ἀφθόρως καὶ ἀπόνως γεγέννηται τὸ κατὰ σάρκα καὶ ἐνεφανίσθη τῷ κόσμῳ, μὴ χωρισθεὶς τῆς πατρικῆς καὶ κρυφίας οὐσίας τοῦ γεννήτορος θεοῦ. Ὥστε δέδεικται ἐν τῷ μοναδικῷ τῆς ἀθανάτου ἡμῶν καὶ νοερᾶς ψυχικῆς οὐσίας ὡς ἐν εἰκόνι τρεῖς τινες ὑποστατικαὶ ἰδιότητες, ἀγεννησία ψυχῆς, καὶ γέννησις λόγου καὶ ἐκπόρευσις πνεύματος ἤγουν τοῦ νοός (Anastasius the Sinaite, *Ad imaginem dei et ad similitudinem*, 3.20–40 [CCSG 12:18–19]).

41. Anastasius the Sinaite, *Ad imaginem dei et ad similitudinem*, 3.46–47 (CCSG 12:19).

learn the way in which God, as in a body, has revealed and manifested Himself to the world and how gradually our nature has come to know the mystery of the Trinity.[42]

This is followed by an explicit parallelism between the history of salvation and the development of the human soul: a true exercise in the theology of history based on Trinitarian ontology and anthropology on which the psychological analogy itself is based. Thus, the gift of the Law to Moses is presented as an essential milestone in the understanding of the unity of the soul itself in the face of the risks of polytheism. But after the knowledge of the Father, with the incarnation of the *Logos*, human nature knew its own ternary perfection thanks to the gift of the Holy Spirit, of which the word and mind of the human being are the image.

In the light of this path, Anastasius proposes the method for the correct reasoning on the image of God in the human being:

> But just as in the soul there is the rational part (ψυχὴ λογική) and together with it the reason (λόγος) that is in it, and still together and always in it the vital spirit (τὸ πνεῦμα τὸ ζωτικόν) that gives unity (συστατικόν) and brings to completion (συμπληρωτικόν), so there is the Father, and together with the Father the Word God (Λόγος), and always together with the Son and the Father there is also the Spirit with the Son and the Father. If you separate and divide reason from the soul, your soul remains deprived of reason (ἄλογος); so that, through what is in God's image, you may learn that if you deny the *Logos* God, saying that He is not with God the Father, then you would preach that God is deprived of reason and reduced to the level of beasts. And if you separate the Spirit from God, then He would remain as dead and you would say that God is not a living Person. If you

---

42. Ὅθεν καὶ ἡ τῶν νηπίων φύσις, ὡς ἐκ σκότους εἰς φῶς τικτομένη καὶ προσερχομένη, εὐθέως μὲν τὴν ψυχὴν φανεροῖ ἔχειν εἰς τύπον τοῦ θεοῦ καὶ πατρός, δυνάμει μὲν νοερὰν οὖσαν καὶ οὐσιωδῶς ἐν αὐτῇ ἔχουσαν τὸν λόγον καὶ τὸν νοῦν· κατὰ πρόσβασιν δὲ προκόπτοντος καὶ αὐξοῦντος τοῦ σώματος, δεύτερον ἐμφανίζει τὸν λόγον, καὶ τοῦτον οὐκ ἀθρόως οὐδὲ ἐξαίφνης, ἀλλὰ προψελλίζουσα καὶ οἱονεὶ σκιαγραφοῦσα καὶ προμηνύουσα τὴν τοῦ λόγου διὰ σαρκὸς γέννησιν καὶ τελειοτάτην φανέρωσιν, μεθ᾽ ἣν λοιπὸν ἡ τοῦ νοῦ δηλοῦται παρουσία, ὅτε εἰς ἄνδρα τέλειον προκόψει τὸ νήπιον. Ἀλλὰ τί, φησί, ταῦτα συντείνει εἰς τὴν προκειμένην τοῦ κατ᾽ εἰκόνα καὶ καθ᾽ ὁμοίωσιν τοῦ ἀνθρώπου ὑπόθεσιν; Καὶ πάνυ μὲν οὖν, ὦ ἄνθρωπε, διὰ τούτων μανθάνομεν τὸν τρόπον τῆς τοῦ θεοῦ, ὥσπερ ἔν τινι σώματι, ἐν τῷ κόσμῳ φανερώσεώς τε καὶ ἀναδείξεως, καὶ πῶς κατὰ πρόσβασιν ἡ ἡμετέρα φύσις τὸ τῆς τριάδος ἐπέγνω μυστήριον (Anastasius the Sinaite, *Ad imaginem dei et ad similitudinem*, 4.7–24 [CCSG 12:21–22]).

want to philosophize on what is in the image and likeness of God, you must philosophize in this way: discover the hidden God not from the external realities, but from the inner realities, from the trinity in you; know the Trinity through the realities that exist in you.[43]

It is important to emphasize here that the Spirit gives unity and brings the Trinity to completion, according to Cappadocian pneumatology as we have tried to portray it. Here we see how the immanent personal characteristic of the Third Person is reflected from top to bottom in economic action thanks to the relational conception of the gap, according to the theology outlined in the previous chapters. The linear scheme has been symmetrized preserving the monarchy of the Father. But the psychological analogies presented are not the cause of this dynamic position of the Third Person between the First and the Second, but on the contrary it is the perfection of the pneumatology and the clear distinction between the triune Creator and the human being that makes this kind of theological interpretation of anthropology possible.

At the end of this exposition, it is worth pointing out that for Anastasius the Sinaite the three constitutive elements of the Trinitarian image in the human being are the *psychē*, the *logos*, and the *nous* or *pneuma*. They are always present, even if they occur in succession. The reason for this interpenetration, so profound as to become the image and symbol of divine unity and trinity, is the correlativity of the three elements, similarly to how the Father, the Son, and the Spirit are correlative to each other. Anastasius writes:

> Consider then that our soul possesses being in the image of God figuratively: not only in reality, but also in the words themselves—I say figuratively, but not naturally. How is this possible? I can surely clarify what I am saying. We believe that the God and Father is infinite, as are the Son and the Holy Spirit. Therefore, as they are unlimited, they also have their own

---

43. ἀλλ᾽ ὥσπερ ἐπὶ τῆς ψυχῆς ἅμα ψυχὴ λογικὴ, ἅμα σὺν αὐτῇ ὁ λόγος ὁ ἐν αὐτῇ, καὶ ἅμα, καὶ συνάμα ἐν αὐτοῖς τὸ πνεῦμα τὸ ζωτικὸν καὶ συστατικὸν καὶ συμπληρωτικόν, οὕτως ἅμα πατὴρ, ἅμα θεὸς λόγος σὺν πατρὶ, ἅμα υἱὸς σὺν πατρὶ, συνάμα τὸ πνεῦμα σὺν υἱῷ καὶ πατρί. Εἰ δὲ χωρίζεις καὶ ἀποστερεῖς τὸν λόγον ἐκ τῆς ψυχῆς, ἄλογός σου λοιπὸν ἡ ψυχή· εἰ δὲ διαιρεῖς τὸ πνεῦμα ἐξ αὐτῆς, νεκρὰ λοιπόν, ἀλλ᾽ οὐ ζωτικὴ ἡ ψυχή, ἵνα διὰ τούτου τοῦ κατ᾽ εἰκόνα θεοῦ ὢν μάθῃς ὅτι, ἐὰν ἀρνήσῃ τὸν θεὸν λόγον λέγεις σὺν τῷ θεῷ καὶ πατρὶ, ἄλογον λοιπὸν καὶ κτηνώδη κηρύττεις τὸν θεόν, καὶ ἐὰν χωρίσῃς τὸ πνεῦμα ἐκ τοῦ θεοῦ, λοιπὸν νεκρόν τινα καὶ οὐ ζῶντα λέγεις θεόν. Εἰ φιλοσοφεῖν περὶ τοῦ κατ᾽εἰκόνα σου καὶ ὁμοίωσιν θεοῦ βούλει, οὕτω φιλοσόφησον· οὐκ ἐκ τῶν ἐκτός, ἀλλ᾽ ἐκ τῶν ἐντός σου τὸν κρυπτὸν θεὸν γνώρισον· ἐκ τῆς ἐν σοὶ τριάδος τὴν τριάδα ἐπίγνωθι δι᾽ἐνυποστάτων πραγμάτων (Anastasius the Sinaite, *Ad imaginem dei et ad similitudinem*, 4.66–5.4 [CCSG 12:24]).

mutually referential and mutually connected names: in fact, if you say father, you are evidently declaring the existence of a son of his. Because how can you call yourself a father if you do not have a son? In the same way if you say spirit, God manifests Himself, because God is spirit, as Scripture says. Therefore, go from this holy Trinity to its image, that is to say to the trinity that exists within us, and you will see that the three names of this trinity are also mutually correlated and united (φεραλλήλους καὶ ἡνωμένας). For if you say "rational and intellectual soul," it is evident that you are also referring to the word and the mind; and when you name the word, you certainly manifest the rational soul that generates it; and when you say mind, you manifest the soul and the word as well. Of what, in fact, can it be a mind if not of a soul and a word?[44]

In this way the analogy between the soul and the Trinity can be extended to all the dogmatic elements that have been developed in Trinitarian doctrine to formulate the mystery of the triune God: from correlativity to unity of action, from hypostatic properties to processions. Obviously, it is not a matter of demonstrating the Trinity from below, but of reading humanity from above from its Trinitarian origin, drawing the consequences from the fact that Being itself is the Trinity. The novelty in the ontological architecture and the new understanding of the value of relations allow a synthesis that unites the cosmos and history to the triune God through the inner life of the human being created in His image and likeness. Humanity's life, in fact, is understood as the image and likeness of divine Life, now perceived in its immanent dynamic thanks to the definition of the divinity of the Holy Spirit and the formulation of the distinction of the two eternal processions.

---

44. Ὅρα γοῦν ὅτι οὐ μόνον ἐν πράγμασιν, ἀλλὰ καὶ ἐν αὐτοῖς τοῖς ῥήμασι τὸ κατ᾽ εἰκόνα θεοῦ τυπικῶς ἡ ἡμετέρα ψυχὴ κέκτηται· τυπικῶς λέγω, ἀλλ᾽ οὐκ ἰσοφυῶς. Πῶς δὲ τοῦτο; Εὐθέως τὸ λεγόμενον ποιήσω σαφές. Ἀπερίγραπτον εἶναι τὸν θεὸν καὶ πατέρα, ὁμοίως καὶ τὸν υἱὸν καὶ τὸ ἅγιον πνεῦμα εἶναι πιστεύομεν. Διὸ ὡς ἀπερίοριστοι φεραλλήλους καὶ ἀλληλενδέτους καὶ τὰς οἰκείας προσηγορίας ἔχουσιν· ἐπὰν γὰρ ὀνομάσῃς πατέρα, πρόδηλον ὅτι καὶ υἱοῦ τινος αὐτοῦ ἐμήνυσας ἔμφασιν. Πῶς γὰρ ἂν καὶ κληθήσεται πατὴρ μὴ γνωριζομένου υἱοῦ; Ὡσαύτως καὶ ἐπὰν εἴπῃς πνεῦμα, θεὸν ἐδήλωσας· πνεῦμα γὰρ ὁ θεός, ὥς φησιν ἡ γραφή. Εἶτα ἐλθὲ ἀπὸ ταύτης τῆς ἁγίας τριάδος ἐπὶ τὴν εἰκόνα αὐτῆς, τὴν ἐν ἡμῖν λέγω ἔνδον ὑπάρχουσαν τριάδα, καὶ ὄψει καὶ τὰς τρεῖς προσηγορίας αὐτῆς φεραλλήλους καὶ ἡνωμένας ὑπαρχούσας. Ἐπὰν γὰρ εἴπῃς ψυχὴν λογικὴν καὶ νοεράν, εὔδηλον ὅτι καὶ λόγον καὶ νοῦν ἐσήμανας· καὶ ἐπὰν ὀνομάσῃς λόγον, πάντως ὅτι καὶ τὴν λογικὴν ψυχὴν τὴν τούτου γεννητικὴν ἐδήλωσας· ὡσαύτως καὶ ἐπὰν εἴπῃς νοῦν, ἐκ παντὸς τρόπου ὅτι καὶ τὴν ψυχὴν καὶ τὸν λόγον ἐδήλωσας. Τίνος γὰρ ἂν καὶ ἔσται νοῦς εἰ μὴ ψυχῆς καὶ λόγου (Anastasius the Sinaite, *Ad imaginem dei et ad similitudinem*, 5.64–85 [CCSG 12:27–28]).

V. Conclusion: A Doctrine to Be Rediscovered

Psychological analogy does not enjoy a brilliant reputation in contemporary theology.[45] Yet it represents a key step in the development of the thought transformed by Christian revelation. In an epistemological context that is no longer faithful to apophaticism, it can be disfigured, transformed into a "proof" of the Trinity.[46] However, its interpretation can never be bottom-up, if one reads it in its original context, but only top-down. The presence of this doctrine that is also in the framework of Greek patristics, and especially the Cappadocians, must make one think. It is, in fact, a perspective that can also be valid in the current context.[47]

Ecumenical concerns should not hold back such a rediscovery because only a common return to the roots, that is, to the fathers of the Church, can help rebuild that unity that the Holy Spirit establishes and claims. Therefore, the differences should be clearly highlighted: the thought of the Greek fathers does not make explicit the connection of the procession of the Spirit with that of the will in the human being but sticks to the sphere of love and relations.

However, one can also see the presence of this tradition in Byzantine thought. In fact, in the fourteenth century Gregory Palamas,[48] a reference figure

45. The reason seems connected to the relationship with some philosophical foundations of modernity. See N. Ormerod, "The Psychological Analogy for the Trinity: At Odds with Modernity," *Pacifica* 14 (2001): 281–94.

46. On this point, Thomas Aquinas's criticism of Richard of San Victor and Anselm of Canterbury regarding the implicit tendency in their theological approach to introduce necessary reasons into Trinitarian doctrine is paradigmatic: see Thomas Aquinas, *Summa Theologiae*, pt. 1, q. 32, a. 1, ad 2.

47. See G. Maspero, "Coscienza e relazione: Analogie trinitarie tra filosofia e neuroscienze," *Lateranum* 80 (2014): 355–70.

48. Gregory Palamas (1296–1359) became a monk on Mount Athos in 1316 and immersed himself in the experience of spirituality connected with the Hesychastic method. This consisted of a prayer technique which, based on the conviction that the body is closely united to the spirit, sought to achieve the state of perfect tranquillity (ἡσυχία), making prayer descend from the head to the heart through the continuous repetition of the prayer "Lord Jesus, Son of God, have mercy on me," linked to the rhythm of breathing. The goal was to be able to pray at all times and thus achieve contemplation of the divine light—the uncreated energy of essence—as it was revealed on Tabor. The Hesychastic movement presented itself as a movement of reform in the search for poverty and the independence of the church from the empire. Palamas's opponent was Barlaam the Calabrian, who denied the possibility of theological understanding of the mystical phenomenon to which the monks of Athos referred. The clash had political implications and became a controversy between East and

in orthodoxy, still clearly recognizes the role of the will alongside the intellect as an intradivine principle. The revolution of the Greek philosophical doctrine is evident, since desire is recognized *in divinis*. The theological journey that began with the theology of the *Logos* culminates in the recognition of will and desire as divine and essential realities for man to be authentically the image of God. Thus, in *Capita 150*, Palamas, after repeating considerations similar to those expressed by Gregory of Nyssa in the fourth century about the difference between the *Logos* and the divine *Pneuma* compared to human ones, writes, "That Spirit of the Supreme *Logos* is like an ineffable desire (ἔρως) of the One who generates toward the ineffably generated *Logos*."[49] This affirmation highlights the marvelous path that from the intellectualistic identification of *Eros* with Apollo, and therefore with rationality, as in Plato's *Symposium* led to the recognition of the irreducible role of will and desire, in light of the very inner life of God.

Gregory Palamas therefore defines the Spirit as the eternal joy (προαιώνιος χαρά) of the Father and the Son, precisely because He is common to them.[50] Immediately afterward, the Trinity is presented in terms of psychological analogy:

> And our mind too, created in the image of God, possesses the image of this supreme desire (ἔρωτος) toward the knowledge that always exists from our mind and in it, a desire that is also from it and in it and proceeds (συμπρο-ϊόντα) together with the inner *Logos*.[51]

Gregory Palamas has just stated that the Spirit is the joy that unites the Father and the Son. Therefore, after specifying that the Spirit proceeds (ἐκπορεύται) only from the First Person, he goes on to present the human mind as an im-

---

West due to the Thomist language of Barlaam and his followers. After alternating defeats and victories, Palamas became bishop of Thessalonica in 1347, the seat of which he took possession only three years later. The fight continued to take on dramatic tones. After his death on November 14, 1359, Palamas was canonized by the Church of Constantinople in 1368. For an introductory reading to Gregory Palamas and his doctrine, see J. Meyendorff, *S. Grégoire Palamas et la mystique orthodoxe* (Paris: Editions du Seuil, 1959).

49. Ἐκεῖνο δὲ τὸ πνεῦμα τοῦ ἀνωτάτω λόγου, οἷόν τις ἔρως ἐστὶν ἀπόρρητος τοῦ γεννήτορος πρὸς αὐτὸν τὸν ἀπορρήτως γεννηθέντα λόγον (Gregory Palamas, *Capita 150*, 36, in E. Perrella, ed., *Gregorio Palamas. Che cos'è l'ortodossia* [Milan: Bompiani, 2006], 38).

50. See Gregory Palamas, *Capita 150*, 36 (Perrella, 40).

51. Τούτου τοῦ ἀνωτάτω ἔρωτος τὴν εἰκόνα καὶ ὁ κατ'εἰκόνα τοῦ Θεοῦ κτισθεὶς ἡμῶν ἔχει νοῦς πρὸς τὴν παρ'αὐτοῦ καὶ ἐν αὐτῷ διηνεκῶς ὑπάρχουσιν γνῶσιν, παρ'αὐτοῦ καὶ ἐν αὐτῷ καὶ τοῦτον ὄντα καὶ συμπροϊόντα παρ'αὐτοῦ τῷ ἐνδοτάτῳ λόγῳ (Gregory Palamas, *Capita 150*, 36 [Perrella, 40]).

age of God not only with regard to the *Logos*, but also with regard to love and desire, which are inseparable in knowledge itself. The Spirit is presented here in a common procession together with the Second Person in the verbal form *symproionta* which clearly differs from *ekporeutai*.

In all of this, the line of development of the different Trinitarian analogies, which extends from the Cappadocians, through Maximus, to Anastasius the Sinaite, seems fundamental. The Cappadocian heritage is taken up and extended not only in the family and psychological sense, already present in tradition, but also in the sense of salvific history and personal history in such a way that the emergence of humanity's immanent faculties speaks, for those who believe, of the Trinity from which everything originated and toward which everything tends.

It can be said, therefore, that the Trinitarian analogies drawn by Anastasius revolve around the psychological analogy, which is developed and connected to the entire history of salvation. In this way, a real inversion is apparent with respect to Origen, for whom the events and the bodily dimension were symbols of spiritual and intelligible realities;[52] for the Sinaite, instead, the human soul itself is a symbol of history, whose value is recognized through incarnation. Trinitarian theology, based on a true Trinitarian ontology, naturally translates into Trinitarian anthropology. And this also seems to give rise to a theology of history.

This emerges against the backdrop of the Cappadocian tradition and the development of the ontological understanding of the world in the light of the formulation of Trinitarian and christological dogma without the need to refer to the Western and Augustinian traditions. The terminological distance between Anastasius and Augustine is also evident, yet what seems to separate also allows us to see how the line of development of the psychological analogies of the Trinity both in the West and in the East manifests the existence of a common theological grammar. This seems to be another example of what happens when in research the epistemology is relationally coherent with the objects studied. Gregory of Nyssa wrote that knowledge is possible only through wonder.[53] Maybe this implies that the surprises of the discovery of a role of the Son in the procession of the Holy Spirit and of the psychological analogy are meaningful. Without any risk of projecting an anthropology onto God, rethinking the human being in the light of the mystery of Christ and the

---

52. Origen, *Commentarii in evangelium Joannis*, 10.18.110.4–6 (SC 157:448).
53. Gregory of Nyssa, *In Canticum canticorum*, GNO 6:358.12–359.4.

Trinity allows us to understand the meaning of His creation as revelation and praise of the Trinity itself.

But what about Augustine's thought? Why has he been regarded as the real "culprit" of the *Filioque*? Why is his Trinitarian theology considered to be the origin of the division between East and West? The following chapter will attempt to answer these questions through an analysis of the ontological conception of the relation.

Augustine's Question: Western Metaphysical Poverty

1. Introduction: A Latinizing Interpretation?

As has already emerged at several points, from the perspective of *Dogmengeschichte* it is interesting to note how, in order to formulate the mystery of the triune God in a noncontradictory way, the Trinitarian thought of the fathers of the Church achieved a real accomplishment in ontology, modifying the metaphysical status of relation. In their thinking, this was no longer considered a mere accident and rose to a new ontological position with respect to the substance, being introduced into the immanence of the latter. The very formulation of the divinity of the Holy Spirit and the identification of His personal *proprium* have gone through this ontological rereading. The question that may spontaneously come to mind is whether such approaches to the premises of the *Filioque* and the psychological analogy in the Greek world do not reveal a Latinizing reading of the Eastern fathers. This chapter attempts to resolve this possible doubt (and criticism) through a comparison between the relational ontology of Gregory of Nyssa, whose pneumatological contribution proved, as we have seen, particularly important, and the parallel operation in the work of Augustine, whose influence obviously marks the entire Latin tradition.[1] Our focus is on the main theological repercussions of this metaphysical option in the thought of both.[2]

---

1. The present chapter does not attempt to directly compare the position of Gregory of Nyssa to that of Augustine on the role of the divine Second Person in the procession of the Holy Spirit. Such a comparison can, however, be found in the recent monograph by Ch. Lee, *Gregory of Nyssa, Augustine of Hippo, and the Filioque* (Leiden: Brill, 2021), esp. 276–302.

2. I was stimulated to add this epistemologically bold chapter to the volume by Richard Cross and Piero Coda, whose suggestions came at different moments and for different reasons.

It is clear upon a first look that the Arians and Pneumatomachians share very similar foundations in the Eastern and Western versions of these heresies, at least according to their reading in the works of both of the fathers whom we are discussing. This makes plausible the hypothesis that the Trinitarian ontology they developed, despite its different nuances in language and emphases, is a sort of fundamental theological grammar that emerges from the confrontation of Trinitarian revelation with the metaphysical thought of the time.[3]

This ontology is expressed in two instances: the first and founding one, which places relation alongside substance as a co-principle of the First Principle that is now recognized as triune; and a second instance that reinterprets the world, especially human beings, through their creation in image and likeness in the light of the previous ontological novelty. These two instances correspond to the recognition of the existence of the two ontological orders highlighted in the previous chapters: the first eternal, which identifies with the Trinity, and the second created, marked by participation.

In any case, extreme caution seems necessary when comparing Gregory of Nyssa and Augustine, in part because of the differences between Greek and Latin Neoplatonism at the epistemological level: the former was more Aristotelian at the level of the analysis of knowledge, while the latter remained more Platonic, as evidenced by the theory of illumination that characterizes the thought of Augustine.[4] But, despite these precautions, the identification of the triune God with the *ipsum esse subsistens* leads one to ask the question of the existence of a common Trinitarian grammar and its relationship with ontology, especially in the contemporary postmodern context, which has a burning metaphysical thirst.[5]

The comparison between Gregory of Nyssa and Augustine could be expressed in very different ways. Here it has been divided into three main architectural elements, preceded by a philosophical contextualization: (1) their conception of relation *in divinis*; (2) its reflection on the understanding of the Holy Spirit, who is precisely the Person who transmits divine life to us, linking

3. Some references to Augustine's Trinitarian ontology can be found in K. Kienzler, "Zu den Anfängen einer trinitarischen Ontologie: Augustinus' Bekenntnisse," in *Der dreieine Gott und die eine Menschheit*, ed. M. Albus et al. (Freiburg im Breisgau: Herder, 1989), 45–60. More generally, for a definition of Trinitarian ontology, see P. Coda, "L'ontologia trinitaria: che cos'è?," *Sophia* 2 (2012): 159–70.

4. On illumination theory, see L. Gioia, *The Theological Epistemology of Augustine's De Trinitate* (Oxford: Oxford University Press, 2008), 193–98.

5. See R. Brague, *Anchors in the Heavens: The Metaphysical Infrastructure of Human Life* (South Bend, IN: Saint Augustine's Press, 2019).

immanence and economy; and (3) the relational rereading of creation and, in particular, the solution to the objection to the use of the plural to speak of three distinct people, while the singular is used in the case of the divine Persons, since they are one God. This is a key issue for the understanding of the top-down relational reading of the gap that makes it possible to respond to the possible criticism of an "Augustinian" reading of the Greek patristic sources on the second immanent procession. The analysis of Augustinian thought[6] will be preceded by a synthesis of the philosophical precedents of the metaphysics of relation in both the Greek and Latin traditions, with particular reference to the work done by Gregory of Nyssa.

II. Relation: The Philosophical Background

Some etymological context is necessary before we assess the philosophical precedents of the metaphysical relation in both the Greek and Latin tradition. The root of the Greek *schesis* is linked to the verb "to have" (ἔχειν), while in Latin *relatio* is linked to *referre*, as in "to refer" or "to report." This implies that the gnoseological dimension may have a greater presence in the Latin sense, while the Greek approach is more ontological.

As far as the philosophical precedents are concerned, the fundamental definitions of relation can be found in Aristotle's *Categories*, where it is expressed through the *pros ti*:

> All the realities which are said to be relative (πρός τι) are those which are said to be what they are based on other realities or, as is otherwise the case, by reference (πρὸς ἕτερον) to another one.[7]

The term *schesis* has not yet emerged at this level, but there is already a reference to one's possession, and therefore to the verb *echein*, as is evident in a second definition also by Aristotle:

---

6. Due to the vastness of the production of and on Augustine, the research will be limited to a terminological analysis and to the most essential bibliography, bringing out only the core of the question without any claim to completeness. For a clear and synthetic presentation of the recourse to relationship in Augustine's Trinitarian theology with its tension with respect to substantiality and its linguistic dimension, see J. Brachtendorf, *Selbstreflexion und Erkenntnis Gottes: Die Struktur des menschlichen Geistes nach Augustinus De Trinitate*, Paradeigmata 19 (Hamburg: Meiner, 2000), 63–74.

7. Πρός τι δὲ τὰ τοιαῦτα λέγεται, ὅσα αὐτὰ ἅπερ ἐστὶν ἑτέρων εἶναι λέγεται ἢ ὁπωσοῦν ἄλλως πρὸς ἕτερον (Aristotle, *Categoriae*, 6a36–37).

Relational (τὰ πρός τι) are those realities for which being identifies with having a certain relationship to something (πρός τί πως ἔχειν).[8]

From the definitions themselves it follows, according to the Stagirite, that they are accidental in themselves and that no substance can be counted among them (οὐδεμία οὐσία τῶν πρός τί ἐστιν), as already mentioned.[9]

The contribution of the Stoics was notable for the development of the philosophical question. However, in Sextus Empiricus's opinion, they affirmed that the realities in relation (τὰ πρός τι) were only in thought and could not exist (ὑπάρχει) in the proper sense.[10]

It is precisely in the discussion of the reality of those in relation that the term *schesis* takes on great importance. For, within the Platonic-Aristotelian tradition, the exegesis of the *Categories* leads Alexander of Aphrodisias to deny that there are ideas that correspond to the relative realities:

> Ideas exist in themselves as substances, while the relative realities (τὰ δὲ πρός τι) are in mutual relation (ἐν τῇ πρὸς ἄλληλα σχέσει).[11]

It is extremely interesting that commentators in different times maintained the statement that the relative realities are accidental, that they are similar to an excrescence (παραφυάδι) of being and therefore extrinsic to the substance. The affirmation is found in the *Ethica Nicomachea*[12] and is taken up by both Alexander of Aphrodisias[13] and Plotinus.[14]

The latter has the merit of showing the relationship between *schesis* and *pros ti*: the relative realities are not merely logical realities, but have a foundation in being, even if accidental, thanks to the very *schesis* that gives them existence.[15] The relative realities are thus placed in relation with the formal dimension (λόγος) and with the participation of the Forms.[16]

---

8. ἔστι τὰ πρός τι οἷς τὸ εἶναι ταὐτόν ἐστι τῷ πρός τί πως ἔχειν (Aristotle, *Categoriae*, 8a31–32).

9. Aristotle, *Categoriae*, 8b21. See chapter 5.

10. Sextus Empiricus, *Adversus Mathematicos*, 8.453.1–454.1.

11. τὰς μὲν ἰδέας καθ᾽ αὑτὰς ὑφεστάναι αὐτοῖς οὐσίας τινὰς οὔσας, τὰ δὲ πρός τι ἐν τῇ πρὸς ἄλληλα σχέσει τὸ εἶναι ἔχειν (Alexander of Aphrodisias, *In Aristotelis metaphysica commentaria*, 83.24–26).

12. Aristotle, *Ethica Nicomachea*, 1096a21–22.

13. Alexander of Aphrodisias, *In Aristotelis metaphysica commentaria*, 83.3.

14. Plotinus, *Enneades*, 6.2.16.1–3.

15. Plotinus, *Enneades*, 6.1.7.11–18.

16. Plotinus, *Enneades*, 6.1.9.1–8.

According to Porphyry, then, relation (σχέσις) is like a middle term (μέσον) that unites different subjects and makes the relative realities (τὰ πρός τι) exist as the indication of a certain bond that characterizes them.[17] For this, concludes the disciple of Plotinus:

> [The relative realities] are not in the subjects either as complements of the substance, or as any other accident, which arise in the subjects themselves, for example, as passion or action (ἐνέργεια), but are something external (ἔξωθεν). That is why they arise and disappear without the subjects being affected.[18]

From this perspective, of course, the First Principle must be without relation (ἀσχετός).[19] In Neoplatonic reading, therefore, the relative realities have their own existence, even if minimal, and are only connected to the sensory sphere. Yet they are always incorporeal and have no matter of their own, in such a way that they can never be the object of perception, but only of intellection. It is Iamblichus, according to Simplicius, who introduces the relative realities in the intelligible dimension as well.[20]

It seems that this is also the background of the philosophical doctrine of relations in the Latin context in which Augustine lives. Specifically, Martianus Capella offers two definitions of relative. The first is the following:

> The relative (*relativum*) is what is said in relation to something (*ad aliquid*), like a father or a brother. And these too are certainly in the subject (*in subiecto*). In fact, it is necessary that these names are related to something (*aliquid*). And there are some whose correlatives are obvious to the mind.[21]

The essential point here is the affirmation that relation is an accident that

17. Porphyry, *In Aristotelis categorias expositio per interrogationem*, 125.16–19.

18. Ὅτι ἐν τοῖς ὑποκειμένοις ἐστὶν οὔτε ὡς οὐσίας συμπληρωτικὸν οὔτε ὡς ἄλλο τι τῶν συμβεβηκότων, ἃ ἐν αὐτοῖς τοῖς ὑποκειμένοις γίνεται, οἷον πάθος ἢ ἐνέργεια, ἀλλά τι ἔξωθεν. διὸ καὶ μὴ πασχόντων τῶν ὑπο κειμένων γίνεται καὶ ἀπογίνεται (Porphyry, *In Aristotelis categorias expositio per interrogationem*, 125.25–28).

19. Porphyry, *In Platonis Parmenidem commentaria*, 3.35–4.4.

20. See J. Dillon, "Iamblichus νοερὰ θεωρία of Aristotle's Categories," *Syllecta classica* 8 (1997): 65–77.

21. "Relativum est, quod ad aliquid vocant, ut pater, frater et haec utique in subiecto sunt; nam necesse est, ut haec nomina ad aliquid sint; et nonnulla sunt, de quibus dicantur illa quae dicuntur in anima videbuntur" (Martianus Capella, *De nuptiis Philologiae et Mercurii*, 4.363 [text in J. Willis, ed., *Martianus Capella* (Leipzig : Teubner, 1983), 118, line 7]).

must adhere to a substance. A second element takes up the duplicity of the Aristotelian definition seen before, where the relative being is expressed both by the genitive and by the preposition that refers to something else:

> The relative (*relativum*) being is what is said is of something (*alicuius*) or can in some way refer to something (*ad aliquid*), as it is not possible to think of the son without the father or the mother or the servant without the master, and vice versa with respect to one another.[22]

Martianus Capella shows how neither the first nor the second substance can be considered relative, but that only in the case of the latter could its parts be considered relative, if one considers as a definition of relative to be everything that can be said about something, that is, everything that can be expressed through the genitive case.[23]

Thus, the tradition of the commentaries on Aristotle's *Categories* was kept alive in the Latin context within the liberal arts precisely by *De dialectica*, which flanked *De rhetorica*, to which it provided strength of reasoning and argumentative power. This is why the orientation tends toward the logical and linguistic dimension.[24]

III. Gregory of Nyssa's Rereading

Such philosophical references seem important for getting an idea of the importance of the discussion on the relative in the context of the Arian crisis.[25] The point is that, according to Athanasius, Arius himself denied that the *Logos* could be a relative being:[26]

---

22. "Relativum est, quod hoc ipsum, quod dicitur, alicuius est vel ad aliquid quolibet modo referri potest, ut filius non sine patre vel matre, et servus non sine domino potest intelligi, neque sine his illi vicissim" (Martianus Capella, *De nuptiis Philologiae et Mercurii*, 4.374 [Willis, 122, line 21]).

23. See Martianus Capella, *De nuptiis Philologiae et Mercurii*, 4.378 (Willis, 125, line 14).

24. On the sources of Martianus's *De dialectica*, see I. Ramelli, ed., *Marziano Capella, Le nozze di Filologia e Mercurio* (Milan: Bompiani, 2004), xxxix–xlvi.

25. The discussion of relativities, together with that of apophaticism, does not seem to get the attention it deserves in Johannes Zachhuber's latest and otherwise most valuable volume: J. Zachhuber, *The Rise of Christian Theology and the End of Ancient Metaphysics: Patristic Philosophy from the Cappadocian Fathers to John of Damascus* (Oxford: Oxford University Press, 2020).

26. For the theological perspective, Philo's contribution is relevant; see G. Maspero, *Essere e relazione: L'ontologia trinitaria di Gregorio di Nissa* (Rome: Città Nuova, 2013), 30–32.

For [the *Logos*] is neither eternal, coeternal, nor unengendered with the Father, nor does He have the being with the Father. But some people say that these [Persons] belong to the relative realities (τὰ πρός τι), introducing two unengendered principles (ἀρχάς).[27]

The great importance of the subject in the Eastern discussions can be deduced from the attack that Eusebius of Caesarea launched against Marcellus of Ancyra, who was accused of attributing to God a human *logos*, that is to say a changeable *logos*, which was presented in the last chapter. As we have seen, Eusebius argues that John began the Prologue of his Gospel with the expression "The *Logos* was *with* God" and not "The *Logos* was *in* God" to avoid lowering the *Logos* itself to the level of accidents. The question is purely metaphysical, and it is linked precisely to the category of relation since the preposition *in* traditionally refers to inhering in a substance. The Bishop of Caesarea explicitly denies, therefore, that the *Logos* belongs to the relative realities (τῶν πρός τι).[28]

But Gregory's position, developed in contrast with both the Arians and the Pneumatomachians, is diametrically opposed because in his view the *Logos* belongs precisely to the dimension of the relative beings (τῶν πρός τι λεγομένων).[29] As we saw in chapter 5, in fact, the Bishop of Nyssa reads the Johannine Prologue according to its chiastic structure, interpreting the first verse in light of the last,[30] to affirm that the Son is *in* the Father as the Father is *in* the Son, where *en tini einai* is understood in a relational sense, as testified by the text of *Contra Eunomium III*, 8, which is presented in chapter 4.[31] Here *being in* is no longer synonymous with accident, but is given in the most absolute substantial identity, according to a reinterpretation that recognizes an immanent dimension of the *archē* itself.[32]

This *being in* assumes a fundamental role in preaching the substantial identity of the divine Persons, that is, in identifying each of them with each individual divine attribute. Still in commenting on the Prologue, and specifically

---

27. οὐδὲ γάρ ἐστιν ἀίδιος ἢ συναίδιος ἢ συναγέννητος τῷ πατρί, οὐδὲ ἅμα τῷ πατρὶ τὸ εἶναι ἔχει, ὥς τινες λέγουσι τὰ πρός τι δύο ἀγεννήτους ἀρχὰς εἰσηγούμενοι (Arius, *Letter to Alexander of Alexandria*, in Athanasius, *De synodis*, 16.4 [AW 2.1:244.11]).

28. See the texts in *De ecclesiastica theologia*, 2, at p. 205.

29. See the text of *Oratio cathechetica magna* cited on p. 107.

30. See G. Maspero, *The Mystery of Communion: Encountering the Trinity* (South Bend, IN: Saint Augustine's Press, 2021), 17–19.

31. See p. 106.

32. See the quote from *Contra Eunomium III* on pp. 103–4.

on the final verse, Gregory writes that God, inasmuch as He is fullness, must have in Himself (that is, in His "womb") power, wisdom, light, word, life, and truth. But it is precisely the Son who makes the "womb" of the Father full, because it is impossible for Him to be thought at some moment without what is good. The Son, therefore, must *be* such good realities and must identify with power and life and truth and light and wisdom.[33] All this is expressed by the correlativity of the names of the Father and the Son, which refer to their being "in each other" (τῷ ἑτέρῳ τὸ ἕτερον).[34]

Therefore, the Son who is *in* the Father does not have only a part of the attributes that characterize the latter, but identifies Himself perfectly with them, being incorruptible because He is in Incorruptibility, good because He is in Goodness, powerful because He is in the Father's Power, and so on.[35] Thus we have here a real and proper theologization of divine attributes, as they are reread based on the relational dimension that characterizes divine immanence *in its entirety*.

Gregory's attention is also directed toward divine action through the connection between immanence and economy. Indeed, as we have already seen, the Cappadocians base their theological thought on the distinction without separation of these two dimensions, which makes it possible to formulate the unity of action of the three divine Persons, while highlighting the role that each Person plays in the one action (for example, in creation). This is usually expressed through the *ek - dia - en* prepositions, which, based on action, recall the prepositions that characterize God's immanent being at the level of processions and relations.[36]

With a synthetic expression one could say that Gregory's Trinitarian ontology is expressed by "putting prepositions to being"; that is, by recognizing the immanent relational dimension of the divine substance. Again with a synthetic formula, one could say that for Gregory, God is one *precisely because* He is triune and thus He is truly good, omnipotent, and every other attribute, *precisely because* of the dimension of relation and communion that characterizes divine immanence in a unique and exclusive way.

This is the basis of the possibility of placing the Holy Spirit in a relational position with respect to the Father and the Son, as a bond that unites them. This, as we have seen in the previous pages, was made explicit in the dispute

---

33. See Gregory of Nyssa, *Contra Eunomium* III, 1.48–49 (GNO 2:20.8–21.5).

34. See Gregory of Nyssa, *Contra Eunomium* III, 5.47.3–8 (GNO 2:177.18–21).

35. Gregory of Nyssa, *Contra Eunomium* III, 6.10.7–12 (GNO 2:189.17–22).

36. See Gregory of Nyssa, *Ad Ablabium*, GNO 3.1:47.21–48.8. See in this regard Maspero, *Trinity and Man*, 53–60.

with the Pneumatomachians, who accepted the divinity of the Son as begotten but denied that of the Holy Spirit, considered only the first of creatures. And the solution proposed by Gregory of Nyssa is properly relational: to place the Third Person between the first two as the *Glory* that they eternally exchange and the *Royal Power* that the Father King confers to the Son, who in turn is King and the perfect image of the Father precisely in receiving and giving back such Power.[37] This is demonstrated by attributing to the Third Person the characteristic of being a bond (συνδετικόν) that unites the Father and the Son, and it is even more explicit in the dynamic and relationship with economy.[38] In this way, the divine Persons are presented as one in the other and identified with the Divinity and with each of the divine attributes. The tool that allows one to reach this image is relation and its connection with the immanent processions.

This makes it possible to identify the personal *proprium* of the Father, the Son, and the Spirit from these elements. For this reason, however, it is essential to distinguish the level of substantial attribution from relational attribution.[39] It paves the way for a relational definition of the different levels of reality, so as to distinguish economy and immanence without separating them. At the same time, the relational dimension is referenced through a philosophical neologism, that is, the *pōs einai* which replaces the Aristotelian *pōs echein*,[40] etymologically linked to *schesis*.[41]

It is worth highlighting here that the equivalence of *pōs einai* and *schesis* is also attested by Gregory of Nazianzus and seems to belong to a sort of theological "grammar" that is not limited to Gregory of Nyssa.[42] The high number of recurrences of the word *schesis*—about 140 times—certainly seems to indicate that the latter is the author of the corresponding theological-philosophical shift. In Gregory of Nazianzus there are, in fact, little more than a dozen recurrences of the term *schesis*, but the logic of the discourse goes in the same direction, as evidenced by the following passage:

37. See, in particular, p. 120.

38. This is particularly evident in the commentary on the Canticle; see pp. 131–32.

39. See pp. 103–4.

40. This was taken up both in the Stoic sphere and by Plotinus with πῶς ἔχον; e.g., Plotinus, *Enneades*, 4.7.4.8–21, in Eusebius, *Praeparatio evangelica*, 15.22.18.1–20.1 (SC 338:338–40).

41. See the text of *Contra Eunomium II*, on p. 164.

42. For an analysis of the different stages of the development of the ontology of relation in the Cappadocians and a demonstration of the specific role of Gregory of Nyssa, see Maspero, *Essere e relazione*, 135–65.

Father is neither the name of a substance, nor of an action, but of a relation (σχέσεως) and of the way of being of the Father toward the Son or the Son toward the Father (πῶς ἔχει πρός). In fact, as it also happens among us, these denominations make known the bond of blood and kinship, so they indicate the connaturality (ὁμοφυίαν) of the generated with respect to the generator. But let us admit, for you, that the Father is a substance, then the latter will include the Son at the same time (συνεισάξει) and will not exclude Him, according to the common notions and the meaning of these denominations.[43]

This "grammar" allows us to speak of intra-Trinitarian relational causality without the risk of confusing the Creator with creation precisely because of the clear distinction between economy and immanence, that is, the exegetical reflection of the metaphysical distinction in two different ontologies. Thus, the Bishop of Nyssa presents the distinction of Persons *in divinis* starting from the relations of origin, as it happens in *Ad Ablabium*.[44]

It is significant that in the same treatise Gregory discusses how it is possible that Peter, James, and John are called three men in the plural, while the Father, the Son and the Spirit are called one God in the singular, even though in both cases there are three persons. The question is both anthropological and Trinitarian because it depends on the possibility and opportunity to connect the terms of *nature* and *person* as they are used *in divinis* with their use in the created order.

It is particularly interesting how the theology that we have summarized so far is presented again, distinguishing the divine Persons in a relational way: first the Father as the absolute cause (τὸ αἴτιον) with respect to the Son and the Spirit united in their being "caused" (αἰτιατόν), then distinguishing the Second Person with respect to the Third. The *Ad Ablabium* arises, in essence, from a question concerning "Trinitarian ontology" understood as discussion of the reflection of the Creator's immanence in the creature, but formulates an answer only starting from a "Trinitarian ontology" understood as an extension of classical metaphysics through a new ontological conception of the

---

43. οὔτε οὐσίας ὄνομα ὁ πατήρ, ὦ σοφώτατοι, οὔτε ἐνεργείας, σχέσεως δὲ καὶ τοῦ πῶς ἔχει πρὸς τὸν υἱὸν ὁ πατήρ, ἢ ὁ υἱὸς πρὸς τὸν πατέρα. ὡς γὰρ παρ' ἡμῖν αἱ κλήσεις αὗται τὸ γνήσιον καὶ οἰκεῖον γνωρί ζουσιν, οὕτω κἀκεῖ τὴν τοῦ γεγεννημένου πρὸς τὸ γεγεννηκὸς ὁμοφυίαν σημαίνουσιν. ἔστω δέ, ὑμῶν χάριν, καὶ οὐσίας τις ὁ πατήρ· συνεισάξει τὸν υἱόν, οὐκ ἀλλοτριώσει, κατὰ τὰς κοινὰς ἐννοίας καὶ τὴν τῶν κλήσεων τούτων δύναμιν (Gregory of Nazianzus, *Oratio*, 29.16.10–17 [SC 250:210]).

44. See the quotations on p. 109.

relation. This implies a new understanding of distinction and causality in a relational sense.

The question is not relegated to a single treatise and is not marginal, but seems to belong to the very "grammar" of Gregory's theology, as can be seen in the following passage:

> If, therefore, in Adam and Abel the reason of humanity does not change because of the difference of the origin (γεννήσεως) and neither the order (τάξεως), nor the mode of existence (τρόπου τῆς ὑπάρξεως) produce any change in nature, but there is no change in nature, as everybody agrees that this is the same by common consent of all sober people and no one would say otherwise unless one was completely insane, what need would there be to support this absurdity of thought for the divine nature? Hearing the words *Father* and *Son* from the One who is the Truth [i.e. the Lord], we have learned of the unity of nature in the two subjects (ἐν δύο τοῖς ὑποκειμένοις τὴν ἑνότητα τῆς φύσεως), a unity which is placed on a natural level by the names in mutual relation (δύο ἄλληλα σχέσεως) and again by the same voice of the Lord.[45]

This is a fundamental and inescapable crossroads in thought because the alternative was to consider the notions of person, nature, and relation equivocal and merely metaphorical in the two ontologies, (i.e., in the Trinity and in the world). On the other hand, the same ontological force attributed to the relation in God makes it possible to reinterpret relations at the level of creation.

In this way in the *Ad Ablabium* Gregory provides the answer to the question of why we are not talking about three gods but about three men, starting from what we have seen about the intra-Trinitarian relations as the principle of personal distinction in the one divine nature and through a rereading, again from a relational perspective, of the one nature of the human being. In fact,

---

45.εἰ οὖν ὁ τῆς ἀνθρωπότητος λόγος ἐπὶ τοῦ Ἀδὰμ καὶ τοῦ Ἄβελ τῷ παρηλλαγμένῳ τῆς γεννήσεως οὐχ ὑπαλλάσσεται, οὐδεμίαν οὔτε τῆς τάξεως οὔτε τοῦ τρόπου τῆς ὑπάρξεως τῇ φύσει τὴν παραλλαγὴν ἐμποιούντων, ἀλλ᾽ ὡσαύτως ἔχειν τῇ κοινῇ τῶν νηφόντων συγκαταθέσει διωμολόγηται καὶ οὐδεὶς <ἂν> ἀντείποι τούτῳ μὴ σφόδρα τοῦ ἐλλεβόρου δεόμενος, τίς ἡ ἀνάγκη κατὰ τῆς θείας φύσεως τὸ παράλογον τοῦτο τῆς ἐννοίας κατασκευάζεσθαι; Πατέρα καὶ υἱὸν παρὰ τῆς ἀληθείας ἀκούσαντες ἐν δύο τοῖς ὑποκειμένοις τὴν ἑνότητα τῆς φύσεως ἐδιδάχθημεν, ὑπό τε τῶν ὀνομάτων φυσικῶς [διὰ] τῆς πρὸς ἄλληλα σχέσεως σημαινομένης καὶ ὑπ᾽ αὐτῆς πάλιν τῆς τοῦ κυρίου φωνῆς (Gregory of Nyssa, *Contra Eunomium I*, 497.1–499.1 [GNO 1:170.5–17]).

the Bishop of Nyssa identifies a dual aspect in the human *physis*: an intensive one and an extensive one.[46] Man is not only an individual of the human species. Neither humanity is the mere sum of individuals, but human nature is simultaneously the communion of all men of all times and the individual man. It is a synthesis of the first Aristotelian substance and the second one, which are unified into a single concept to express the revealed novelty. While in God these two aspects do indeed perfectly coincide, in humanity they are distinct; but at the same time they cannot be separated.

Gregory differentiates the two creations of Genesis 1:26–28 and 2:7, stating that in the first the whole human being was created,[47] as a set of individuals intentionally present in the divine mind.[48] Humanity is recognized as an image of God not only in its individuality, but also as a communion of persons from which the essential role of human relationships logically follows.[49] The step is fundamental and also has immediate consequences on the practical level, since Gregory is the first father of the Church who explicitly and blatantly condemns slavery.[50]

Thus the relational rereading of the creatural dimension seems to be the foundation of the development, in the Greek context too, of the analogies between the immanent structure of the human soul and the Trinity itself, to which the last chapter was dedicated.

The resemantization of the relation at an ontological level makes it possible for Gregory to deeply understand creation and especially the human being. The inclusion of the *schesis* in the Trinitarian immanence allows us both to recognize the personal characteristic of the Spirit as a bond between the Father and the Son and to reconsider the relationship between the Trinity and the world, rereading human nature and the immanent dimension of the individual human from a Trinitarian and, therefore, relational perspective.

---

46. J. Zachhuber, *Human Nature in Gregory of Nyssa: Philosophical Background and Theological Significance* (Leiden: Brill, 2000), 74.

47. See Gregory of Nyssa, *De opificio hominis*, PG 44, 185BC.

48. See J. Daniélou, *Le IVe siècle: Grégoire de Nysse et son milieu* (Paris: Institut catholique de Paris, 1964), 62. Gregory explicitly excludes the fact that it is the preexistence of souls, as Origen maintains (cf. *De Anima*, PG 46, 113BC). See G. Maspero, "Anthropology," *The Brill Dictionary of Gregory of Nyssa*, 37–47.

49. See G. Maspero, "Ontologia trinitaria e sociologia relazionale: Due mondi a confront," *PATH* 10 (2011): 19–36.

50. I. Ramelli, *Social Justice and the Legitimacy of Slavery: The Role of Philosophical Asceticism from Ancient Judaism to Late Antiquity* (Oxford: Oxford University Press, 2016).

IV. AUGUSTINE'S ONTOLOGICAL NOVELTY

In very briefly summarizing the Trinitarian ontology of Gregory of Nyssa together with the "strategic" relevance of this ontology for the whole of the theology of the great Cappadocian, we have also tried to highlight the harmony with his friend and fellow Gregory, the bishop of Nazianzus. This seems particularly relevant when viewed through the lens of the comparison between the Bishop of Nyssa and Augustine. In fact, several authors agree that the Bishop of Hippo knew a now lost translation of Gregory of Nazianzus's *Oratio* 29.[51] This may have been one of the sources of inspiration for Augustine's thought.[52]

A thorough analysis of the occurrences of the semantic family of *relatio* in his works immediately highlights how the properly theological use of the relationship terminology is not linked to the term *relatio* itself, which instead has the literary and juridical meaning, but to *relativum* and the corresponding adverb. This indicates the metaphysical matrix of Augustine's approach.[53]

In fact, a search of the occurrences of *relativum* in Latin literature reveals its presence in the work of the aforementioned Martianus Capella in the part of his *De nuptiis Philologiae et Mercurii* dedicated to the dialectic. It is difficult to determine whether there is a direct influence, partially because of uncertainties about the dating of the life of Capella, or whether Augustine and his compatriot share a common Varronian source. The influence of Plotinus's Latin translations is also probable, especially the lost *Enneades* by Marius Victorinus, and in general the exegetical tradition of the Aristotelian Categories.

In the absence of Latin translations of Gregory of Nazianzus's *Orationes theologicae*, the analysis of theological thought cannot be a discussion of the sources; rather, the main and practically only determining element would be a comparison between the Trinitarian ontology of Gregory of Nyssa and Augustine.[54]

---

51. See I. Chevalier, *S. Augustin et la pensée grecque: Les relations trinitaires* (Fribourg: Librairie de l'Université Fribourg en Suisse, 1940), 141–52, and B. Altaner, *Kleine patristische Schriften* (Berlin: Akademie-Verlag, 1967), 284.

52. On the possibility of Cappadocian sources in Augustine's thought, see R. Kany, *Augustins Trinitätsdenken: Bilanz, Kritik und Weiterführung der modernen Forschung zu "De trinitate,"* Studien und Texte zu Antike und Christentum 22 (Tübingen: Mohr Siebeck, 2007), 92–97.

53. For a deeply theological presentation of Augustine's Trinitarian doctrine, see L. Ayres, *Augustine and the Trinity* (Cambridge: Cambridge University Press, 2010).

54. Sarah Heaner Lancaster studied the relationship between substance, person, and relations in the work of the Bishop of Hippo, trying to respond to the criticism of those who, like Catherine Mowry LaCugna, see a substantialism in his thought. See S. Heaner

In Augustine's *corpus* the absence of the semantic family linked to *relatio* in his Commentary on John and in the explicitly anti-Arian writings, with the exception of *De Trinitate*, is striking. Chapters five through seven of *De Trinitate* must have been written between 413 and 416 after the sack of Rome in 410, an event that prompted various Arians to seek refuge in Africa.[55] This could explain the introduction of relation in these chapters, based on what has been said about Arius's denial that the *Logos* belonged to the relative beings.[56] Despite the difficulties of a diachronic analysis of Augustine's work, it does not seem possible to give chronological reasons for this dearth. It must therefore have theological reasons.[57]

Relation is a key element of the Augustinian interpretation of the data offered by revelation and tradition discussed in the first four chapters of his work. As we can see in the summary presented in book 15, it is precisely in book 5 where the reference to the relational dimension appears explicitly:

In the fifth book, for those who think that the substance of the Father and the Son is not the same, because they believe that all that is said of God is said according to substance, and for this reason they maintain that to generate and be generated or to be begotten and unengendered, being different, refer to different substances, it is shown that not all that is said of God is said according to substance, as according to substance they say good and great or the other attributes that are preached in a substantial way (*ad se*). There is, instead, also the being said in a relative sense (*relative*), that is, not in a substantial way (*ad se*), but in relation to something else (*ad aliquid*), as *Father* is said in relation to *Son*, or *Lord* with respect to the creature who serves Him.[58]

Lancaster, "Three-Personed Substance: The Relational Essence of the Triune God in Augustine's *De Trinitate*," *Thomist* 60 (1996): 123–39. We believe that a comparison with Gregory of Nyssa's theology and attention to the differences in metaphysical traditions can help to further examine the relationship between relations and substance in Augustine's thinking.

55. On the controversial question of the chronology of the *De Trinitate*, see Kany, *Augustins Trinitätsdenken*, 31–46.

56. S. Heaner Lancaster, "Divine Relations of the Trinity: Augustine's Answer to Arianism," *Calvin Theological Journal* 34 (1999): 327–46, esp. 333.

57. On the specifics of Western Arianism, see M. Simonetti, "S. Agostino e gli ariani," *Revue des études augustiniennes* 13 (1967): 55–84.

58. "In quinto, propter eos quibus ideo videtur non eamdem Patris et Filii esse substantiam, quia omne quod de Deo dicitur, secundum substantiam dici putant, et propterea gignere et gigni, vel genitum esse et ingenitum, quoniam diversa sunt, contendunt substantias esse diversas, demonstratur non omne quod de Deo dicitur secundum substantiam dici,

This is the only occurrence of relation in book 15. Therefore, it seems that for Augustine the central nucleus of his relational theology should be sought in book 5.

Here the Bishop of Hippo establishes apophaticism as a starting point for the new part of *De Trinitate* (books 5–7), which is in his view a true fundamental epistemological principle of Trinitarian theology. The object of the investigation is, in fact, unattainable and inexpressible. God is always beyond the capabilities of human thought, so that the human being experiences the paradox of always having to think of Him, without ever being able to do so in a worthy way (*de quo digne cogitare non possumus*).[59]

This principle is based on the ontological discontinuity that separates divine nature from created nature. This constitutes humanity's field of view, in terms of both the material and spiritual dimensions of the inner life. The intellect is the best part of the human being through which wisdom is learned, yet even the human mind cannot be understood. Thus, it is even more futile to try to understand God.[60] The intellect has no materiality and is not linked to the categories which characterize creation, so such accidents will certainly not be found in God, who is good without quality and great without quantity (*sine qualitate bonum, sine quantitate magnum*), as well as all divine attributes without creatural limit.

God is without a doubt substance (*sine dubitatione substantia*), that is essence, a new term that comes from *esse* (i.e., being), as in Latin *sapientia* comes from *sapere* (i.e., tasting). This expression corresponds to no one more so than to God, because He does not change and cannot change, thus identifying with Being itself.[61]

The refutation of the Arian theses therefore begins with a reaffirmation of apophaticism, that is, further explanation that we are moving into an area where neither expression can match thought nor thought comprehend reality.[62] The classical Arian position is presented through the distinction between substantial and accidental predication. The latter is impossible in the case of God, for whom only the former can be given. But the Father is called *unbegotten*, while the Son is *begotten*, and to be *unbegotten* and to be *begotten* are

---

sicut secundum substantiam dicitur bonus et magnus, et si quid aliud ad se dicitur; sed dici etiam relative, id est non ad se, sed ad aliquid quod ipse non est; sicut Pater ad Filium dicitur, vel Dominus ad creaturam sibi servientem" (Augustine, *De Trinitate*, 15.3.5 [CCSL 50:463–64]).

59. See Augustine, *De Trinitate*, 5.1.1 (CCSL 50:206).
60. See Augustine, *De Trinitate*, 5.1.2 (CCSL 50:206).
61. See Augustine, *De Trinitate*, 5.2.3 (CCSL 50:206–7).
62. See Augustine, *De Trinitate*, 5.3.4 (CCSL 50:208).

manifestly different realities, so that, according to the Arians, the substances of the first two divine Persons should be different.[63]

Their refutation is a *reductio ad absurdum* based on John 10:30: the Arian affirmation that in God everything is necessarily said according to substance is assumed to be good to show that, if this were true, then when Jesus says that He and the Father are one, this should mean that they are one substance, in clear contrast to the Arian position. But then one must admit that it is possible to say something of God in a nonsubstantial sense, so *unengendered* and *generated* do not necessarily need to be said in that sense. In fact, the accidental dimension is identified with that of mutability according to the common fact in the philosophical tradition, which for this reason excluded the possibility of putting it in relationship with God, who is immutable.[64]

From here we proceed rigorously, assuming that nothing can therefore be preached about God according to accidents. At the same time, revelation compels one to recognize that it cannot be said that in God everything is preached according to substance:

> So in God, nothing is said according to accident, for in Him nothing changes. But not even everything that can be said is said according to substance. In fact, there is also the relative (*ad aliquid*) predication, as the Father with respect to the Son and the Son with respect to the Father, and this is not accidental, since the former is always Father and the second always Son. And *always* is said not in the sense that the Father does not cease to be Father from the moment the Son is born, or that the latter does not cease to be Son from that moment, but *always* because the Son has always been born and has never begun to be Son. For, if at a certain moment He had begun or at a certain moment He ceased to be Son, it would be said in an accidental sense.[65]

---

63. On the relation between the Father and the Son in *De Trinitate*, see M. Weedman, "Augustine's *De Trinitate* 5 and the Problem of the Divine Names *Father* and *Son*," *Theological Studies* 72 (2011): 768–86.

64. Augustine, *De Trinitate*, 5.4.5 (CCSL 50:209).

65. "In Deo autem nihil quidem secundum accidens dicitur, quia nihil in eo mutabile est; nec tamen omne quod dicitur, secundum substantiam dicitur. Dicitur enim ad aliquid sicut Pater ad Filium, et Filius ad Patrem, quod non est accidens: quia et ille semper Pater, et ille semper Filius; et non ita semper quasi ex quo natus est Filius, aut ex eo quod numquam desinat esse Filius, Pater esse non desinat Pater, sed ex eo quod semper natus est Filius, nec coepit umquam esse Filius. Quod si aliquando esse coepisset, aut aliquando esse desineret Filius, secundum accidens diceretur" (Augustine, *De Trinitate*, 5.5.6 [CCSL 50:210]).

Here we see the effect of the second Arian principle according to which God had begun to be Father since the Son was not eternal. In the quoted passage the *relative* term translates the *ad aliquid*, that is, the Latin version of Aristotle's *pros ti*, whose categories are explicitly mentioned. This makes the ontological dimension of the response evident. The *relativum*, corresponding to *schesis*, appears in the conclusion of the section:

> For this reason, although it is different to be Father and to be Son, the substance is not different, because this is not said according to the substance (*secundum substantiam*), but according to the relation (*relativum*). And the relation (*relativum*) is not accidental because it is not mutable.[66]

Then Augustine explains that the Arians would deny that *unengendered* and *begotten* are names that express relations, as is the case for *Father* and *Son*. According to them, these would be absolute terms, which is why they affirm the substantial difference between the first two divine Persons. Augustine replies that *generated* must necessarily be a relative name, because it refers to a *generator* and is synonymous with *son*.[67] The point is that *father* and *son* are not correlative terms like *friend* and *neighbour*, which imply reciprocity, but the *Father* refers back to the *Son* maintaining a distinction and an order with respect to Him, which excludes the interchangeability of the two, since the *Son* is not called *Father* and vice versa:

> And since the Son is not said in relation to the Son, but in relation to the Father, the Son is not equal to the Father according to what is said in relation to the Father. It follows that He is equal according to what is said in an absolute sense (*ad se*). But whatever is said in the absolute sense, it is said according to the substance. So it follows that equality is according to the substance. That is why the substance of both is the same. But when you say that the Father is unengendered, you are not saying what He is, but what He is not. And when one builds the negative of a relative term, one does not deny the substantial dimension, since the relative itself is not said according to the substance (*ipsum relativum non secundum substantiam dicitur*).[68]

66. "Quamobrem quamvis diversum sit Patrem esse et Filium esse, non est tamen diversa substantia, quia hoc non secundum substantiam dicuntur, sed secundum relativum; quod tamen relativum non est accidens quia non est mutabile" (Augustine, *De Trinitate*, 5.5.6 [CCSL 50:211]).

67. See Augustine, *De Trinitate*, 5.6.7 (CCSL 50:211).

68. "Quia vero Filius non ad Filium relative dicitur sed ad Patrem, non secundum hoc

The negative meaning of *unengenerated* is the subject of the following point: starting from the equivalence of begotten and son, it is shown that *unengenerated* actually means "not son," that is, *non genitus*. The point is that "the negative particle does not make what in its absence was in a relative sense to now predicate according to substance."[69] The conclusion is that *unengenerated* is a relative term, because it denies the relation with respect to a parent and does not leave the relative dimension. For Augustine it is therefore clear that what is said in a relative sense cannot refer to the substance.

Then the Bishop of Hippo continues his reasoning by showing how divine attributes should be indicated in the singular because God, and therefore each divine Person, identifies totally with them:

> Therefore, we affirm specifically that any attribute predicated of that divine sublimity in an absolute sense (*ad se*) is said in a substantial sense (*substantialiter*), while when it is predicated in relation to something else (*ad aliquid*) it is not said in a substantial sense, but in a relative sense (*relative*). And we also affirm that in the Father, in the Son, and in the Holy Spirit such is the strength of the identity of substance, that whatever attribute is said of them in the absolute sense (*ad se*) must be taken not in the collective plural, but in the singular. In fact, in the same sense the Father is God and the Son is God and the Holy Spirit is God, an affirmation that no one doubts being predicated according to the substance, and yet they are not three gods, but let us say that the Supreme Trinity is one God.[70]

This is where the expressions that are echoed in the Athanasian Symbol come

---

quod ad Patrem dicitur aequalis est Filius Patri. Restat ut secundum id aequalis sit quod ad se dicitur. Quidquid autem ad se dicitur, secundum substantiam dicitur. Restat ergo ut secundum substantiam sit aequalis. Eadem est igitur utriusque substantia. Cum vera ingenitus dicitur Pater, non quid sit, sed quid non sit dicitur. Cum autem relativum negatur, non secundum substantiam negatur quia ipsum relativum non secundum substantiam dicitur" (Augustine, *De Trinitate*, 5.6.7 [CCSL 50:212]).

69. "Negativa porro ista particula non id efficit ut quod sine illa relativi dicitur eadem praeposita substantialiter dicatur" (Augustine, *De Trinitate*, 5.7.8 [CCSL 50:213]).

70. "Quapropter illud praecipue teneamus, quidquid ad se dicitur praestantissima illa et divina sublimitas substantialiter dici; quod autem ad aliquid non substantialiter, sed relative; tantamque vim esse eiusdem substantiae in Patre et Filio et Spiritu Sancto, ut quidquid de singulis ad se ipsos dicitur, non pluraliter in summa, sed singulariter accipiatur. Quemadmodum enim Deus est Pater, et Filius Deus est, et Spiritus Sanctus Deus est, quod secundum substantiam dici nemo dubitat, non tamen tres deos sed unum Deum dicimus eam ipsam praestantissimam Trinitatem" (Augustine, *De Trinitate*, 5.8.9 [CCSL 50:215]).

from: the Father is great, the Son is great, the Holy Spirit is great but they are not three greats, and this is true of goodness and all the other attributes of the three divine Persons, which are always predicated in the singular because for them to be and to be great, good, or omnipotent does simply coincide.

After discussing the formula "one essence and three persons," connecting the meaning with the corresponding Greek expressions,[71] it becomes clear that there can be no participation in God. This brings us to one of the most complete statements in book 5 on the question of the attribution of the different names to the Father, the Son, and the Holy Spirit:

> Instead, what is said about the individual Person in the Trinity is in no way predicated in an absolute sense (*ad se*), but in the sense of reciprocal relation (*ad invicem*) or in relation to the creature (*ad creaturam*), and it is clear for this reason that it is not said in a substantial sense, but in a relative one (*relative non substantialiter*).[72]

It should be noted that the plane of language and that of being are clearly distinct, but connected in such a way that it does not seem possible to reduce relations to the purely linguistic dimension.

v. The Holy Spirit as Relation

For Augustine, the affirmation of the uniqueness of God and the attribute *Lord* in Deuteronomy 6:4 is interpreted as a reference to the three divine Persons, while the Trinity cannot be called Son. The discourse is more complicated for the Holy Spirit, because both *Spirit* and *Holy* can be said of the three Persons in the absolute sense, while when the two terms appear together they form an expression that is only personal and should therefore be understood in the relative sense, as the Spirit of the Father and the Son (cf. Matt 10:20; Gal 4:6):

> But the relation itself does not appear in this name, it appears instead when we speak of God's Gift. For the Gift is of the Father and the Son, for it "proceeds from the Father" (John 15:26), as the Lord says. And with the words "Whoever does not have the Spirit of Christ does not belong to him"

---

71. See Augustine, *De Trinitate*, 5.8–9 (CCSL 50:215–17).

72. "Quod autem proprie singula in eadem Trinitate dicuntur nullo modo ad se ipsa, sed ad invicem aut ad creaturam dicuntur, et ideo relative non substantialiter ea dici manifestum est" (Augustine, *De Trinitate*, 5.11.12 [CCSL 50:218]).

(Rom 8:9) the Apostle is surely speaking about Him. So, when we talk about "the Donor's Gift" and "Donor of the Gift," we are using both these expressions in a mutually relative sense (*relative to invicem*). Therefore, the Holy Spirit is a certain ineffable communion (*ineffabilis quaedam communio*) of the Father and the Son, and perhaps He is referred to in this way precisely because the same denomination can be appropriate for both the Father and the Son. In fact, for Him one uses as a name what is attributed to the Father and the Son as a common name, because both the Father and the Son are spirit, just as both the Father and the Son are holy. In this way, the Holy Spirit is called the Gift of both, so that He who is the communion of both may be indicated by a name that suits both. And this Trinity is one God, single, good, great, eternal, omnipotent: unity, divinity, greatness, goodness, eternity, omnipotence in itself.[73]

Thanks to this reflection on the divine Third Person and His proper name, which expresses in its very form the communion of the first two Persons, we reach an effective formulation of the difference between absolute and personal, or relative, use of a name. Augustine also explains the problem of identifying the correlative name of the Holy Spirit: if for *father* we immediately have the term *son* and in the same way for *master* we have *servant*, then in the case of the Third Person we cannot reverse the expression "Spirit of the Father and the Son" by saying "Father of the Spirit" or "Son of the Spirit": "In fact, in many related terms it happens that there is not a term in which the realities that refer to each other correspond to each other."[74] Thus, for the Spirit one can say that He is a gift of the Father and the Son, but one cannot speak of the Father or the Son of the gift. The correlativity can only be expressed as Donor's Gift and Donor of Gift (*donum donatoris, et donatorem doni*).

73. "Sed ipsa relatio non apparet in hoc nomine; apparet autem cum dicitur donum Dei. Donum enim est Patris et Filii, quia et a Patre procedit, sicut Dominus dicit, et quod Apostolus ait: Qui Spiritum Christi non habet, hic non est eius, de ipso utique Spiritu Sancto ait. "Donum" ergo "donatoris" and "donator doni," cum dicimus, relative utrumque ad invicem dicimus. Ergo Spiritus Sanctus ineffabilis quaedam Patris Filiique communio, et ideo fortasse sic appellatur, quia Patri et Filio potest eadem appellatio convenire. Nam hoc ipse proprie dicitur quod illi communiter quia et Pater spiritus et Filius spiritus, et Pater sanctus. Ut ergo ex nomine quod utrique convenit, utriusque communio significetur, vocatur donum amborum Spiritus Sanctus. Et haec Trinitas unus Deus, solus, bonus, magnus, aeternus, omnipotens; ipse sibi unitas, deitas, magnitudo, bonitas, aeternitas, omnipotentia" (Augustine, *De Trinitate*, 5.11.12 [CCSL 50:219–20]).

74. "In multis enim relativis hoc contingit, ut non inveniatur vocabulum quo sibi vicissim respondeant quae ad se referuntur" (Augustine, *De Trinitate*, 5.12.13 [CCSL 50:220]).

The doctrine set forth makes it clear that the name *principle* admits both an absolute use, referring to the three divine Persons, and a relative sense, referring only to the Father. In an absolute sense the Son can also be called the Principle with respect to creation, and in the same way this applies to the Holy Spirit, but *Son*, *Image*, and *Word* have only relative meanings.[75]

The study of the term "principle" in Trinitarian immanence is therefore connected to the question of the relation between the Father and the Spirit. Can the former be called the Principle of the latter? The answer is positive because the Father is not only the Principle of what He generates, but also of what He gives. This is helpful for understanding why the Third Person is not generated, but given:

> For what is born of the Father, being called Son, is relative only to the Father. That is why He is the Son of the Father and not Son of us. Instead, what is given is relative both to the One who has given and to those to whom He is given. Thus, the Holy Spirit is said to be not only of the Father and the Son who have given Him, but also of us who have received Him.[76]

From this perspective the Father and the Son are one Principle of the Spirit, while the three divine Persons are one Principle of created realities.

This seriously poses the problem of the distinction between the immanence and the divine economy, because the relational definition of the Third Person in terms of gift seems to join Him to creation. Therefore, Augustine explains that the Spirit is Gift in eternity, in that He proceeds in eternity while He is given in time. Indeed, it is possible to be a gift without having been given yet. Thus, the Spirit proceeds eternally as Gift even before being given temporally. When this happened, God obviously did not change at all, while the creatures did change. Thus, divine relations are neatly distinguished from those relations with creation, which do not involve change in the Trinity:

> It is clear, then, that what one begins to attribute to God in time, and that was not said before time, is said in a relative sense (*relative*), but this is not an accidental predication as if something happened to God. Instead, it is accidental with respect to what begins to be said of God in a relative sense (*relative*).[77]

75. See Augustine, *De Trinitate*, 5.13.14 (CCSL 50:221).

76. "Quod enim de Patre natum est, ad Patrem solum refertur cum dicitur Filius, et ideo Filius Patris est, non et noster. Quod autem datum est et ad eum qui dedit refertur et ad eos quibus dedit; itaque Spiritus Sanctus non tantum Patris et Filii qui dederunt, sed etiam noster dicitur qui accepimus" (Augustine, *De Trinitate*, 5.14.15 [CCSL 50:222–23]).

77. "Quod ergo temporaliter dici incipit Deus quod antea non dicebatur manifestum

It is evident how Augustine is led by his theological grammar to analyze the Trinity and the world at the same time. This can be a serious difficulty, because it requires a continuous reformulation of difference, but at the same time this approach compels a reinterpretation of creation in the light of the ontological novelty discovered through Trinitarian revelation.

It should be noted that the danger of what will be later called Filioquism resides here, as the relation between the Father and the Son, at least in this formulation, seems to be perfect in itself without any reference to the Spirit, because from the linguistic perspective the Son refers to the Father and not to the Third Person.

This is a key element in verifying the strength of the Trinitarian ontology of Augustine, who recovers the relational dimension of the Spirit, not on a formally metaphysical level but on that of communion and love. Working on the correlativity of the names of Father and Son, he excludes the use of the ontological instrument of relation in the definition of the personal *proprium* of the Third Person, however, as *Donum* expresses the link between economy and immanence more intensely.[78] Clearly Augustine has an ontological conception of the Spirit, but this does not formally go through the reshaping of the metaphysical status of relation. In fact, book 6 explains how the Spirit is connected to the unity of the Father and the Son:

> So even the Holy Spirit is in this very unity of substance and equality [with the Father and the Son]. In fact, whether we speak of the unity of both, or of their holiness, or of their charity, or their unity because this is charity or of charity because it is holiness, in any case it is clear that He in whom both [the Father and the Son] are united is not one of the two of them, precisely He who is the one in whom the Generated is loved by His Generator and in whom He Himself loves His Generator, so as to maintain "the unity of spirit in the bond of peace" (Eph 4:3), not by participation but in His own essence, i.e., nor by the gift of someone superior but their own.[79]

---

est relative dici, non tamen secundum accidens Dei quod ei aliquid acciderit, sed plane secundum accidens eius ad quod dici aliquid Deus incipit relative" (Augustine, *De Trinitate*, 5.16.17 [CCSL 50:227]).

78. On the personal *proprium* of the Holy Spirit, see K. Reinhard, "Somebody to Love? The Proprium of the Holy Spirit in Augustine's Trinity," *Augustinian Studies* 41 (2010): 351–73.

79. "Quapropter etiam Spiritus Sanctus in eadem unitate substantiae et aequalitate consistit. Sive enim sit unitas amborum, sive sanctitas sive caritas, sive ideo unitas quia caritas et ideo caritas, quia sanctitas, manifestum est quod non aliquis duorum est quo uterque coniungitur, quo genitus a gignente diligatur generatoremque suum diligat, sintque non

The personal characteristic of the Holy Spirit is therefore to be the communion of the first two divine Persons, as their love with whom the Son is loved by the Father and with whom the latter loves Him back. In this sense the danger of Filioquism is absolutely excluded, that is, there is no place for a closed conception of the relationship between the first two divine Persons where the third becomes a mere addition.[80] Yet Augustine cannot express this at the ontological level, because in this approach relation is juxtaposed with substance and is not placed within it, as seen in the doctrine of the Greek fathers. But the Bishop of Hippo founds a true metaphysics of love, adding below:

> Therefore the Holy Spirit is something common (*commune aliquid*) between the Father and the Son, whatever it may be, the very consubstantial and coeternal communion; and if it could be conveniently called friendship, let us call it so. But it would be better to call it charity; and the latter is also substance, because God is substance and "God is charity" (1 John 4:16), as Scripture says. But just as it is called substance with the Father and the Son, so it is also called great and good and holy and whatever other attribute is predicated in an absolute sense (*ad se*), because being God is nothing other than being great and good and everything else that has been shown above.[81]

This is the theological element that brings Augustine to affirm that the Third Person proceeds *communiter* from the Father and the Son, while *principaliter* proceeds only from the first One.[82] The strength of this perspective is that it makes it possible to express that the origin of creation itself is the joyful rela-

---

participatione, sed essentia sua, neque dono superioris alicuius sed sua proprio servantes unitatem spiritus in vinculo pacis" (Augustine, *De Trinitate*, 6.5.7 [CCSL 50:235]).

80. For a concise and complete presentation of Augustine's pneumatology and the *Filioque*, see Kany, *Augustins Trinitätsdenken*, 216–27. Especially important is page 219, where the tensions in the different readings with respect to the Eastern sources are apparent.

81. "Spiritus ergo Sanctus commune aliquid est Patris et Filii, quidquid illud est, aut ipsa communio consubstantialis et coaeterna; quae si amicitia convenienter dici potest, dicatur, sed aptius dicitur caritas; et haec quoque substantia, quia Deus substantia et Deus caritas, sicut scriptum est. Sicut autem simul substantia cum Patre et Filio, ita simul magna et simul bona et simul sancta et quidquid aliud ad se dicitur, quoniam non aliud est Deo esse, et aliud magnum esse vel bonum, et cetera sicut supra ostendimus" (Augustine, *De Trinitate*, 6.5.7 [CCSL 50:235–36]).

82. Cf. Augustine, *De Trinitate*, 5.11.12 and 15.17.29 (CCSL 50:219 and 503–4). On this pair of adverbs in Augustine's pneumatology, see G. Catapano, "La processione dello Spirito Santo nel *De Trinitate* di Agostino," in *Contra Latinos et Adversus Graecos: The Separation*

tionship between the Father and the Son. Augustine comments here on Hilary of Poitiers, who had defined the personal properties of the Father, the Son, and the Holy Spirit with the following statement: "Eternity is in the Father, the form in the Image, the fruition (*usus*) in the Gift."[83]

The Bishop of Hippo starts from the relation between the First and the Second Persons, where the latter is image in such a perfect sense that He is identical to the reality of which He is image (*ad identidem respondens ei cuius imago est*). For this reason in the Son there is that Life which for God coincides with Being (*idem et esse et vivere*). In the same way, in Him there is a perfect knowing that once again coincides with living and being (*id quod est intellegere, hoc vivere*). And everything created is in this *Verbum perfectum* in which God knows every creature. This is not known because it comes to being; on the contrary, it comes to being because it is eternally known in God, in the intradivine relation of the Father and the Son. And in this relation the Spirit is the joy that floods everything as Love of the first two divine Persons:

> Therefore, that ineffable embrace (*ineffabilis complexus*) of the Father and His Image is not without fruition, charity, or joy. Therefore that delight, pleasure, happiness or bliss, if any human word expresses it in a worthy way, is in short called by him [Hilary] *fruition*. And in the Trinity He is the Holy Spirit, who is not begotten, but is the suavity of the Generator and the Generated, who with great abundance and generosity fills all creatures according to their capacities, so that they may maintain their order and rest in the places that correspond to them.[84]

This vibrant mystical language interprets creation in the light of the relation between the three divine Persons. All things are themselves resting in the order that in the Spirit pours out from the superabundant joy of divine knowledge that characterizes the relation between the Father and the Son. From this

---

between Rome and Constantinople from the Ninth to the Fifteenth Century, ed. Alessandra Bucossi and Anna Calia (Leuven: Peeters, 2020), 65–87.

83. Hilary of Poitiers, *De Trinitate*, 2.1.1 (SC 443:276).

84. "Ille igitur ineffabilis quidam complexus Patris et Imaginis non est sine perfruitione, sine caritate, sine gaudio. Illa ergo dilectio, delectatio, felicitas vel beatitudo, si tamen aliqua humana voce digne dicitur, usus ab illo appellatus est breviter, et est in Trinitate Spiritus Sanctus, non genitus, sed genitoris genitique suavitas ingenti largitate atque ubertate perfundens omnes creaturas pro captu earum, ut ordinem suum teneant et locis suis acquiescant" (Augustine, *De Trinitate*, 6.10.11 [CCSL 50:242]).

perspective the world is presented as the overflowing of God's inner life, of His love and happiness.[85]

The step is essential in the whole design of Augustine's *De Trinitate*. He shifts his gaze to creation and to the human being in particular, letting himself be carried away by a double movement that, like the waves of the sea, brings thought from the Trinitarian vestige (*vestigium*) in the world to its divine origin, and then to descend again following the flow of everything from this highest origin, which is in itself Beauty and absolute Joy. The unity of creation, where one thing together is not equal to three things and two things are bigger than one, appears as the refraction of the divine unity, where each divine Person is as great as the other two as infinite, so that "each is in each, all are in each, and all are in all, and all are one" (*singula sunt in singulis, et omnia in singulis, et singula in omnibus, et omnia in omnibus, et unum omnia*).[86]

VI. THE RELATIONAL DESCENT

This establishes the possibility of the relational descent, the strong point of Augustine, who manages to articulate relations at the creatural level with relations *in divinis*. Augustine's own method leads him to analyze the Trinity and the human being together, not to confuse them but to highlight the differences. Thus, in his *In Iohannis Evangelium tractatus*, the affirmation of apophaticism is repeated in a magnificent comparison between the three Persons of the Trinity and three human beings. Here the Pneumatological tension emerges again because in God, unlike in creation, "the number serves only to indicate their mutual relations, not what they are in themselves" (*Hoc solo numerum insinuant quod ad invicem sunt, non quod ad se sunt*).[87] The relational dimension is expressed here not with the term *relativum* but with *ad aliquid*, as opposed to *ad se*. The central point is that the correlativity of the divine Persons is not extended by Augustine also from the Spirit to the first two Persons, unlike what we see in Gregory of Nyssa and the answers to the Pneumatomachians. In fact, the Bishop of Hippo writes that "Considered the Father in Himself, He is God; in relation to the Son He is Father. The Son in Himself is God, in

---

85. Chungman Lee has highlighted the role of the *scientia-sapientia* pair in Augustine: the former is related to the created dimension, while the latter characterizes the contemplation of the uncreated. The human being is called to move from *scientia* to *sapientia*: see Lee, *Gregory of Nyssa*, 179–81. The distinction is relevant for the role of apophaticism and its relationship with illumination theory.

86. See Augustine, *De Trinitate*, 6.11.12 (CCSL 50:243).

87. Augustine, *In Iohannis Evangelium tractatus*, 39.4 (CCSL 36:347).

relation to the Father He is Son" (*Id enim quod Pater ad se est, Deus est; quod ad Filium est, Pater est: quod Filius ad seipsum est, Deus est; quod ad Patrem est, Filius est*)[88] and "Well then, God the Father is Father in relation to another, to the Son; and God the Son is Son in relation to another, that is to the Father; these however are not two gods, as those are two men" (*At vero Pater Deus ad aliquid est Pater, id est ad Filium; et Filius Deus ad aliquid est Filius, id est ad Patrem: sed non quomodo illi duo homines sunt, sic isti duo dii*).[89] The relationship between the Father and the Son thus seems to be closed in on itself, in such a way that the Spirit is distinct insofar as He is relative to the first two persons, while the latter are not relative to Him:

> Since, however, the Father is not Father in Himself but in relation to the Son; and the Son is not Son in Himself but in relation to the Father; and the Spirit is not Spirit in Himself but insofar as He is the Spirit of the Father and the Son, it cannot be said that they are three, but only that the Father and the Son and the Holy Spirit are one God, one almighty.[90]

It is sufficient to compare the quoted text with the full correlativity in Epiphanius, *Panarion*, 74 in chapter 3.[91] This is confirmed in the later books of *De Trinitate*. The Bishop of Hippo actually discusses the Person in God in the seventh book and raises the issue already seen in Gregory of Nyssa: the issue of why we should not talk about three gods while using the expression three men, in this case Abraham, Isaac and Jacob. But the structure of the seventh book of *De Trinitate* and the role that relation plays in it is highlighted by the summary that introduces book eight. The center of the previous book would be precisely the distinction of what is predicated in the Trinity about the Persons, that is, the names that imply the mutual relationship (*relative dicuntur ad invicem*) and what is said about the Persons considered each in oneself (*ad se*), for which only the singular is always used. That is why we do not speak of three gods, but of one God for the Father, the Son, and the Holy Spirit.[92] So there are not three Goods or three Almighties, but one Good and one Almighty.

---

88. Augustine, *In Iohannis Evangelium tractatus*, 39.3 (CCSL 36:346).

89. Augustine, *In Iohannis Evangelium tractatus*, 39.4 (CCSL 36:346).

90. "Quia vero non ad se est Pater, sed ad Filium; nec Filius ad se est, sed ad Patrem; nec Spiritus ad se, in eo quod dicitur Spiritus Patris et Filii; non est quid dicam tres, nisi Patrem et Filium et Spiritum sanctum unum Deum, unum omnipotentem" (Augustine, *In Iohannis Evangelium tractatus*, 39.4 [CCSL 36:347]).

91. See p. 81.

92. On the connection of this topic with Porphyry in Augustine's approach, see R. Cross,

Therefore, the Father is not greater than the Son, nor are the Father and the Son together greater than the Holy Spirit, nor is a single divine Person lesser than the Trinity.[93] In this regard, Augustine, in a significant way, reproposes a clear affirmation of apophaticism, saying that in this area what is true is more true than what one can say and more true than what one can think (*verius enim cogitatur Deus quam dicitur, et verius est quam cogitatur*).[94]

Thus, the Bishop of Hippo wonders about the sense of the word *not* when used for Abraham, Isaac, and Jacob to say that one is *not* the other. In recognizing that there are three persons, we use the indication in the plural, saying that they are three *men* with a specific name in the plural, or three *animals* with a generic name, but always in the plural. When you then ask what a horse, an ox, and a dog are, you do not say that they are three horses, three oxen, or three dogs, but three animals, using a generic term because they are not of the same species. And so more generally you could say three substances, three creatures, or three natures. In this way switching to the generic dimension allows one to include in the plural denomination what cannot be indicated with a specific term because it belongs to different species. This generic term indicates something that the three subjects have in common, such as being animals in the case mentioned, or being men in the case of Abraham, Isaac, and Jacob. Returning to the Trinity, Augustine writes:

> So, since the Father, the Son, and the Spirit are three, we wonder what three they are and what they have in common. In fact, it is not common to them what the Father is in such a way as to be fathers to each other, like friends, being called in a relative way to each other (*relative ad alterutrum*), three friends can be called friends, because they are friends to each other. But this does not apply here, because only the Father is a father and not even a father of two, but only of the only Son. And there are not three children, for the Father is not the Son and neither is the Holy Spirit. Neither are there three holy spirits, for neither the Father nor the Son is the Holy Spirit according to the proper sense by which He is indicated as the "Gift of God" (Acts 8:20; John 4:10). So what are the three? In fact, if they are three Persons (*tres Personae*), it is common to them what the person is. So they have a specific name and a generic name, if we accept the custom of language. But where

---

"Quid Tres? On What Precisely Augustine Professes Not to Understand in *De Trinitate* V and VII," *Harvard Theological Review* 100 (2007): 215–32.

93. See Augustine, *In Iohannis Evangelium tractatus*, 8.1.1 (CCSL 50:268).

94. Augustine, *In Iohannis Evangelium tractatus*, 7.4.7 (CCSL 50:255).

no diversity of nature is given, some realities can be enunciated in a generic as well as a specific sense. In fact, the difference in nature means that the laurel, myrtle, and olive tree or horse, ox, and dog are not indicated by a species name, i.e., three laurels for the first or three oxen for the second, but by a generic name, i.e., three trees or three animals. But indeed, where there is no difference in essence, it is necessary that the three also have a name of species, which however is not found. In fact, person is a generic name, since the human being can also be defined as such despite the great distance between man and God.[95]

The text shows the strength with which Augustine raises the question of the relationship between God and man and this profound linguistic inquiry. The Father, the Son, and the Spirit have in common being Person, a name which in common language can be both general and specific. But the distinction at the creatural level is possible because of the difference in nature, which forces us to move from the specific name to the generic one. In the absence of such a difference it should be possible to find both a generic and a specific name, but in the case of the Trinity the latter is not found, so much so that man is also called a person.[96] The statement is apophatic and discusses the difference *in divinis* at the level of names and language. Note that the Bishop of Hippo does not exploit the relational difference, because for him the relationship is not included in the substance.

---

95. "Pater ergo et Filius et Spiritus Sanctus quoniam tres sunt, quid tres sint quaeramus, quid commune habeant. Non enim commune illis est id quod Pater est ut invicem sibi sint patres; sicut amici, cum relative ad alterutrum dicantur, possunt dici tres amici quod invicem sibi sunt; non autem hoc ibi quia tantum Pater ibi pater, nec duorum pater sed unici Filii. Nec tres filii cum Pater ibi non sit Filius, nec Spiritus Sanctus. Nec tres spiritus sancti, quia et Spiritus Sanctus propria significato qua etiam donum Dei dicitur, nec Pater nec Filius. Quid igitur tres? Si enim tres Personae, commune est eis id quod persona est. Ergo special hoc aut general nomen est eis, si consuetudinem loquendi respicimus. Sed ubi est naturae nulla diversitas, ita generaliter enuntiantur aliqua plura, ut etiam specialiter enuntiari possint. Naturae enim differentia facit ut laurus et myrtus et olea, aut equus et bos et canis non dicantur speciali nomine, istae, tres lauri, aut illi, tres boves, sed generali, et istae, tres arbores; et illa, tria animalia. Hic vero ubi nulla est essentiae diversitas, oportet et speciale nomen habeant haec tria, quod tamen non invenitur. Nam persona generale nomen est, in tantum ut etiam homo possit hoc dici, cum tantum intersit inter hominem et Deum" (Augustine, *In Iohannis Evangelium tractatus*, 7.4.7 [CCSL 50:256–57]).

96. On the relationship between divine and human person in Augustine, see A. Turchi, "Persona divina—persona umana: Nota di cristologia e di filosofia; Commento di un testo del *De Trinitate*, V,5," *Angelicum* 76 (1999): 341–65.

The importance of the conceptual passage seems to be marked by the fact that Augustine reiterates the affirmation of the excess of the Trinitarian mystery over the capacity of human thought, which in its indigence (*humana inopia*) must resort to terms suitable for human understanding. So, discussing the formula "one essence and three substances or persons" (*una essentia, tres substantiae vel personae*), where substance is etymologically traced back to subsistence and therefore equated with the person, Augustine writes:

> Since if for God it is the same being and existence, then we must not speak of three substances, just as we do not speak of three essences, in the same way, because for God it is the same being and knowledge, just as we do not speak of three essences we do not speak of three wisdoms. In fact, just as for God it is the same being and being what He is, it is not permitted to speak of three essences and three gods. But if it is different for God to be and to subsist, as it is different for God to be, to be Father, and to be Lord, because what He is is said in an absolute way (*ad se*), while Father is said in relation to the Son (*ad Filium*) and Lord in relation to the creature who is subject (*ad servientem creaturam*), then God subsists in a relative way (*relative*), as in a relative way generates and in a relative way is Lord. Thus, however, the substance will no longer be substance, because it will be a relative reality (*relativum*). In fact, just as the term essence derives from the fact of being (*esse*), so from the fact of subsistence we speak of substance. But it is absurd that the substance is said in a relative sense (*ut substantia relative dicatur*). For every entity subsists in itself (*ad se*); and how much more must this apply to God?[97]

God is therefore an essence and *tria quaedam* "three something," which one cannot name and which are indicated by the term "person" because one has nothing better at one's disposal.[98] But the path that Augustine fol-

97. "Nam si hoc est Deo esse quod subsistere, ita non erant dicendae tres substantiae, ut non dicuntur tres essentiae, quemadmodum quia hoc est Deo esse quod sapere, sicut non tres essentias, ita nec tres sapientias dicimus. Sic enim quia hoc illi est Deum esse quod est esse, tam tres essentias quam tres deos dici fas non est. Si autem aliud est Deo esse, aliud subsistere, sicut aliud Deo esse, aliud Patrem esse vel Dominum esse; quod enim est ad se dicitur, Pater autem ad Filium, et Dominus ad servientem creaturam dicitur; relative ergo subsistit, sicut relative gignit et relative dominatur; ita iam substantia non erit substantia quia relativum erit. Sicut enim ab eo quod est esse appellatur essentia, ita ab eo quod est subsistere substantiam dicimus. Absurdum est autem ut substantia relative dicatur; omnis enim res ad se ipsam subsistit. How much *magis deus*?" (Augustine, *De Trinitate*, 7.4.9 [CCSL 50:259–60]).

98. See Augustine, *De Trinitate*, 5.9.10 (CCSL 50:217).

lows to show the expressive insufficiency of the proposed terms is extremely significant, especially if contemplated over the background of Gregory of Nyssa's theology.

The first step leads to the affirmation of the identity of essence and subsistence, from which derives the impossibility of speaking of three substances because the essence, precisely, is unique, being one God. But in this way one would no longer know how to formulate personal plurality, because if one were to distinguish being and subsisting in God, according to the difference between being in the absolute sense, the being of the immanent relationship, and that of the relationship with creation, then one would come to a stalemate. The substance would, in fact, cease to be such by identifying itself with a relationship. This would be absurd because it would deny the proper and defining characteristic of the substance, which is to be in itself.[99] It is clear that the introduction of the relation in the divine substance is not envisaged here, as a substance relative in itself—rather than *ad se*—is not admissible from this metaphysical perspective.

In the interpretative hypothesis proposed here, in the text of Augustine there is a philosophical conception similar to that of Martianus Capella, who excluded that both a first and a second substance could belong to the relative realities. Piero Coda, for this reason, concludes that Augustine probably considered the *relativum* to be a *tertium quid* between substance and accident.[100]

But this favors the possibility of also finding this relational dimension in human immanence. In fact, after dealing with the relationship between human and divine persons, showing the ontological difference between the two levels, Augustine takes the way of interiority and traces the magnificent path of psychological analogy, whose prodromes, as seen in the previous chapter, are already present in Cappadocian thought of both Gregory of Nyssa and Gregory of Nazianzus. As in their case, for Augustine it is precisely the role of the Trinitarian relation that makes it possible to read the metaphysical structure of the rational being in the light of that "relationship" between humanity and God that is the creation in image and likeness (cf. Gen 1:27).[101]

99. Clearly, Augustine affirms the *subsistentia personarum* founded on the identification in God of being and having, where the personal distinction is traced back only to relational opposition because God "quod habet hoc est, excepto quod relative quaeque persona ad alteram dicitur" (Augustine, *De civitate Dei*, 11.10.1 [CCSL 48:330]).

100. P. Coda, *Sul luogo della Trinità: rileggendo il "De Trinitate" di Agostino* (Rome: Città Nuova, 2008), 60.

101. See H. U. von Balthasar, *The Glory of the Lord: A Theological Aesthetics. II: Studies in Theological Style: Clerical Styles*, trans. A. Louth et al. (San Francisco: Ignatius, 1984), 114.

This last aspect grounds the psychological analogy, which the Bishop of Hippo recognizes at three different ontological levels:[102]

1. A more phenomenological sensitive level consisting of the triad *memoria - intelligentia - voluntas*.
2. The triad *mens - notitia - amor* that characterizes the properly spiritual level.
3. The highest analogy constituted by the very relationship with God articulated in *memoria Dei - intelligentia Dei - amor in Deum* that properly concerns the sphere of contemplation and the relationship with the divine source, of whose immanence the human spirit is image.[103]

In the first triad, Augustine fixes his attention directly on humanity's psychic faculties, showing their mutual coexistence. To speak of the Trinity and Unity in God without introducing any separation of the divine Persons, he refers to the psychology of the human being as it is known in natural science. The fundamental concept with which the Bishop of Hippo works is Life, which is God but is given analogically in the creature and is especially perfect in the rational creature through creation in image and likeness. Conscious life is thus directly connected to the Trinity:

> So these three realities—memory, intelligence, and will—given that they are not three lives, but one life, and that they are not even three spirits (*mentes*), but one spirit (*mens*), therefore, they are certainly not even three substances, but one substance. Memory, of course, as it is called life, spirit, and substance, is predicated in an absolute sense (*ad se*), but as memory it is predicated in the relative sense of something else (*ad aliquid relative*). And I could also say this about intelligence and will, because both intelligence and will are predicated with respect to something else (*ad aliquid*). But each in itself (*ad se*) is life, spirit, and essence. And "these three things are one" (1 John 5:7–8), for the same reason that they are one life, one spirit, one essence.[104]

102. See J. Brachtendorf, "Der menschliche Geist als Bild des trinitarischen Gottes-Ähnlichkeiten und Unähnlichkeiten," in *Gott und sein Bild: Augustins De Trinitate im Spiegel gegenwärtiger Forschung*, ed. J. Brachtendorf (Paderborn: Schöningh, 2000), 155–70.

103. In a valuable monograph on *De Trinitate*, Lewis Ayres recently de-emphasized, or better, contextualized, the role of psychological analogy in Augustine's theology; see Ayres, *Augustine and the Trinity*, 325.

104. "Haec igitur tria, memoria, intellegentia, voluntas, quoniam non sunt tres vitae, sed una vita; nec tres mentes, sed una mens, consequenter utique nec tres substantiae sunt,

It is clearly a summit of the theological thought, which does not claim to create a univocal correspondence between divine and human immanence, but simply reads the latter in the light of the former. There is no projection of an anthropology in the Trinity itself from the bottom up. But the resemantization of the relation makes it possible to recognize the greatness of the intimate structure of the human person in an absolutely original way compared to the philosophical anthropologies of the time.[105]

It should be noted that, in the Augustinian reading of humanity's psychological faculties, what allows them to be used as images of God's immanence is precisely their relational dimension. And it is, in fact, because of relations that these faculties, belonging to the sensitive sphere, can be recognized as expressions of a deeper level, which is the spiritual one consisting of *mens*, *notitia*, and *amor*:

> The spirit (*mens*) cannot love itself if it does not know itself; how can it love that which it does not know? (. . .) How does a spirit know another spirit if it does not know itself? (. . .) But just as the spirit and its love are two things when the spirit loves itself, so are the spirit and its knowledge (*notitia*) when it knows itself. So the spirit, its love, and its knowledge are three things, and these three things make but one, and when they are perfect, they are equal. (. . .) But when the spirit is known and loved, in those three realities—spirit, knowledge, love—there is a trinity; and there is neither a mixing nor a confusion, although each one is in itself, and all of them are found interchangeably in all, each in the other two, and the other two in each. Therefore, all in all (1 Cor 15:28).[106]

---

sed una substantia. Memoria quippe, quod vita et mens et substantia dicitur, ad se ipsam dicitur; quod vero memoria dicitur, ad aliquid relative dicitur. Hoc de intellegentia quoque et de voluntate dixerim; et intellegentia quippe et voluntas ad aliquid dicitur. Vita est autem unaquaeque ad se ipsam, et mens, et essentia. Quocirca tria haec eo sunt unum, quo una vita, una mens, una essentia" (Augustine, *De Trinitate*, 10.11.18 [CCSL 50:330–31]).

105. In this sense, the present analysis differs from that in the following: A. Fokin, "St. Augustine's Doctrine of the Trinity in the Light of Orthodox Triadology of the Fourth Century," in *The Trinity: East/West Dialogue*, ed. Melville Y. Stewart (Dordrecht: Kluwer Academic, 2003), 131–52.

106. "Mens enim amare se ipsam non potest, nisi etiam noverit se. Nam quomodo amat quod nescit? [. . .] Unde enim mens aliquam mentem novit, si se non novit? [. . .] Sicut autem duo quaedam sunt, mens et amor eius, cum se amat; ita quaedam duo sunt, mens et notitia eius, cum se novit. [. . .] Ipsa igitur mens et amor et notitia eius tria quaedam sunt, et haec tria unum sunt, et cum perfecta sunt, aequalia sunt. At in illis tribus, cum se novit mens et amat se, manet trinitas: mens, amor, notitia; et nulla commixtione confunditur,

Our thought or spirit loves itself, and this love is nothing more than the natural affirmation of its existence. Thus, we have two distinct but inseparably united realities: thought and love. And such love would be impossible if thought had no self-awareness, that is, if it had no *notitia* of its own existence. And thought, which by its nature is knowledge, cannot but be knowable to itself. Thus, in the inner life of the human being, immanent operations provide an image of the inner unity and distinction of the divine Persons and of their mutual being in one another. From the sensitive level we have passed to the properly spiritual one, which escapes the analysis of the empirical sciences but is the source and prototype of what they can analyze, that is, the faculties seen in the first triad.

And this second triad situated on a spiritual level in the human being is such because it is the image of a superior triad, which consists of the very relations with the one and triune God, who created humanity, in body and spirit, in His own image and likeness. Thus, above these analogies there is that of the *memoria Dei, intelligentia Dei*, and *amor Dei*, which is the most important triad of all, because it studies the soul not in relation to itself but in its vital relationship with God, of Whom it is image. Memory is understood here as memory of God, knowledge as knowledge of God, and love as love for God. These are acts performed by the soul by grace and not simply by natural forces. In fact, the image of God in the soul acquires its authentic perfection precisely because of the elevation of grace:

> Therefore, this trinity of the spirit is not an image of God, because the spirit merely remembers itself, understands itself, and loves itself, but because it can also remember, understand, and love Him by whom it was created. When the spirit does this, it becomes wise. If it does not so, even when it remembers itself, understands and loves itself, it is foolish. Therefore, remember your God, in whose image you were created, understand Him, and love Him.[107]

---

quamvis et singula sint in se ipsis, et invicem tota in totis, sive singula in binis, sive bina in singulis. Itaque omnia in omnibus" (Augustine, *De Trinitate*, 9.3.3; 4.4; and 5.8 [CCSL 50:295–97, 300]).

107. "Haec igitur trinitas mentis non propterea Dei est imago, quia sui meminit mens, et intelligit ac diligit se: sed quia potest etiam meminisse, et intelligere, et amare a quo facta est. Quod cum facit, sapiens ipsa fit. Si autem non facit, etiam cum sui meminit, seque intelligit ac diligit, stulta est. Meminerit itaque Dei sui, ad cuius imaginem facta est, eumque intellegat atque diligat" (Augustine, *De Trinitate*, 14.12.15 [CCSL 50:442–43]).

Even though God is always in the human being, the human being is not always in God; in fact, to be in God means to remember Him, to know Him, and to love Him. And this is tantamount to renewing the divine image in us, because with this memory, this intelligence, and this will we participate in that life in which God knows and loves us.[108] Thus the human is only truly fulfilled as a saint, that is, by participating fully in the intimate life of God in knowledge and love.

In introducing these analogies, Augustine knows very well that they are only images since the reality of the Trinity always remains beyond description. He simply seeks to represent Life with life, the True Life of the triune God with that participation in that which God has granted to humanity by creating and elevating them. Therefore, in the last book of *De Trinitate* the Bishop of Hippo strongly emphasizes the differences between God and the image. At the same time, the affirmation of the possibility of distinguishing the three levels of (1) the phenomenological dimension (i.e., the psychic faculties); (2) the properly spiritual dimension of the faculties in the soul; and (3) the contemplative dimension founded in humanity's relationship with God, is a precious inheritance.

This Augustinian process highlights how the analogical structure is made possible by a relational understanding of human faculties and spirit, which are such precisely because they are the image of God who is three eternal relations and who therefore creates relations and enters into relationship.

VII. Conclusion: The Metaphysical Deficit

In conclusion, it can be said that the main difference between the resemantization of the relation done by Gregory of Nyssa and that introduced by Augustine is as follows:

1. Gregory changes the ontological statute of relation and includes it in the divine substance. Its resemantization therefore concerns both relation and substance, since this "opens up" the relationship to its immanence.

2. The Bishop of Hippo recognizes a new ontological dimension to relation, but does not include it in the substance, limiting himself to approaching it as a new reality. Thus he formally changes the conception of relation while that of substance remains unchanged.

---

108. See G. Bardy, "Trinité," in *Dictionnaire de théologie catholique* (Paris: Letouzey et Ané, 1950), 1690–91.

Augustine does not stop at the linguistic level, but rethinks being starting from love. On the contrary, his whole theology is moving toward a rereading of the universe in the light of Trinitarian revelation. The metaphysical tools at his disposal are, however, inferior to what happens in the East. That is why the ontological language does not allow him to reach a total interpenetration between substance and relation, shifting the balance of his wonderful mystical-theological construction toward a metaphysical understanding of anthropology.[109]

This could help explain the Eastern suspicions against the Bishop of Hippo, who was accused of violating the apophatic veil by anthropologising the Trinity. Even a simple glance at the content of *De Trinitate* would be enough to disprove such an interpretation. Yet it is understandable how from the Greek perspective the recourse to the anthropological dimension in the absence of a resemantization of all ontological categories could be misunderstood. The point is clearly the initial imbalance between the Eastern metaphysical heritage, with the powerful work done within the Platonic-Aristotelian tradition by the Middle and Neoplatonic commentators of Aristotle's *Categories*, and the Western one, which is poorer and circumscribed within the *De dialectica*.[110]

Augustine's genius overcomes these limitations with the power of his mystical gaze, achieving a more anthropological result, in which, however, the ontological language is less integrated. This highlights how fundamental the study of the history of ontology is for *Dogmengeschichte* and suggests as a possible path of fruitful development a greater integration of theological and philosophical research.

From a Latin perspective, however, the question about the origin of Thomas Aquinas's *relatio subsistens* arises: Was it an original elaboration on the Augustinian legacy that led the *Doctor Angelicus* to overcome its limitations, or did other sources (especially new patristic translations available in medieval times) intervene? The answer is beyond the scope of this work. We can say for certain here that with different tools and choices about perspective (even if they are in part complementary), Gregory of Nyssa and Augustine of Hippo share a common theological grammar that tries to understand the creature

---

109. For an interpretation of the enlightenment in relational terms, see A. Pârvan, "La relation en tant qu'élément clé de l'illumination augustinienne," *CHORA. Revue d'études anciennes et médiévales* 7–8 (2010): 87–103.

110. On the Augustinian reading of the *Categories*, see P. Thom, *The Logic of the Trinity: Augustine to Ockham* (New York: Fordham University Press, 2012), 22–24; and on its relationship with the liberal arts, see C. G. Vaught, *The Journey toward God in Augustine's Confessions: Books I–VI* (Albany: SUNY Press, 2012), 111–14.

in a relational way, in the light of the Trinitarian dimension of the Creator, in order to contemplate the world in the light of the Trinity and to show the true nature of the theological act in the latreutic dimension.

At the same time, however, the daring comparison in this chapter comes to the surprising conclusion that the proposed reading of the Son's role in the procession of the Spirit in Greek patristics, as well as the psychological analogies found there, are not Latinizing projections, because Augustine's work itself seems less radical than the theological solutions seen in the Greek world. Aquinas is certainly responsible for the great development, particularly in the Middle Ages, of both the *Filioque* and the psychological analogy in Latin theology, which he articulates with great precision at the different levels of being.[111] The misunderstandings on the side of Orthodox tradition can instead be traced to the metaphysical *deficit* of the theological tools developed by Augustine, which do not reach the perfection of those found in Greek Trinitarian theology. In fact, this offers an ontologically and theologically more elaborate thought that is capable of recognizing the relation in the very immanence of the one and triune God, thus rereading the whole world and the human being in the light of this category, now recognized as another principle of being together with substance.

From this perspective, the role of the Son in the procession of the Spirit does not depend on psychological analogy, as some simplifications have suggested about Augustine. On the other hand, what the two theological elements in the Cappadocians and the Bishop of Hippo have in common is the Trinitarian ontology that rereads creation from the perspective of Trinitarian revelation, that is, from top to bottom without any undue projection in the opposite direction. Thus it could be said that the opposite of what is generally said is true: it is the psychological analogy that depends on the recognition of the role of the Second Person in the procession of the Third, since the new relational understanding of divine immanence has allowed the two processions to pass to a true correlativity, and therefore the Father, the Son, and the Spirit.

---

111. On the development of the psychological analogy in medieval Trinitarian doctrine with the loss of the moderation preserved in patristic times by apophaticism, see R. L. Friedman, *Medieval Trinitarian Thought from Aquinas to Ockham* (Cambridge: Cambridge University Press, 2010).

An Ecumenical Proposal

At the end of this long journey, the narrative presented in this book can be conceived as an ellipse centered on two focus points, which, as such, are the cornerstones of the narrative itself: (1) the responses of the Greek fathers of the Church to Pneumatomachian criticism; and (2) apophaticism as the fundamental methodological touchstone of theological epistemology. Both of these elements have been overshadowed in previous literature. Having paid close attention to these elements here, what is the picture that now emerges?

At the beginning of this book we encountered Origen, who sharply distinguished the three Persons of the Trinity from the created world, making recourse to pure spirituality. His solution is ingenious but imperfect, as demonstrated by the subsequent Arian misunderstandings of his work, which were due to the participative language used by Origen to formulate the intra-Trinitarian distinction. The differentiation of the sphere of action of the divine Persons also depends on this way of expressing the hypostatic distinction. Such a path is linked to the two main schemes introduced by Origen to illustrate the relations between the Father, the Son, and the Holy Spirit. A linear conception is combined with a more ancient and Semitic triangular one, in which the Second and Third Persons form each of the two bottom corners. In light of the outlined narrative one can recognize how, from its beginning, all of the dogmatic discussion on the subject was already focused on the relational dimension, even if unconsciously.

From the standpoint of the premises of the *Filioque* and the patristic affirmation of an active, but not causal, role of the Son in the procession of the Spirit, the two schemes with their interaction and tension, as highlighted by the Pneumatomachians, are obviously very interesting because the linear form presents precisely the mediation of the Second Person in the relationship of the Third Person with the first, while the triangular form leads the Spirit directly back to the Father.

At the beginning of the fourth century these tensions were highlighted in the pneumatological discussion between Marcellus and Eusebius, which showed the imperfect success of the linear model. The former criticized the latter's Trinitarian theology by contrasting John 15:26 with John 16:14. For if the Spirit proceeded directly from the Father, as according to the first verse, it should be perfect and there would be no need for the Son. But if the Third Person depended on the Son, as John says in the second verse, then the Spirit would no longer proceed from the First Person. In his reply, Eusebius tried to reconcile the two verses of John, overcoming the dialectic of his opponent. At the same time, he was unable to completely free the linear scheme from the participatory structure because he did not yet have the instrument of relation (*schesis*). He actually denies that the *Logos* belongs to the relative realities, as Arius also does, blocking *a priori* the way to any approach in the line of psychological analogy.

In response to this problem, Athanasius introduced a fundamental solution in conformity with the linear scheme through a reconfiguration of ontological architecture. In fact, he recognizes how Arian criticism demands that the *Logos*-theology of apologist inspiration be overcome; despite having been corrected by Origen's theology, it had left its traces in the participatory conception of divine immanence. This hampered the formulation of the relationship between God and the world in terms of absolute freedom. Therefore, the formulation of the radical distinction between the triune Creator and the created world in terms of *Physis*-theology allowed the Bishop of Alexandria to purify Origen's heritage from those elements that were invoked by the Arians. This process saw the success of the linear model, which, however, lent itself to Pneumatomachian criticism because, in Athanasius's formulation, it distinguished the two processions only in numerical terms without clarifying the differences between the procession of the Spirit and generation. Hence the accusation that the Father was the grandfather of the Third Person or that the Son was His brother, which would go against the name "Only Begotten."

Basil synthesizes what he inherited from Athanasius, that is, the linear scheme, and what he receives from Origen, that is, the difference between the divine Persons regarding the sphere of action. But this synthesis led the Bishop of Caesarea to introduce the unity of action, affirming that the Spirit is creator, and to recognize the link between economy and immanence, through the analysis of the prepositions in his *De Spiritu Sancto*. Here too the relational dimension is already present, as well as the intuition of bringing the distinctive characteristic of the Third Person back to the communion of the first two. This choice was logical from the perspective of the dogmatic development, as the Pneumatomachians denied the authentically creative role of the Spirit, bringing the issue to the forefront in the debate. This is why the Cappadocians' affirmation of unity of action proved fundamental. In order to arrive at this solution, it was necessary to go through the affirmation of the distinction without separation of economy and immanence, where the element of correspondence between the two spheres was identified precisely in the relational dimension that distinguishes and unites the divine Persons.

Through this process, it was Gregory of Nyssa who, together with Gregory of Nazianzus in the context of the First Council of Constantinople, managed to fully formulate the difference between the two processions through the definition of the personal *proprium* of the Third Person. This has the Father as His only cause, according to the positive principle highlighted by the triangular scheme, but He is "manifested" by the Son in accordance with the dynamics indicated by the linear scheme. The Spirit, who (like the other two Persons) is uncreated and is in a full and absolute way, because He is identified with the only divine substance, is not singled out by the quality of being generated nor by that of being unbegotten. Instead, it is precisely His double reference to both of the first two Persons that constitutes His personal characteristic. In fact, His only cause is the Father, His principle, but He is also relationally "manifested" by the Son in the Trinitarian immanence, through whom He proceeds because He is the royal Power and the Glory that the Father, the origin of all things, gives to the Son in generating Him and that the Son, the Image of the Father, gives back to the latter. Thus, the Spirit is the *bond* of the Father and the Son, their communion (i.e., their hypostatized relationship), as the term *syndetikon* reveals.

And this solution is not a *unicum*, but is part of the pattern of responses to the Pneumatomachians: it protects the divinity of the Third Person by placing Him relationally between the first two, or by bringing His origin back to both of them without violating the monarchy. The pneumatology of Gregory of Nazianzus followed this strategy, recognizing that the Spirit is the immanent *meson* of the Father and the Son. In this way, the divinity of the Third Person was affirmed and "protected" through His insertion between the first two Persons. The intra-Trinitarian order, with the monarchy of the Father, was not violated by this choice, because the personal distinctions were expressed in relational terms.

The resemantization of the relation-*schesis* thus proved to be the fundamental element that allowed the Trinitarian doctrine to proceed from the Nicene *homoousios* to the Constantinopolitan one. As John Zizioulas rightly observed, in the Symbol of 381 the expression *ek tēs ousias tou Patros*, which was present in 325, disappears.[1] In fact, the conflicts following the first Council

---

1. J. Zizioulas, *Communion and Otherness: Further Studies in Personhood and the Church* (London: T&T Clark, 2009), 120.

had shown the insufficiency of an approach centered only on substance. The generation, and in parallel the *ekporeusis*, could not be interpreted only as the communication of the substance of the Father to the Son, and then from the Son to the Spirit, according to the linear scheme. It was necessary, instead, to make explicit that *homoousios* implies the numerical identity of the one substance of the three divine Persons, whose distinction is given in immanence only by the difference of origin, expressed by the *schesis*, without any element of ontological participation.

But this step required a new ontology. In fact, the apologists' *Logos*-theology had been reshaped as *Physis*-theology by Athanasius, which would later be transformed into the *Schesis*-theology of the Cappadocians. It is important to remember that all these steps are moments upon a single path, not disjointed moments that can be overcome and forgotten since each of them is based in the previous one. The *Physis*-theology would not be possible without the *Logos*-theology and the *Physis*-theology itself is the basis of the *Schesis*-theology. This is the framework that demonstrates the necessity of reading the language of manifestation applied to the relationship of the Spirit to the Son in the second procession, in the immanent sense, as reference to the relational dimension.

In fact, to respond to the Pneumatomachians it was necessary to bring the economic relationship between the Spirit and the Son into immanence, as was done in the response to the Arians, thereby bringing the relationship of the Son and the Father into immanence itself. But this relational interpretation presents the Spirit as the bond between the Father and the Son, the hypostasis of their very personal communion. In this sense the Third Person is from the First and the Second, without diminishing the monarchy in the slightest. The *Filioque* therefore appears theologically, and even literally, in Greek patristics too, but this cannot be read in the sense that the Second Person is the cause of the Third.[2]

The surprising conclusions of this journey required us to conduct a triple check at the theological level, first to make sure that it was not just a Latinized reading, for the Western understanding of the relationship between the two divine processions, or as a consequence of Augustine's psychological analogy and a projection of his categories of thought on the Greek fathers, and then to try to explain the conflict that has plagued relations between East and West on this very point.

---

2. It is interesting that these theological elements are not present in Photius's arguments. See V. Polidori, "L'attualità della Mistagogia di Fozio alla luce della recente edizione critica," *Studi sull'Oriente Cristiano* 24 (2020): 59–73.

Thus, the study of Syriac pneumatology and the translations of the Greek fathers in this area served as a litmus test for the results this research suggests. The language that characterizes this tradition has in common with Latin the absence of a specific verb to indicate the origin of the Spirit from the Father as His principle. Consubstantiality is indicated by the use of the Syriac expression "being the son of" substance or nature, making it difficult to formulate the procession of the Third Person in His difference with respect to the generation of the Son. The presence of Syriac texts that indicate a role of the Second Person in the procession of the Spirit, even at the level of the translation of the Nicene Creed, suggests that the Latin *Filioque*, according to the definition proposed here, is not the result of an undue rationalization on the Latin side, but can be a real necessity when Trinitarian doctrine is translated into a language other than Greek and transposed into a different geographical area.

The second verification concerns the alleged connection of the *Filioque* with the psychological analogy typical of Augustine's Trinitarian doctrine. The usual scheme that identifies the reinterpretation of the tripartition of human interiority in the light of the relationships of the three Persons in the divine immanence as hallmark of the Latin tradition is challenged. In fact, a similar trend can be found in the Greek fathers based precisely on the new relational ontology introduced by the Cappadocians in view of the Council of Constantinople. This suggests the need to radically rethink the relationship between the *Filioque* and the psychological analogy, excluding the route that the former be caused by the latter. On the contrary, this happened the other way around, as the theology which led to the distinction between the two immanent processions had as a natural consequence the rereading of the human being's internal faculties without any undue projection from the bottom up.

The last test of this book therefore tried to explain the misunderstanding about Augustine through a daring comparison of the rereading of the ontology of relation in his thought and in that of Gregory of Nyssa. Here a clear difference emerges, as the latter reshaped both the metaphysical understanding of substance and relation, while the Bishop of Hippo simply juxtaposed the two, resemantizing relation (which could no longer be considered an accident) without radically changing the conception of substance. The cause of this is to be found in the poverty of the metaphysical tools with which the Bishop of Hippo worked, since the tradition of commentary on Aristotle's *Categories* in Western Neoplatonism was situated within the dialectic, therefore more focused on the linguistic level and less powerful on the ontological level.

But how does this reconstruction tie in with the previous data? If we compare it with the testimony of Maximus the Confessor it seems that the possibility that the Son had an active but not causal role in the procession of the Spirit was contemplated not only in the Latin tradition but also in the Greek tradition with Cyril of Alexandria:[3]

> On the first question, they have cited the unanimous testimonies of the Roman fathers and, with greater certainty, those of Cyril of Alexandria in his sacred study on the Gospel of St. John. Starting from these, they showed that they do not make the Son the cause of the Holy Ghost; they know, in fact, that the Father is the unique cause of the Son and of the Holy Spirit, of the former by generation and of the latter by procession, but they stated that the Spirit comes through the Son (δι' αὐτοῦ), thus showing the unity and immutability of the substance.[4]

In fact, in Cyril's commentary on the Fourth Gospel, there are several passages with references to the procession of the Spirit from or through the Son. Two examples immediately offer the perspective of Cyrillian pneumatology,[5] the first which comments on John 15:26: "For just as the Spirit is by nature (φυσικῶς) proper to the Son, subsisting in Him and proceeding through Him (δι' αὐτοῦ προϊόν), so is He also proper to the Father."[6] The presence of the adverb *physikōs* clearly indicates that Cyril's concern is focused on affirming the identity of nature, rather than on clarifying the difference between the first and second procession. A second example confirms this perspective: "the

---

3. On the letter to Marinus, see A. E. Siecienski, *The Filioque: History of a Doctrinal Controversy* (Oxford: Oxford University Press, 2010), 78–86. For an original reading of the cited letter, see C. dell'Osso, "Il Filioque in Massimo il Confessore," in *Il Filioque: A mille anni dal suo inserimento nel credo a Roma (1014-2014)*, ed. M. Gagliardi (Vatican City: LEV, 2015), 147–64.

4. Καὶ τό μέν πρῶτος, συμφώνους παρήγαγον χρήσεις τῶν Ῥωμαίων Πατέρων· ἔτι γε μὴν καὶ Κυρίλλου Ἀλεξανδρείας, ἐκ τῆς πονηθείσης αὐτῷ εἰς τὸν εὐαγγελιστὴν ἅγιον Ἰωάννην ἱερᾶς πραγματείας· ἐξ ὧν, οὐκ αἰτίαν τὸν Υἱὸν ποιοῦντας τοῦ Πνεύματος, σφᾶς αὐτοὺς ἀπέδειξαν· μίαν γὰρ ἴσασιν Υἱοῦ καὶ Πνεύματος τὸν Πατέρα αἰτίαν· τοῦ μὲν κατὰ τὴν γέννησιν· τοῦ δὲ, κατὰ τὴν ἐκπόρευσιν· ἀλλ' ἵνα τὸ δι' αὐτοῦ προϊέναι δηλώσωσι· καὶ ταύτη τὸ συναφὲς τῆς οὐσίας καὶ ἀπαράλλακτον παραστήσωσι (Maximus the Confessor, *Epistula ad Marinum*, PG 91:136a–b).

5. On Cyril's Trinitarian theology, see the excellent M.-O. Boulnois, *Le Paradoxe Trinitaire chez Cyrille d'Alexandrie: Herméneutique, Analyses Philosophiques et Argumentation Théologique* (Paris: Institut d'études augustiniennes, 1994).

6. ὥσπερ γάρ ἐστιν ἴδιον Πνεῦμα τοῦ Υἱοῦ φυσικῶς, ἐν αὐτῷ τε ὑπάρχον καὶ δι' αὐτοῦ προϊόν, οὕτω καὶ τοῦ Πατρός (Cyril of Alexandria, *In Joannis evangelium*, 15.26.27 [text from P. E. Pusey, ed., *Commentary on John*, 3 vols. (Oxford: Clarendon, 1872), 2:607 lines 19–21]).

Holy Spirit is not alien to the Son but is consubstantial (ὁμοούσιον) to Him and (δι᾽ αὐτοῦ) proceeds (προϊόν) from the Father through Him."[7] Here the adjective *homoousion* shows how the Spirit's being from the Father through the Son is proof of consubstantiality. The doctrine is repeated both in the same commentary on John[8] and in other works by Cyril. In *De adoratione* the expression *di' autou* is presented as equivalent to a literal Greek version of the *Filioque*, since it says of the Third Person "who is the Spirit of God the Father and also of God the Son, from both (ἐξ ἀμφοῖν) as concerns substance, that is, proceeding from the Father through the Son (δι᾽ Υἱοῦ)."[9] Similarly in *Thesaurus de sancta et consubstantiali Trinitate* it is said that the Spirit comes from the Father and the Son.[10] But such expressions must always be read from the standpoint of consubstantiality because being from the Son means proceeding from the substance of the Son, just as the Second Person proceeds from the substance of the Father—an affirmation that can be inferred from other passages of the same work.[11] And this is also present in the commentary on the fourth gospel, where Cyril writes that the Spirit cannot be considered extraneous to the substance of the Son, because He proceeds by nature from this very essence (πρόεισι δὲ φυσικῶς ἐξ αὐτῆς).[12]

This pneumatology is an excellent test for the proposed narrative. In fact, Cyril's authority has always been mentioned in the *Filioque* dispute. But if his texts are examined in the light of the path illustrated here, it becomes clear that his concern is not to distinguish the procession of the Spirit from the generation of the Son.[13] It is a more Nicene than Constantinopolitan pneumatology. And this is not because Cyril's Trinitarian theology is not developed, but because his concern is essentially christological and soteriological.[14] The same role of the ninth of his *anathematismata* in the third letter to Nestorius of September

---

7. οὐκ ἀλλότριον τοῦ Υἱοῦ τὸ Ἅγιον Πνεῦμά ἐστιν, ἀλλ᾽ ὁμοούσιον αὐτῷ, καὶ δι αὐτοῦ προϊὸν τὸ ἐκ τοῦ Πατρός (Cyril of Alexandria, *In Joannis evangelium*, 20.22.23 [Pusey, 3:131 lines 28–29]).

8. Cf. Cyril of Alexandria, *In Joannis evangelium*, 16.12.13 (Pusey, 2:629 lines 15–19).

9. εἴπερ ἐστὶ τοῦ Θεοῦ καὶ Πατρὸς καὶ μὴν καὶ τοῦ Υἱοῦ τὸ οὐσιωδῶς ἐξ ἀμφοῖν, ἤγουν ἐκ Πατρὸς δι᾽ Υἱοῦ προερχόμενον Πνεῦμα (Cyril of Alexandria, *De adoratione*, PG 68:148a).

10. Cyril of Alexandria, *Thesaurus*, 34 (PG 75:585a).

11. Cyril of Alexandria, *Thesaurus*, 33 and 34 (PG 75:573c and 608b).

12. Cyril of Alexandria, *In Joannis evangelium*, 16.12.13 (Pusey, 2:628 lines 14–18). See also 16.16.17 (Pusey, 2:467 lines 6–12).

13. Cf. Boulnois, *Le Paradoxe Trinitaire*, 513–14 and 524.

14. Cf. B. E. Daley, "The Fullness of the Saving God: Cyril of Alexandria on the Holy Spirit," in *The Theology of St. Cyril of Alexandria*, ed. G. Weinandy and Daniel A. Keating (London: T&T Clark, 2003), 145.

430 demonstrates this: Cyril's focus is to avoid that the Holy Spirit could be understood as a power extraneous to Christ, hence the emphasis on the correspondence between economy and immanence.[15] The essential issue is that the substance of the Father passes to the Son and from the Son to the Spirit, so that the Third Person is immanent to the Second and not external to Him.

It is important to note that Cyril is consistent with the Cappadocians' pneumatology. For example, he states that the Spirit brings the Trinity to completion.[16] But this is not expressed in terms of correlativity between the three divine Persons. Therefore, only the Father and the Son belong to the relative realities (*pros ti*), while the Spirit cannot be considered just as a relationship (*schesis*) exterior to Christ. Here the role of *schesis* itself also comes into play in the confrontation with Nestorius, as the basis of a weak union between the two natures. Thus, our analysis confirms the position of Brian Daley, who denies that Cyril's pneumatology can be invoked in favor of the *Filioque*.[17]

The situation of Maximus the Confessor is quite different. As we have already seen, Maximus also supports an immanent *per Filium* and presents a Greek version of the psychological analogy.[18] If we read the following text taken from his commentary on the Lord's Prayer against the backdrop of the narrative proposed here, we can understand how much Maximus owes to Gregory of Nyssa and Gregory of Nazianzus:

> In fact, the words of prayer indicate the Father, the name of the Father, and the kingdom of the Father, to teach us from the very beginning to worship, invoke, and venerate the one Trinity. For the Name of God the Father who essentially subsists is the only Son, and the Kingdom of God the Father who essentially subsists is the Holy Spirit. In fact, here Matthew calls "kingdom" what elsewhere another evangelist has called "Holy Spirit," saying "may your Holy Spirit come and purify us." The Father, in fact, has not acquired the Name, nor should we understand the Kingdom as a dignity that has been conferred upon Him. For He does not begin to be Father or King; but since He is always, He is also always Father and King. Neither has He ever begun to be absolutely, nor has He ever begun to be Father and King. If, therefore, He always is and also always is Father and King, so certainly the Son and the

---

15. Cf. Boulnois, *Le Paradoxe Trinitaire*, 519–21.

16. Cyril of Alexandria, *Thesaurus*, 34 (PG 75:608b).

17. Cf. Daley, "Fullness of the Saving God," 148.

18. See chapter 7. On the *per Filium*, see also Maximus the Confessor, *Quaestiones ad Thalassium*, 63 (CCSG 22:155).

Holy Spirit also coexist essentially with the Father, being from Him and in Him by nature, beyond all cause and reason, but not after Him, as if They had come into existence posteriorly with or through a cause. In fact, relation (σχέσις) possesses the strength to simultaneously indicate the realities of which it is and is called relation, without the elements in relationship (σχέσις) having to be considered one after the other.[19]

The Spirit is here called "Kingdom" again starting from the variant to the Lord's Prayer already seen in chapter 4. But above all, the intra-Trinitarian distinction of the divine Persons is expressed through the *schesis*, including the Spirit in this relational rereading. This makes it possible to interpret the *per Filium* of the Confessor in the (Constantinopolitan) line of the immanent distinction of the procession from generation and not as a simple (Nicene) affirmation of consubstantiality. Therefore, although both Cyril and Maximus have been mentioned in the discussions on the *Filioque*, the reconstruction of Greek pneumatology proposed in this volume makes it possible to clearly appreciate the difference in their position.

To confirm the importance of the proposed conclusions we can cite the pneumatology of Nikephoros Blemmydes who, in the middle of the thirteenth century, read the patristic data precisely in the line of an active but not causal role of the Son in the procession of the Holy Spirit, expressing the connection between economy and immanence in relational terms.[20]

19. Πατρός γάρ, καί ὀνόματος Πατρός, καί βασιλείας Πατρός δήλωσιν ἔχει τῆς προσευχῆς τά ῥητά· ἵν᾽ ἀπ᾽ αὐτῆς διδαχθῶμεν τῆς ἀρχῆς τήν μοναδικήν Τριάδα σέβειν, ἐπικαλεῖσθαί τε καί προσκυνεῖν. Ὄνομα γάρ τοῦ Θεοῦ καί Πατρός οὐσιωδῶς ὑφεστώς ἐστιν ὁ μονογενής Υἱός· καί βασιλεία τοῦ Θεοῦ καί Πατρός, οὐσιωδῶς ἐστιν ὑφεστῶσα, τό Πνεῦμα τό ἅγιον. Ὁ γάρ ἐνταῦθα Ματθαῖος φησι βασιλείαν, ἀλλαχοῦ τῶν εὐαγγελιστῶν ἕτερος Πνεῦμα κέκληκεν ἅγιον, φάσκων, Ἐλθέτω σου τό Πνεῦμα τό ἅγιον, καί καθαρισάτω ἡμᾶς. Οὐ γάρ ἐπίκτητον ὁ Πατήρ ἔχει τό ὄνομα, οὔτε μήν ὡς ἀξίαν ἐπιθεωρουμένην αὐτῷ νοοῦμεν τήν βασιλείαν. Οὐκ ἦρκται γάρ τοῦ εἶναι, ἵνα καί τοῦ πατήρ ἤ βασιλεύς εἶναι ἄρξηται· ἀλλ᾽ ἀεί ὤν, ἀεί καί πατήρ ἐστι καί βασιλεύς· μήτε τοῦ εἶναι, μήτε τοῦ πατήρ ἤ βασιλεύς εἶναι τό παράπαν ἠργμένος. Εἰ δέ ἀεί ὤν, ἀεί καί πατήρ ἐστι καί βασιλεύς, ἀεί ἄρα καί ὁ Υἱός καί τό Πνεῦμα τό ἅγιον οὐσιωδῶς τῷ Πατρί συνυφεστήκασιν, ἐξ αὐτοῦ τε ὄντα, καί ἐν αὐτῷ φυσικῶς, ὑπέρ αἰτίαν καί λόγον, ἀλλ᾽ οὐ μετ᾽ αὐτόν, γενόμενα δι᾽ αἰτίαν ὕστερον. Ἡ γάρ σχέσις συνενδείξεων κέκτηται δύναμιν, τά ὤν ἔστι τε καί λέγεται σχέσις, μετ᾽ ἄλληλα θεωρεῖσθαι μή συγχωροῦσα (Maximus the Confessor, *Expositio orationis dominicae*, CCSG 23:41–42).

20. Cf. M. Stavrou, "Nicéphore Blemmydès en dialogue théologique avec les Latins (1234–1250)," in *Contra Latinos et Adversus Graecos: The Separation between Rome and Constantinople from the Ninth to the Fifteenth Century*, ed. Alessandra Bucossi and Anna Calia (Leuven: Peeters, 2020), 343–58.

From this point of view, the present path leads to a paradox, because in light of the data proposed here we can say that Cyril and Augustine, considered in the medieval debates as true champions of the *Filioque*, are actually less consistent with it, if it is understood as the elaboration on the difference between the procession of the Spirit and the eternal generation of the Son. Instead, a line of development emerges that is linked to the rereading of the pneumatology of Origen, with the tension inherent to it, to the thought of the Cappadocians, and to the responses to Pneumatomachian criticism. This tradition presents an active, but not causal, role of the Son in the procession of the Spirit without in any way affecting the monarchy of the Father. This step is made possible by a new ontological reshaping of the instrument of relation, which is introduced into the intra-Trinitarian dimension, continuing what was initiated in the response to Arianism, to present all three divine Persons with the two processions in a correlative sense. Augustine and Cyril remain anchored to a pneumatology of gift, which highlights the consubstantiality and continuity between economy and immanence. Both clearly affirm the apophatic dimension, but their reflection is less refined at the level of the theological reworking of metaphysics. Perhaps this point has contributed to the generation of tension in the controversy linked to the *Filioque*. Hopefully the narrative proposed here can be of help in the path toward unity.[21]

In all likelihood, when the emperor Heraclius decided in 615 that Latin would no longer be the official language of the empire he was simply stating a fact, but this can now also be recognized as a deeper cause of the loss of relational capacity in the dialogue between West and East. The hermeneutical proposal put forward here is that the positions of Cyril of Alexandria and Maximus the Confessor should also be interpreted against this ontological and theological backdrop preceding the loss of the relational perspective in our theological epistemologies. This would also make it possible to put forward an ecumenical proposal[22] which, similar to what happened with the Petrine primacy, suggests the possibility that the different Christian traditions

---

21. Sarah Coakley, in her clear and passionate Duquesne University Holy Spirit Lecture in 2016, spoke of "a point of *rapprochement*" between East and West, in reference to some of the pneumatological elements here presented, as Gregory of Nyssa's reading of the Holy Spirit as bond between the Father and the Son: see S. Coakley, "Beyond the *Filioque* Disputes? Re-Assessing the Radical Equality of the Spirit through the Ascetic and Mystical Tradition" (forthcoming).

22. An excellent presentation of the *status quaestionis* of the documents of the ecumenical dialogue on the *Filioque* can be found in Ch. Lee, *Gregory of Nyssa, Augustine of Hippo, and the Filioque* (Leiden: Brill, 2021), 26–80.

could confess together the active, but not causal, relational role of the Son in the immanent procession of the Spirit according to the reconstruction of the pneumatological thought of the Greek fathers that is proposed here. In fact, it would simply be a matter of returning to that communion in which they were united in the patristic era with the Latin (and Syriac) fathers. This would also profoundly correspond to the spirit of the Orthodox tradition, which is completely directed toward the liturgy and is the keeper for everyone of a truly profound sense of the mystery.

In fact, the very spirit of patristic theology is embodied by the icon, whose purpose is essentially latreutic:[23] the image is not the mystery and does not replace it, but to the extent that it is "written" with faith, piety, and love, it helps to enter into relationship with the three divine Persons. Perhaps it is no coincidence that both theological treatises and icons are *written*. But the condition for this *writing* to make sense is respect for the fact that God's mystery exceeds our concepts, which we cannot allow to lead us to idolatry, moving away from that communion which ontologically is the meaning of everything and the very condition of possibility for our thinking.

So, following Gregory of Nyssa's warning, we must avoid turning concepts into idols through a common effort to recover the sense of the Christian mystery.[24] The conflict over the *Filioque* can in fact be traced back to the weakening in the theological epistemology of the essential role of apophaticism, understood as affirmation of the fact that the revealed reality exceeds our ability to formulate it. This epistemological loss characterizes the turn from the patristic era, which coincides with that of the first seven Ecumenical Councils, to the medieval and Byzantine era. This seems to suggest the need to study the development of thought in the first eight centuries of the Christian era in search of a common theological grammar.

The extraordinary definition of the true theologian presented by Gregory of Nazianzus seems to lead us in this direction:

> But by getting some idea of what concerns Him [God] (τὰ κατ' αὐτόν) from the realities surrounding Him (ἐκ τῶν περὶ αὐτόν), we piece together

23. Vladimir Zielinsky notes that in Orthodoxy, dogmas primarily have a protective function with respect to heresies, while in Western tradition they also have a latreutic dimension and a glorifying function, which Orthodoxy essentially assigns to liturgy (V. Zielinsky, "Le mystère de Marie, source d'unité," *La Nouvelle revue théologique* 121 [1999]: 90).

24. This seems to be in line with Jean-Luc Marion's latest research on the Trinity and the icon; see J.-L. Marion, *D'ailleurs, la révélation* (Paris: Gallimard, 2020), 467–93, and *Givenness and Revelation* (Oxford: Oxford University Press, 2016), 89–115.

(συλλέγομεν) a dark and uncertain image from different things (ἄλλην ἀπ' ἄλλου). And so, in our opinion, the best theologian is not the one who has understood the whole, because the limited does not contain the whole, but rather the one who has been able to imagine (φαντασθῇ) more than others and to better unite in his mind (συναγάγῃ) the mental image of the truth or a shadow of it or whatever we would like to call it.[25]

The true theologian knows very well that our thought is limited, as the most blessed Trinity is eternal and infinite, that is, always beyond our capabilities. At the same time, the possibility for the knowledge and worship of the Father, the Son, and the Holy Spirit is always open, at the relational level. In fact, the correspondence of the verbs *syllegō* and *synagō* in the quoted text recalls precisely the drawing of the connection between the different moments and signs of God's giving of Himself in history, in imitation of the *symballō* that according to Luke 2:19 characterizes the meditation of the Heart of Mary.

We do not know if this narrative and the resulting proposal will be accepted by many or just a few. What we are persuaded of is that, if the imaginary dialogue over a beer of the two ninth-century monks with their patristic dossier and the young man protesting in London with the sign "Drop the *Filioque*" could be in harmony with the Mother of God's form of thought, then the writing on the pizza box could become "Drop the medieval *Filioque* and let's keep that of the (Greek) fathers."

---

25. ἀλλ' ἐκ τῶν περὶ αὐτὸν σκιαγραφοῦντες τὰ κατ' αὐτόν, ἀμυδράν τινα καὶ ἀσθενῆ καὶ ἄλλην ἀπ' ἄλλου φαντασίαν συλλέγομεν. καὶ οὗτος ἄριστος ἡμῖν θεολόγος, οὐχ ὃς εὗρε τὸ πᾶν, οὐδὲ γὰρ δέχεται τὸ πᾶν ὁ δεσμός, ἀλλ' ὃς ἂν ἄλλου φαντασθῇ πλέον, καὶ πλεῖον ἐν ἑαυτῷ συναγάγῃ τὸ τῆς ἀληθείας ἴνδαλμα, ἢ ἀποσκίασμα, ἢ ὅ τι καὶ ὀνομάσομεν (Gregory of Nazianzus, *Oratio*, 30.17.9–14 [SC 250:262]).

Abramowski, Luise. "The Confession of Gregor Thaumaturgus with Gregor of Nyssa and the Problem of Its Authenticity." *Zeitschrift für Kirchengeschichte* 87 (1976): 145–66.

Aldenhoven, Herwig. "Trinitarische Analogien und Ortskirchenekklesiologie." *Internationale kirchliche Zeitschrift* 92 (2002): 174–75.

Alexandre, Monique. "La variante de Lc 11, 2 dans la Troisième Homélie sur l'Oraison Dominicale de Grégoire de Nysse et la controverse avec les pneumatomaques." Pages 163–89 in *Grégoire de Nysse: La Bible dans la construction de son discours*. Edited by M. Cassin et al. Paris: Brepols, 2008.

Altaner, Berthold. *Kleine patristische Schriften*. Berlin: Akademie-Verlag, 1967.

Anatolios, Khaled. *Athanasius: The Coherence of His Thought*. London: Routledge, 1998.

———. *Deification through the Cross*. Grand Rapids: Eerdmans, 2020.

———. *Retrieving Nicaea: The Development and Meaning of Trinitarian Doctrine*. Grand Rapids: Baker Academic, 2011.

Aranda, Antonio. "El Espíritu Santo en la Esposición de Fe de S. Gregorio Taumaturgo." *Scripta Theologica* 10 (1978): 373–407.

Assemani, Josephus Simonius. *Bibliotheca Orientalis Clementino-Vaticana*. 4 vols. Rome: Sacrae Congregationis de Propaganda Fide, 1719–1728.

Ayres, Lewis. *Augustine and the Trinity*. Cambridge: Cambridge University Press, 2010.

———. *Nicaea and Its Legacy: An Approach to Fourth-Century Trinitarian Theology*. Oxford: Oxford University Press, 2006.

———. "Not Three People: The Fundamental Themes of Gregory of Nyssa's Trinitarian Theology as Seen in *To Ablabius: On Not Three Gods*." *Modern Theology* 18 (2002): 445–74.

Balás, David L. "The Idea of Participation in the Structure of Origen's Thought: Christian Transposition of a Theme of the Platonic Tradition." Pages 257–75 in vol. 1 of *Origeniana*. Bari, Italy: Istituto di letteratura cristiana antica, 1975.

Balthasar, Hans Urs von. *The Glory of the Lord: A Theological Aesthetics. II: Studies in Theological Style: Clerical Styles*. Translated by A. Louth et al. San Francisco: Ignatius, 1984.

———. *Présence et pensée: Essai sur la philosophie religieuse de Grégoire de Nysse*. Paris: Beauchesne, 1988.

Barnes, Michel R. *The Power of God: Dunamis in Gregory of Nyssa's Trinitarian Theology*. Washington, DC: CUA Press, 2001.

Batllo, Xavier. *Ontologie scalaire et polémique trinitaire: Le subordinatianisme d'Eunome et la distinction κτιστόν/ἄκτιστον dans le Contre Eunome I de Grégoire de Nysse*. Münster: Aschendorff, 2013.

Beatrice, Pier Franco. "The Word 'Homoousios' from Hellenism to Christianity." *Church History* 71 (2002): 243–72.

Beck, Edmund. *Ephräms Trinitätslehre*. CSCO 425. Leuven: Peeters, 1981.

———. *Des Heiligen Ephraem des Syrers Hymnen de Fide*. CSCO 154. Leuven: Peeters, 1955.

———. *Des Heiligen Ephraem des Syrers Sermones de fide*. CSCO 212. Leuven: Peeters, 1961.

Bedjan, Paul. *Acta martyrum et sanctorum*. Vol. 1. Leipzig: Harrassowitz, 1890.

Bendinelli, Guido. "Il dibattito sullo Spirito Santo in ambito latino prima di Agostino." Pages 195–224 in *Pneuma: Il divino in/quieto; Lo Spirito santo nelle tradizioni antiche*. Edited by Francesco Pieri and Fabio Ruggiero. Supplementi di Adamantius 6. Brescia: Morcelliana, 2018.

Berardino, Angelo di, ed. *Patrology: The Eastern Fathers, 451–750*. Cambridge: James Clarke, 2006.

Bernardi, Jean. *La prédication des Pères Cappadociens: Le prédicateur et son auditoire*. Paris: Presses Universitaires de France, 1968.

Bizer, Christoph. "Studien zu pseudathanasianischen Dialogen der Orthodoxos und Aëtios." PhD diss., University of Bonn, 1970.

Blanc, Cécile. "Jésus est fils de Dieu: L'interprétation d'Origène." *Bulletin de littérature ecclésiastique* 84 (1983): 5–18.

Böhnke, Michael, Assaad Elias Kattan, and Bernd Oberdorfer, eds. *Die Filioque-Kontroverse: Historische, ökumenische und dogmatische Perspektiven 1200 Jahre nach der Aachener Synode*. Freiburg im Breisgau: Herder, 2011.

Boulnois, Marie-Odile. *Le Paradoxe Trinitaire chez Cyrille d'Alexandrie: Hermeneutique, Analyses Philosophiques et Argumentation Theologique*. Paris: Institut d'études augustiniennes, 1994.

Brachtendorf, Johannes. "Der menschlische Geist als Bild des trinitarischen Gottes-Ähnlichkeiten und Unähnlichkeiten." Pages 155–70 in *Gott und sein Bild: Augustins De* Trinitate *im Spiegel gegenwärtiger Forschung*. Edited by Johannes Brachtendorf. Paderborn: Schöningh, 2000.

———. *Selbstreflexion und Erkenntnis Gottes: Die Struktur des menschlichen Geistes nach Augustinus* De Trinitate. Paradeigmata 19. Hamburg: Meiner, 2000.

Brague, Rémi. *Anchors in the Heavens: The Metaphysical Infrastructure of Human Life*. South Bend, IN: Saint Augustine's Press, 2019.

Brock, Sebastian. "L'apport des Pères grecs à la littérature syriaque." Pages 9–26 in *Les Pères grecs dans la tradition syriaque*. Edited by Andrea Schmidt and Dominique Gonnet. Paris: Geuthner, 2007.

———. "The Holy Spirit as Feminine in Early Syriac Literature." Pages 73–88 in *After Eve: Woman, Theology, and the Christian Tradition*. Edited by J. Martin Soskice. London: HarperCollins, 1990.

———. *The Luminous Eye: The Spiritual World Vision of Saint Ephrem*. Kalamazoo, MI: Cistercian, 1992.

———. "Towards a History of Syriac Translation Technique." In *III Symposium Syriacum*. Edited by R. Lavenant. Orientalia Christiana Analecta 221. Rome: Pontificium Institutum Orientalium Studiorum, 1983.

Brufau, Miguel Brugarolas. *El espíritu santo: De la divinidad a la procesión; El desarrollo pneumatológico en los escritos dogmáticos de los tres grandes capadocios*. Pamplona, Spain: Eunsa, 2012.

Bruns, Peter. "Bemerkungen zur Rezeption des Nicaenums in der ostsyrischen Kirche." *Annuarium historiae conciliorum* 32 (2000): 1–22.

Bucossi, Alessandra, and Anna Calia, eds. *Contra Latinos et Adversus Graecos: The Separation between Rome and Constantinople from the Ninth to the Fifteenth Century*. Leuven: Peeters, 2020.

Bucur, Bogdan Gabriel. *Angelomorphic Pneumatology: Clement of Alexandria and Other Early Christian Witnesses*. Leiden: Brill, 2009.

Caldarelli, Giuliana. *S. Gregorio di Nissa: La preghiera del Signore*. Milan: Edizioni Paoline, 1983.

Cassin, Matthieu, Hélène Grelier-Deneux, and Françoise Vinel, eds. *Gregory of Nyssa: Homilies on the Our Father; An English Translation with Commentary and Supporting Studies*. Leiden: Brill, 2021.

Castagno, Adele Monaci, ed. *Dizionario Origene*. Rome: Città Nuova, 2000.

Catapano, Giovanni. "La processione dello Spirito Santo nel *De Trinitate* di Agostino." Pages 65–87 in *Contra Latinos et Adversus Graecos: The Separation between Rome and Constantinople from the Ninth to the Fifteenth Century*. Edited by Alessandra Bucossi and Anna Calia. Leuven: Peeters, 2020.

Cattaneo, Enrico. "La Bestemmia Contro Lo Spirito Santo (Mt 12,31–32) in S. Atanasio." *Studia Patristica* 21 (1989): 421–25.

Cavalcanti, Elena. *Dialoghi contro i Macedoniani.* Turin: SEI, 1983.

Chadwick, Henry. *East and West: The Making of a Rift in the Church; From Apostolic Times until the Council of Florence.* Oxford: Oxford University Press, 2003.

Cherniss, Harold F. *The Platonism of Gregory of Nyssa.* Berkeley: University of California Press, 1930.

Chevalier, Irene. *S. Augustin et la pensée grecque: Les relations trinitaires.* Fribourg: Librairie de l'Université Fribourg en Suisse, 1940.

Cipriani, Nello. "La processione dello Spirito Santo in sant'Agostino." Pages 99–116 in *Il Filioque: A mille anni dal suo inserimento nel credo a Roma (1014-2014).* Edited by Mauro Gagliardi. Vatican City: LEV, 2015.

Clément, Olivier. *The Roots of Christian Mysticism.* New York: New City, 1995.

Coakley, Sarah. "Beyond the *Filioque* Disputes? Re-Assessing the Radical Equality of the Spirit through the Ascetic and Mystical Tradition." Forthcoming.

———. *God, Sexuality, and the Self: An Essay 'On the Trinity'.* Cambridge: Cambridge University Press, 2013.

Coda, Piero. "L'ontologia trinitaria: che cos'è?" *Sophia* 2 (2012): 159–70.

———. *Sul luogo della Trinità: rileggendo il "De Trinitate" di Agostino.* Rome: Città Nuova, 2008.

Coetzee, Michelle. *The Filioque Impasse: Patristic Roots.* Piscataway, NJ: Gorgias, 2012.

Cross, Richard. "Quid Tres? On What Precisely Augustine Professes Not to Understand in *De Trinitate* V and VII." *Harvard Theological Review* 100 (2007): 215–32.

———. "Two Models of the Trinity?" *Heythrop Journal* 43 (2002): 275–94.

Cureton, William. *Ancient Syriac Documents Relative to the Earliest Establishment of Christianity in Edessa and the Neighbouring Countries from the Year after Our Lord's Ascension to the Beginning of the Fourth Century.* London: Williams & Norgate, 1864.

Daley, Brian E. "The Fullness of the Saving God: Cyril of Alexandria on the Holy Spirit." Pages 113–48 in *The Theology of St. Cyril of Alexandria.* Edited by G. Weinandy and Daniel A. Keating. London: T&T Clark, 2003.

Daniélou, Jean. "La chronologie des oeuvres de Grégoire de Nysse." *Studia Patristica* 7 (1966): 159–69.

———. *Le IVe siècle: Grégoire de Nysse et son milieu.* Paris: Institut catholique de Paris, 1964.

———. *Théologie du Judéo-christianisme.* Tournai: Desclée, 1958.

DelCogliano, Mark. "Eusebius of Caesarea on Asterius of Cappadocia in the Anti-

Marcellan Writings: A Case Study of Mutual Defense within the Eusebian Alliance." Pages 163–287 in *Eusebius of Caesarea: Tradition and Innovations*. Edited by Aaron P. Johnson and Jeremy M. Schott. Cambridge: Harvard University Press, 2013.

Delogu, Paolo. "Leone III, santo." Pages 695–703 in *Enciclopedia dei papi*. Rome: Treccani, 2000.

Detienne, Claude. "Grégoire de Nazianze dans la tradition syriaque." Pages 175–83 in *Studia Nazianzenica*. Edited by Bernard Coulie. CCSG 41. Turnhout: Brepols, 2000.

Dillon, John. "Iamblichus νοερὰ θεωρία of Aristotle's Categories." *Syllecta classica* 8 (1997): 65–77.

———. "Origen's Doctrine of the Trinity and Some Later Neoplatonic Theories." Pages 19–23 in *Neoplatonism and Christian Thought*. Edited by D. J. O'Meara. Norfolk, VA: International Society for Neoplatonic Studies, 1982.

Douglass, Scot. *Theology of the Gap: Cappadocian Language Theory and the Trinitarian Controversy*. New York: Lang, 2007.

Draguet, René. *Dadišo Qatraya: Commentaire du Livre d'Abba Isaïe*. CSCO 326. Leuven: Peeters, 1972.

Drecoll, Volker H. *Die Entwicklung der Trinitätslehre des Basilius von Cäsarea: Sein Weg vom Homöusianer zum Neonizäner*. Göttingen: Vandenhoeck & Ruprecht, 1996.

———. "How Binitarian/Trinitarian Was Eusebius?" In *Eusebius of Caesarea: Tradition and Innovations*. Edited by Aaron P. Johnson and Jeremy M. Schott. Cambridge: Harvard University Press, 2013.

———. "Maced: Adversus Macedonianos, De Spiritu Sancto." Pages 464–66 in *The Brill Dictionary of Gregory of Nyssa*. Edited by Lucas Francisco Mateo-Seco and Giulio Maspero. Leiden: Brill, 2009.

Dupont, Jacques. "Le chrétien, miroir de la gloire divine d'après II Cor., III, 18." *Revue biblique* 56 (1949): 392–41.

Edwards, Mark J. "Did Origen Apply the Word 'Homoousios' to the Son?" *Journal of Theological Studies* 49 (1998): 658–70.

Esbroeck, Michel van. "The Credo of Gregory the Wonderworker and Its Influence through Three Centuries." *Studia Patristica* 19 (1989): 255–66.

Eyzaguirre, Samuel Fernández, ed. *Origenes: Sobre los principios*. Fuentes patrísticas 27. Madrid: Ciudad Nueva, 2015.

Farina, Raffaele. *L'impero e l'imperatore cristiano in Eusebio di Cesarea: La prima teologia politica del cristianesimo*. Zurich: PAS Verlag, 1966.

Fokin, Alexei. "St. Augustine's Doctrine of the Trinity in the Light of Orthodox

Triadology of the Fourth Century." Pages 131–52 in *The Trinity: East/West Dialogue*. Edited by Melville Y. Stewart. Dordrecht: Kluwer Academic, 2003.

Frend, William H. C. *The Rise of the Monophysite Movement*. Cambridge: Cambridge University Press, 1972.

Friedman, Russell L. *Medieval Trinitarian Thought from Aquinas to Ockham*. Cambridge: Cambridge University Press, 2010.

Froehlich, Karlfried. "The Lord's Prayer in Patristic Literature." Pages 59–77 in *A History of Prayer: The First to the Fifteenth Century*. Edited by Roy Hammerling. Leiden: Brill, 2008.

Froidevaux, Leon. "Le symbole de saint Grégoire le Thaumaturge." *Recherches de science religieuse* 19 (1929): 193–247.

Gagliardi, Mauro, ed. *Il Filioque: A mille anni dal suo inserimento nel credo a Roma (1014–2014)*. Vatican City: LEV, 2015.

Garrigues, Jean-Miguel. "À la suite de la Clarification romaine sur le 'Filioque.'" *La nouvelle revue théologique* 119 (1997): 321–34.

———. "Procession et ekporèse du Saint Esprit: Discernement de la tradition et réception oecuménique." *Istina* 17 (1972): 345–66.

Gemeinhardt, Peter. *Die Filioque-Kontroverse zwischen Ost- und Westkirche im Frühmittelalter*. Berlin: de Gruyter 2002.

Gieschen, Charles A. *Angelomorphic Christology: Antecedents and Early Evidence*. Leiden: Brill, 1998.

Gioia, Luigi. *The Theological Epistemology of Augustine's* De Trinitate. Oxford: Oxford University Press, 2008.

Girardi, Mario. *Basilio di Cesarea interprete della Scrittura: Lessico, principi ermeneutici, prassi*. Bari: Edipuglia, 1998.

Gleede, Benjamin. *The Development of the Term ἐνυπόστατος from Origen to John of Damascus*. Leiden: Brill, 2012.

Gnilka, Christian. *Chrēsis: Die Methode der Kirchenväter im Umgang mit der antiken Kultur; Der Begriff des "rechten Gebrauchs."* Basel: Schwabel, 2012.

Grohe, Johannes. "Storia del Filioque prima del 1014 e il suo inserimento nel Credo." Pages 15–38 in *Il Filioque: A mille anni dal suo inserimento nel credo a Roma (1014–2014)*. Edited by Mauro Gagliardi. Vatican City: LEV, 2015.

Guidi, Ignazio. *La lettera di Filosseno ai monaci di Tellʿaddâ (Taleda)*. Rome: Reale Accademia Nazionale dei Lincei, 1886.

Günthör, Anselm. "Die 7 pseudoathanasianischen Dialogen ein Werk Didymus' des Blinden von Alexandrien." PhD diss., Pontifical Atheneum of St. Anselm, 1940.

Gwynn, David M. *The Eusebians: The Polemic of Athanasius of Alexandria and the Construction of the "Arian Controversy."* Oxford: Oxford University Press, 2007.

Habets, Myk. *Ecumenical Perspectives on the Filioque for the 21st Century.* London: T&T Clark, 2014.

Haddad, Rachid. *La Trinité divine chez les théologiens arabes, 750–1050.* Paris: Beauchesne, 1985.

Haelewyck, Jean-Claude, ed. *Orationes XXVII, XXXVIII et XXXIX.* Vol. 3 of *Sancti Gregorii Nazianzeni opera: Versio Syriaca.* CCSG 53. Turnhout: Brepols, 2005.

Haidacher, Sebastian. "Rede über Abraham und Isaak bei Ephraem Syrus und Pseudo-Chrysostomus—ein Exzerpt aus Gregor von Nyssa." *Zeitschrift für katholische Theologie* 29 (1905): 764–66.

Halleux, André de. "*Manifesté par le Fils*: Aux origines d'une formule pneumatologique." *Revue théologique de Louvain* 20 (1989): 3–31.

———. *Philoxène de Mabbog.* Leuven: Imprimerie Orientaliste, 1963.

———. "Le symbole des évêques perses au synode de Séleucie-Ctésiphon (410)." Pages 161–90 in *Erkenntnisse und Meinungen.* Edited by Gernot Wiessner. Wiesbaden: O. Harrassowitz, 1977.

Hammerling, Roy. "The Lord's Prayer: A Cornerstone of Early Baptismal Education." Pages 167–82 in *A History of Prayer: The First to the Fifteenth Century.* Edited by Roy Hammerling. Leiden: Brill, 2008.

Haneberg, Daniel Bonifacius de. *Canones S. Hippolyti arabice e codicibus romanis cum versione latina annotationibus et prolegomenis.* Münster: Academiae Regiae Boicae, 1870.

Hanson, Richard P. C. "Did Origen Apply the Word 'Homoousios' to the Son?" Pages 293–303 in *Epektasis: Mélanges Jean Daniélou.* Paris: Beauchesne, 1975.

———. "The Holy Spirit in Creeds and Confessions of Faith in the Early Church." Pages 291–302 in vol. 1 of *Credo in Spiritum Sanctum: Atti del Congresso Teologico Internazionale di Pneumatologia.* Edited by J. Saraiva Martins. Rome: LEV, 1983.

Harb, Paul. "La conception pneumatologique chez Philoxène de Mabbug." *Parole de l'orient* 5 (1969): 5–15.

Harl, Marguerite. "From Glory to Glory: L'interprétation de 2 Co 3, 18b par Grégoire de Nysse et la liturgie baptismale." Pages 730–35 in vol. 2 of *Kyriakon: Festschrift Johannes Quasten.* Edited by Patrick Granfield. Münster: Aschendorff, 1970.

Hauschild, Wolf-Dieter. *Gottes Geist und der Mensch: Studien zur frühchristlichen Pneumatologie.* Munich: Chr. Kaiser, 1972.

———. "Die Pneumatomachen: Eine Untersuchung zur Dogmengeschichte des vierten Jahrhunderts." PhD diss., Hamburg University, 1967.

Haykin, Michael A. G. *The Spirit of God: The Exegesis of 1 and 2 Corinthians in the Pneumatomachian Controversy of the Fourth Century.* Leiden: Brill, 1994.

Hermanin de Reichenfeld, Giovanni. "The Role of the Holy Spirit in the Gospel of John within Origen's and Augustine's Commentaries." PhD diss., University of Exeter, 2018.

Hill, Kevin Douglas. *Athanasius and the Holy Spirit: The Development of His Early Pneumatology.* Minneapolis: Augsburg Fortress, 2016.

Horn, Cornelia B. "Überlegungen zur Rolle der Pneumatologie Ephräm des Syrers im Umfeld des Ersten Konzils von Konstantinopel." Pages 29–52 in *Syriaca II.* Edited by Martin Tamcke. Münster: LIT, 2004.

Hupsch, Piet Hein. *The Glory of the Spirit in Gregory of Nyssa's* Adversus Macedonianos: *Commentary and Systematic-Theological Synthesis.* Leiden: Brill, 2020.

Iammarrone, Luigi, ed. *Atanasio: Lettere a Serapione.* Padua, Italy: Ed. Messaggero, 1983.

Jacobs, Nathan A. "On 'Not Three Gods'—Again: Can a Primary-Secondary Substance Reading of *Ousia* and *Hypostasis* Avoid Tritheism?" *Modern Theology* 18 (2002): 431–58.

Kaniyamparampil, Emmanuel. *The Spirit of Life.* Kottayam: OIRSI, 2003.

Kannengiesser, Charles. "Athanasius of Alexandria and the Holy Spirit between Nicea I and Constantinople I." *Irish Theological Quarterly* 48 (1981): 166–80.

Kany, Roland. *Augustins Trinitätsdenken: Bilanz, Kritik und Weiterführung der modernen Forschung zu "De trinitate."* Studien und Texte zu Antike und Christentum 22. Tübingen: Mohr Siebeck, 2007.

Kienzler, Klaus. "Zu den Anfängen einer trinitarischen Ontologie: Augustinus' Bekenntnisse." Pages 45–60 in *Der dreieine Gott und die eine Menschheit.* Edited by Michael Albus et al. Freiburg im Breisgau: Herder, 1989.

Klijn, Albertus F. J. *The Acts of Thomas.* Leiden: Brill, 2003.

Kochlamazashvili, Tamaz. "Thaum. De vita Gregorii Thaumaturgi." Pages 718–20 in *The Brill Dictionary of Gregory of Nyssa.* Edited by Lucas Francisco Mateo-Seco and Giulio Maspero. Leiden: Brill, 2009.

Kretschmar, Georg. *Studien zur frühchristlichen Trinitätstheologie.* Tübingen: Mohr, 1956.

Ladaria, Luis F. *El Espíritu Santo en San Hilario de Poitiers.* Madrid: Eapsa, 1977.

Laird, Martin. "Apophasis and Logophasis in Gregory of Nyssa's *Commentarius in Canticum Canticorum.*" *Studia Patristica* 37 (2001): 126–32.

Lamy, Thomas J. *Sancti Ephraem Syri hymni et sermones.* Vol. 2. Mechlin: H. Dessain, 1882.

Lancaster, Sarah Heaner. "Divine Relations of the Trinity: Augustine's Answer to Arianism." *Calvin Theological Journal* 34 (1999): 327–46.

———. "Three-Personed Substance: The Relational Essence of the Triune God in Augustine's *De Trinitate.*" *Thomist* 60 (1996): 123–39.

Larson, Mark J. "A Re-examination of *De Spiritu Sancto*: Saint Basil's Bold Defence of the Spirit's Deity." *Scottish Bulletin of Evangelical Theology* 19 (2001): 65–84.

Lee, Chungman. *Gregory of Nyssa, Augustine of Hippo, and the Filioque.* Leiden: Brill, 2021.

Leloir, Louis. *Saint Ephrem: Commentaire de l'Évangile concordant texte syriaque (manuscrit Chester Beatty 709).* Dublin: Hodges Figgis, 1963.

Loofs, Friedrich. "Zwei macedonianische Dialoge." *SPAW* (1914): 526–51.

Luislampe, Pia. *Spiritus vivificans: Grundzüge einer Theologie des Heiligen Geistes nach Basilius von Caesarea.* Münster: Aschendorff, 1981.

Magne, Jean. "La réception de le variante 'Vienne ton Esprit saint sur nous et qu'il nous purifie' (Lc 11,2) et l'origine des épiclèses, du baptême et du 'Notre Père.'" *Ephemerides liturgicae* 102 (1988): 81–106.

Marion, Jean-Luc. *D'ailleurs, la revelation.* Paris: Gallimard, 2020.

———. *Givenness and Revelation.* Oxford: Oxford University Press, 2016.

Maspero, Giulio. "Anthropology." Pages 37–47 in *The Brill Dictionary of Gregory of Nyssa.* Edited by Lucas Francisco Mateo-Seco and Giulio Maspero. Leiden: Brill, 2009.

———. "Coscienza e relazione: Analogie trinitarie tra filosofia e neuroscienze." *Lateranum* 80 (2014): 355–70.

———. "Dallo Spirito vivificatore allo Spirito Creatore: L'esegesi cappadoce di Sal 32(33),6." Pages 407–26 in *Creazione e salvezza nella Bibbia.* Edited by M. V. Fabbri and M. Tábet. Rome: EDUSC, 2009.

———. *Dio trino perché vivo: Lo Spirito di Dio e lo spirito dell'uomo nella Patristica greca.* Brescia: Morcelliana, 2018.

———. *Essere e relazione: L'ontologia trinitaria di Gregorio di Nissa.* Rome: Città Nuova, 2013.

———. "Life from Life: The Procession of the Son and the Divine Attributes in Ch. VIII of Gregory of Nyssa's *Contra Eunomium III*." Pages 401–28 in *Gregory of Nyssa's* Contra Eunomium III: *An English Translation with Commentary and Supporting Studies; Proceedings of the 12th International Colloquium on Gregory of Nyssa (Leuven, 14–17 September 2010).* Edited by Johan Leemans and Matthieu Cassin. Leiden: Brill, 2014.

———. "The Logos in Us and the Logos in the Principle according to Origen." Pages 843–56 in *Origeniana undecimal: Origen and Origenism in the History of Western Thought.* Edited by Anders-Christian Jacobsen. Leuven: Peeters, 2016.

———. *The Mystery of Communion: Encountering the Trinity.* South Bend, IN: Saint Augustine's Press, 2021.

———. "Ontologia trinitaria e sociologia relazionale: Due mondi a confront." *PATH* 10 (2011): 19–36.

———. "La perichoresis e la grammatica teologica dei primi sette Concili ecumenici." *Theologica* (2020): 161–81.

———. "Remarks on Origen's Analogies for the Holy Spirit." Pages 563–78 in *Origeniana Decima*. Edited by Henryk Pietras and Sylwia Kaczmarek. Leuven: Peeters, 2011.

———. "Tradition and Translation: The *Filioque* and the Procession of the Holy Spirit in Syriac." *Parole de l'orient* 36 (2011): 87–109.

———. "The Trinitarian Reading of the Lord's Prayer: The Third Homily." Pages 326–54 in *Gregory of Nyssa: Homilies on the Our Father; An English Translation with Commentary and Supporting Studies*. Edited by Matthieu Cassin, Hélène Grelier-Deneux, and Françoise Vinel. Leiden: Brill, 2021.

———. "The Trinity." Pages 125–38 in *The Routledge Handbook of Early Christian Philosophy*. Edited by Mark Edwards. London: Routledge, 2021.

———. *Trinity and Man: Gregory of Nyssa's Ad Ablabium*. Leiden: Brill, 2007.

Mateo-Seco, L. F. "El Espíritu Santo en el Adv. Macedonianos de Gregorio de Nisa." *Scripta Theologica* 37 (2005): 475–98.

Mateo-Seco, Lucas Francisco, and Giulio Maspero, eds. *The Brill Dictionary of Gregory of Nyssa*. Leiden: Brill, 2009.

May, Gerhard. "Die Chronologie des Lebens und der Werke des Gregor von Nyssa." Pages 51–66 in *Ecriture et culture philosophique dans la pensée de Grégoire de Nysse*. Edited by Marguerite Harl. Leiden: Brill, 1971.

McIntyre, John. "The Holy Spirit in Greek Patristic Thought." *Scottish Journal of Theology* 7 (1954): 353–75.

Meinhold, Peter. "Pneumatomachoi." *Paulys Real Encyclopädie der classischen Altertumswissenschaft* 21.1 (1951): 1066–87.

Meredith, Anthony. "Origen and Gregory of Nyssa on the Lord's Prayer." *Heythrop Journal* 43 (2002): 344–56.

———. "The Pneumatology of the Cappadocian Fathers and the Creed of Constantinople." *Irish Theological Quarterly* 48 (1981): 196–211.

Meyendorff, John. *S. Grégoire Palamas et la mystique orthodoxe*. Paris: Editions du Seuil, 1959.

Michelson, David A. "Philoxenos of Mabbug: A Cappadocian Theologian on the Banks of the Euphrates?" Pages 151–74 in *Motions of Late Antiquity: Essays on Religion, Politics, and Society in Honour of Peter Brown*. Edited by Jamie Kreiner and Helmut Reimitz. Cultural Encounters in Late Antiquity and the Middle Ages 20. Turnhout: Brepols, 2016.

———. *The Practical Christology of Philoxenos of Mabbug*. Oxford Early Christian Studies. New York: Oxford University Press, 2014.

Mimouni, Simon-Claude. *Le judéo-christianisme ancien*. Paris: Cerf, 1998.

Mitchell, Stephen. "The Life and Lives of Gregorius Thaumaturgus, in Portraits of

Spiritual Authority." Pages 99–137 in *Religious Power in Early Christianity, Byzantium, and the Christian Orient.* Edited by Jan Willem Drijvers and John W. Watt. Leiden: Brill, 1999.

Moreschini, Claudio. "Osservazioni sulla pneumatologia dei Cappadoci: Preannunci del Filioque?" Pages 117–46 in *Il Filioque: A mille anni dal suo inserimento nel credo a Roma (1014–2014).* Edited by M. Gagliardi. Vatican City: LEV, 2015.

Moser, Maureen Beyer. *Teacher of Holiness: The Holy Spirit in Origen's Commentary on the Epistle to the Romans.* Piscataway, NJ: Gorgias, 2005.

Moutsoulas, Elias D. "Β´ Οἰκουμενικὴ Σύνοδος καὶ Γρηγόριος ὁ Νύσσης." Θεολογία 55 (1984): 384–401.

———. Γρηγόριος Νύσσης. Βίος, Συγγράμματα, Διδασκαλία. Athens: Eptalophos, 1997.

Murray, Robert. *Symbols of Church and Kingdom: A Study in Early Syriac Tradition.* London: T&T Clark, 2006.

Ormerod, Neil. "The Psychological Analogy for the Trinity: At Odds with Modernity." *Pacifica* 14 (2001): 281–94.

Orphanos, Markos A. "The Procession of the Holy Spirit: According to Certain Greek Fathers." Θεολογία 50 (1979): 763–78.

Osso, C. dell'. "Il Filioque in Massimo il Confessore." Pages 147–64 in *Il Filioque: A mille anni dal suo inserimento nel credo a Roma (1014–2014)*, ed. M. Gagliardi. Vatican City: LEV, 2015.

Parmentier, Martien. "St. Gregory of Nyssa's Doctrine of the Holy Spirit." PhD diss., University of Oxford, 1972.

———. "Syriac Translations of Gregory of Nyssa." *Orientalia Lovaniensia Periodica* 20 (1989): 143–93.

Pârvan, Alexandra. "La relation en tant qu'élément clé de l'illumination augustinienne." *CHORA. Revue d'études anciennes et médiévales* 7–8 (2010): 87–103.

Parys, Michel van. "Réfutation, Grégoire de Nysse, Réfutation de la profession de foi d'Eunome." PhD diss., Université de Paris–Sorbonne, 1968.

Penido, Maurilio T.-L. "Prélude Grec à la Théorie Psychologiche de la Trinité." *Revue thomiste* 45 (1939): 665–74.

Perrone, Lorenzo. "Origenes alt und neu: Die Psalmenhomilien in der neuentdeckten Münchner Handschrift." *Zeitschrift für Antikes Christentum* 17.2 (2013): 193–214.

———. "La pneumatologia di Origene alla luce delle nuove 'Omelie sui Salmi.'" Pages 101–17 in *Pneuma: Il divino in/quieto; Lo Spirito santo nelle tradizioni antiche.* Edited by Francesco Pieri and Fabio Ruggiero. Supplementi di Adamantius 6. Brescia: Morcelliana, 2018.

———. *La Preghiera Secondo Origine: L'impossibilità Donata.* Brescia: Morcelliana, 2011.

Pieri, Francesco, and Fabio Ruggiero, eds. *Pneuma: Il divino in/quieto; Lo Spirito santo nelle tradizioni antiche.* Supplementi di Adamantius 6. Brescia: Morcelliana, 2018.

Pitra, Jean Baptiste. *Analecta sacra Spicilegio Solesmensi parata.* Vol. 4. Paris: Jouby et Roger, 1883.

Pochoshajew, Igor. *Gregory of Nyssa:* De Beatudinibus *IV,* Ad Ablabium, *and* Adversus Macedonianos. Frankfurt am Main: Lang, 2008.

Polidori, Valerio. "L'attualità della Mistagogia di Fozio alla luce della recente edizione critica." *Studi sull'Oriente Cristiano* 24 (2020): 59–73.

Porrino, Giovanna Maria. *Le poids et la gloire: Splendeur de Dieu, splendeur de l'homme, de la Genèse aux Psaumes.* Paris: Cerf, 2016.

Pruche, Benoît. "Autour du traité Sur le Saint-Esprit de saint Basile de Césarée." *Revue des sciences religieuses* 52 (1964): 204–32.

Radde-Gallwitz, Andrew. *Gregory of Nyssa's Doctrinal Works: A Literary Study.* Oxford: Oxford University Press, 2018.

Ramelli, Ilaria, ed. *Marziano Capella, Le nozze di Filologia e Mercurio.* Milan: Bompiani, 2004.

———. "Origen's Anti-Subordinationism and Its Heritage in the Nicene and Cappadocian Line." *Vigiliae Christianae* 65 (2011): 21–49.

———. *Social Justice and the Legitimacy of Slavery: The Role of Philosophical Asceticism from Ancient Judaism to Late Antiquity.* Oxford: Oxford University Press, 2016.

Ratzinger, Joseph. *Theologische Prinzipienlehre: Bausteine zur Fundamentaltheologie.* Donauwörth: Wewel, 2005.

Reinhard, Kathryn. "Somebody to Love? The Proprium of the Holy Spirit in Augustine's Trinity." *Augustinian Studies* 41 (2010): 351–73.

Riedel, Wilhelm Johann. *Die Kirchenrechtsquellen des Patriarchats Alexandrien.* Leipzig: Wilhelm Johann, 1900.

Rordorf, Willy. *Liturgie, foi et vie des premiers chrétiens: Études patristiques.* Paris: Beauchesne, 1986.

Scher, Addai. "Joseph Hazzâyâ, écrivain syrien du VIIIme siècle." *Rivista degli studi orientali* 3 (1910): 45–63.

Schmaus, Michael. *Die Psychologische Trinitätslehre des Hl. Augustinus.* Münster: Aschendorff, 1927.

Segovia, Augusto. "Contribucion al estudio de la tradicion manuscrita dei pseudo-atanasiano: Dialogo I contra un Macedoniano o pneumatomaco." *Archivio teológico granadino* 1 (1938): 87–107.

Siecienski, Anthony E. *The Filioque: History of a Doctrinal Controversy.* Oxford: Oxford University Press, 2010.

Simonetti, Manlio. "Il regresso della teologia dello Spirito Santo in Occidente dopo Tertulliano." *Augustinianum* 20 (1980): 655–69.

——. "Note sulla teologia trinitaria di Origene." *Vetera Christianorum* 8 (1971): 273–307.

——. "La processione dello Spirito Santo nei Padri Latini." *Maia* 7 (1955): 308–24.

——. "S. Agostino e gli ariani." *Revue des études augustiniennes* 13 (1967): 55–84.

——. "Spirito Santo." Pages 450–56 in *Dizionario Origene*. Edited by A. Monaci Castagno. Rome: Città Nuova, 2000.

Stavrou, Michel. "Nicéphore Blemmydès en dialogue théologique avec les Latins (1234–1250)." Pages 343–58 in *Contra Latinos et Adversus Graecos: The Separation between Rome and Constantinople from the Ninth to the Fifteenth Century*. Edited by Alessandra Bucossi and Anna Calia. Leuven: Peeters, 2020.

Stramara, Daniel F. "Gregory of Nyssa's Terminology for Trinitarian *Perichoresis*." *Vigiliae Christianae* 52 (1998): 257–63.

Stroumsa, Gedaliahu G. "Le couple de l'Ange e de l'Esprit: Traditions juives et chrétiennes." *Revue biblique* 88 (1981): 42–61.

Strutwolf, Holger. *Die Trinitätstheologie und Christologie des Euseb von Caesarea: Eine dogmengeschichtliche Untersuchung seiner Platonismusrezeption und Wirkungsgeschichte*. Göttingen: Vandenhoeck & Ruprecht, 1999.

Studer, Basil. "La foi en l'Esprit Saint dans l'Église Ancienne." In *Mysterium Caritatis: Studien zur Exegese und zur Trinitätslehre in der Alten Kirche*. Rome: Pontificio Ateneo Sant'Anselmo, 1999.

——. *Trinity and Incarnation: The Faith of the Early Church*. Collegeville, MN: Liturgical Press, 1994.

Taft, Robert F. *A History of the Liturgy of St. John Chrysostom: The Precommunion Rites*. Rome: Orientalia Christiana, 2000.

Taylor, David G. K. "Les Pères cappadociens dans la tradition Syriaque." Pages 43–61 in *Les Pères grecs dans la tradition syriaque*. Edited by Andrea Schmidt and Dominique Gonnet. Paris: Geuthner, 2007.

——, ed. *The Syriac Versions of the* De Spiritu Sancto *by Basil of Caesarea*. CSCO 575–576. Leuven: Peeters, 1999.

Thom, Paul. *The Logic of the Trinity: Augustine to Ockham*. New York: Fordham University Press, 2012.

Torrance, Thomas F. "The Doctrine of the Holy Trinity according to St. Athanasius." *Anglican Theological Review* 71 (1989): 395–405.

Troiano, Maria Silvia. "Il concetto di *perichoresis* in Gregorio di Nissa." *Studi storico-religiosi* 2 (1978): 81–92.

Turchi, Athos. "Persona divina—persona umana: Nota di cristologia e di filosofia; Commento di un testo del *De Trinitate*, V,5." *Angelicum* 76 (1999): 341–65.

Uthemann, Karl-Heinz, ed. *Anastasii Sinaitae Sermones duo in constitutionem hominis secundum imaginem Dei necnon Opuscula adversus Monotheletas.* CCSG 12. Turnhout: Brepols, 1985.

———. "Anastasius the Sinaite." Pages 313–32 in *Patrology: The Eastern Fathers, 451–750.* Edited by A. di Berardino. Cambridge: James Clarke, 2006.

Vaschalde, Adolphe. *Babai Magni Liber de unione.* CSCO 79. Leuven: Peeters, 1915.

———. *Three Letters of Philoxenus: Bishop of Mabbôgh (485–519); Being the Letter to the Monks, the First Letter to the Monks of Beth-Gaugal, and the Letter to Emperor Zeno.* Rome: Tipografia della R. Accademia dei Lincei, 1902. Repr. Whitefish, MT: Kessinger, 2010.

Vaught, Carl. *The Journey toward God in Augustine's Confessions: Books I–VI.* Albany: SUNY Press, 2012.

Verbeke, Gérard. *L'évolution de la doctrine du pneuma.* Leuven: Desclée de Brouwer, 1945.

Vööbus, Arthur. "New Sources for the Symbol in Early Syrian Christianity." *Vigiliae Christianae* 26 (1972): 291–96.

Weedman, Mark. "Augustine's *De Trinitate* 5 and the Problem of the Divine Names *Father* and *Son*." *Theological Studies* 72 (2011): 768–86.

Weinandy, Thomas G. *The Father's Spirit of Sonship: Reconceiving the Trinity.* Edinburgh: T&T Clark, 1995. Repr. Eugene, OR: Wipf & Stock, 2011.

Yanguas, José María. "La divinidad del Espíritu Santo en S. Basilio." *Scripta Theologica* 9 (1997): 485–539.

Zachhuber, Johannes. *Human Nature in Gregory of Nyssa: Philosophical Background and Theological Significance.* Leiden: Brill, 2000.

———. "Philosophy and Theology in Late Antiquity." Pages 52–77 in *Eastern Christianity and Late Antique Philosophy.* Edited by Ken Parry. Leiden: Brill, 2019.

———. *The Rise of Christian Theology and the End of Ancient Metaphysics: Patristic Philosophy from the Cappadocian Fathers to John of Damascus.* Oxford: Oxford University Press, 2020.

Zielinsky, Vladimir. "Le mystère de Marie, source d'unité." *La Nouvelle revue theologique* 121 (1999): 72–91.

Zizioulas, John D. *Communion and Otherness: Further Studies in Personhood and the Church.* London: T&T Clark, 2009.

———. "The Teaching in the 2nd Ecumenical Council on the Holy Spirit in Historical and Ecumenical Perspective." Pages 29–54 in *Acts of the International Theological Congress of Pneumatology.* Vol. 1. Rome: Libreria Editrice Vaticana, 1983.

Index of Authors

Index of Scripture

Index of Ancient and Medieval Sources